Praise for *Leadership Matters*

"Cronin and Genovese have written a compelling and original book. It is terrific—a real addition to the leadership canon."

—**Warren Bennis,** *Marshall School of Business, University of Southern California*

"*Leadership Matters* is a highly sophisticated, deeply probing, and remarkably comprehensive treatment of this dynamic and crucial subject."

—**James MacGregor Burns,** *Williams College (Emeritus), Pulitzer Prize–winning political scientist, historian, and biographer*

"This book offers unique insights into the field of leadership with stunning examples about what historical and popular leaders can teach us. Cronin and Genovese give us an entirely different perspective on the field. This is a must-read for anyone interested in leadership!"

—**Nicole Cundiff,** *Director of the Northern Leadership Center, University of Alaska–Fairbanks*

"This book is an absolute tour-de-force—one of the most wide-ranging, fascinating, intricate studies of leadership I have ever read."

—**Doris Kearns Goodwin,** *Pulitzer Prize–winning author and presidential historian*

"Cronin and Genovese present leadership as 'the most baffling of the performing arts.' They unpack the paradoxes of leadership, provide memorable illustrations, and include nuggets of wisdom for anyone interested in learning more about this complex human activity."

—**Nannerl O. Keohane,** *President Emeritus of Wellesley College and Duke University and Lawrence S. Rockefeller Distinguished Visiting Professor of Public Affairs and the University Center for Human Values at Princeton University*

"This is a terrific book…destined to become a classic."

—**James O'Toole,** *former Executive Vice President, Aspen Institute*

"*Leadership Matters* is the book my course on leadership has been waiting for—a volume that intelligently embraces, rather than avoids, the paradoxes inherent in the subject."

—**Norman W. Provizer,** *Leadership Scholar, Director of the Golda Meir Center, Metropolitan State University–Denver*

"A unique, well-researched, and well-written book on leadership that has been needed for a long time. This book is the one I have been thinking about writing. Now I won't have to, because Cronin and Genovese have already done it very well."

—**William E. Rosenbach,** ***former Chair of Leadership Programs, U.S. Air Force Academy, and Gettysburg College***

"*Leadership Matters* is simply terrific. This is a superb book—it will have an important place in the literature and in the classroom, and might well become a classic."

—**J. Thomas Wren,** ***Jepson School of Leadership, University of Richmond***

LEADERSHIP MATTERS

To Tania and Gabriela—love matters!

LEADERSHIP MATTERS

Unleashing the Power of Paradox

Thomas E. Cronin
Michael A. Genovese

Paradigm Publishers
Boulder • London

Published in the United States by Paradigm Publishers, 5589 Arapahoe Avenue, Boulder, CO 80303 USA.

Paradigm Publishers is the trade name of Birkenkamp & Company, LLC, Dean Birkenkamp, President and Publisher.

Library of Congress Cataloging-in-Publication Data

Cronin, Thomas E.
  Leadership matters : unleashing the power of paradox / Thomas E. Cronin, Michael A. Genovese.
    p. cm.
  Includes bibliographical references and index.
  ISBN 978-1-61205-142-0 (hardcover : alk. paper)—
  ISBN 978-1-61205-143-7 (pbk. : alk. paper)
  1. Political leadership. 2. Leadership. I. Genovese, Michael A. II. Title.
  JC330.3.C76 2012
  303.3'4—dc23

2011049942

Printed and bound in the United States of America on acid-free paper that meets the standards of the American National Standard for Permanence of Paper for Printed Library Materials.

Designed and Typeset by Straight Creek Bookmakers.

16 15 14 13 12   2 3 4 5

Contents

Preface

Leadership is about making things happen that otherwise might not happen. It is a process of getting people to work together to achieve mutually shared aspirations.

Leadership invariably involves an infusion of vision, purpose, and energy into an enterprise. It entails mobilizing both people and resources in order to achieve results.

Leaders have been responsible for liberating breakthroughs in public affairs, commerce, and the arts. But they have been responsible as well for failed states, failed enterprises, extravagant follies, and horrible crimes. For better or for worse, leaders and leadership matter.

Still, "leadership" for most people is a hazy and confusing abstraction. People wonder whether leaders are born or made, and whether leadership is a result of individual agency or social context. Did Martin Luther King Jr., for example, serve as a leader in creating the civil rights movement, or was he largely shaped by that movement? And what role do followers play? How much do followers guide their leaders? Can leaders take us where we don't want to go?

While most leadership books emphasize specific rules for effective leadership, we see a more fluid and contradictory leadership universe, where rules only occasionally apply, and "how-to-do-it" prescriptions can obscure rather than enlighten our understanding of leadership.

Our book challenges common myths about leadership, such as these:

Leaders are born, not made.
Leadership is a rare and uncommon talent.
Leaders are necessarily charismatic.

Leadership is found only at the top of an organization.
Office holders are necessarily leaders.
Organizational or group members are either leaders or followers.
Leaders are smarter and more creative than most of us.
Power is the dominant currency of leadership.

We see leadership as a series of dilemmas, choices, and paradoxes that challenge would-be leaders in every sector. Clashing expectations and demands, and unexpected occurrences must be regularly confronted and dealt with.

Four basic premises guide this book. First, leadership is a process that encourages the accomplishment of group purposes. Second, the key and enduring tasks of a leader are to learn, build morale, motivate, educate, and create human communities. Third, leaders not only need followers, their very legitimacy is granted by followers. Leadership always involves followers as well as leaders and context. Finally, we contend that much of what we call leadership can be learned. There are some things, to be sure, that can't be taught. Much indeed is learned in the trenches, in the crucible of challenges that are unexpected or unprecedented.

In the chapters that follow, we wrestle with these central themes:

- *Leadership matters.* Leaders can encourage ordinary people to undertake and sometimes achieve extraordinary things. Yet when examined more closely, the consequential agent of change is more often the leadership of teams, of social or political movements, of ideas and innovations, rather than the leadership of a lone hero, a storybook Lone Ranger, or a transformational High Noon Superman.
- *Leadership remains as hard to define today* as it was for the ancient Greek philosophers and playwrights. It is hard to define and measure because it is contextual—leaders invariably act in the stream of history. It is similarly hard to define and measure because it is part purpose, part process, part product, part decisions, part implementation, and part artistry. Leaders can lead or mislead, clarify or confuse, bring out our best or our worst.
- *Leadership has to do with reconciling diverse values, interests, and ambiguities,* juggling contradictions and paradoxes, adapting to change, and trying to find the right balance between competing claims while recognizing the limits of politics and opportunity.
- *Leadership requires a combination* of optimism and skepticism, of strength and compassion, of mastering quantitative information and yet believing in one's intuition.
- *Can leadership be taught? is the wrong question. Can leadership be learned? is the better question. Much of what we think of as leadership can be learned.*

Some things are not easily taught. Thus one gets game- or battle-ready by being on the field, in the trenches, tested in crises. Still, apprentices, interns, understudies, and disciplined go-getters can develop, hone, and exercise leadership in their own right, and in their own way—just as development league athletes do in every sport and understudies do in opera or on Broadway. Leadership in so many ways is a performing art and thus it is that leadership skills can be fruitfully studied, learned, and developed. The soul of a leader—courage, character, empathy, and public virtue—may be more exacting, and indeed harder to get right; yet leadership skills and values are learned anew in every generation and in every culture.

We believe that the most effective leaders are synthesizing and integrative thinkers who resiliently adapt to the opportunities, luck, and paradoxes that confront every venture.

We turn first to the enduring paradoxes of leadership.

Thomas E. Cronin (tom.cronin@coloradocollege.edu)
Michael A. Genovese (Michael.Genovese@lmu.edu)

Chapter One
The Paradoxes of Leadership

> Of course, life would be easier if leadership was just a list of simple rules, but paradoxes are inherent in the trade.
>
> —***Former General Electric chairman Jack Welch***[1]

General Douglas MacArthur is described by his biographer as a great thundering paradox of a man, "noble and ignoble, inspiring and outrageous, arrogant and shy, the best of men and the worst of men.... For each of MacArthur's strengths, there was a corresponding MacArthur weakness."[2]

"My life, my work, my position, everything I've done, seems intertwined with a suspiciously large number of paradoxes," writes Vaclav Havel, the writer and intellectual who became Czechoslovakia's president in 1989 after the collapse of the Soviet empire. Havel says that conflict, tensions, and misunderstandings upset him. Yet both his writings and his life as a political activist were full of conflict, tension, and controversy. He writes, "I'm very unsure of myself, almost a neurotic. I tend to panic easily ... I'm plagued by self-doubts ... yet I appear to many as someone who is sure of himself, with an enviable equanimity." Havel liked people and bringing people together, yet was happiest when he was alone and could escape into solitary introspection as a rabble-rousing Don Quixote. "For many people I'm a constant source of hope and yet I'm always succumbing to ... uncertainties."[3]

Being a leader is a complex fate. Although contradictions and clashing expectations are part of life, they are especially present in the exercise of leadership. Leaders with great strengths often have great weaknesses as well. And what may be a leader's strength in one area, or at one time, can prove a weakness later on. Or as in the case of Winston Churchill, vice versa. A quality that may be a strength in one context may be a weakness in another. A leader's life is usually, as the MacArthur and Havel examples attest, a collage of conflicting expectations, dilemmas, and necessities.

We both admire and fear power. We admire and fear leaders. Likewise, we yearn for self-confident, tough-minded heroic leadership yet are also inherently suspicious of it. We at times desire decisive hierarchical leaders yet later wish to be left alone. We want leaders who are like us yet better than us. We yearn for leaders to serve the common good yet simultaneously serve particular interests. We lament the lack of leadership, yet we are harsh critics of the leaders we get. We want leaders to tell us the truth yet often get upset with them when they do. We want effective political leadership yet wish we could have it without politicians. We value leaders who have humility and compassion yet also know that sometimes it is the demanding perfectionist, control freak with narcissistic personality disorders, like Apple's Steve Jobs, who produce valuable breakthroughs. Somehow leaders like Havel, MacArthur, and Jobs learned to live with, if not master, the paradoxes confronting them.

We ask leaders to resist being overly wed to the status quo, tradition, or convention, yet we want them to possess a sense of history and a sensitivity to human experience. We are impressed with leaders who display fearless resolve, yet we also respect those who are self-effacing, acknowledge their fallibility, and learn from mistakes.

Leaders of genius and creativity have been vital in guiding us toward liberty, economic progress, peace, and social justice. Yet if leaders have often been a source of freedom and liberation, they have almost as often been responsible for war, horrible repressions, and crimes against humanity.

Leaders learn to live and cope with contradictions. Effective leaders learn to exploit contrary and divergent forces. They become savvy synthesizers of disparate information, integrative thinkers who can anticipate and read changing contexts. In Joseph Nye's useful phrase, they develop their contextual intelligence. Leadership commonly requires successive displays of contrasting characteristics. Thus leaders learn to live with ambiguous demands, shifting expectations, and sometimes fickle followers.

The effective leader in business, government, and elsewhere, much like a first-rate conductor, knows when to bring in the various sections, when to increase and diminish the volume, and how to balance opposing groups to achieve satisfying results.

Leaders are constantly buffeted by competing demands, constituencies, and policies, and must often strike a balance in order to be effective. Compromise and patience may be required in one situation, yet too much compromise or patience in other situations may be fatal.

Certain clashing expectations or contradictions are sometimes resolved by proper timing. Others have to be juggled or balanced. Effective leaders manage their time wisely while trying as well to appreciate and balance the endless stream of conflicting demands. They redefine their roles, recast strategies, reposition budgets, reorganize staff, and reorient their organizations—constantly.

This chapter explores the contradictions, paradoxes, clashing expectations, and competing demands leaders live with.

There are few fixed rules regarding leadership. It is mostly a moving target. That is why the study of leadership is more art than science.

Leadership, like life, is too complex for simplistic answers. Leadership and life are complex, contradictory, paradoxical. That is why life—and leadership—are about balance and flexibility, not absolutes and rigidity. Good leaders and healthy individuals seek a balance, deal with competing demands, are flexible.

Leadership Contradictions and Paradoxes

- We want decent, just, compassionate, and moral leaders, yet at times we admire and need tough, assertive, cunning, manipulative, and even intimidating leaders.
- Effective leadership involves self-confidence, the audacity of hope, and sometimes even a fearless optimism. However, humility, self-doubt, and self-control are also essential.
- Leaders must be representative—yet not too representative; they need to consult and engage followers, and they need to respond to them. Yet they also must educate, motivate, and unlock the best in everyone.
- Leaders must be visionaries guided by ideas, ideals, and principles, yet we also want pragmatic realists guided by logic, evidence, and level-headed rational analysis.
- Leaders invent and reinvent themselves. Their leadership usually is intentional, not accidental. Yet people also want their leaders to be open, relaxed, "authentic," sincere, spontaneous, and to somehow emerge from within rather than be imposed upon a group.
- Leadership often calls for intensity, enthusiasm, passion, dramatization, and self-promotion—yet too much highly personalized volcanic energy can paralyze an organization. Too much of a "cult of personality" can create dependency or other organizational dysfunctions.
- Leaders need to unify their organizations or communities through effective negotiation and alliance building, yet leaders also have to stir things

up and jolt their organizations out of complacency. In short, we ask them to be uniters *and* dividers.
- Leaders are supposed to lead, not follow the polls, yet they are often followers as much as they are leaders. One of the grand paradoxes of leadership is that leaders often follow, and followers often point the way or lead more than is appreciated. Change often comes from the bottom up rather than from the top down. And it often comes from the young rather than from establishment elites.
- Although we may reject the General George Patton or the Godfather model of leadership for most of our organizations most of the time, we still want to believe leaders make a significant difference—yet idealistic and romantic theories exaggerate the impact of leaders. Most of the time, "leaders" are agents of their organizations or are at least shaped by them more than they are agents of change.

Moral versus Manipulative

Most people want leaders to be decent, just, and "proper" in their personal conduct. Others, more focused on results, look for hard-driving personalities and insist that leaders be opportunistic, realistic, and masters of trading, accommodation, and guile.

We want leaders to be ferocious or compassionate, mean-spirited or sensitive, ruthless or cooperative, depending on what we want done, depending on the situation, depending on how much time is available, and to some extent, depending on the agreed-upon "successful" role models of the recent past.

No magic formula exists. Leaders need to be sensitive to the varying expectations of their followers and aware, too, of the shifting nature of their followers' dispositions.

However much we admire transparency, vulnerability, and an emphasis on teamwork, many of our most effective business and societal leaders have been vain, crafty, and deceitful. Thus Franklin D. Roosevelt may have devoted himself to advancing the ends of social justice and peace, but his biographers agree he was often duplicitous, vain, manipulative, and had a passion for secrecy.

Change is scary and organizations sometimes need scary, in-your-face leaders to steer them through tough times. "Great intimidators may create disharmony," writes Stanford University professor Roderick Kramer, "but they also can create value." He points to Bill Gates, Steve Jobs, Martha Stewart, and Michael Eisner as abrasive, forceful, and sometimes intimidating bosses.[4]

Management writers such as Jim Collins, Max De Pree, and Robert Greenleaf have famously argued that the best chief executives are humble, self-effacing, resolute, yet not flamboyant egotists. They find many examples to back up their contention.[5] But others contend that the corporate and political worlds sometimes need flamboyant visionaries and narcissists. "Think of the people who have shaped the modern business landscape, and 'faceless' and 'humble' are not the first words that come to mind," writes a columnist for *The Economist*.[6]

> Henry Ford was as close as you get to being deranged without losing your liberty. John Patterson, the founder of National Cash Register and one of the greatest businessmen of the gilded age, once notified an employee that he was being sacked by setting fire to his desk. Thomas Watson ... the founder of IBM, turned his company into a cult and himself into the object of collective worship. Bill Gates and Steve Jobs are both tightly wound empire-builders. Jack Welch and Lou Gerstner are anything but self-effacing. These are people who have created the future, rather than merely managing change, through the force of their personalities and the strength of their visions.[7]

Americans can become supercritical of would-be leaders who are viewed as soft, wimpy, or afraid to make unpopular decisions. This is as true in politics as it is in business. Among others, Adlai Stevenson, Jimmy Carter, Gerald Ford, Michael Dukakis, John Kerry, and Barack Obama were faulted at times for indecision, timidity, or failure to be pragmatists. Journalists merely said they did not know how to play "hardball."[8] And yet, the opposite can also lead to poor performance, as the apparent certainty of George W. Bush and Dick Cheney sometimes demonstrated.

A leader "must know when to dissemble, when to be frank. He must pose as a servant of the public in order to become its master," wrote Charles de Gaulle in *The Edge of the Sword*.[9] He also said leaders had to have a strong dose of egotism, pride, and hardness. Former president Richard Nixon goes even further in one of his many memoirs: "Guile, vanity, dissembling—in other circumstances these might be unattractive habits, but to the leader they can be essential."[10]

We do not openly admire cunning as a quality, and we know that too much of it can destroy a dedicated leader. Yet as political scientist Clinton Rossiter noted, "a president cannot get the best out of the dozens of able figures around him or keep them under his command unless he is a master in the delicate art of manipulating men."[11]

Leaders have to be uncommonly active, attentive listeners. They must "squint" with their ears. But they can't listen forever. Eventually they must act, decide, and make judgments. People such as Hamlet waited too long to act. Others like King Lear, Othello, or Sophocles' King Creon listened poorly, if at all, and acted in foolish haste.

Ambition is essential if a leader is to make a difference. To gain and retain power one must have a love of power, and this love of power can be incompatible with moral goodness. In fact, ambition is more often linked to qualities of pride, narcissism, duplicity, and cruelty and often raises all the worst fears associated with questionable ends justifying unacceptable means.

The intentional use of coercion, force, and even killing may, under certain circumstances, be morally justified. Leaders can't always combat evil with goodness. Some just causes, such as just wars, require unjust means. The moral dilemma sometimes becomes a choice between two competing evils.

Leaders who are transformational can also be impatient and can display deep-seated hostility toward the status quo. They can be driven and angry, with a compulsive darker side that can make them impossible and dangerous personalities.

Leaders invariably combine toughness and softness. "Where results must be achieved quickly he must, on occasion, be ruthless if it is possible to be ruthless without injuring the confidence of his employees or the claimants to his service."[12]

Yet the successful leader must also be fair. "If he becomes arbitrary, capricious, and dictatorial, he may become feared but he will also lose his qualifications for leadership. Morale has never yet flourished in an organization based largely upon fear," writes management writer Marshall Dimock. "Sooner or later the members of such an institution find it possible to secure their revenge."[13]

A leader takes care not to become too self-absorbed. Self-preoccupation becomes one's own prison.

Leadership, divorced from worthy purposes, is merely manipulation of deception and, in the extreme, the wielding of repressive and tyrannical power.

Still a paradox remains. "Power, or organized energy, may be a man-killing explosive or a life-saving drug," writes Saul Alinsky. "The power of a gun may be used to enforce slavery, or to achieve freedom."[14] And so it is with leadership. Leaders must respect the preciousness of human life. Elements of calculation, abrasiveness, manipulation, and egoism are endemic in positions of authority. But a leader must also be able to consider people in the wholeness of their lives, not just for getting a job done or as a means for enhancing a bottom line.

Leaders who are hell-bent on success rarely ponder whether the ends justify the means. Consequently, their means often undermine their ends.

Thus leaders have to choose between democratic and autocratic styles, and how open or secretive, how honest or cunning, they should be in a particular situation. Much depends on their community's accepted values. Yet even within a culture or communities, there are marked variations in how leaders wrestle with this dilemma.

Few things, Abraham Lincoln said, are wholly good or wholly evil. Most choices are an inseparable mix of the two. Judgment about balance between good and evil is continually demanded. Effective leaders are balanced individuals; they are self-aware and self-assured yet willing to learn from their mistakes.

They weigh conflicting good and evil among alternative courses, and strike a balance that weighs on the side of the good.

Do leaders occupy a different moral universe than the rest of us? One of the paradoxes of leadership is that the public demands leaders be of high moral quality yet at times do things that are morally reprehensible. On one level, they must behave in ways that we as individuals do not condone. Because of the responsibilities that weigh on leaders, they occupy a different moral world than ordinary citizens. The responsibilities on a leader's shoulders grant more latitude than mere citizens possess.

As individuals, we choose the moral or religious guidelines by which we live our lives. This choice is ours and we accept the consequences. And as we are directly responsible only to ourselves and our families, the fallout of moral and religious choices is limited. The leader, on the other hand, does not have the luxury of living only for oneself and is responsible for and to the larger community. The leader may or may not share our own religious and moral convictions, but that is of little consequence. Leaders cannot impose their own religious views on the society as a whole, nor can they abandon their greater responsibility, which is to serve and protect the entire community.

The ethics of leadership are, and must be, *situational* and *positional.* They are contingent on the circumstances confronting the legitimate leader of the community in an uncertain, complex, and sometimes violent world. As Machiavelli reminds us, a leader "must be prepared to vary his conduct as the winds of fortune and changing circumstances constrain him ... and not deviate from right conduct, but be capable of entering upon the path of wrongdoing when this becomes necessary."[15] And although all religions have universal ethical principles or "oughts," such as thou shalt not kill or lying is wrong, these rules are not absolutes. After all, if it is wrong to kill, then all wars are wrong, all death penalties are wrong. So we make exceptions. The mark of a sophisticated mind is the ability to think in degrees, to form a hierarchy of values. Such a mind asks when and under what circumstance is one justified in breaking with the moral norms of society?

Machiavelli also reminds a would-be prince that to accomplish great things, he may on occasion have to act in rough or even evil ways. But Machiavelli's insight is not a green light for a leader to behave badly. The evil of which he speaks must be entered into only as the situation demands. He did not advise the prince to be evil, only that there would be times and circumstances when to either protect his power or the state, he must be ready to use evil for strategic ends. Yet the prince would be prepared to act immorally only "when this becomes necessary." *When this becomes necessary.* Of course, we are all selfish judges of our own cases; so on this Machiavelli opens himself up to criticism, but his general principle has merit. When dealing with evil or dangerous people, only a fool would take the moral high ground when it would undermine his interests.

The goal, as Terry L. Price writes in *Understanding Ethical Failures in Leadership*, is that "leaders must differentiate between those requirements that apply to them and those with respect to which a deviation would be justified.... The main challenge in leadership ethics is to clarify and to give precision to the justificatory force of leadership." Price adds that "leaders are excepted from moral requirements only on the condition that there are some reasons or set of reasons that legitimates the exceptions." Perhaps the most important feature of this model environment is "the expectation that leaders make explicit appeal to the reasons that legitimate deviations from moral requirements by which the rest of us are bound."[16]

Of course, that does not mean leaders get a free ride to be or do anything they wish. The leader's freedom to act is not a license to act in any way he desires. Leaders are confined by moral codes, just not the moral codes that apply to the rest of us. Leaders have greater freedom to act, yet this freedom is not limitless. Ironically, there are few restrictions placed upon most leaders. Most restrictions are self-imposed.

If leaders must act in ways that are morally questionable, they must fully justify those acts. Abraham Lincoln, during the Civil War, acted in ways that would, in normal times, have led to his impeachment. But Lincoln, facing the crisis of civil war, appealed to the Congress and public that, based on the crisis, the *doctrine of necessity* governed his behavior. This doctrine forgives many but not all sins. Lincoln believed he had pursued all other avenues, exhausted all other options, and had no other choice but to act as he did. In Lincoln's own words, "As our case is new, so we must think anew, and act anew." And he did so publicly and invited the Congress to legitimize his acts.

It is praiseworthy to be a good person. And we esteem leaders who possess the qualities we think are admirable. But the chief goal of a national leader is to serve the needs and interests of the larger commonwealth, which means that there may be times when leaders cannot observe the demands of goodness that bind private individuals. But the burden of proof is exceptionally high, and when leaders choose to transgress a moral norm, they must be on the steadiest of grounds. Thus, they need to answer: Is this truly a case of necessity? Has one exhausted all the normal options? Do these acts promote the rights, security, and welfare of the people-at-large, or are they merely a case of despotism or empire building? And, finally, were these decisions or actions effective?

Although not everyone believes there should be a "moral exceptionalism" for leaders, in practice that is precisely what occurs.[17] Better to face up to and deal constructively with the moral dilemma than bury one's head in the sand with moral considerations. One does not have to have a leader-centric view to give the leader some latitude here. As Machiavelli noted, and Lincoln practiced, *necessity* can be a powerful, if unsatisfying moral imperative. Leaders on occasion have "dirty hands" because—for us—they sometimes engage in a dirty (as well as at other times ennobling) business.[18]

We'll return to this paradox again in Chapter 11. For now we would only note that leaders such as George Washington and Abraham Lincoln taught us productive methods of dealing with or synthesizing this particular paradox.

Self-Confidence versus Humility

A leader needs contagious confidence, drive, and focus. Humility—the ability to view and evaluate oneself honestly and without defensiveness—is admirable, yet excessive humility paralyzes. "Most of the significant advances in the world have been made by people with at least a touch of irrational confidence in themselves."[19]

Leaders must believe in themselves. Israeli general Moshe Dayan talked of this calculated self-confidence in battle situations: "When I go into battle, I am 100 percent sure I will win and come out safely. I believe, with my luck and skill, that I'll manage between the bullets and they will not get hold of me. You have to feel this way or you'll never come out of it."[20] Dayan added, "You can show no doubt—only black and white. Except at night, when you are alone, you can look at it and wonder if maybe you were wrong. But you never show it."[21]

Leaders face all the complexities of the situation, yet, in the end, they must act. Shakespeare's *Henry V* provided this gamble-it-all, whatever-the-odds call to arms in his famed pre-Agincourt battle talk to his troops. Winston Churchill in the midst of World War II displayed a similar quality.

"Any self-doubts the leader may have, especially in the battlefield, must be concealed at all costs," writes military historian John Keegan. "The leader of men in warfare can show himself to his followers only through a mask, a mask that he must make for himself. But a mask made in such form as will mark him to men of his time and place as the leader they want and need."[22]

The politician who does not with every fiber of his body want to be a leader, says management guru Peter Drucker, is not likely to be effective or remembered. "To be more than a 'journeyman' requires a man who is conceited enough to believe that the world—or at least the nation—really needs him and depends on his getting into power."[23]

But untempered confidence is dangerous. Hitler oozed it. So did Herman Melville's mad Captain Ahab. Yet both had vision, purpose, and drive.

The critical test is whether a large ego is subject to reasonable self-control. Self-discipline is key. An undisciplined large ego that constantly needs to be fed and isn't placed in disciplined service of worthy ends is an ego that doubtless corrupts the individual.[24]

Having a *strong ego* can be usefully distinguished from having a *big ego.* A person with a strong ego has plenty of drive and ambition yet is open and flexible and has a connective sense of relationships. A *strong ego* pays attention to others and context. A *big ego* craves flattery and attention. A big ego is often rigid and controlling. A big ego quickly loses rather than earns our respect.[25]

Leaders believe in *themselves* yet cannot afford to discredit the ideas, counsel, or criticism of others. Leaders who embrace thoughtful dissent in their organizations are likely to encourage better organizational decision making. Good leaders acknowledge criticism without retaliating against critics. Hitler and Saddam Hussein eliminated their critics. Ahab ignored his.

Sophocles' King Creon, in the play *Antigone,* listened almost entirely to himself and this proved fatal. His son chided him, famously saying, "let not your first thought be your only thought. Think if there cannot be some other way. Surely, to think your own the only wisdom, and yours the only word, the only will, betrays a shallow spirit, an empty heart. It is no weakness," says Haemon to King Creon, "for the wise man to learn when he is wrong, know when to yield." So, "father, pause, and put aside your anger. I think for what my young opinion's worth, that good as it is to have infallible wisdom, since this is rarely found, the next best thing is to be willing to listen to wise advice."[26]

But Creon dismisses his son's advice, saying, "Indeed, am I to take lessons at my time of life from a fellow of his age?" He ignores everyone else as well, until, of course, it is too late. His self-centeredness and arrogance, just as is the case with Shakespeare's Lear, invite the tragedy.

The moral is, of course, that we are all a little like Creon, we are all a little like Douglas MacArthur or any hardheaded, determined individual. A fine line separates self-confidence from pigheaded pride, boldness from recklessness.

Leaders balance the need to be self-assured and the need to keep learning. Timing and balance are crucial. They need to have the will to act and the humility to listen. Morgan McCall and colleagues write that "we are a contradictory, paradoxical, and miscellaneous jumble of vices and virtues. And this is why balance is so basic. Every strength can also turn out to be a weakness, and great strengths or weaknesses can grow unjustifiably overblown."[27] The challenge is how to blend competing impulses and wisely combine them.

How can we safeguard against the mistake-prone, overly confident, impulsive big-ego types? Prizewinning psychologist Daniel Kahneman says the well-functioning organization can serve as an appropriate check and balance. "Organizations are better than individuals when it comes to avoiding errors, because they naturally think more deeply and have the power to impose orderly procedures."[28] Yes, organizations slow things down, but they can also upgrade the quality of the decision-making processes that produce good judgment.

Representative Yet Not Too Representative

We yearn for leaders with vision or dreams of what might be, people who have lofty standards and will relentlessly pursue success and excellence. This is the perennial search for the heroic. When we witness these visionaries we say they are great because they are original and remind us of no one else. On the other hand, we also yearn for representative leaders—those who are a lot like us. Heroic or charismatic leaders, by nature, are often aloof, distant, and detached. They conceal their real selves from their followers.

Hence the paradox: we want great leaders but also leaders who are not too different from us. A president must have "common opinions" but it is equally imperative that he be an "uncommon man," writes Harold Laski in discussing the ideal qualities for an American president. "The public must see themselves in him, but they must at the same time be confident that he is something bigger than themselves."[29]

Then, too, we yearn for flawless leaders; yet a dose of vulnerability can often add to their accessibility, likeability, and even charm.

On many issues, however, people must wait for their so-called leaders to catch up. On other issues, associates or constituents need to be lifted out of their old routines and need galvanizing leaders to bring the best out of everyone. In the end, the exercise of leadership is the act of balancing ideals and realities, the views of the people and the realities of what can be and what should be done. Again, it is a matter of balance and timing. A friend of ours, who served his state as an effective governor, once noted in yet another variation of this paradox: "The people always want you to tell them the truth yet they get madder than hell at you when you do."

"I do not believe that any man can lead who does not act, whether it be consciously or unconsciously, under the impulse of a profound sympathy with those whom he leads," said Woodrow Wilson. This is, he added, "a sympathy which is insight—an insight which is of the heart rather than of the intellect."[30]

The question, of course, is how sympathetic can one be. Writers such as Walter Lippmann and Hans J. Morgenthau counsel that leadership or "statesmanship" consists of giving the people not what they may want at a given moment but rather what they will learn to respect later on. *Politicians* accept public opinion, Lippmann held, whereas *leaders* reeducate their public and place opinion in larger contexts. Lippmann warned about being too representative: "The chief element in the art of statesmanship under modern conditions is the ability to elucidate the confused and clamorous interests which converge upon the seat of government. It is an ability to penetrate from the naïve self-interest of each group to its permanent and real interest." Lippmann added, "It is a difficult art that requires great courage, deep sympathy, and a vast amount of information. That is why it is so rare."[31]

Morgenthau, writing at least a generation later, agrees. The will to lead, he writes, can be paralyzed by an unfounded fear of and a "misplaced deference to public opinion. Presidents must reverse the established pattern of subservience to public opinion and become its molder, for this subservience does nothing but enfeeble the will to govern."[32] Machiavelli, of course, had put it even more strongly.

Authentic leadership, however, is always a collective process, an inevitable engagement, a meshing of the views of the leader as well as the led. It emerges, says James MacGregor Burns, from the clash and the congruence of motives and goals of both followers and leaders. It requires that leaders neither slavishly adapt their own motives and goals to those of their followers, nor the reverse. Still, the essence of the art of leadership is the reality that people can be, and often want to be, motivated and lifted into their better selves.[33]

Visionary or Realistic?

Vision is incredibly important. Yet so is execution and getting things accomplished, often even small things. "Yes, we need vision," goes the old lament, "but we also need somebody to tell us what to do." So the best vision is often supervision.

Idealism and realism are at war with one another in every community. Effective leaders blend them in ways that are appropriate to the times, circumstances, and community values. Leaders in the middle must integrate, coordinate, harmonize, and bring extremes into some form of a coherent whole. Only then will leaders become architects of shared value and community. But leaders in the middle continually risk being torpedoed by rival forces.

The oft-cited biblical proverb warns, "where there is no vision, the people perish." Victor Hugo added that "there is nothing so powerful as an idea whose time has come." A primary task of a leader is to discern the compelling needs of the time and then develop a vision to address both needs and possibilities. Leaders often relate to followers through stories (Lincoln) or parables (Jesus) or example (Mohandas Gandhi and Nelson Mandela). They paint word pictures or offer hopeful narratives that articulate what is often unspoken within the people.

An effective vision allows us to see where we want to go, and when the circumstances are right, to move in that direction. Vision is purpose exposed and made clear.

A vision guides action, is about the future, draws people to its premise and logic, is about empowerment, defines meaning, and is goal oriented. The best vision reminds us who we are, is simultaneously backward looking and aspirational; it accentuates what we hope to achieve.

Visions rarely spring full blown from the mind of a leader. Enabling and empowering visions emerge instead from mutually shared interests, values, and aspirations; flow from the past; and reflect the new requirements of the present and future.

A solid vision is a dream of a more desirable future, a dream realistic enough to appear attainable, compelling enough to inspire, and attractive enough to gain consent and commitment. It is mostly about encouraging hope: this is what tomorrow can be, this is how we can get there, this is what it will take, this is how you can play a significant role in making it happen, and this will be how we can "change history." Effective visions grab our attention, stir our imagination, and call on us to become the very best we can become.

Leadership requires radiating confidence, yet grounding in reality. "Become passionately dedicated to 'visions' and fanatically committed to carrying them out—but be flexible, responsive, and able to change direction quickly," writes Harvard Business School professor Rosabeth M. Kanter.[34] A leader must be a realist and a pragmatist yet also a creative dreamer. An equilibrium is needed, reconciling dreams and reality, intuition and logic.

"We need leaders of inspired idealism," said Theodore Roosevelt, "leaders to whom are granted great visions, who dream greatly and strive to make their dreams come true; who can kindle the people with the fire from their own burning souls."[35] We admire leaders who refuse to compromise their values; yet TR, Ronald Reagan, Bill Clinton, Barack Obama, and indeed almost all of our presidents were accomplished compromisers.

We occasionally look to idealists and prophets because we know major breakthroughs often come from "conviction leaders" rather than conventional leaders. This is true, in part, because majority opinion often stifles new approaches. As every politician knows, "If you oppose your constituents too directly on an issue too close to their hearts, you are not going to get elected," or reelected.[36]

Leadership, however, does not always wear the harness of compromise. Leaders sometimes are motivated by the purest of ideals. Such reformers or agitators don't bow to the conventions of their times but challenge them. These reformers "wear no armor, they bestride no chargers; they only speak their thoughts.... But the attacks they sustain are more cruel than the collisions of arms," writes Woodrow Wilson. "Friends desert and despise them. They stand alone, and oftentimes are made bitter by their isolation. They are doing nothing less than defying public opinion." Wilson captures the difficulty faced by idealistic reformers:

> These men who stood alone at the inception of the movement and whose voices then seemed as it were the voices of men crying in the wilderness, have in reality been simply the more sensitive organs of society—the parts first awakened to consciousness of a situation. With the start and irritation of a rude and sudden

> summons from sleep, society at first resents the disturbance of its restful unconsciousness, and for a moment racks itself with hasty passion. But, once completely aroused, it will sanely meet the necessities of conduct revealed by the hour of its awakening.[37]

Arousing, agitational consciousness-raising leadership is often indispensable for social progress. Thomas Paine, Frederick Douglass, Harriet Beecher Stowe, and Susan B. Anthony played such roles in America.

We expect leaders to provide us with bold, creative, and forceful initiatives, yet society resists radical change. We commonly embrace "new" initiatives only after they have achieved wide consensus. In a sense, we elect leaders to "make things better," then fight them nearly every step of the way.

Elected officials regularly fear taking a controversial stand too early on important issues. Thus the old saw: "I'm a person of fixed and unbending principles—but my first fixed and unbending principle is to be flexible at all times."

Franklin D. Roosevelt knew voters liked candidates with firm opinions, yet he also knew that to get elected and to govern he needed to keep his options open. He once explained to an adviser that although he could educate voters about the merits of his proposals after he became president, as a candidate he had to accept people's prejudices and do what he could to work with them and "turn them to good."[38]

FDR later proclaimed the presidency is preeminently a place for moral leadership, but, as noted, he was as pragmatic and opportunistic as most of the occupants of his position. Roosevelt knew political leadership in America required sometimes taking bold stands and yet at other times remaining vague or uncommitted. Timing shapes success or failure.

We want leaders to inspire creativity and organizational efficiency. Creativity, however, involves taking risks. Creative initiatives often fail and can be disruptive. Creative organizations are willing to accept disruption, failure, mistakes, and instability. But how much is enough? What's the balance?

Leaders have to decide how much instability can be tolerated. They have to know when to nurture creativity and also when to abandon a venture when this is required.

We ask leaders for visionary idealism *and* tough realism, optimism *and* logic, intuition *and* rationality, creativity *and* organizational stability. They need to balance bold dreams with accurate, reliable information and pragmatic implementation.

Business organizations constantly experience the tensions between relying on intuition and rational analysis. Creative, innovative solutions are required to solve complex problems, but corporate promotion systems often discourage innovative people from assuming leadership positions. Thus, however much we yearn for this kind of visionary leadership, we often prevent these types from rising to the top. We suspect those who might strike off on their own and disrupt existing habits and ideas.

Excessive reliance on visionaries can be fatal to any organization. Melville's Captain Ahab had plenty of passion and vision. He took a bold stand—committing his crew and his ship to a mighty mission: get Moby Dick. Logic and reason were not common on his ship. John Brown of Harpers Ferry fame had plenty of vision too. Vision, unchecked by clearheaded rational evaluation, proved costly for Ahab and Brown and their associates.

Cold Calculation versus Spontaneity

Leadership is seldom a random act. Much of what leaders do is intentional.

Peter Drucker says that in all his years of advising businesses he never came across a "natural" executive, that is, an executive who was born successful. "Leaders invent themselves," says Warren Bennis. "Leaders have nothing but themselves to work with."[39]

In effect leaders have to be actors or actresses who become the makers and directors of their own lives. They reject randomness. They embrace destiny. They redefine luck as, just as the cliché has it, when preparation and learning meet opportunity.

Bennis finds leaders rise to the top because they are self-made; they have lived in their organization yet have brought creativity and original ideas to it. "I cannot stress too much the need for self-invention," writes Bennis. "To be authentic is literally to be your own author ... to discover your own native energies and desires, and then to find your own way of acting on them."[40]

Successful leaders understand the importance of theater and self-promotion. If they have the ideas and reform impulses but lack a stage, their ideas are unlikely to gain much attention. The two go hand in hand—self-promotion and policy substance.

France's Charles de Gaulle held that nothing great can be achieved without great leaders, and that individuals "are great only if they are determined to be so."[41] Note the role willpower plays in Bennis, de Gaulle, and others. They are saying that leaders are necessarily promoters—promoters of self as well as ideas. They set about learning to be effective, seizing opportunities to display their leadership. "He must outbid his rivals in self-confidence, and only after a thousand intrigues will he find himself entrusted with full power," writes de Gaulle.[42]

Leaders are often obsessed with making a difference. "I have always had an absolutely obsessive focus, obsessive to the point that people have wanted to cage me up at times," says Portia Isaacson, chair and CEO of Intellisys Corporation.

She says that when she starts a project she drops everything else and intensely concentrates on it. "This absolutely obsessive focus is not necessarily a positive trait," she adds. "It drives some people away.... Being a compulsive workaholic, I have to be very conscious about not demanding that kind of behavior from other people. I am sensitive to the fact that some people like balance in their lives—even though I guess I don't."[43]

Constituents, however, also want leaders who are "natural" or "organic." Authenticity is crucial for a leader's believability. Spontaneity is also needed. Calculations and plans can and often do go awry. Adaptability and flexibility are essential.

This raises our familiar question whether leaders shape events or are shaped by social forces and events. The quick answer, of course, is that organizations, culture, circumstances, and resources shape leaders more than leaders shape their environments. Social forces play an obvious part in the development and exercise of leadership. It varies, of course, depending on the organizational setting—and that is the heart of this ambiguity.

In practice, leaders shape as well as are shaped. Nelson Mandela is a good example. His people—black South Africans—yearned for political and economic rights. Mandela was a product of the large community of which he was just a singular part. But by intense discipline and personal sacrifice, Mandela earned the respect of his people by giving voice and meaning to their inchoate feelings. Was Mandela shaped by the needs and aspirations of the movement? Definitely. Did he invent and earn a role of leadership for himself? Definitely. "He is a man whose life instructs that people can assert control of their personal destiny no matter what the force of the hardships they incur and that they can by their own conduct overwhelm the odds against them."[44]

Culture shapes the character of leaders, and the requirements or needs of a cultural community define the contributions of a leader. We look for leaders within ourselves, our groups, our communities and organizations. But we also look for leaders who have left the "tribe," who have gone away and gained a range of different experiences and insights. They return to our groups no longer exactly as one of us. Thus leaders in part invent themselves and in part we invent them. But it is complicated further, for leaders and their cultures are forever shaping one another as well. After his analysis of Moses as a political and religious leader, political scientist Aaron Wildavsky concludes that just as there are no great leaders for all seasons, no single concept of leadership can serve every purpose. "By conceiving of leadership as contingent on context, we are at least warned that it is futile to search for single types."[45]

Just as seasons change, so too do the seasons of leadership. Some seasons require a leader with a firm hand; others, a leader who is able to collaborate. Some require representative leaders who follow our directions; others, inventive leaders who show us the way. Office holders who are unable to identify the changing seasons and who cannot alter their leadership styles to the changing climate are doomed to fail.

Passion versus Reason

A leader must stir our blood *and* appeal to our reason. Enthusiasm lifts all enterprises, and yet excessive enthusiasm can destroy the integrity of an operation. Both enthusiasm and optimism can be "force multipliers"; yet both, in excess, are dysfunctional or worse.

A few years ago we encountered a gentleman who shared the following problem. He had a volunteer who was exuberant and passionate about her tasks, so much so that she was painfully disruptive. Such was her enthusiasm and energy that she caused stress and derailed rather than advanced the goals of the organization. The executive in charge could hardly fault her for lack of commitment, yet he had to calm her down or transfer her to a job where her enthusiasm could be more properly channeled.

Business and political leaders emphasize the importance of showmanship. Churchill, Gandhi, TR, de Gaulle, Mao Zedong, FDR, MacArthur, Reagan, Mikhail Gorbachev, Havel, Obama, and many other national leaders often dramatized their initiatives with theatrical personal visits or similar symbolism. Sometimes it was an unannounced visit to their troops in battle. Sometimes it took the form of a stirring oration. In Gandhi's case it took the form of fasts or a long march to the sea. On still other occasions leadership flare manifested itself in mingling with constituents. Whatever the approach, leaders are remembered for an uncommon spark of passion for what they believed.

"A great leader must have a certain irrational quality, a stubborn refusal to face facts, infectious optimism, the ability to convince us that all is not lost even when we're afraid it is," writes Michael Korda. Confucius suggested, adds Korda, that "while the advisors of a great leader should be as cold as ice, the leader himself should have fire, a spark of divine madness."[46]

Public opinion polls highlight this contradiction. When asked to describe in their own words the qualities they would like to have in national leaders, respondents give high marks to honesty and trustworthiness. They favor leaders with simple rather than imperial tastes. On the other hand, they express a strong preference for a spellbinding speaker, someone like John F. Kennedy or Ronald Reagan who inspires the nation. An old Greek saying holds that there are basically two types of leaders, the hedgehogs and the foxes. The hedgehog knows only one or two things but is dogged in pursuit of these goals. Foxes, on the other hand, are said to know many things and pursue multiple priorities.

Lincoln, FDR, and Reagan are archetypal hedgehogs. They were driven by single-minded devotion to specific large causes. They regularly simplified their goals to dramatize the need. They were wholesalers. Herbert Hoover and Jimmy Carter are likened to foxes that get caught up with so many unclear undertakings that they eventually become buried under the load.

Effective leaders learn to be both hedgehogs and foxes, wholesalers as well as retailers. They have macro agendas as well as a concern for the details. They dramatize their missions yet know that displays of passion and rhetoric need to be balanced by reflective reasoning.

Unifiers and Dividers

Leaders relish the role of serving as a uniter. President George W. Bush even campaigned on this theme. "I'll be a uniter and not a divider," he boasted in 2000. But, as with the Bush example, leaders invariably become dividers. The country did unite briefly after the 9/11 terrorist attacks. And Bush tried to take some credit for this. Yet he divided the nation with his Iraq war and Social Security reform policies, among others.[47]

Leadership involves unifying and pulling people together. But crises and change necessitate priority setting, decision, and often division.

Leaders break deadlocks and rally support around new goals. In breaking deadlocks leaders make decisions that inevitably disappoint supporters of alternative plans, as well as adherents of the status quo. Machiavelli famously describes this well:

> There is nothing more difficult to carry out, nor more doubtful of success, nor more dangerous to handle, than to initiate a new order of things, for the reformer has enemies in all those who would profit by the old order and only lukewarm defenders in all those who would profit by the new order.[48]

The strength of a leader often lies in knowing how to deal with competing factions, knowing when to compromise and when to heighten or sharpen conflict in an organization. Although shared values are essential to the smooth functioning of most organizations, leaders occasionally need to stir things up.

Saul Alinsky, a legendary Chicago community organizer, like most organizers of "the have-nots," sought change. Outsiders, he believed, had to fight for change. One of his maxims for organizers was to pick the target, freeze it, personalize it, and polarize it. The first law of community organizing, Alinsky said, is community disorganizing.[49] Yet even Alinsky counseled that conflict should not be allowed to go on for too long.

Effective corporate leaders know the usefulness, at least on occasion, of sweeping reorganizations and infusing a spirit of change in their organizations. They may not use the word "conflict," but they come to see the need for realigning and, in effect, disturbing the settled culture.

A major insurance company we watched closely had this type of top leadership. The president of the firm made it plain he was dissatisfied with the rigidity and lack of imagination in his company. His remedy was to shake things up: fire people, reorganize divisions, bring in new leaders from the outside, introduce new planning procedures, and require the top 2,000 managers to take a series of competency workshops including one on "Executive Leadership." He was seeking to unify the company and refocus its priorities. He had, he believed, to jolt his lumbering organization. They needed to adapt to new realities. They needed new competencies, new methodologies, and new attitudes. Conflict and a certain amount of disequilibrium were the price he was willing to pay as a means of turning his organization around.

Creativity and innovation often arise out of tension, passion, conflict, and paradox. "Paradoxical qualities within an organization have value because they force people to think outside the box, and to break away from convenient categories and patterns," writes business consultant Richard T. Pascale. "The puzzle in a paradox serves as an impulse; it energizes our minds to 'jump the rails' in search of a reconciling insight."[50] Smart leaders embrace conflict and paradox and occasionally introduce it into their organizations as a means of enhancing self-renewal. Cultivating these opportunities can help liberate an organization to see more clearly.

Leaders regularly decide how much harmony or how much tension is needed to achieve their organizations' objectives. Organizations need action and decisiveness; yet they also need harmony, shared values, community, and integration. Effective leaders understand how to use selective conflict for revitalization.

Reasonable people, as George Bernard Shaw noted, adjust to reality and cope with what they find. Unreasonable people dream dreams of a different, better world and try to adapt the world to themselves. This discontent or unreasonableness is often the first step in the progress of an organization or a nation-state.

Yet, innovators, "stirrer-uppers," disrupters, and conflict polarizers are threatening people. In the kingdom of the blind, the one-eyed man is king. This may be as the proverb states, but in the kingdom of one-eyed people, the two-eyed person is looked upon with profound suspicion. Leaders are often those two-eyed, twice-born types, who perceive things differently and who think differently. And thus they challenge the status quo, they war on complacency, they become "movers and shakers"—all of which done too fast or too much can create instability.

How do leaders transcend or at least cope with this paradox? One way is to focus on underlying *values*. If these are understood and shared, considerable organizational or societal change can be permitted in their pursuit. Another way is to develop integrative strategies that can harness the creative energy of the disruptive catalysts without paralyzing the overall enterprise. Then there is the Steve Jobs example. Fire him. But bring him back at the appropriate time and let him be in charge. That might not work for most organizations, but it worked for Apple and, in some ways, may be a quintessential example of unleashing the power of paradox.

The Leader/Follower Paradox

We customarily think of leaders as taking bold initiatives, as preoccupied with tomorrow rather than today, and as being out in front, pulling followers along. In short, a leader's job is to lead, "not to follow the polls."[51] Although this conception of leaders has some merit, in reality it is not entirely accurate.

Leaders are usually as much created by their organization as the other way around. Leaders lead as well as follow, and those who follow also often—at least in some way—lead.

Motorola's Bob Galvin said to lead well presumes the ability to follow smartly. The test of leadership, he suggests, is not to direct or command but to work with followers in such a way as they will become leaders and develop an ability to make the right decisions on their own. Under this kind of leadership it is not always clear just who is leading whom. What is important is that everyone learns to lead even as they collaborate as team members.[52]

If one defines leadership as a process of empowering a group to adapt wisely to change and achieve its goals, then leaders must have a solid grasp of what their followers wish to achieve. Yet they must also set goals that their followers might not otherwise appreciate. In this sense leaders are listeners who anticipate the cues of those they lead. If they fail to do so their leadership is jeopardized; leaders are nothing without followers. As noted, leadership is conferred and legitimized by followers. As management scholar Chester Barnard put it, "The decision as to whether an order has authority or not lies with the persons to whom it is addressed, and does not reside in 'persons of authority' or those who issue these orders."[53] Followers need to be persuaded.

Most people can be led only where they want to go. Effective leadership, writes James MacGregor Burns, is a collective process. It emerges from a sensitivity or appreciation of the motives and goals of both followers and leaders. The test of leadership, says Burns, "is the realization of intended, real change that meets people's enduring needs." Thus a key function of leadership is "to engage followers, not merely to activate them, to commingle needs and aspirations and goals in a common enterprise, and in the process to make better citizens of both leaders and followers."[54]

Courageous followers help keep a leader honest and out of trouble—that is, if leaders listen. In a *Harvard Business Review* essay, "In Praise of Followers," Robert E. Kelley says the success of a company depends as much on the nurturing of effective followers as it does effective leaders. Self-confident followers see colleagues as allies and their leaders pretty much as equals. Good leaders know how to follow even as they set an example for others. Effective followers regularly see themselves, except in terms of line responsibility, "as the equals of the leaders they follow," writes Kelley. "They are more apt to openly and unapologetically disagree with leadership and less likely to be intimidated by hierarchy and organizational structure. At the same time, they can see that the people they follow are, in turn, following the lead of others, and they try to appreciate the goals and needs of the team and the organization."[55]

Effective followers are willing to tell the truth, as in speaking truth to those in power. "Followers who tell the truth, and leaders who listen to it, are an unbeatable combination."[56]

It is in this sense that several writers conceptualize a leader as a servant, or servant leader. Robert K. Greenleaf, a former AT&T executive, says his ideas about the leader as servant, or servant as leader, came from his reading of Hermann Hesse's *Journey to the East.* In that story a band of men are on a mythical journey. A central figure in the story is Leo, who accompanies the party as their servant, performing menial chores yet also sustaining the group with songs and spirit. He becomes a special presence. All goes well until Leo disappears, at which point the group falls into disarray and the journey is abandoned. They are lost without their servant leader. The moral to Greenleaf's borrowed allegory is that the indispensable leader is often seen as servant, and this simple reality is the key to the leader's effectiveness. A second lesson is that those who are leaders don't always look like leaders.[57]

Greenleaf says leaders are only as good as their ability to win the confidence of those they lead. An old military manual observed: "No man is a leader until his appointment is ratified in the minds and hearts of his men."

Not everyone is comfortable with this conception of leadership. Military and sports leaders, long accustomed to hierarchical command and control systems, are understandably uncomfortable with these notions.

Thus Arnold "Red" Auerbach, legendary coach and former president of the Boston Celtics, chides the leader-as-follower theory summarized in the preceding paragraphs. "Can you imagine a team in which players picked other players and decided on substitutions? It is absolutely ludicrous," writes Auerbach. "Or can you imagine a business run by people without authority or by people who are not in a position to assume the responsibility of failure?" Auerbach, echoing Plato, asks, "Can a ship be run without a captain? It would undoubtedly flounder."[58]

Auerbach probably misunderstands Kelley's and Greenleaf's suggestions, yet he too has a point. Even a team occasionally forces its coach or captain to resign or relinquish command as the crew did on the minesweeper *Caine* in Herman Wouk's *Caine Mutiny,* or as countless teams have done with athletic coaches who have failed to lead. Votes of no confidence come as often from the followers as they do from the board of directors or their functional equivalent. Economist Larry Summers learned that in his short tenure as president of Harvard University. The leader who refuses to heed his or her followers, just like the coach who fails to "read" his or her team, is eventually dismissed, or encouraged to take early retirement.

The American people have often been out in front of their so-called political leaders on many issues. Thus, the public wanted to get out of Vietnam before Congress and the White House fully caught on. The public knew Richard Nixon had to go before he fully appreciated that reality. Tax revolts and populist measures such as term limits for legislators or the Tea Party and "Occupy" movements are other instances where followers can, rightly or wrongly, point the way. Officials are sometimes the last to learn about the new directions so-called followers have decided on. The "wave elections" of 2006, 2008, and 2010 were illustrative as voters sent messages to their presidents and parties (something that in the past was more periodic such as in 1966, 1974, and 1994).

Civil rights leader and congressman John Lewis sees leaders as standing with and beside followers, not above or even out in front of the people. "A person does not become a leader simply by assuming a position, filling a chair, or earning a title. A real leader doesn't see himself as standing out in front of the people. He sees himself as standing *beside* them, *among* them," writes Lewis. "He doesn't tell people to dig a ditch; he gets down in the ditch with them and digs it himself. That's why people believe so strongly in and follow so faithfully a figure like Mother Teresa, Gandhi, Cesar Chavez, or Nelson Mandela—because they spent a lot of time getting down in the ditch and digging."[59]

Thus, we have the paradox that all of us are followers, and, to a large extent, most of us are also leaders or at least have leadership instincts. Those who temporarily serve as leaders are no exception. Effective organizations need effective leaders as well as effective followers who provide the energy, ideas, and legitimacy. In the end, it is an engagement and a mutual dependency.

The larger lesson here is to embrace the paradox that we are all leaders and all followers, all leaders and all managers, and we need to recognize when we should emphasize one or the other. "It has been my observation," writes management and leadership scholar William Rosenbach, "that in high performing groups or organizations, leaders and followers are very comfortable switching roles when the situation calls for it."[60] In such organizations you'll often find that followers mentor their "leaders," and the forward-thinking leader, who may be rather rigid or fixed about the organization's values, is strikingly flexible in how the values are operationalized.

Those who have worked in community and civic development are similarly struck at how often a redefinition of leadership detached from formal positions and formal authority enables self-authorizing individuals to step forward and provide fresh solutions and imaginative, collaborative policymaking. "Rather than characterizing civics as the interaction of citizens with government focused on its oversight and operation," writes David Crislip, "this emerging understanding broadens this description to include the role of ordinary citizens and others in the organization and workings of society in order to address common concerns." Crislip adds, "Embedded in this enlarged understanding is the notion that each of us shares directly in both the problems and opportunities of civic life and so bear some of the responsibility for making progress."[61]

The "Is It the Leader or Is It the Context?" Paradox

One of the oldest and most debated paradoxes is the fascinating debate as to whether history is shaped by heroic change agents or whether leaders and their followers are primarily and more decisively shaped by their times, by events, and by the economic, social, and physical circumstances in which they live.

Be forewarned: we necessarily revisit this paradox at several places in our book because this "agency" versus "context" is such an iconic debate. Context shapes and limits opportunities, but individual agency (a rational, responsible, impactful individual) is always possible and is always "in play." Prophets and visionaries are often among us, yet we are not necessarily listening.

Scottish historian Thomas Carlyle (1795–1881) held that great leaders, by which he meant individuals of genius and original insight, made all the difference. To Carlyle, heroic and powerful men made history, forced change, got things done. The history of the world is but the biography of "great men."[62] Carlyle's distaste for democracy and celebration of the charismatic leader led him to oversimplify reality and glorify strength and power. Carlyle is by no means alone. Plutarch, Machiavelli, Confucius, Ralph Waldo Emerson, and many others celebrated the indispensable impact of notable leaders. "The notion that a people can run itself and its affairs anonymously," wrote the philosopher William James, "is now well known to be the silliest of absurdities. Mankind does nothing save through initiatives on the part of inventors, great or small . . . these are the sole factors in human progress."[63]

Biographers invariably leave the impression that the subjects of their biographies—generals, presidents, corporate chieftains, famous coaches and conductors—made a significant difference.[64] "All roads lead to Lincoln," says historian James McPherson in explaining both the conduct and the outcome of the Civil War.[65]

Many historians would agree with President Harry Truman who once said: "Men make history and not the other way around. In periods where there is no leadership, society stands still. Progress occurs when courageous, skillful leaders seize the opportunity to change things for the better."[66] Truman is a good example. He made a difference in the Berlin Airlift, in the Marshall Plan, in the Truman Doctrine, in dropping the atomic bomb.

This is not to say that citizens can expect saviors or that people can sit around passively waiting for another Lincoln, Churchill, Martin Luther King Jr., or Mandela. Still, people in business, politics, the media, and higher education regularly lament the absence of visionary leaders in their fields. Those in high positions are depicted as pygmies compared to leaders of the past, or in contrast to certain leaders in other companies or other countries. Thus: "I wish we had leaders with vision in my company; they just don't think big or long term here." "If we only had a leader with a capital 'L' this could be a far better place." "Our leaders are stuck up there (on those high floors) where the rubber meets the air, but they don't lead and I'm afraid they don't know what leadership is all about." Or as Lee Iacocca asked a few years ago: "Where are the voices of leaders who can inspire us to action and make us stand taller? ... Where have all the leaders gone?"[67]

Social scientists, however, say that our preoccupation with heroic or savior agents is wrongheaded. Indeed many scholars question the impact of leaders in general. It is hard, they say, to measure the precise influence or effects of top leaders. One student of top federal executives concluded that even those who "hurled themselves into the fray" had little impact on the policies and program accomplishments of their organizations. They make their mark "in inches, not miles," and their overall influence is incremental, not dramatic.[68]

A second student of organizational decision making finds that much of the job of an administrator in most organizations involves the mundane work of making a bureaucracy run efficiently. "It is filled with activities quite distant from those implied in a conception of administration as heroic leadership." He adds that, when an organization's system is working well, "variations will be due largely to variables unrelated to variations in top leaders. Where top leadership affects variation in outcomes, the system is probably not functionally well."[69]

Another report concludes that our faith in leadership usually exceeds the reality of measurable control by leaders and is used "to account for variance that is in fact uncontrollable." We may think leaders count for a lot in part because leaders spend so much time claiming credit and symbolically inflating their role and control. "It may be that the romance and the mystery surrounding leadership concepts are critical for maintaining follower-ship and that they contribute significantly to the responsiveness of individuals to the needs and goals of the collective organization."[70]

The British writer C. P. Snow put it succinctly when he wrote that he didn't much believe in the idea of the great leader because "great leaders emerge from circumstances and normally don't create them." Psychologist Daniel Kahneman acknowledges that business leaders, for example, do influence organizational performance, but the efforts are much smaller than a reading of most of the best-selling business press books suggests.[71]

If we conceive of leaders as people who make things happen that otherwise would not have happened, we are conceiving of leadership as a causal relationship. But we know that the cause is often attributable to followers, or stakeholders, or constituents, new technological inventions, bold new ideas, or favorable external developments. "There are as many leaders as there are causes," says political scientist Aaron Wildavsky, and "there is much trouble distinguishing one from the other or assigning them relative weights."[72]

Then, of course, there are those who are in Russian novelist Leo Tolstoy's school, or who are economic or social determinists of one variety or another. Larger social forces and events, they contend, explain why companies or nations succeed or fail. Leaders, Tolstoy (1828–1910) said, are mostly the pawns rather than the game changers of history. Leadership, for Tolstoy and his supporters, is significant only as illustrative human responses or reactions to events and social and economic developments. Leaders, they posit, seldom act alone—they are caught up in the web of social, economic, and geophysical phenomena. It is these factors, not temporary power-wielders, that shape the important outcomes.[73]

Tolstoy was skeptical of the idea that larger-than-life leaders make a big difference. Leaders or office holders, to Tolstoy, were more often confused, clueless, and seldom in control of what was going on. His writings in *War and Peace* suggest that history is full of ambiguity and arises from complex interaction of countless, often contradictory and insignificant, impersonal events. Thus leaders are shaped by their environments more than they are the shapers.[74]

This may be an old and defining debate, yet there are few signs of resolution. Understanding this debate, however, helps remind us of the enigmatic aspects of the leadership process.

We are rarely sure what causes people to follow a leader, and we are seldom sure either how much leaders lead or are being led, whether by the followers or the requirements of culture and context. It may be more useful to conceptualize the leader as an intervening rather than the primary variable, for plainly there are always a number of shaping factors—social, economic, organizational, cultural, and psychological—that cause leaders to do what they do.

Leaders obviously like to think they make a difference and some doubtless do. Americans like to think of George Washington and Abraham Lincoln as indispensable men or at least something close to that.[75] Yet it is sometimes hard to measure precisely the difference even they, and leaders like them, made. Among the important tasks of a leader are symbolic and psychological roles—of evoking loyalty and affirming significance, purpose, and meaning in an organization—and these are as elusive to measure as they are vital to the health of complex organizations.

Conclusion

Leadership will always mean different things to different people. For most of us it is an evocative word rich in positive meaning, as in empowerment and liberation. Yet for others it connotes manipulation, deception, intimidation, or coercion. And everyone is partly right.

Life is a struggle for many and a paradoxical puzzle for most in part because so much of life is made up of opposites. The life of leaders is paradoxical because it asks them to live in a world of simultaneous dichotomies and equilibriums, mixed with disequilibriums often in search of yet some new balance or order. A dialectical process of thesis versus antithesis in search of some new type of synthesis comes with the leadership territory.

Business theorist Charles Handy adds, "Paradox confuses us because things don't behave the way we expect them to behave!"[76] He could well have added that things often don't behave the way we "want" or "need" them to.

Leaders find ways to understand the dialectics and paradoxes, to put them to use and reframe them to shape better organizations and bringing about progress. Sometimes this involves a creative integrating of normal opposites. When the noted diplomat Richard Holbrooke was asked whether he was a Wilsonian idealist or a ruthless "realpolitiker," he rejected the either/or formula: "We cannot choose between the two; we have to blend the two." He was comfortable with American power, yet he could hardly forsake the American idealism that had inspired his Jewish parents as they sought refuge in America.[77]

Certain cultures and communities celebrate decisive assertiveness and dominant styles of leadership. Others yearn for more modest servant leaders, if they are willing to tolerate leaders at all. Societal and organizational expectations of leaders vary enormously from setting to setting, according to the requirements of context. In virtually every society and setting, we require leaders to be alternately collaborative and competitive.

Leaders find themselves in a web of mutual engagements with both fellow leaders and followers. Our expectations shift. We send mixed signals. The job description of nearly any leader is full of ambiguities. Leaders are forever having to redefine and reimagine their contributions in response to how they read the requirements of context as well as expectations.

Ultimately, effective leaders wrestle with the paradoxical aspects of leadership and learn to improvise and synthesize as best they can. Effective leaders not only learn to live with these and related paradoxes but they also develop a contextual intelligence and an "integrative thinking" approach that helps them look beyond either/or decision making. Roger Martin urges leaders to learn how to integrate the obvious advantages of one possible solution without canceling out the advantage of alternative solutions. Integrative thinking, Martin adds, involves "generative reasoning, a form of reassessing that inquires into what might be rather than what is. Generative reasoning helps build a framework for creative resolutions that are sturdy enough to withstand the rigors of the real world."[78]

John Heider in *The Tao of Leadership* writes that because most behaviors contain their opposites, we need to "learn to see things backwards, inside out, and upside down."[79]

Psychologist Howard Gardner emphasizes that effective leaders must have, among other skills, the ability to knit together information and ideas from competing sources into a coherent strategy. "As synthesizers, they will need to be able to gather together information from disparate sources and put it together in ways that work for themselves and can be communicated to other persons."[80]

No leader can be all things to all people at all times, and yet this is precisely what we would often like. An appreciation of these contradictions and paradoxes helps explain why we complain so much about leaders. It may also explain why many people shy away from what they consider the seemingly no-win situation we visit upon leaders.

In the chapters that follow, we examine more fully how leaders have coped with these enduring paradoxes and contradictions. We are especially interested in how effective leaders have often, at least for a while, managed paradoxes, learned to coexist with them, or found "ways around or out of" them. We are equally interested in examining leaders who can unlock or unleash the power of paradox. But first we tackle the challenge of defining leadership.

Chapter Two
Defining Leadership

> If your actions inspire others to dream more, learn more, do more, and become more, you are a leader.
>
> —*John Quincy Adams*[1]

The scene is one of the most powerful in the dramatic canon, and is one of the most celebrated speeches ever delivered. It rallied a band of vastly outnumbered warriors to an unlikely victory in one of Europe's most notable battles. It moved underdogs to fight against great odds and secure victory for England. And it is still considered a sublime act of leadership at its best. Or was it?

We are referring to William Shakespeare's dramatic representation of Henry V's St. Crispin's Day speech, delivered in late October 1415 on the eve of the Battle of Agincourt between the English and the French.

> Enter the King
> WESTMORELAND. O that we now had here
> But one ten thousand of those men in England
> That do no work to-day!
> KING. What's he that wishes so?
> My cousin Westmoreland? No, fair cousin;
> If we mark'd to die, we are enow
> To do our country loss; and if to live,
> The fewer men, the greater share of honour.
> God's will! I pray thee, wish not one man more....
> Rather, proclaim it, Westmoreland, through my host,
> That he which hath no stomach to this fight,

Let him depart; his passport shall be made,
And crowns for convoy put into his purse;
We would not die in that man's company
That fears his fellowship to die with us.
This day is call'd the feast of Crispian.
He that outlives this day, and comes safe home,
Will stand a tip-toe when this day nam'd,
And rouse him at the name of Crispian.
He that shall live this day, and see old age,
Will yearly on the vigil feast his neighbours,
And say "To-morrow is Saint Crispian."
Then will he strip his sleeve and show his scars,
And say "These wounds I had on Crispian's day."
Old men forget; yet all shall be forgot,
But he'll remember, with advantages,
What feats he did that day. Then shall our names,
Familiar in his mouth as household words—
Harry the King, Bedford and Exeter,
Warwick and Talbot, Salisbury and Gloucester—
Be in their flowing cups freshly rememb'red.
This story shall the good man teach his son;
And Crispin Crispian shall ne'er go by,
From this day to the ending of the world,
But we in it shall be remembered;
We few, we happy few, we band of brothers;
For he to-day that sheds his blood with me
Shall be my brother; be he ne'er so vile,
This day shall gentle his condition;
And gentlemen in England now-a-bed
Shall think themselves accurs'd they were not here,
And hold their manhoods cheap whiles any speaks
That fought with us upon Saint Crispin's day.
(*Henry V*, Act 4, Scene 3)

This inspiring speech, this bold act of heroic leadership, we are led to believe, is what spurred the outmanned English troops to an unlikely victory. Perhaps, yet perhaps not. Even if the speech was real and not a dramatic flourish from the pen of the Bard, it is likely that this iconic inspirational battlefield pep talk did not in fact win the battle that day.

The English discovered that the wood of the yew tree could be made into a longbow, and thus, English archers could kill French fighters at a long distance. Most of the French troops were thus struck down long before they even engaged in the hand-to-hand, close-range battle they might have won.[2]

Henry's leadership, it now seems, probably mattered less than Shakespearean verse suggested.

The Greek playwright Euripides once wrote that ten soldiers wisely led will best one hundred without a head. And this may also have helped the English at Agincourt, for the French national leaders were overconfident and perhaps in disarray. Leo Tolstoy would suggest that ambiguities and events may well have been beyond the control of the leaders that day. But, in the event, new technology, more than rhetorical leadership, carried the day for the English.

What does this teach us about leadership? Leadership matters. But in this case what proved consequential was the leadership and innovation of developing new weaponry as much as, if not more than, battlefield pep talk or the heroics of the twenty-nine-year-old King Henry V.

Great leaders sometimes do make history; yet so do new inventions, social movements, organizational breakthroughs, and timely innovations of all kinds. Change and success have many parents and multiple causes. It is often easy to highlight a single person and exclaim, "See, he (or she) did it!"; yet what is easy can often be wrong.

This book defines and analyzes leadership, yet we do not contend leaders alone make history, win battles, or cause change. Nor do we contend leaders are inconsequential. Leaders and leadership matter. Not all leaders matter all of the time. Of course leadership matters, yet it is not the only thing that matters. As agents of change or achievers of group goals, social movements or concerted efforts may be important, coalitions of various groups and interests may make a difference, the exercise of force or raw power may be important, technological innovations might cause great changes, the power of an idea may be vital. Leadership matters, yet it is not the be-all and end-all. It is only a part of the puzzle.

On the other hand, what about Winston Churchill's dogged leadership that propelled England to stand up to the Nazis during the darkest days of World War II? Did his grit, drive, and unrelenting determination turn the tide, or might the British on their own have risen to the challenge? We can never definitively know the answer, yet one cannot help but think that Churchill mattered, and mattered greatly.[3]

Another case for the "leadership matters" argument is Mikhail Gorbachev.[4] Who would deny that Gorbachev opened doors in the former Soviet Union that led to dramatic changes, liberating Eastern Europe, breaking up the moribund Soviet dynasty, ending the Cold War, and helping bring about the downfall of communism?[5]

What of Florence Nightingale? After her service as a nurse during the Crimean War, she returned to England where she revolutionized the field of nursing by making it more professional and better grounded in medical science. Her book,

Notes on Nursing, plus her extraordinary leadership, had a profound impact on public health.

Or Nelson Mandela? If charisma is in part defined as creating a presence, Mandela's absence, in prison, paradoxically created for his colleagues an indelible presence. After spending twenty-seven years in prison, Mandela emerged as the leader of his cause and people. His strength, moral courage, example, and personal narrative inspired a peaceful transition that toppled apartheid in South Africa and led to his becoming South Africa's president.[6]

Absent Mandela, would the apartheid government of South Africa have fallen? Yes, but later rather than sooner. Would a bloody revolution have ensued? One is hard-pressed to imagine a positive outcome absent the moral and political leadership of Mandela. Yes, at times, leadership *can* matter. Surely the *roles* required to achieve group ends have to be performed by an individual or individuals.

When, why, and how much is leadership likely to matter? Consider a baseball analogy. In baseball, some managers matter greatly. Good and bad managers can have a significant impact. When Joe Torre left the New York Yankees (where his teams won four World Series championships) to manage the Los Angeles Dodgers in 2008, he took a mediocre team and made them into winners. A good manager can do that.

What was Torre's "magic"? He knew the game (he was an all-star) and had experience managing several teams before the Dodgers. As a successful, quietly confident coach, he supported his players and earned their trust. As a strategist, he knew just which players to use and when. He helped hire talented players and skilled coaches and built his team around the dimensions of the home field. When his high-maintenance superstar Manny Ramirez was suspended for fifty games for violating the Major League's performance-enhancing drug policy during the 2009 season, Torre's team continued to win (in fact, during Ramirez's absence the Dodgers had the best record in baseball).

Joe Torre was a great player *and* a great manager. Contrast Torre to Ted Williams. Williams was one of the greatest hitters in the history of the game. He is the last player to hit over .400 in a season, and was a two-time winner of the American League Most Valuable Player award, led the league in hitting six times, and won the Triple Crown. The Hall of Famer had a career batting average of .349.

Williams managed the Washington Senators for three seasons and the Texas Rangers for one (the Senators moved to Texas in 1972). In his four years as a manager, he won 273 games *and* lost 364, a dismal .429 winning percentage. His only winning season was his first, with an 86–76 record. His teams got worse each year he managed. In his fourth season, his team finished with a 54–100 record.

Why was so great a player so poor a manager? Williams was a hitter's manager. He knew hitting. Yet, hitting is only part of the game. Williams was notorious for being short with pitchers and he often openly displayed contempt for his pitchers. He was less savvy about overall strategy and could be short-tempered when his team failed. Some players say they felt uncomfortable and anxious playing for Williams, who expected, even demanded, that his team play up to *his* skill level. It was a formula for failure.

If good managers matter a great deal in bringing about positive results and bad managers have a decidedly negative impact, what can be said about "most" managers who are mediocre or merely capable? Thus, a few good managers matter, a few bad managers matter, but most managers have little impact and matter little.

The same is true of leaders in general. Leaders *can* matter, for better or worse. Yet most "leaders" (office holders) matter little.

This is a book about leaders and leadership. It is not a "how-to" book, although we offer classical as well as contemporary insights for leaders. We don't promote a specific theory of leadership although we discuss and analyze many theories and put them to the test. This is not a book that glorifies the cult of leadership, although there are leaders we admire. It looks at how leaders lead, why and when followers follow, what leadership is and how it works, what the limits and possibilities of leadership are, what happens when leaders "go bad," and how leadership can be valued, empowered, *and* constrained in a democratic culture.

We employ a distinct thematic approach to leadership. As discussed, we believe leadership can best be understood by using the conceptual framework of *paradoxes*. It requires the balancing of competing demands, contradictory lessons, and clashing expectations. Leaders learn to live with, navigate through, and master paradoxes. Thus, there are few absolute rules for leadership. What works for one leader, at one time, under one set of circumstances, may not work for another leader. What leads to success today may condemn a leader to failure tomorrow. For leaders to succeed they must learn to lead, adapt, and improvise within the harsh confines of paradox, reality, context, and culture.

The Need for Leadership

Leadership is universal and inescapable—unless, of course, one chooses to live alone in a cave. Sociologist Robert Michaels's "iron law of oligarchy"[7] holds that in all forms of organization, whether democratic or autocratic, leaders emerge, or oligarchies form. Leadership is indispensable and thus ubiquitous.

Humans need organization as well as some form of hierarchy. As soon as our ancestors started living in groups, government became necessary. And as soon as government became necessary, leaders became necessary. Collective work requires coordination, thus government and leadership.

Living systems seek equilibrium or balance. And when knocked out of equilibrium, "living systems summon a set of restorative responses" designed to *adapt* to the new challenges that jolted us out of balance.[8] Leadership helps identify threats to equilibrium and proposes constructive measures to adapt to threats to social balance.

Real leadership is not afraid to confront the threats of disequilibrium. As Ronald Heifetz points out, "In times of distress, we turn to authority."[9] False leaders lie or give us sugar pills; true leaders give us the truth, as hard as that may be to swallow. It is the difference between maladaptive and adaptive leadership.[10]

Studying Leadership

Given the multidisciplinary nature of leadership studies, to master the field (just as to master the actual practice of leadership) one must be a *generalist.* To map the terrain of the discipline demands that we *integrate* a wide range of material from a wide range of fields. Thus, we try to fit the many parts into an understandable whole.

In some ways, the study of leadership began with the study of politics. Socrates, Plato, Aristotle, and Thucydides explored what made for the good state and what a leader must know in order to govern.

Early studies of leadership tended to focus on the "ought" of leadership: how leaders ought to behave. Acting justly, exercising virtue, and developing goodness were seen as the keys to unlocking the door to good leadership. Thus, to know virtue and to act on virtue were essential in the instruction of would-be leaders.

Then, along came Niccolò Machiavelli, and the study of leadership turned upside down. Machiavelli focused on how effective leaders got things done rather than how they should behave. Machiavelli was on to something: leaders were less concerned with virtue and justice than with what was necessary to create the stable and successful city-state.

Although we still criticize Machiavelli for his preoccupation with power politics, we remain indebted to him for grounding the study of leadership in the real world of behavior and politics.

Leaders: Born or Made?

A persistent and vexing question in the field of leadership is: Are leaders *born* or *made*? One can argue that leaders are *both* born and made. To use another sports analogy, Michael Jordan was born with physical gifts that gave him advantages over the rest of us. Yet to become the great basketball player he became, he had to work long, hard hours for years to develop his natural physical talents. Jordan was doubtless born with good athletic and basketball genes, but so were thousands of others. Why did Michael Jordan sparkle while others remained ordinary? Plenty of hard work, discipline, good coaching, drive, and ambition. And when he was surrounded by good teammates and master coaches, he won individual as well as team awards.

Leaders may be born with good leadership genes. They may be attractive, have high intelligence, physical stamina, and so on. All of these traits help but are not enough. Leaders must develop, train, learn, be disciplined, have the hunger (drive and ambition for achievement) to succeed.

The key is they make the most of what they have, learn skills they do not possess, know themselves, know the world, and work, work, work. Leadership *can* be learned. Here are the phases of leadership "learning."

Phase I: The Accident of Birth. Some are born with better genes or qualities and attributes (attractive, good speaking voice, etc.) that give them an early boost.

Phase II: Early Childhood Development. Teachers, coaches, ministers, scout leaders, and parents model different styles of leadership. Early childhood experiences or unusual challenges can also have an impact on leadership. For example, losing a parent often forces a child to mature faster and take on family leadership roles early in life.

Phase III: Education and Growth. In school, on teams, and in other groups, some students emerge (self-selected or peer-selected) as formal or informal leaders. Team captains, class presidents, debating teams, and other groups foster leadership growth. Later in life, formal training in leadership skills can have a significant impact. West Point, the Stanford Business School, the Center for Creative Leadership, the Young Presidents Organization, the White House Fellows program, and the Junior League are some of the "developmental leagues" and "finishing schools" that prepare nascent leaders.

Phase IV: Experience. As people grow, opportunities to assume leadership positions abound. Some seek them, others retreat. At this stage, mentors can be especially important for would-be leaders. And although experience itself does not always produce learning, experience *plus* careful, honest *reflection* on experience often does. The wise among us extract lessons from experience and especially from our mistakes and the mistakes of others.

Leadership *can* be learned. That is not to say it can be easily or completely mastered.

Most anyone can become competent in most endeavors. What is required are three things: practice, practice, practice. Mastery, however, requires more. It requires innate talent, incredible commitment, and judgment, and not everyone has the God-given natural talent of a Michael Jordan or a Leonard Bernstein.

Defining Leadership

Despite the impressive writings of Plato, Plutarch, Machiavelli, Shakespeare, Sigmund Freud, Thomas Carlyle, Tolstoy, Max Weber, James MacGregor Burns, and others, no grand, unifying theory of leadership exists.[11] One may never exist. Yet we now know a lot about leadership and leaders, and it is these ideas that are discussed throughout this book. We'll set the stage.

People regularly yearn for transcending leadership for their communities, companies, unions, universities, political parties, and nations. Yet we have ambivalence about power wielders and those who exercise great influence. As noted, we dislike anyone who tries to boss us around. We admire leaders like Washington and Churchill, but Richard Nixon and Hitler and Saddam Hussein were leaders, too—and this highlights a central problem: leadership can be exercised in service of noble, liberating, life-enriching ends; yet it can also be used to manipulate, mislead, and repress.

"One of the most universal cravings of our time," writes James MacGregor Burns, "is a hunger for compelling and creative leadership."[12] But exactly what is creative leadership? Leadership defies simple definition, but it is ultimately a relationship or chemistry between leaders and associates. We understand much of what is involved in leadership—shared values, community goals, vision, collaboration, strategy, cooperation, trust, adaptation, synthesizing, motivation, mobilization, decision making, judgment, and productivity—yet leadership for many people is often a hazy and confusing abstraction. One of the puzzling paradoxes about leaders is that invariably a leader is a follower who emerges as a leader and remains a leader only so long as the followers are willing to follow. Yet exactly when these transitions occur is typically unclear to everyone, including the leader.

Leadership is about making things happen, both good and bad, that might not otherwise happen and preventing things from happening that ordinarily would. It is the process of getting people to work together. Leadership transforms intentions into actions, visions into realities. It turns a group of people into a community with a purpose. It involves the infusion of vision into an enterprise. It entails mobilizing people and resources to undertake desired patterns of cooperation. It often involves directing followers where only their better selves are willing to go.

Leadership is a process of persuasion and example, whereby leaders or a leadership team motivate colleagues to take an action and achieve shared goals.[13] Leadership in common with coaching and conducting is a process where leaders empower the rest of us to rise to our potential, to become engaged and excel. Leadership is about getting people in an organization to discover their comparative advantages and getting them to concentrate their resources on those advantages. It involves conflict, challenge, learning, collaboration, adaptation, renewal, and disciplined, tenacious action in pursuit of desired results.

Bernard Bass, in his *Handbook of Leadership,* suggests leadership should be defined broadly, arguing that "leadership occurs when one group member modifies the motivation or competencies of others in the group."[14]

Other definitions emphasize similar themes:

- Leadership is the process of capturing people's attention and getting people to think about what is important and how this can be achieved.
- Leadership refers to someone or a team who helps a larger group create and achieve mutual goals.
- Leadership involves diagnosing the collective situation, designing ways of dealing with it, and mobilizing support for both a diagnosis and proposed adaptive responses.
- Leadership is the capacity to shape organizations and mobilize and inspire members to achieve results; the cooperation must be purposeful and the executive exercise of authority involves management as well as vision and imagination.
- Leadership involves intentional action that allocates resources to achieve desired shared aspirations.

What Leaders Do

Any effort to define leadership necessarily involves an analysis of what leaders do. A leader guides the group and, as noted, is at the same time paradoxically guided by the group. No one can lead except from within. Not only must leaders be part of the group, they also must acknowledge their common bonds with the group. Leaders are defined by what they do for others rather than by who they are. The wise leader is dedicated not only to his or her own career but the careers of colleagues and associates. One of the first maxims of leadership is to take care of those one works with and a lot of good things will happen.

Leaders interpret our experiences to us. They are often able to see the different points of view that underlie our activities. Leaders are often better than the rest of us in seeing beyond the horizon, in comprehending the bigger picture, and in sharing storytelling narratives that help us make sense of our story, our situation, and our possibilities and where we should be going. This is sometimes called the "helicopter" factor—the ability to rise above ongoing operations and take a more encompassing view of one's self and one's organization in a societal or global context.

Leaders empower us less by dominating than by expressing our hopes and values and unlocking our collective energies in pursuit of those goals. Leaders inspire us to believe in ourselves and in our power and responsibility to improve our situation, and leaders help convince us of our strengths and help us focus on what we want to achieve. An effective college president, for example, gets the important constituencies to believe their school could and should be an outstanding institution. An effective corporate executive sets goals, articulates vision, and aligns the organization's personnel, resources, and structure to execute its plans. "He is a leader who gives form to the inchoate energy in every man," wrote Mary Parker Follett in the 1920s. "The person who influences me most is not the person who does great deeds but he who makes me feel I can do great deeds."[15]

The effective leader is variously a listener, learner, teacher, mentor, negotiator, pragmatist, coach, and politician. But too much focus on the function of *the leader* can undermine the effort to understand *leadership*. Leadership needs in contemporary organizations—public and private—are necessarily understood as an *engagement* between partners and collaborators.

To study leaders separate from the loyalties and complex interactions they have with followers, constituents, and team members is to miss the essence of leadership. It is always a two-way loyalty, a two-way communication, and the mutual engagement of leaders and the "led" that are crucial. Leadership scholars rightly insist on putting the "ship," or the followers, back in the leadership equation. Leadership is a collective enterprise: the ongoing, if subtle, interplay between common desires and a leader's capacity to understand and respond to these shared aspirations. The success of effective leadership becomes apparent primarily among the so-called followers. Are they learning? Are they succeeding? Are they productive, efficient, effective? Are they achieving their common goals?

Leadership may be a mutual process of influence among a group's members. Yet normally, we single out one or a few members who exert the most influence and we designate those people as leaders—especially when their exercise of influence has an impact on the group's attainment of a specified set of goals. Still, followers can have considerable influence over their so-called leaders. Influence "between leaders and followers is seldom unidirectional."[16] Indeed, as Keith Grint perceptively notes, "What distinguishes a successful from a failed leader is whether the subordinates can and will save the organization from mistakes of its leader."[17]

The mind's eye often sees leaders as larger-than-life figures who act boldly, often alone, make things happen, have and use power. Yet this is seldom the case. Most of the time, leaders stand on the shoulders of others, derive their strength and authority from others, benefit from being a member of an effective team, and build on the previous work of others.

Let us clarify some of the definitional ambiguities. Leadership is not *management*; it is not *command* and it is not *office holding*. Management is the practice of directing and coordinating organized activity within a group or organization. It is process oriented, a technical skill, designed to do things right.

Command, as in the military command model, grants someone authority to decide and dictate. In command, an authoritative person has recognized rights to issue orders that are expected to be followed.

Office holding is not leadership. Merely holding office may grant a modicum of authority, an opportunity to lead, and resources to command; yet, mere office holding falls far short of leadership.

Leadership is about mobilizing and inspiring others to get something done for the benefit of the group or the common good. It is interactive and requires leaders to lead and followers to become activated.

In the simplest form, leaders find ways to get things done. There is a telling aphorism that holds: one doesn't need a title or a special position to lead. Leaders may or may not occupy an institutional position or office, yet they see a need and fill it, see a problem and get it solved, see an opportunity and make the most of it. They do not do this alone, but in concert with others. They work with others to get things done, to fill needs, to solve problems.

- Leadership is a *process,* not a single act by a lone individual.
- Leadership involves a leader *and* followers—it is a *group process.*
- Leadership is *influence,* much more than the exercise of raw power.
- Leaders ignite a spark in others.
- Followers *willingly* follow a legitimate leader, just as followers generally validate a leader's legitimacy.
- Leadership is about attaining *mutually desired goals* for the group.
- A key to effective leadership is good judgment.
- Good judgment requires rationality *and* empathy, passion *and* a sense of proportion.

The U.S. Army, which for obvious reasons has one of the world's most sophisticated leadership training models, strives to create what it calls "pentathlete" leaders. These are the ideal leaders, and are defined as officers "who are not only competent in their core warrior skills, but who are also scholars; men and women who are creative, innovative, strategically minded, culturally competent, and skilled in all aspects of peace, war, politics, and civil administration."[18] That's asking a lot. And it sets the bar high.

With some tweaking, that is a definition of an effective leader in most contexts. It is a lot to ask of anyone. But leaders aren't just "anyone." And although anyone can become a better leader, not everyone can become a pentathlete leader.

In the United States, the words "leader" and "leadership" generally have positive associations with the public. Not so in some other cultures. In German, "leader" is translated as *Führer,* a red flag warning if ever there was one. And in many Asian societies, anyone who stands out as above or apart from "the group" risks being resented and resisted.

All leaders have some power, but not all office holders (who have positions of power) are leaders. Leadership is the ability to mobilize a group to achieve a common purpose. Power is the capacity to control decisions and actions via the authoritative use of force or sanctions. Leadership is about working with and for others. Power is the ability of an individual to get his or her way. Leadership is about persuasion, influence, and agreement building. Power is about having one's desires implemented. In leadership, followers *agree* to follow. In power, "followers" have little choice.

Effective leadership remains in many ways the most baffling of the performing arts. There is an element of mystery about it. Intuition, passion, flare, and even theatrical ability come into play. Individuals with ample leadership qualities do not necessarily become effective leaders, often because of cultural or situational factors. Sometimes, it is because they are insufficiently optimistic or insufficiently tenacious or unwilling to dramatize their values, visions, and ideas. The genius of leadership sometimes comes too early or too late; an effective person in one setting can be a failure in another.

Leaders often emerge as products of newly coalescing interest groups or movements rather than sole instigators or initiators of such movements. Thus, Lincoln was an emerging star within the recently formed Republican Party in 1860. Not to belittle or slight their courage, contributions, or talents, leaders are often unduly singled out as founders and catalysts of parties and movements that hoisted them to prominence. Textbook writers too often, for example, define eras or movements by the actions of famous individuals—almost as if they acted alone. In Lincoln's case, for example, his role was crucial but so was the rise of the Republican Party, the agitational might of the Abolitionists, and the increasing rebellion and yearnings of African Americans led by Frederick Douglass and others.

By idolizing Mount Rushmore leaders, we underestimate everyone's ability to lead. At the end of his prizewinning biography of Martin Luther King Jr., David J. Garrow approvingly quotes a friendly observer of King and the civil rights movement: "If people think that it was Martin Luther King's movement then today they—young people—are more likely to say, 'Gosh, I wish we had

Martin Luther King here today to lead us. . . .' If people knew how the movement started, the question they would ask themselves is, 'What can I do?'"[19]

If a group or community wishes to have leaders to follow, they often must first show the way. Citizens, groups, and movements often get the leadership they nurture, encourage, inspire, and ultimately deserve. Here again, leadership is more a bottom-up than a top-down proposition.

There are a number of generic tasks leaders typically perform. Leaders direct and coordinate the effort of a group toward goals. "The leader generally plans, organizes, directs, and supervises the activities of group members and develops and maintains sufficient cohesiveness and motivation among group members to keep them together as a functioning unit."[20]

Leaders get organizations interested in what they are going to become as well as remind them of what they have been. They show the direction and help people get there.

Leaders help groups to plan, gather data, develop action strategies, understand their challenges and competition, understand both the positive and negative technological developments of the day, and then make decisions and assess outcomes. Leaders also motivate and rally people to make commitments that permit the group to achieve much more than they thought possible.

Leaders have ideas. Yet leaders seldom come up with all or even most of the ideas as much as they are users and integrators of available new ideas. Still, leaders must contribute to the substantive thinking necessary to move an organization beyond problems and toward achievements. A leader helps to define reality, to clarify options and opportunities, and to remove the obstacles that make it difficult for the members of an organization to succeed in their work. A leader helps to set the agenda, spelling out strategies, timetables, and objectives for achieving an organization's mission. Leaders are listeners, yet they also raise group consciousness and unlock the energies and talents of fellow associates.

Leaders define, defend, and promote values. They also help redefine values and understand, in Abraham Lincoln's phrase, when the dogmas of the past are inadequate for the stormy present, when new circumstances call for new vision. "Good business leaders create a vision, articulate the vision, passionately own the vision, and relentlessly drive it to completion," wrote former General Electric chairman Jack Welch.[21] Leaders carefully appreciate their colleagues' values, beliefs, and passions.

Leaders merge hopes and needs with organizational purposes and shared aspirations. The task of leadership is one of closing the gap between an individual's needs and abilities and the organization's goals. In this sense, leaders mediate, direct, negotiate, motivate, and in general, "mesh things up."

Leaders capitalize on the strengths of their talented members while simultaneously upgrading the competencies and the morale of their less prepared members.

Although everyone needs motivation or training, some people need more of one than the other. Some top performers are can-do, will-do contributors. But certain laggards need more specialized skills training. Still others need additional motivation and clarification about the central purpose and meaning of a venture. Yet others need better skills and inspiration. The leader's job never ends.

Leaders recruit new blood and, preferably, the right type of blood. They are responsible for identifying, developing, and nurturing future leaders. A primary job of a leader is helping talented people blossom. Equally important, they fire people who need to be let go. As management consultant Jim Collins famously wrote, leaders get the right people in the right seats on the bus and the wrong people off the bus as well as making sure the bus is headed in the proper direction.[22]

As important as anything, however, a leader has to nurture trust and self-confidence in an organization. Associates expect leaders to have sensible visions and to pursue them with enthusiasm. People being led require a mission or vision that is simply stated, enthusiastically endorsed, and sufficiently inspiring to induce extraordinary effort. They want to be members of organizations that radiate significance. They yearn for communities of trust, competence, shared values, and meaning.

According to the mountain climbing classic *Mountaineering: The Freedom of the Hills,* fellow climbers look instinctively to the person who inspires confidence. This may not be the person with the most experience, nor is it always the person with the most skill. It is, mountaineering experts say, the person who displays the most common sense and sensible judgment. What matters is the climbers' willingness to follower a leader's judgment and decisions. Consideration of both safety and success is important. "Knowledge, experience, and climbing skills help meet these responsibilities, but of far greater importance is the ability to deal with others, to be sensitive to their attitudes, physical requirements and limitations, to inspire and encourage them and to guide them in the exercise of their own initiative so that their efforts contribute to the achievement of their goals." It is in this sense that effective leaders give us an idea not only of who they are, but also of who we are, and where we are going.[23]

Of course, leaders do much more. They delegate. They thank people. They listen. They teach. They motivate. They evaluate. They praise. They get everyone involved and focused. "Leadership is diving for a loose ball, getting the crowd involved, getting other players involved," said basketball legend Larry Bird. "It's being able to take it as well as dish it out. That's the only way you're going to get the respect of the players."

Leaders are expected to see farther and more accurately than others to balance present and future, to think big and take certain risks, and to use their intuition and imagination as well as their analytic reasoning abilities to define meaningful relations with followers, customers, and important external stakeholders. It often falls to presidents and corporate leaders, for example, to be the necessary intermediaries between internal and external forces, between micro and macro, between national and transnational relations.[24]

Hockey great Wayne Gretzky used to credit some of his legendary success to a key point in sports as well as leadership. "I go," he said, "where the puck is going to be, not where it is." In a similar way, effective leaders read the context, diagnose the current situation, and see where things are headed before the fact. This is strategic anticipation or contextual intelligence, and it allows a leader to be ahead of the wave rather than swallowed up by it. This was, we are told, the genius Steve Jobs provided for Apple.[25]

Leaders have to prepare, modify, and simplify plans so everyone understands and "owns" a share in the organization's goals. They must have a personal vision of where they want to lead, yet just having a vision isn't enough. Effective leaders get the best people they can find to improve, share, help implement, and achieve their vision. Leaders also shape their organization's culture, ideology, and values. And since values can decay over time, leaders are constantly reviewing, renewing, and reaffirming the values and integrity of an organization.

Leaders are hope dealers. They activate positive emotions and imagination. They create, in Ted Turner's phrase, "infectious enthusiasm." Exuberance enlists followers and inspires support.[26]

Humans do not live by reason alone. Dreams and myths are an age-old form of motivation as well as entertainment and escape. People turn to civic and societal leaders just as tribesmen turn to shamans—searching for meaning, healing, improvement, legitimacy, assurance, and a sense of purpose. Leaders lead us in part by tapping into the myths, legends, symbols, and aspirations of our culture. Alexander the Great did this, Henry V did this, Lincoln did this, MLK Jr. did this, Mandela did this.

What Motivates Leaders?

Why do leaders do what they do? A mix of both conscious and unconscious motives explains why most leaders seek positions of power and seek to influence change. Some leaders are primarily motivated by ideals, others by personal, political, or material interests. For others, it is a mixture of these factors, including the exhilaration of solving problems; the honor of holding positions; affection, love, a need for approval, and a desire to feel relevant; money and status, and the psychological need to prove one's worth; and, in some cases, revenge.

For most leaders it is the desire to be where "the action is," to have a larger voice in how their lives are lived and make a difference in the lives of their community or profession, to advance fresh ideas and approaches, and to contribute to progress. Some leaders are galvanized to action because of a vision, faith, or ideology. Most leaders, however, gradually rise to prominence because they are competitive as well as competent; they can communicate better than others or they have certain skills in negotiating, managing, planning, or finance that propel them competitively into ever larger spheres of responsibility.

Psychological factors are harder to understand. Yet most leaders, at least in part, want the attention that comes from effective performance of leadership roles. Some seek the trappings of power. Some thirst for the excitement of conflict, danger, and risk taking. Others have developed, for whatever reason, a deep-seated sense of destiny. Lawrence of Arabia (T. E. Lawrence) is a fascinating yet complex case study of a blend of this motive.[27]

Some contend that political and leader types are characterized by intense craving for esteem and deference.[28] One provocative, if not entirely persuasive, personality analysis of Woodrow Wilson concluded that his unquenchable thirst for accomplishment and vindication as well as his lifelong interest in power and leadership were based on his need to compensate for damaged self-esteem.[29]

Leadership, most assuredly, does not always come from contented people. Leaders often have an edge to them, are discontented with the status quo, want something different. Also, many leaders seem to have demons, are dyslexic, or have some form of melancholy or depression.

Of course, to a degree, we all have demons. For some, the demons are so big and powerful they destroy us or lead to self-destruction. Effective leaders learn to control and channel their demons into constructive and productive action. Our demons, under control, help provide us energy, drive, passion, discipline, and focus. They also help give us the courage to take on great odds and the great responsibility of leadership. The key is to control passions, not be controlled by them; to make them allies, not adversaries; to make the demons work for us, not against us.

The great leader often has in common with the great runner and the great composer a need to achieve, excel, and make a difference. Ambition is invariably a driving element. The role of ambition, drive, and the need for self-affirmation is doubtless a causal factor that is always present in the shaping and making of a leader. Leaders may deny it. They also may camouflage it, yet self-serving motivation doubtless exists as at least one part of the leadership equation.

A few analysts have studied the paradoxical internal psychic theater of leaders. Management scholar and psychiatrist Manfred Kets de Vries, for example, concludes that entrepreneurs are often double-sided in this respect. On the positive side they loved taking responsibility for decisions, had high energy, contagious enthusiasm and tenacity, and a pronounced willingness to take risks. But, on the other hand, entrepreneurs are often driven by a need to control and become manipulators or loners.[30]

Arrogance is yet another motivator. Certain people believe they are better, brighter, more competent, more able to lead. Some "aim for the top" because they know "it's less crowded there." They push and discipline themselves in order to distinguish and set themselves apart from the crowd.

We believe that in every leader there is a mix of idealism, service, opportunism, vanity, ambition, narcissism, thrill seeking, and arrogance, which compels or at least encourages them to lead. Any of these traits in addition to the powerful motivators of challenge, mentors, and exemplary role models are clearly at work.

The "soul" of a leader is impossible to penetrate, yet it is probably some combination of empathy and duty on the one hand and ambition and arrogance on the other. Empathy drives one to serve, help, and improve things. High self-esteem helps one believe that he or she is the person who will actually get the job done.

Understanding Leaders and Leadership

We all have multiple experiences dealing with leaders. Our *teachers* in school, *coaches* in sports, *bosses* at work, *mayors* in our cities, *parents* in our families, *ministers, priests,* and *rabbis* in our churches, and *presidents* on television are all examples of leaders with whom we have had to deal. Some we liked, others we loathed; some made us feel good, others made us feel awful; some commanded us, others persuaded us; some were kind, others cruel; some encouraging, others humiliating; some unlocked the best in us, others got little out of us.

The point is, we all have countless data with which to evaluate leaders and leadership. The data may be personal, filtered through our biases and expectations, but at our disposal is a wealth of information from which we can begin to understand helpful as well as inadequate leadership. The data may be unmoored of theoretical structure, scattered, and confusing, but they are there. It isn't data we lack, but the right way to understand the information and the right means of providing analogies.

How are we to make sense of all these data? One useful method is to *compare* similar situations and leaders. We have all had multiple teachers, some of us have had multiple coaches, most of us have two parents (or more), and we have watched several presidents. Which teachers did we *like* the most, and why? Which teachers got the *most* from us, and how? How did the best teachers behave? How did they treat us? Were they easy on us, or did they demand a great deal of us? Were they tough or gentle?

And what about "reverse mentors"—supervisors we really dislike? Some people think we learn more from them, as we dedicate ourselves to be much better examples than the negative role models they provide.

Another method is a *performance*-based means. Which coaches won the most games? The most championships? Which military leaders prevailed in battle? Which teachers got the highest performance from students on standardized tests? Results matter and perhaps those who get the highest results—by whatever means—are the best.

There are a variety of ways we might judge and evaluate leaders and leadership. Our task is made all the more difficult in that we have leaders from so many different fields in the public, private, and not-for-profit sectors. We look at politicians, corporate executives, military commanders, university presidents, club leaders, coaches, ministers, teachers—and the list goes on and on.

Conclusion

Leadership is hard to define and even harder to quantify. We do know, however, that leadership always involves leaders, followers, and context. Leadership needs vary depending on context, culture, and changing circumstances. Leadership is typically dispersed throughout a society.

Leadership involves teams of people. Moreover, leadership necessarily involves friction and conflict. Leadership is revealed in acts of change and especially in efforts to repudiate and overcome past policies and courses of action. Societies and organizations experience peaks as well as valleys, and leaders and leadership teams help everyone to ride out the storms.

In the end, as discussed in Chapter 1, leadership is about embracing and trying to master paradoxes and challenge. We never escape the conflicting demands, clashing expectations, and contradictory elements that make leadership so difficult, so frustrating, so promising, and so confounding. Those wishing to master leadership must first learn to embrace, understand, and master the complex and confusing context of paradox. In addition, a variety of leadership realities, the subject we treat in Chapter 3, need to be fully understood by leaders and those who study leadership.

Chapter Three
Leadership Realities

> Holding a formal leadership position is like having a fishing license; it does not guarantee you will catch any fish.
>
> —*Joseph S. Nye Jr.*[1]

Leaders face a series of challenges that test them every day. The following list is hardly exhaustive, yet it provides compelling realities leaders regularly face.

1. Leadership is a means by which groups confront change and adapt to new realities. It should not be confused with individuals who merely occupy positions of authority.
2. Leadership is more broadly dispersed and decentralized than most people appreciate.
3. Leadership requires leaders to act as organizational politicians and "social architects," representing, mediating, negotiating, and forging alliances as they go about making decisions.
4. Leadership involves the use of intuition more than is generally acknowledged.
5. Leadership itself is morally neutral; it can be used for good and for evil ends; leaders can lead in the most positive sense of that term as well as "mislead."
6. Leadership often involves conflict, manipulation, and even coercion.
7. Leadership is different from management, yet successful organizations need plenty of both.

8. Leadership is more of an art than a science and has more to do with strategy, attitudes, judgment, and values than tactics and technical or managerial problem solving; yet these too are needed.
9. Leadership recognizes the liberating power of diversity, capitalizes on both the so-called feminine and masculine strengths, and understands that effectiveness often alternates or combines soft and hard power strategies to match changing contexts.
10. Leadership is often a thankless job, subject to hostile backlashes as well as high stress.
11. Leadership is shaped and constrained by context and culture.

1. Leadership is a means by which groups confront change and adapt to new realities. It should not be confused, as we have emphasized, with individuals who merely occupy positions of authority. One of the most common misconceptions about leadership is that people in high positions or of high status are inherently leaders. Certain people may look like leaders—they may hold fancy titles, win high elective or appointive offices, inherit royal or corporate status—yet none of these guarantee much. Most of us know of high officials who are so inept they couldn't "fight their way out of a paper bag," or who relinquish leadership responsibilities and merely preside.

Leaders emerge in situations when choices and decisions are confronted, when change occurs. We call people leaders when they are able to win support for their views and visions, and when they are able to mobilize people to act in the common interest.[2]

Leadership scholar Ronald Heifetz points out that living biological systems adaptively seek equilibrium. "These responses to disequilibrium are the product of evolutionary adaptations that transformed into routine problems what were once nearly overwhelming threats."[3]

Similarly, social systems, governments, and businesses under threat seek ways to restore their equilibrium. *Paradoxically,* notes Heifetz, vital organizations may seek equilibrium yet sometimes also need certain periods of stressful disequilibrium to prepare themselves for necessary adaptive change.

> Generally, equilibrium means stability in which the levels of stress within the political, social and economic areas of the society are not increasing. Yet there is nothing ideal or good about a state of equilibrium per se. Indeed, achieving adaptive change probably requires sustained periods of disequilibrium. A society may operate without increasing levels of stress, quite oblivious to the bankruptcy that lies ahead. Without a general climate of urgency—the feeling that something must change—the society may do nothing until it is too late.[4]

Leaders diagnose what situations call for adaptive change or for more routine strategies. But whatever the situation a leader needs diagnostic skills to understand the constantly changing interrelated contexts they and their organizations confront.

No one leads without engaging with a group or society. No leader exists "fully formed" before such encounters; "he finds his style and identity in the course of interacting with the led."[5]

Note that although challenges from the outside may force a leader to adapt his or her organization to change, internal challenges can also plague an organization. It is a well-known tendency for most organizations to seek out "comfort zones" where work becomes routinized and dissent or disruptive ideas get marginalized. Complacency creeps in and people become all too comfortable with the status quo. At such times leadership involves shaking things up, reframing, recontextualizing, revitalizing. Sometimes it may require reinvention, rebellion, and even revolution.

Leadership involves a two-way set of loyalties, trust and collaboration. It is less a case of a single, dominant leader exercising control over others than of considerable power residing in the hands of the so-called followers. Members in an organization have influence, or at least potential influence. It is in this sense, as noted, that followers in effect grant both power and legitimacy to a leader.

Leaders emerge all the time, yet especially when organizations face changing circumstances, most notably during emergencies. It is here where they help diagnose new realities. The Civil War, the Depression of 1929, Pearl Harbor, and 9/11 all highlighted the need for leaders and strong leadership in the United States. At such times leaders help fellow citizens adapt, change, or stay the course.

Leadership doesn't always come from those we assume are leaders. Leadership can just as easily come from the nonelected or the nonappointed. Nonconstituted leaders are citizens-at-large who advance a definition of a public situation and a prescription for collective action to deal with it. Further, they succeed in mobilizing a following.[6] Rachel Carson, a woman with a love of wildlife and considerable technical expertise and writing skill, published a book in 1962 called *Silent Spring*. Her analysis of how 200 or more chemical pesticides were polluting our world triggered much of the environmental policy agenda and movement of the 1960s and 1970s. Martin Luther King Jr.'s "Letter from a Birmingham Jail" similarly served as a catalyst for policy change in civil rights. Russian nuclear physicist and human rights leader Andrei Sakharov helped initiate momentous political changes in the former Soviet Union even while, for several years, he remained under house arrest.

Sakharov forswore a life of privilege as a Nobel Prize physicist to wage a three-decade battle against repressive Soviet policies. In a period of painful repression, his was a voice urging political freedom, human rights, and an end to the nuclear arms race. He became the intellectual leader of a movement that refused to submit to an authoritarian regime. And, like many consciousness-raising leaders, he paid dearly. He was stripped of his medals, ostracized, threatened, and exiled to the remote and closed city of Gorky. Shortly before Sakharov's death, Mikhail Gorbachev permitted him to return to Moscow where he was elected to the Soviet Parliament. But Sakharov still attacked Gorbachev for amassing too much power. Throughout his life, and even after his death, Sakharov's voice rang like a great bell calling Russians and Eastern Europeans to continue their fight for freedom.

The signs that leadership is succeeding appear mainly in the behavior of the followers. Are followers learning, mobilizing, performing effectively, and achieving commonly desired results? Although leaders and their actions are vital, it is the accomplishments of the community that attest to the effectiveness of its leaders.

2. Leadership is usually more broadly dispersed and decentralized than most people appreciate. Thus we have consciousness-raising leaders; warrior leaders; national leaders; community leaders; civic activists; liberation leaders; inventors and innovators; intellectual, political, and business leaders. Not to be forgotten, too, are artistic and cultural leaders.

In pluralistic societies like the United States, leadership is dispersed throughout multiple levels and segments of society; and this, it appears, is how most people want it. Citizens in democracies are distrustful of too much power being concentrated in any one institution or person.

Rarely can one person meet an organization's entire range of leadership needs. Leadership is almost always provided by a team of people and not by a solo performer. Behind every Lech Walesa, there were scores of Polish union leaders, intellectuals, and church activists who helped pave the way and helped perform many of the crucial supporting leadership roles indispensable to Solidarity's success. Behind every Martin Luther King Jr., there were countless attorneys litigating in the courts, scores of volunteers and deputies planning a march or a boycott, and dozens of others comprising a movement's team.

Most organizations and societies have all kinds of leaders at various levels. These diverse leaders, in turn, are dependent on other leaders for their own success. Certain leaders are excellent at creating new movements or structures. Others are imaginative consciousness raisers or social architects, helping to enrich morale and renew the spirit of an organization or a people. These leaders are indispensable in providing the human glue holding us together.

Still other leaders command influence because of their integrity, character, and moral authority. They compel us to ask: Is this justice? Is this right? They raise their voices on behalf of the powerless and those who have been left behind. They are mentors and exemplary moral leaders who remind us of the tragedies of the past, such as the Holocaust and Rwanda, and urge us on toward social responsibility and social justice. They remind us that power wielded justly today may be wielded corruptly tomorrow. They rally us to protest when they know a policy is wrong or when our sisters or brothers find their rights diminished.[7]

Yet another set of leaders are those who, because of their study and preparation in the art of war, act as defenders of national security. Machiavelli preached that security must be the first priority of societal leaders. "A prince must have no other objective, no other thought, or take up no other profession but that of war, its methods and its discipline, for that is the only art expected of a ruler.... The first cause of losing [states] is the neglect of this art, just as the first means of gaining them is proficiency in it."[8] George Washington served eight years as commanding officer of the American rebels and insurgents well before he or anyone else could serve as president of the United States. Most nations were created or re-created (such as in the Arab Spring of 2011) as a result of some form of military struggle, wars of liberation, or turbulent regime change.

Douglas MacArthur emphasized that other leaders in a society will debate the controversial issues of the day, but trained military leaders have the fixed, determined, and inviolable mission to win wars. "All other public purposes, all other public projects, all other public needs, great or small, will find others for their accomplishment; but you [speaking to the cadets at West Point] are the ones who are trained to fight: yours is the profession of arms—the will to win, the sure knowledge that in war there is no substitute for victory; that if you lose, the nation will be destroyed."[9]

Leadership can also be intangible and noninstitutional. Thus, there is the leadership fostered by ideas embodied in social, political, or artistic movements; in books, documents, and speeches; and in the memory of lives greatly lived. Spirited critical discussion about leadership and the moral and virtuous use of power is important. Artists, poets, critics, scientists, writers, theologians, and scholars of all kinds can help us determine whether we are using power or whether power is using us.

Intellectual leadership at its best is provided by those—often not in high political or corporate offices—who clarify values and explore the implications of such values for policy. They are leaders, too, who help generate the defining narrative symbols and metaphors that shape our values and commitments. The point here is that leadership is not only dispersed and diverse, but also interdependent. There are many forms and faces of leadership.

Leadership also varies in direction—top down, bottom up, and mixtures of the two. Programmatic policy breakthroughs in a nation are more likely to come between elections, and from the grassroots up rather than from the top down. There are exceptions, but most social, educational, and political-rights breakthroughs in the United States took root around the country—not in Washington, DC. These innovations were incubated by neighborhood, city, and statewide groups and advocates before they attracted political support from established leaders. This fact proves equally true for policy reforms pushed by the Right as well as the Left. The suffragettes found little leadership help at the top in their day. Environmentalists, tax reformers, term-limit crusaders, Mothers Against Drunk Driving, and Tea Party advocates also have to take on their current elite leaders and bring pressure on the system from the outside. Presidents and other leaders, even though they may deny it, often yearn to have the real leadership provided first by grassroots leaders and political movements. John F. Kennedy needed the civil rights movement to "encourage" his leadership. Also, a grassroots movement to, for example, balance the federal budget might just empower a president to make possible the politically difficult discussions necessary to cut programs and/or raise taxes. This is how democratic systems have worked for a long time. This is also the genius of a democratic system: the acknowledgment that "genius" is not invested in the few, but in the collective intellect of a nation.

3. Leaders act as organizational politicians and "social architects," representing, mediating, negotiating, and forging alliances and coalitions as they go about making decisions. People look for strong, dynamic leaders when they are in distress. Wartime emergencies, for example, have created leaders like George Washington, Abraham Lincoln, Winston Churchill, Ulysses S. Grant, General George Patton, and General David Petraeus. The terrorism of 9/11 and Hurricane Katrina as well as the massive 2010 Gulf of Mexico oil spill encouraged U.S. citizens to turn to their national elected officials in the hope of some form of adaptive, proactive, or even redemptive leadership.

In more normal times, however, people are often ambivalent or hostile to change and to would-be leaders. Leaders often confront multiple factions who resist collaboration. Sectionalism, parochialism, nationalism, racism, tribal loyalties, ethnic ties, specialization, and a variety of other forces, including the desire to score political points in a partisan environment, tend to divide the ranks, even as leaders try to unify and mobilize.

In such times leaders act as politicians in the best sense of the term. They define the possibilities and put together teams of people or build communities of trust that can respond to change and bring about progress. The ability to communicate is crucial. Leadership and politics involve listening to as well as convincing people.

Leaders at their best are expert listeners and communicators, understanding the basic wants, higher aspirations, and passions of their constituents. Leaders help set priorities, formulate budgets, raise revenues, and implement plans of action. Most of these functions require superb "people skills" and social and political negotiation. Leaders listen and consult, recognizing it will seldom be possible to please everyone. No group or subgroup is ever pleased for long no matter how artful a compromise on priorities or budget or taxes may be. The leadership challenge is to keep people talking with one another and to keep people fired up about the significance and urgency of their role, their work, and their sacrifices.

Leaders need to be able to understand and consult people and represent their true needs. President Ted Hesburgh at the University of Notre Dame had a policy that anyone at his university could visit him at any time—students, faculty members, staff, anyone. "The big thing you learn is that you don't want to be isolated or insulated."[10] Chairman and CEO Bill Gates of Microsoft in his early years encouraged everyone in his sprawling software giant to communicate with him via electronic mail, and they did so by the hundreds every week. Thus effective leaders are open. "They go up, down, and around their organizations to reach people. They don't stick to established channels. They're informed. They're straight with people. They make a religion out of being accessible."[11]

But leadership involves more than mere mechanical representation or re-presenting the views of others. Effective leaders somehow unlock the best impulses within others. They are wheelers and dealers, yet also dreamers; and they inspire others to dream, think, act boldly, and excel.

Consensus is difficult to achieve and rarely characterizes any group or community for long; yet a certain amount of consensus is needed if an organization is to cooperate and work together to introduce a new course of action. Leaders are continually fashioning alliances and negotiating agreements. This is as true for small towns that have to put out forest fires or build roads from one county to another as it is for those working to prevent nuclear terrorism or to lessen the effects of global warming.

4. Leadership involves the use of intuition. Intuition defies easy definition. Intuition is not wild or blind guessing; it is appropriate knowledge with minimal use of reasoning. Most students of intuition believe intuitive feelings are grounded in life experiences or prior knowledge we cannot immediately or explicitly recall. In this sense, intuition is not a substitute for reason. It is building on what one already knows and making inferences about what might work, even when a fair amount of uncertainty exists. Leaders understand they cannot know everything. Making decisions with less than complete information or solving new problems is something they accept as part of their job. They recognize the role intuition, "educated hunches," and "soft" data play in their lives.

Leaders, as noted, see change as healthy, inevitable, and necessary. They also recognize the inevitability of uncertainty and acknowledge that modern leaders must work in a world of "permanent white water."[12] Leaders must help their organizations adapt to and exploit change and view it as an opportunity, even as they admit they do not fully comprehend the change that may be needed. Effective leaders often warn their colleagues that if they don't like change, they'll like irrelevance, failure, or bankruptcy a lot less.

In helping their organizations transform visions into reality, leaders must often live in two worlds—the world of imagination, intuition, and dreams, as well as the world of strategic planning, computer spreadsheets, hard evidence, and pragmatic analysis.

Nobel Prize winner Herbert Simon warns rightly that it is a fallacy to contrast "analytic" and "intuitive" styles of administrative leadership. Although every manager, Simon writes, must analyze problems systematically with all the tools of operations research and management science, he needs also to be able to respond to situations rapidly, a skill that requires the cultivation of intuition and judgment over many years of experience and training. "The effective manager does not have the luxury of choosing between 'analytic' and 'intuitive' approaches.... Behaving like a manager means having command of the whole range of management skills and applying them as they become appropriate."[13]

We all have occasional intuitive flashes or hunches. Sometimes we refer to these as "street smarts" in contrast to book learning. Executives tell of occasions when a person they interview for a job appears highly qualified, perhaps even the best qualified, yet their intuition suggests otherwise. In another example, legal and financial advisers may counsel against buying a firm, as was the case when Ray Kroc decided to buy McDonald's. Against considerable contrarian advice, Kroc went ahead and bought McDonald's anyway, guided as much by his intuition as by logic or legal and financial considerations. Sometimes things don't appear logical and yet work.

Intuition can be the wellspring of visions. Intuitive leaders, relying perhaps on their greater peripheral vision, sometimes see what others fail to see. They see the interrelationships and sense the connections between disparate facts and past experience. Intuition is a way of knowing; yet it is also, in Buckminster Fuller's phrase, a form of "cosmic fishing" or gut reaction. When we know something intuitively, it usually has the ring of truth even if we do not exactly know how we came to this knowledge.

Although the use of intuition is commonplace among executives, "they are very reluctant to talk about it. Hard-bitten senior managers see it as too soft and mystical to openly acknowledge."[14] Perhaps this has to do, in part, with pride—with being or seeming in charge, objective, and unemotional. Many people understandably have difficulty trusting something as ephemeral as intuition, in part because they don't understand the origins of these insights and are unsure which of them should be trusted and which ignored, or whether just plain luck was involved.

Veteran diplomats, however, such as Henry Kissinger and Harland Cleveland claim there is, in virtually every important national security emergency, always a shortage of information and a surplus of uncertainty. Key decisions at such times must frequently ride more on a president's intuition than on his briefing books.

Cleveland says that in the 1960s when he worked in the State Department, he noticed that whenever a major question could be addressed by rational argument and reasoned compromise, the matter usually could be settled or negotiated without having to send it to the White House. "The issues that went to the secretary of state or the president were those that could be decided in any of several ways, each way eminently reasonable. So the top political leaders were mostly using their intuition, deciding by educated hunch."[15]

A body of research on entrepreneurial leadership concludes that effective business leaders use their intuition or right brain faculties more than was once appreciated. This enables them to process all kinds of information, not just hard data. "Organizational effectiveness does not lie in that narrow-minded concept called 'rationality'; it lies in a blend of clear-headed logic *and* powerful intuition."[16] Intuitive leaders are able to live with a sense of uncertainty. They use their analytical abilities as far as they will reach, yet appreciate they sometimes have to make intuitive leaps relying on the knowledge, experience, feelings and sensations that lie buried in their subconscious. They free the imaginative subconscious from the sometimes paralyzing constraints of the conscious mind. They appreciate that a case can be made for daydreaming, for brainstorming in committees, for discarding preconceptions, for looking at things and ourselves differently, for loosening structures and leaving people to their own devices, for encouraging more autonomy and individual responsibility, and for giving people with ideas a chance to see if they will work. They understand, too, the need for time, relaxation, openness, courage, nonjudgmental attitudes, and trust of both experience and the inner self.[17]

Leaders know, too, that extensive consensus building doesn't always result in a decision. When a decision needs to be made and group decision processes get bogged down, a leader often has to step up and make the decision, integrating what the group has considered with a host of other factors.

Another body of research has acknowledged that while we all regularly rely on intuitive thinking, our intuitions often suffer from a whole variety of biases. Our thinking, especially initial hunches, is influenced more than we realize by the environment of the moment. Daniel Kahneman warns about halo effects and factors such as "focused illusion" instances where merely because we are focused on something we posit its importance as greater than it is.

Effective executives and effective organizations nurture their intuitive capabilities but also learn how to discipline their intuition with appropriate skepticism and with slower, more systematic methodologies of evaluation.[18]

5. Leadership can "mislead" as well as "lead." Strong leaders can lead us astray as well as in desirable directions. Leaders, to be sure, are credited with moving humanity toward individual freedom, social justice, and tolerance. But leaders have also been responsible for the most horrible crimes and extravagant follies that have disgraced the human race.

There will always be those who seek to rule on the basis of fear, hatred, and paranoia, along the way becoming destroyers of our civilized process. Evil leaders gradually make us dependent, rob us of our mature judgment, and ultimately—as in the cases of Hitler, Stalin, Idi Amin, the Duvaliers of Haiti, Colonel Qaddafi, and James Jones of Guyana notoriety—return us to mental infancy.

Positive leaders bring out the best in us; expand our choices, options, and freedoms; and encourage each of us to become leaders in our own right.

The framers of the U.S. Constitution understood the problem of the darker side of leadership. They had suffered under autocratic royal governors and an inflexible monarch who had become, in Jefferson's words, a tyrant and absolute despot.

Our rich mosaic of checks and balances, constitutional safeguards, and especially our Bill of Rights is a testimony to a permanently embedded fear of the potential abuse of public power. Americans are fond of quoting Lord Acton's phrase "power tends to corrupt" even if we also know that the absence of power can paralyze if not corrupt.

We are mindful, too, of the haunting aphorism that "strong leaders make for a weak people." A leader strong enough to do everything we would like done for us, warns political theorist Benjamin Barber, is also likely to be strong enough to deprive us of the capacity to do anything at all for ourselves. Barber reminds us of the story of Eugene Debs, the renowned radical, who once shouted to his adoring followers who craved his leadership: "Too long have the workers of the world waited for some Moses to lead them out of bondage. He has not come; he will not come. I would not lead you out if I could: for if you could be led out, you could be led back again."[19]

There is, as we have noted, a dark side to leadership. The qualities often needed to gain power or run for public office require at least some narcissism, pride, and a love of power that may indeed be incompatible with goodness.

Anthropologist F. G. Bailey wrote a contrarian analysis contending that leaders are often liars, villains, and deceitful manipulators. Leadership, Bailey writes, is the art of cutting into the chaos and imposing a simplified definition on the situation. It is often a process of encouraging followers to act as if the simplified picture were reality.[20]

Top business, military, and government leaders are sometimes correctly described as having narcissistic personality features. One thinks, for example, of Ross

Perot, Donald Trump, General Patton, FDR, and Charles de Gaulle, to name a few. That is, they have a keen and sometimes disproportionate interest in their own appearance and importance. Part of this may be an extra dose of self-confidence. It is, however, the wedding of self-confidence and ability that makes for success or effective performance in many executive roles. But narcissism carried too far, "malignant narcissism," can be unhealthy for the leader and the led. It can lead to self-absorption and self-centeredness at the expense of serving followers.[21]

Creative leaders, along with geniuses, sometimes behave unconventionally and become single-minded in service of worthy goals. They ignore old rules and invent new rules; they become crafty, cunning, daring, nonconforming risk takers. But there is a hard-to-define line here. Some would-be leaders are, sadly, consumed by narcissistic needs of pride, self-promotion, and the exploitation of others.[22]

Just as good leadership requires good followership, so also leadership needs to be balanced by a healthy skepticism from constituents. Our preference for democratic over autocratic procedures requires us to be assertive citizens, questioning leaders and never being too trusting of any one group or individual with a lot of power.

We need constantly to ask about the ends that prompt the exercise of leadership. Effective leadership involves serving and empowering people, not encouraging passivity. Effective leadership motivates by positive example, reminding associates of their responsibilities, about the importance of change or stability as needed, yet always remaining focused on the needs and aspirations of the common enterprise.

6. Leadership often involves conflict, manipulation, and coercion. Most of us are made uncomfortable by and shy away from conflict. Yet leaders recognize the inevitability of conflict and disequilibrium as a means to some desired end. George Washington, Susan B. Anthony, and Martin Luther King Jr. all had to engage in conflict before needed breakthroughs could occur. They recognized they had to go against the establishment of their day in order to guide their associates and bring about desired change.

James MacGregor Burns helps clarify the role of leaders in responding to conflict when he says leadership acts as a triggering force in the conversion of conflicting demands and values into significant behavior. Leaders, writes Burns, don't shy away from or shun conflict; they express it, shape it, and turn it to the advantage of their organizations. They exploit it—as Washington, Lincoln, Anthony, and MLK did. They may even welcome it as a chance to reorganize, reshape, or renew their organizations.[23]

Great progress or causes are seldom won by accident, luck, or minimal effort. Nor are they won in a month, a year, or even a decade. Nor can they be won alone by prayers or by the most artfully crafted constitutional charter.

Battles for social justice, fairness, human rights, quality education for all, economic development, and sensible conservation of our environmental resources are all long-term struggles that can never be wholly won or lost. They must be taken up anew and with intense resolve by every generation.

Reform seldom happens because of luck. For significant changes to occur, people are needed who are willing mavericks, reformers, champions, pathfinders, and sometimes even disruptive revolutionaries. A business acquaintance put it this way, "It's very nice just to be quiet and not to create any waves. But if you want to do something, one inevitably creates or makes some waves, and not everybody will like those waves."

Those people who wish to change the status quo invariably must engage in struggles and outright conflict. Those who enjoy a disproportionate share of privileges and power rarely, if ever, yield those privileges without a struggle. Thus, those who have struggled for women's or children's rights or for tax reform measures all learn that conflict is a necessary element of the overall fight.[24]

But does leadership also involve manipulation and coercion? Yes. Are such elements necessary? Many lament this reality, yet a close look at the exercise of leadership teaches that leaders usually have to simplify reality and establish priorities. Seldom will everyone in an organization be equally pleased with the precise statement of an organization's goals, budgetary allocations, or plan of action. If unity is needed, it sometimes has to be achieved through a certain amount of manipulation or coercion. Military or athletic units plainly live with greater amounts of coercion than socialist discussion groups or egalitarian neighborhood associations. To deny the presence of manipulation and coercive arrangements in large, complex organizations is to be naïve about human nature and the character of organizations.

Similarly, to deny the need of executives to make decisions and exercise executive power, especially in emergency situations, is to ignore the lessons of history.[25] Leaders do not have the luxury of governing only in calm, prosperous times. Crises happen. And when they happen, there is a tendency to turn to the leader and ask, expect, even demand that he take over and solve the problem.

Our search for heroic leadership is nowhere more evident than when crisis strikes. After the terrorist attacks of 9/11, the public looked to President George W. Bush to protect them and then get revenge. The president on such an occasion was a protector, avenging angel, military strategist, shaman, and high priest, all rolled into one.

In a major crisis we often elevate the president to a near-dictatorial state and invest virtually all authority and power in his hands alone. We take a risk when we grant to one individual so much power. And in a crisis, so much can go wrong.

By "crisis" we mean a situation with the following characteristics: (1) occurs suddenly or by surprise, (2) heightens tension, (3) creates a high level of threat to a vital interest, (4) gives limited time to decide, and (5) fosters an atmosphere of uncertainty. "Crisis management" involves *precrisis* planning and preparation, and *during crisis* steerage. To say that a crisis can be "managed" suggests that it isn't really a crisis. Management, after all, implies order, control, direction. Crisis implies a loss of control and lack of order. So one can never fully manage a crisis, but one must attempt to do so or at least cast that appearance. A crisis often marks the final step between peace and war, and can serve as a stepping-stone to, or away from, armed conflict.

In a crisis, we tend to stop thinking, narrow the search for information and alternatives, and rush to judgments. Sometimes this is just the opposite of what we *ought* to do. High-stress situations shut down rather than heighten our critical decision-making skills and make us more, not less, prone to making mistakes. Just when we most need heightened skills, we are less able to employ them.[26]

How a leader organizes and interacts with top staff during a crisis matters. The first leadership decision is whom to bring into the inner decision circle. Depending on the leader's "comfort zone" and past experiences, there are a wide range of options. It would be optimal for this core group to be operational before a crisis so that they can familiarize themselves with crisis processes and interaction, but this remains unlikely. It is important to solicit a wide range of ideas and opinions, to avoid yes-men, to avoid the pitfalls of "groupthink," and to insist on the presence of a "devil's advocate" within the proximate structure of the decision.

Although bureaucratic routines and roadblocks are reduced in a crisis, leaders must still be cognizant of potential problems that may arise if the leader's decisions are not implemented. No policy gets automatically implemented, and during a crisis it is especially important that the leader's orders are clearly communicated and executed.

7. Leadership is different from management, yet we need both. Although it is true that an effective manager is sometimes an effective leader, and leadership requires, among other things, many of the skills of an effective manager, the two roles are not the same. Leaders are people who infuse vision and energy into an organization or a society. They are preoccupied with values and the longer-range needs, dreams, and aspirations of their followers. Leaders are people who create communities, renew the spirit, and concern themselves with far more than the mechanics of an effective organization. A good manager is concerned, justifiably, with efficiency, with keeping things going, with routines and standard operating procedures, and with reaffirming ongoing systems. A creative leader acts as an inventor, risk taker, and general entrepreneur, forever asking or searching for what is right, what is true, what is worth doing, where a group is headed, and keenly sensing new possibilities.

Leadership as opposed to management involves asking something of those who will follow. "Anyone can lead where people already want to go; true leaders take them where only their better selves are willing to tread. That's where the leaders' own values come in. They must want to do something with their power, not just be powerful."[27]

Managers are traditionally concerned with efficiency and doing things the right way, whereas good leaders are concerned with overall effectiveness and doing the right thing.[28]

Table 3.1 suggests that not only are there differences between managers and leaders; these individuals in turn are different from the dictatorial power wielders.

Leadership and management are different yet complementary systems of action. Both are necessary. Business scholar John Kotter explains that "management is about coping with complexity.... Good management brings a degree of order and consistency to key dimensions like the quality and profitability of products."

> Leadership, by contrast, is about coping with change. Part of the reason it has become so important ... is that the business world has become more competitive and more volatile.... More changes are more and more necessary to survive and compete effectively in this new environment. More change always demands more leadership.[29]

Efficiency is doing things the most expeditious way—with the best results. Effectiveness is doing the right thing for everybody involved. "Leaders can delegate efficiency, but they must deal personally with effectiveness!"[30] Another way of saying this is to distinguish between purpose and process. *Purpose* is all about why we are doing something. *Process* is all about how we are doing it. Still another way of emphasizing this distinction is to say that some people serve as creators and others as implementers. Healthy organizations have many of both types and not necessarily in a superior-subordinate relationship. Most organizations need creators, inventors, and resourceful people to push and guide them as well as imaginative, wise implementers and managers to achieve results.

Table 3.1 Power Wielders, Managers, and Leaders: Some Suggestive Characteristics

Power Wielders	Managers	Leaders
Command	Tell	Persuade
Force	Sanction	Influence
Demand	Expect	Motivate
Use	Structure	Empower
Control	Efficiency	Effectiveness
Do Things My Way	Do Things Right	Do the Right Thing

Managers are practical people who often become attached (sometimes too attached) to their procedures and structures. They set up bureaucracies that are often needed; yet bureaucracies are often implicitly, if not explicitly, designed to be conservative and routinize the existing order. Managers can be methodical, mechanical, and impersonal. Leaders, in contrast, embrace change—they even enjoy stirring things up and "rocking the boat." "Whereas managers focus on process, leaders focus on imaginative ideas," writes Abraham Zaleznik.[31]

Zaleznik says leaders, as opposed to managers, are more dramatic in style, more like artists and divas, more emotional, unpredictable, and sometimes inconsistent. They demand a lot. They may yell and push people. They have a sense of urgency. But leaders think big, experiment more, take more risks, are more at home with conflict and emotion, and rise above conventional structures and strategies. Leadership can be messy, volatile, and perilous. Although good managers seldom get fired, influential leaders often do.

Managers and experts provide technical competence and human relations skills. Leaders need to have these abilities as well, but it especially falls to the leaders to provide the imagination, passion, enthusiasm, confidence, and emotional energy that give an organization its meaning, its heart, and its soul. These leaders are meaning makers, sense makers, community builders, and opportunity creators. This style and this gift enable them to help make things happen that otherwise would not. Leaders have to engage their colleagues on both rational and emotional levels.

Yet these differences should not be overstated. Effective leaders need to work in complex organizations, and such organizations cannot run on creative ideas and entrepreneurial energy alone. Healthy organizations need effective managers, lots of them. Society needs all the talented managers it can get, as effective leaders are only effective as long as they can recruit managers who can help make things work.

In the past it was fashionable to say that the difference between a leader and a manager was that a manager gets someone to do what he or she wants and a leader, in contrast, gets someone to want what the leader wants. Yet nowadays this is too simplistic. Managers, too, are concerned with community and collaboration. More importantly, the effective leader today consults, listens, and learns from colleagues and, in most instances, needs to negotiate "buy-in" from his or her colleagues.

Moreover, to complicate matters, many aspects of leadership are also a form of managing. Thus planning, agenda setting, priority setting, capital formation, institution building, implementation, and accounting, as well as keeping the ongoing system functioning, are tasks for both leaders and managers. "There is a considerable overlap between the functions of leadership and management," writes John W. Gardner, "and it is one of the dependable characteristics of contemporary leadership that leaders must accomplish their purposes through large and complex organized systems."[32]

James MacGregor Burns, in *Leadership,* offers an additional distinction of leadership forms. Ultimately, Burns says, there are two overriding types of social and political leadership: *transactional* and *transformational* leadership. The transactional leader engages in an exchange, usually for self-interest and with short-term interests in mind. The exchange is a marketplace or bargain situation: "I'll vote for your bill if you vote for mine." Or "you do me a favor and I will shortly return it." Transactional people are power brokers or power wielders unaware or perhaps indifferent to the fact that people have higher needs. Most office holders practice transactional leadership most of the time. It is common practice. We see it in its crassest form in "pay to play" politics.[33] Such transactions are the general way people do business and get their jobs done—and engage in self-preservation. In certain ways the transactional types are managers as previously defined—more process oriented than substance oriented, more pragmatic than programmatic.

The transformational leader, in contrast, is the person who so engages with followers as to bring them to heightened political, social, and moral consciousness. In the process the transforming leader, acting as teacher and steward, converts many followers into first-rate citizen leaders in their own right. Transformational leadership is concerned with liberty, justice, and equality. It focuses on pointing out possibilities, the hopes, and the often only dimly understood dreams of a people. It inspires associates to undertake the preparation and the jobs needed to realize these goals. Transforming leaders encourage personal renewal that in turn can lead to organizational and societal renewal.

Burns talks about Mohandas Gandhi and Mao Zedong as transforming types and most American party officials as transactional types. He also suggests there are types of leadership that fall in between. Thus, if one views transformational and transactional leadership as a continuum, as illustrative approaches, there may also be transcending, catalytic, or innovative leadership approaches between these contrasting types.

Both the leader/manager and the transforming/transactional distinctions illustrate again the many faces of leadership and the reality that no one formula can precisely define leadership for all situations.

8. Leadership is more of an art than a science and has at least as much to do with strategy, attitudes, judgment, and values as tactics and technical or managerial problem solving. Leaders can delegate logistical activities, but they must deal personally with strategic vision. Leaders, if they do nothing else, must educate, explain, show the way, set the tone, and provide direction. How is this done? First, by understanding their organizations' challenges and the larger context they are operating in. Second, by understanding and listening to people, appreciating their values, and by getting colleagues and followers to focus on a realistic and desirable mission.

Leaders have to deal in the realm of values and attitudes. They may have been financial, legal, technical, or manufacturing experts in the past, but organizational leaders have to transcend their specialist expertise. They must become generalists and interpreters of what is important and what can be achieved.

Of the qualities necessary for effective leadership, one of the most important is exercising good judgment. As Tichy and Bennis note, "The essence of leadership is judgment. . . . With good judgment, little else matters. Without it, nothing else matters."[34]

Good judgment requires clear and critical thinking. It is a skill that involves experience, training, intelligence, understanding of self and context, hunger for information, positive discrimination of ideas, foresight, and the exercise of reason.

Consider what distinguishes the all-star from the journeyman point guard in basketball. The truly gifted point guard sees the whole court, knows what his or her teammates are capable of, senses where player X is likely to go in situation Y, has practiced his or her craft for many years, can anticipate what is likely to happen next, makes quick but not snap judgments, is flexible and able to process new and evolving information, has uncommon peripheral vision, is in command of self, is able to lead others, and in the end, delivers the strategic pass to the right teammate at the right time in the right way so that teammate (and the team) can achieve success.

Leaders inspire organizational members to dream new dreams. Leaders help change attitudes. Those who are successful in politics as well as in business get people to think differently about needed innovations. Leaders constantly fight smugness, complacency, and the mentality of the losers who complain that they will lose because they have lost so often in the past. Leaders like Richard Branson at Virgin enterprises or Steve Jobs at Apple were always pushing their colleagues and seizing new opportunities. They had seemingly inexhaustible energy and enormously high aspirations to innovate, to improve things, and to achieve.

Leaders have to motivate people to believe in themselves and to believe in the importance of their joint undertakings. Leaders explain and emphasize the *why* at least as much as the *how to*. Many leaders spend as much as one-half or two-thirds of their time sharing and repeating their vision with the hope of reinforcing the right message and tone and of creating a vibrant human community. They create organizations where creativity can flourish.

Legal contracts have little to do with encouraging people to reach their potential. The letter of the law or of contracts is cold and formal and fails to take advantage of the full range of human possibilities. A legal contract, Herman Miller CEO Max De Pree argues, almost always breaks down under the inevitable duress of change and conflict. What works best, he suggests, is "covenantal" rather than mere contractual relationships. Note his emphasis on values and attitudes.

> A covenantal relationship rests on shared commitment to ideas, to issues, to values, to goals, and to management processes. Words such as love, warmth, and personal chemistry are certainly pertinent. Covenantal relationships are open to influence. They fill deep needs and they enable work to have meaning and to be fulfilling. Covenantal relationships reflect unity and grace and poise. They are an expression of the sacred nature of relationships.
>
> Covenantal relationships enable corporations to be hospitable to the unusual person and unusual idea. Covenantal relationships tolerate risk and forgive errors.[35]

Effective leadership requires leaders who will turn their organizations into learning organizations, constantly profiting from mistakes. Effective leadership often involves a heavy dose of optimism. There is an old saying that the difference between an optimist and a pessimist is that pessimists are better informed. Leaders are those who may know the odds are against them (and their teams or companies) yet still infuse enthusiasm, optimism, and the winning attitudes that are necessary for success. Leaders lift expectations and emphasize the possibilities. Leaders are those undaunted types who help the rest of us banish fear and tackle projects we never dreamed we could undertake.

9. Leadership recognizes the liberating power of diversity and values feminine and masculine strengths and soft and hard power strategies. Leaders realize it is what you know and what you are able to do that are more important than who you are, your gender, color, or ethnicity. What Archimedes said of the lever is even more important in our increasingly borderless and boundary-spanning, knowledge-based world: "If I stand in the right place, I can move the world." One person, one employee, one citizen who keeps on pushing can often make a difference, can matter.

Leadership was long conceptualized in decidedly gendered stereotypes suggesting that alpha males should exercise command and control powers. This alpha male proposition doubtless evolved from military and warrior king examples. An Achilles, Alexander, Caesar, or similar commander embellished the role definitions.

Until recently, with only a few exceptions, military, business, and political leadership was seen as almost a "men's club" where assertiveness, decisiveness, and physical strength were required and rewarded. Alpha male leadership, or so the stereotyping had suggested, was assumed to be analytical, rational, quantitatively talented, and able to probe for engineered solutions to problems.

There were, to be sure, exceptions: Cleopatra, Catherine the Great, Joan of Arc, Golda Meir, Katharine Graham, Margaret Thatcher, and Hillary Clinton are examples. Still, leadership was long viewed, narrowly, as a man's profession.

This has changed. A score or more nations around the world have now been led by women. Half of the American states have had women governors. Giant corporations like IBM, PepsiCo, DuPont, Kraft Foods, and Hewlett-Packard have been, or are being, run by women. Women now assume leadership responsibilities in every profession.

Some advocates contend that women have certain strengths and advantages that make them more desirable leaders. Thus former U.S. ambassador Swanee Hunt and others have celebrated women as more consultative, better listeners, more caring and responsible, more people oriented, better diplomats, better networkers, and more democratic.[36]

Globalization and the information/Internet revolution are changing how both nations and corporations are run. Women, it is often argued, are less hierarchical than men, more effective at flattening pyramids, more skilled at both collaboration and bringing diversity of opinion to decision-making processes. Women, some add as well, are less narcissistic than men and more likely to be motivated by an organization's or a community's best interests. The so-called more feminine or beta-style leadership is often thought to be more intuitive, more tolerant of diversity and value preferences, and more concerned with quality.

"If leadership opportunities are finally opening for women, it has been a long time coming," writes Joseph S. Nye Jr. "Their non-hierarchical style and relational skills fill a leadership gap in the new world."[37]

Caution is needed here. Discussions of alpha or beta styles of leadership can lead to overly simplistic if not sexist analysis.

Political scientist Nan Keohane, who served, with notable success, as president of Wellesley College for more than a decade and again as president of Duke University for another eleven years, suggests that "labeling some styles of leadership 'feminine' and others 'typically male' itself imposes stereotypes on complex behavior and helps perpetuate biases that have provided obstacles for women throughout history."[38]

Keohane concludes that most women leaders display a rather mixed style of leadership. She concludes too that the effects of organizational culture and the expected role demands of institutional leadership generally outweigh the effects of gender. "Some women (surely not all) in some contexts do lead differently from men; but insofar as there is a pattern here it stems from socialization and cultural expectations, rather than hormones or genes."[39]

The larger lesson here is that effective leaders creatively call upon a variety of styles of leadership. Creative leaders are able to transcend traditional gender role stereotyping. Psychologist Mihaly Csikszentmihalyi suggests this is sometimes misunderstood in purely sexual terms and confused with homosexuality. "But psychological androgyny is a much wider concept referring to a person's ability to be at the same time aggressive and nurturant, dominant and submissive, regardless of gender." An androgynous leader, in effect, enhances his or her leadership resources. "Effective leaders are more likely to have not only the strengths of their own gender but those of the other one, too."[40]

Similarly, effective leaders embrace diversity of all kinds, harnessing the advantages of differing points of view. Smart leaders recognize too that leadership is always contextual and that different situations and different challenges call for different leadership styles and different leadership strategies. No strategy fits all situations. Joseph Nye's valuable writings on the need to alternate or combine hard and soft power strategies depending on circumstances are compelling on this matter.[41]

10. Leadership is often a thankless job. We may yearn for transcending leaders, yet we are also tough on them. Followers can be jealous, fickle, and mean, and they often have a "what have you done for me lately?" attitude. Some people dislike all leaders all the time, and we all worry about leaders who overstay their welcome or overplay their hand. There is an old yarn about the veteran baseball manager who jokes that much of his time is spent keeping the ten players who hate him from the ten who haven't yet made up their minds about him.

History is full of visionary leaders—rebels who are martyred by one generation only to be revered by the next: Socrates, Jesus, Buddha, Joan of Arc, Thomas More, Martin Luther King Jr., Robert Kennedy, and many more.

Joan of Arc, or Saint Joan, is a prime example. She was a teenage, illiterate, peasant farm girl. But she was also a consciousness raiser, an organizer, a mobilizer, and a militant activist. She led on the basis of visions she "received" from her mentoring saints. And she enjoyed stunning military success against the English. But she so aroused the passion of her followers that she also ignited fear and jealousy in the leaders of her church and country. They demanded from her a loyalty that she would not give in absolute terms, so they burned her at the stake.

Many would later change their minds. And still later her church would elevate her to sainthood. George Bernard Shaw's splendid play *Saint Joan* depicts the teenage Joan as brilliantly effective yet turned upon by those who feared her brand of visionary leadership and independence. They loathed her irreverence to the existing secular and religious establishments.[42]

We want our leaders to succeed, but we don't want leaders to get too much of the credit. There is a Japanese adage that says, "The nail that sticks up will get hammered down." Other cultures have similar sayings and similar traditions. Perhaps it is in part "the king must die" syndrome. Or the idea that a tribe sometimes needs to sacrifice or vote out its leaders in order to purify or regenerate itself. Leaders can become scapegoats when things go wrong, even if they have been wonderfully successful at earlier stages.

Part of the explanation may lie in the inevitable arrogance that can set in after leaders have been successful. Early success breeds a certain amount of fame and glory, and these in turn may beget arrogance, which breeds resentment. Eventually the public's hammer is lowered.

It is sometimes said, no government likes its truly great writers because the two are in competition with one another. Each interprets the truth. Each talks or writes about justice. Each commands followers. The same is true of gifted or emerging leaders. New leaders very often will challenge the status quo and engender fear in the hearts of people.

Leaders divide as well as unite people. Lincoln, Churchill, Franklin D. Roosevelt, Malcolm X, Martin Luther King Jr., Lyndon Johnson, Richard Nixon, Ronald Reagan, Margaret Thatcher, Bill Clinton, George W. Bush, and Barack Obama inspired as well as infuriated. Churchill valiantly rallied the British in wartime only to be turned out of office once the war had been successfully concluded. He was awarded, he later joked, "The Order of the Boot." Johnson and Nixon won landslide victories in 1964 and 1972 in part for their leadership efforts in civil rights and détente. But later they were thanklessly and ignominiously turned on even by their own party leaders.

Leaders are often viewed as useable yet disposable, rather like fast food items. Flamboyant leaders are often "paid back" in harsh and equally flamboyant ways. Leadership as exercised by Socrates, Saint Joan, Thomas More, Lincoln, JFK, MLK, Malcolm X, and the Chinese students in Tiananmen Square cost lives. Behind-the-scenes leaders are rarely thanked, and labor in exchange for few if any worldly rewards.

This is a compelling reality. Leadership is not only potentially dangerous and fraught with friction, stress, and burnout, but much of what leaders do is done because of the personal challenge of the job rather than for appropriate pay, prizes, or public acclaim.

Leaders learn not to expect much praise. No matter how much they may do for their followers, leaders get few letters of praise and more often hear whining of the "what can my country do for me?" and "what will you do for me tomorrow?" variety.

Father Ted Hesburgh, a legendary president of Notre Dame, said college and university presidents, like everyone else, enjoy an occasional pat on the back. But as he reflected on his own years as a university leader, he advised it is far more realistic to expect numerous "kicks in another part of your anatomy when you make a mistake."

> Criticism is a far greater part of presidential life [in the university] than plaudits and gratitude. One of the best early decisions I made elicited only one letter of thanks from the several hundred faculty who greatly benefited from the decision. I thought things might get better as the years passed, but believe me, they do not.... You will sleep better if you don't court disappointment and personal hurt by expecting what you will not get.[43]

Corporate and political leaders also often say their leadership activities leave them lonely, take them away from their families, and leave them with headaches, stomachaches, worries, and other ailments. This isn't always the case, yet a pattern of stress and burnout often comes with the territory.

A leader is always under scrutiny, being judged, satirized, sometimes picked apart. The scrutiny is 24/7—especially if you are a CEO, national football coach, or president of the United States. Think of the scrutiny Obama and George W. Bush received. As it is always harder to drive well when one is being followed by a police officer, so too it is more challenging to lead when every word and movement is dissected.

A larger point here is that although followers may grant legitimacy, followers are notoriously suspicious of leaders and leadership. We give "credits" to effective, adaptive leaders, but these credits or legitimacy can swiftly be taken away if the "leader" fails to serve the interests of the people.

11. Leadership is shaped by context and culture. Leadership success in one setting does not guarantee leadership effectiveness in another. A union organizer may make an ineffectual community organizer. An athletic coach will not usually also be a good conductor. Business and political leaders can fail when hired to lead universities. A brilliant military leader like U. S. Grant can fail as a U.S. president.

An ideal leader in some settings is merely a team player, or first peer, who does not seek any credit or the limelight. In many cultures the best leader is a person who helps people in such a way that his followers eventually believe they did it nearly all by themselves. Often, too, the desired leader is the person who after a short while is no longer needed. This is in contrast to many traditional American corporate leaders who, at least in the past, have been highly expressive, self-promoting, and individualistic. Jack Welch, T. Boone Pickens, Ross Perot, Steve Jobs, Donald Trump, and George Steinbrenner are examples.

For a long while students of leadership believed certain traits such as height or good looks or great energy were predictive of leadership effectiveness regardless of the setting. Such theories have long been thoroughly debunked. Contextual, situational, or contingency analysis replaced trait analysis. Being seven feet tall might help in basketball yet is a disadvantage for serving as a coxswain of a crew shell. Weighing 340 pounds might be an asset for an NFL football tackle but is a liability for a sprinter. How we behave as leaders, we know now, is determined more by environment and situations than by personal traits.[44]

Would-be leaders have to know the cultural contexts and the cultural values of those they lead. The kind of leadership we get, political scientist Aaron Wildavsky contends, is a function of political or organizational culture. Thus, leadership is expected and relatively easy to exercise in a hierarchical culture such as in the marines. "Prospective leaders [in hierarchies] are expected to lead; their authority inheres in the position. The regime that guides and constrains them gives consistent advice; leadership is necessary and therefore should be supported."[45] The reverse happens in egalitarian societies. Those who try to lead in egalitarian communities have a difficult time because leadership implies followership and hence inequality.

Lovers of equality, egalitarians, have always distrusted and criticized leaders, sometimes to the point of denying the need for leaders. They refuse to acknowledge the inevitability of leadership, and even when they grudgingly accept it, they still note its undesirability. Egalitarians yearn for a community of strong citizens, a "leaderless community" where leadership isn't needed—where there are neither leaders nor followers but feisty individuals who talk, discuss, collaborate, and eventually arrive at an acceptable "sense of the community."

Egalitarians by definition dislike inequality. So how do things get done in such a culture? "Mutual persuasion is what egalitarians approve of. Meetings are lengthy, discussions interminable," writes Wildavsky. "Would-be leaders must dissemble, at once being persuasive about the right course to follow and self-effacing. For if they push themselves forward, attempting to lead rather than merely convening or facilitating discussion, they would soon be attacked for attempting to lord it over others."[46] He cites certain civil rights and feminist organizations as examples of egalitarian organizations. Leadership is tolerated, if at all, in egalitarian organizations only insofar as it will further equality.

Anthropologists have also discovered varying cultural patterns that appear to shape and prescribe leadership styles. Some societies have matriarchal as opposed to patriarchal leadership patterns. Other societies are consensual as opposed to faction oriented. Although activism and talk are much valued in many societies, silence, stillness, restraint, and "mindful" rituals are revered elsewhere.[47]

The rules of the game and the boundaries that permit or constrain leadership activities vary enormously depending on cultural or community context.

Conclusion

Leadership is always needed yet is especially needed when an organization confronts challenges and when fresh deliberation, innovations, and adaptive judgment are required.

Leaders at their best are people who, precisely because they are good listeners and perceive what is needed, know how to inspire people and mobilize resources to accomplish mutual goals. Leaders build on strengths: their own, their colleagues', their superiors', and their subordinates', and on the strength and opportunities afforded by the situation.

Ideal leaders help create options and opportunities—help clarify problems and choices, build morale and coalitions, inspire others, and provide a vision of the possibilities and promise of a better organization, community, or world. Leaders empower and help liberate others, instilling in followers the conviction that they have the responsibility, ability, and plausible answers for the problems they face. They affirm the possibilities for freedom, change, and free choice against the inevitabilities of history. Finally, they so engage with their followers that they inspire them to become leaders in their own right.

Many of these realities highlight additional aspects of the paradoxes of leadership. Effective leaders need to appreciate both the paradoxes and these defining realities of leadership. Leaders learn to embrace and adapt to these realities.

We turn next to the invaluable lessons the classics teach us about both leadership paradoxes and the possibilities for wise and adaptive leadership.

Chapter Four
What the Classics Teach Us about Leadership

From Gilgamesh to the Bible

> The lust for power, for dominating others, inflames the heart more than any other passion.
>
> —***Tacitus, Roman historian***[1]

The classics serve as the foundation of the study of leadership. They offer timeless wisdom and compelling insight into leadership, human nature, and power across the ages and across cultures. We can learn from the lessons of success and failure as practiced by historical, mythical, and even fictional leaders.

The Importance of the Classics for the Study of Leadership

Why study the work of mostly old, dead, white males? In part because it is the foundation of Western civilization; also because most of the important questions we deal with today were asked by these thinkers; partly because the framework of our culture and politics is grounded in that era. Partly also because classical writings often argued with each other, and many of their old arguments, Aristotle versus Plato, Machiavelli versus the church, Locke versus Hobbes, Hamilton versus Jefferson and Madison, Adam Smith versus Marx, for just a few examples, are still relevant today. Also, the classics serve as the foundation for who we are, what we think, what we believe to be important. How could leadership students *not* study the classics?

We examine the classics not to the exclusion of other voices, cultures, races, religions, genders, or excluded and marginalized voices, but in addition to these many rich contributions. As the study of leadership must be, by definition, inclusive and encompassing, it must embrace a wide range of approaches, perspectives, and voices. Thus we study the classics not to exclude, not to assert superiority, but to illuminate how we got here and why that matters.

The Early Classics

Gilgamesh.[2] Earlier classic works were handed down by word of mouth from one generation to the next. One of the earliest of the epic poems to survive is the story of Gilgamesh. Part god, part man, he lived around 2700 BCE. The king of Uruk in Babylonia (today's Iraq), Gilgamesh is represented as a heroic figure and the strongest man who ever lived.

But Gilgamesh is young, unprepared, and oppresses his people. They call to the god Anu for relief. Anu delivers to the people a wild man, Enkidu, to confront Gilgamesh.

Enkidu, living in the forest, is discovered by a young man, who gets a woman, Shamhat, to give herself to the wild man in hopes that this carnal knowledge will strip the man-beast of his wildness. And indeed this happens. In exchange, Enkidu gains wisdom and knowledge.

After living with a group of shepherds and learning the ways of civilization, Enkidu finally goes to meet Gilgamesh. Upon first seeing the king, Enkidu is shocked that Gilgamesh claims the right to sleep with all new brides on their wedding day. Enkidu blocks Gilgamesh's entry into the home of a newlywed, and a furious battle ensues. Gilgamesh wins the fight, but in the end, the two become friends.

Gilgamesh proposes a grand adventure, a trip to the great Cedar Forest to cut down all the trees. But to gain entry to the forest, they must kill the demon Humbaba the Terrible, Guardian of the Cedar Forest. Enkidu tries to talk Gilgamesh out of this adventure, but Gilgamesh insists.

Gilgamesh and Enkidu enter the Cedar Forest and begin cutting down trees. Humbaba hears them, confronts the two, and threatens them. A battle ensues and, with the help of the gods, Humbaba is defeated. Humbaba begs for his life and offers all the trees in the Cedar Forest along with his eternal service to Gilgamesh. However, Gilgamesh beheads the demon.

Gilgamesh's fame grows as word of his grand deeds spreads, attracting the attention of the goddess Ishtar who offers herself to the king. But Gilgamesh rejects the offer and insults the goddess. She goes to her father Anu pleading with him to destroy Gilgamesh. Anu agrees, and sends the Bull of Heaven to Uruk to destroy the king. But along with Enkidu, Gilgamesh slays the beast.

Shortly, Enkidu dies and Gilgamesh is devastated. He embarks on his most ambitious journey, a trip to visit Utnapishtim, who possesses the secret to eternal life. Utnapishtim offers Gilgamesh the chance at immortality, but Gilgamesh fails the test.

Gilgamesh returns to Uruk having failed in his personal task, but having built a great empire in the Uruk region. This tale of heroic, individualistic leadership and agency might lead the reader (or listener in the age of storytelling) to conclude, consciously or otherwise, that great men make things happen. We will see in Gilgamesh and many of the stories that follow a bold articulation of the heroic myth of individualistic accomplishment (leadership).

Beowulf. The tale of Beowulf is also a tale of great adventures and grand achievements.[3]

The kingdom of Hrothgar, king of the Danes, is menaced by the monster Grendel. Beowulf of the Geats goes to help Hrothgar and rid him of the monster. Beowulf battles the monster and kills him. Yet, all is not right with the Danes. Grendel's mother wants to avenge the death of her son.

Beowulf and his men go after the monster and eventually behead her. Celebrations ensue as Beowulf is hailed as the hero.

Fifty years later, Beowulf, then king of the Danes, faces another monster, a dragon who is terrorizing the people. In this battle, Beowulf is killed.

Homer's *Iliad* and *Odyssey*. In *The Iliad* and *The Odyssey,* the two legendary epic poems by Homer, we again see themes of leadership, courage, and heroism presented on a grand scale.

The Iliad pits two monumental figures, Agamemnon and Achilles, against one another. Our story takes place in the tenth year of the Trojan War as they and their "Greek" forces try to besiege Troy. Agamemnon, an arrogant, autocratic leader, has his troops at the walls of Troy, trying to conquer the city. But their attempts are rebutted by the Trojans. Agamemnon appears more concerned with his reputation than his expedition, and he becomes envious of his colleague Achilles' successes as a warrior. Instead of enlisting the help of Achilles, he sees him as a rival. He attempts to take Achilles' war prizes from him, declaring: "I shall take the fair-cheeked Briseis, your prize, I myself going to your shelter, that you may learn well how much greater I am than you." Achilles responds by contending that he, not Agamemnon, has done the lion's share of the fighting and that he deserves his prized maiden. So when it comes time to divide the spoils, Achilles complains his commander unfairly wants the greater rewards. That's unfair.

Agamemnon succeeds only at turning his most legendary warrior against him. He is unable to control his big ego and has alienated his most talented colleague. Thus embittered, Achilles refuses to fight for Agamemnon and, at least temporarily, withdraws his warriors.

Agamemnon tries to lure Achilles back to the fold, yet fails to bring back the disgruntled warrior. The damage has been done and Agamemnon let his own personal weakness jeopardize his real goal: the defeat of Troy. (Troy is eventually conquered, though Achilles, who is lured back to battle not by Agamemnon but to avenge the death of a friend, dies in epic battle.)

The Odyssey is the tale of Odysseus, a stalwart soldier leader who is confronted with a series of challenges as he attempts to return to his homeland after the Trojan War. In the process, he and his crew must overcome the Cyclops, resist the temptation of the island of the Sirens, and avoid the monster Scylla and the whirlpool at Charybdis. One after the other in an especially long and exacting journey, Odysseus overcomes these challenges to finally arrive home, where he must reclaim his throne from ambitious rivals.

Odysseus is successful because he is able to exercise a wide range of skills that are appropriate to the demands he faces. He exercises agility and flexibility when confronting different problems. Some situations call for fight, others for flight; some require guile, and others creativity. Odysseus is smart, skilled, resourceful, goal oriented, and decisive. He is a well-rounded leader.

Gilgamesh, Beowulf, and Homer's *Iliad* and *Odyssey* are stories of compelling, larger-than-life, powerful men who make things happen. From these and other ancient classic tales comes the cult of leadership, the hero worshipping of great men, the iconic figures of power and greatness. We come to see many leaders as courageous saviors and other leaders as failures because of arrogance and hubris. The people are mostly portrayed as merely passive observers waiting for heroic great men to save them.

These epic poems create epic heroes: saviors we admire, respect, fear, and yearn to find, even yearn to become. They are great men with drive, courage, and self-confidence who accomplish great deeds, who are leaders to worship; and that, as we shall see, is one of our problems. And sometimes they are failed, flawed actors who fall short of the test of leadership.

The received wisdom, for the most part, is that history is made by great men acting boldly on a big stage. Men of consequence cause change. Leadership is largely about the individual leader. Or so we are led to believe.

Confucius, Lao-Tzu, and Zen Leadership

Confucius. Leadership classics come to us not just from the Western tradition but from across the globe. One of the most influential of the non-Western voices is Confucius (551–479 BCE). His emphasis is on personal and governmental morality and justice. His works form the basis of what became known as *Confucianism.*

He handed down no commandments and claimed no divine source of inspiration. In his lifetime he accomplished no great goals, performed no miracles, freed no enslaved people. In fact, he seemed to have little impact on his own time and claimed few disciples. His efforts to reform China's bureaucracy failed. He never achieved high office or led troops to victory. And yet, his message ended up resonating in a China marked by chaos and conflict. He offered hope out of this chaos.

Confucius enjoined people to face the future by looking to the past. The wisdom of the ancients was the wisdom of all ages. His lessons were found in simple sayings, maxims (found in his Analects) that speak to us today. Some seem cliché, as when he advises a ruler to "govern for the benefit of the people, reduce taxes, and recruit superior men."[4]

Confucius's simple yet profound message to commoner as well as ruler was to respect *Family* (the wisdom of the ancients), live by *Morals* (be good), and act for the *People* (the mark of a good leader).

He developed a training program for would-be bureaucrats based on the question "What has one who is not able to govern himself to do with governing others?"

Confucius believed we were defined not by our words but by our actions. When he was on his deathbed, one of his followers asked if he could pray for his mentor, but Confucius was skeptical. "My kind of praying was done long ago," he said, "not in words, but deeds."

The goal was to become a "superior man," which meant someone imbued with benevolence (*Jen*), the mean, or moderation (*chung yung*), and propriety (*Li*); someone in harmony with nature (*T'ien*); and someone with the ability to recognize the true nature of things and to give them the correct names (*cheng ming*).

In short, Confucius's teaching took the form of pithy aphorisms written during chaotic days in China. Rulers were to be devoted to the good of the state as they sought personal as well as societal perfection. These virtuous rulers would lead by example. The people, seeing a just and virtuous ruler, would seek to emulate his good behavior, and this would spread to the entire nation.

Confucianism emphasizes personal growth more than the imposition of rules and laws to compel compliance. Thus, Confucius's version of the Golden Rule forms a basis for both personal and governmental behavior:

Kung asked: "Is there any one word that could guide a person throughout life?" The Master replied: "How about 'shu' [reciprocity]: never impose on others what you would not choose for yourself?"[5]

Although Confucius's thoughtful leader rules by the power of personal example, one still sees a form of admiration, even hero worship, in the people looking up to the leader for guidance and direction. Rather than the people leading or instructing the leader, once again, the people look up to and are dependent on the leader. Confucius insists that a great deal of respect be paid to the leader, thereby subjugating the people to the ruler.[6]

Lao Tzu. The great Chinese philosopher and creator of Taoism (or Daoism), Lao Tzu (sixth century BCE), which translated means "old master," may have been a single person or a composite of several influential figures. *Daodejing* is his most famous treatise, written in the form of wise sayings and aphorisms; it calls for a return to nature and de-emphasizing action.

In some ways, Lao Tzu is a "less is more" proponent. He promoted humility and restraint in leaders, and called for rulers to reject personal glory. It is the people, not the individual leader, who are most important.

Leaders should be quiet and reluctant agents of change. Too much change threatens nature and disrupts order. The leader may lead by example but must not force change. In the end, the people choose whether or not to follow. Both modern conservatives and libertarians sometimes trace their intellectual lineage back to Lao Tzu.

An example from the Daodejing will illustrate the point:

Chapter 17: Like a Midwife

The wise leader does not intervene unnecessarily. The leader's presence is felt, but often the group runs itself.

Lesser leaders do a lot, say a lot, have followers, and form cults.

Even worse ones use fear to energize the group and force to overcome resistance.

Only the most dreadful leaders have bad reputations.

Remember that you are facilitating another person's process. It is not your process. Do not intrude. Do not control. Do not force your own needs and insights into the foreground.

If you do not trust a person's process, that person will not trust you.

Imagine that you are a midwife. You are assisting at someone else's birth. Do good without show or fuss. Facilitate what is happening rather than what you think ought to be happening. If you must take the lead, lead so that another is helped, yet still free and in charge.

When the baby is born, the mother will say: we did it ourselves.[7]

What is perhaps most interesting about Lao Tzu is that whereas most of the classical voices promote some form of hero worship, Lao Tzu clearly portrays the leader more as a servant of the people. The leader does not really lead; he presides, facilitates, nurtures.

Zen. Out of the teaching of the "Dao" has come the development of Zen thinking. Zen seeks a harmony that often comes from recognizing the connection of opposites (e.g., "where there is possibility, there is impossibility"). This is the "Wu-Wi" or Yin and Yang of life. Here, Wu refers to action, Wi to inaction.

In Zen leadership, rulers are minimalists.[8] They are also adaptable and flexible. Yoga is an excellent metaphor for leadership in the Zen tradition. Truths and lessons are revealed in metaphors, and the central tenets of Zen leadership include a preference for inaction or less intrusive action by the leader, the goal of seeking harmony by following nature, the pursuit of individual goodness, a focus on "being" (not doing), leadership as service, and leadership by example.

The Tao (Dao) teaches that the wise leader is like water that cleanses and refreshes all; and like water, the leader is powerful when he is yielding. Zen philosophy communicates via metaphor and koans (short aphorisms), such as "Water that is too pure has no fish."

We see in the teachings of Confucius, and several other prominent Asian voices, a distinctly different orientation to leadership than the one developed and embraced in the West. The West will accept a great man/heroic leadership orientation, although several Asian philosophers and practitioners provide us with a counterexample, a "less is more" type of leadership that is less domineering, less obtrusive, and more of a guiding hand than a clenched fist.

The Greeks and the Romans (the Classical Era)

There are two approaches we pursue in employing the classics to study leadership: questions of philosophy and matters of history. The first set of questions that emerges from the study of political philosophy will be essentially normative: who *ought* to rule, what *ought* to be, and *why*? The second set is descriptive and asks: *who* actually rules, *how*, and on *what basis*?

Normative theory from the classical period asks several questions that continue to vex us today: *Who should rule and on what basis? How should society be organized? How should "the people" be defined and what role should they have in politics, and who should get what and on what basis?*

Among the first in the classical era to ask the question "who should rule" was the Greek historian Herodotus, who wrote in the late fifth century BCE. Herodotus not only posed the question in terms of authority but literally staged the debate in the court of the Persian king Darius. Herodotus explored the tripartite classification of political regimes, suggesting three different models of leadership—rule by the *one* (monarchy), rule by the *few* (oligarchy), and rule by the *many* (democracy)—that had earlier been posed by the poet and statesman Solon in the sixth century BCE.[9] This model, to which philosophers and historians would return throughout antiquity, was a product of the Athenian democracy of the later fifth century BCE. It was an era dominated by Pericles.

Pericles was one of several demagogues or popular leaders ("demagogue" acquires its negative connotation after Pericles) in the fifth century BCE. He promoted several reforms that dramatically changed Athenian democracy. He resisted Spartan overtures in the conflicts that later resulted in the catastrophic Peloponnesian War (431–404 BCE), and although his rule was admirable to some, it also contributed to the greatest disaster that befell the Greeks.

The historian Plutarch supports the view of Periclean greatness that began with the historian Thucydides. Thucydides saw Pericles as a skilled statesman and orator, who led Athens' democracy with a vision of greatness, best seen in the famous Funeral Oration. In honoring the Athenian dead of the Peloponnesian War's first year, Pericles spoke of the ideals of a democratic system, and how such a society stands apart from other political forms. Plutarch wrote of Pericles' bold and decisive leadership, and how Pericles' leadership sharply contrasted with the pandering and demagogic policies of those who succeeded him.[10]

Socrates would argue that politics, leadership, and knowledge generally must be taught (leaders, he believed, are made, not born). This would lead to Plato who, in the fourth century BCE, argued that leadership was a specialized task requiring training, discipline, wisdom, and the right temperament. Plato's Academy, established ca. 387 BCE, became a training ground for prospective leaders and attracted students not only from Athens itself but from across the Greek world.[11] The skills of a leader were not seen as natural but were the result of instruction and training (made). In his *Republic,* Plato argues that what was needed were "Philosopher Kings."[12] Only when philosophers were kings, and kings philosophers, might all be right with the leadership of the polis.

Herodotus. Herodotus of Halicarnassus (484–425 BCE) was a Greek historian, regarded as the "Father of History." He attempted to systematically collect material for his histories and is most famous for his work *The Histories,* which deals with the origins of the Greco-Persian Wars.

Although he wrote of powerful leaders, Herodotus was mindful that history was not always the story of great men. "Circumstances rule men; men do not rule circumstances," he wrote. This profound insight was all but lost on subsequent generations who focused on and celebrated the "great man" theory of history.

Herodotus saw leaders as deeply human and susceptible to flattery and manipulation, as when Atossa, wife of King Darius of Persia, appeals to his male vanity in bed, while at the same time pressing her husband to invade Greece. Reason and self-interest may give way to passion and flattery—and at great cost.

Herodotus sees our personal passions, obsessions, ambitions, and emotions as playing a significant part in our decision making, opening us up to blunders that are otherwise avoidable. As Robert D. Kaplan notes, "The essence of Herodotus's *History,* then, is that the more hideous and intractable are the ways of humankind, the more glorious are the heroes who rise above such circumstances. To focus on the worst is not to give oneself up to fate, but to take a necessary step before calculating the possibilities of overcoming it."[13]

No leader starts with a clean slate. Our decisions cannot be purely rational because of the personal perspectives, prejudices, and "baggage" we bring to each decision. The most effective leaders understand *themselves,* the *cultural context,* and accurately *read the situation.* Less effective leaders believe what they want or need to believe. As Kaplan writes: "While Herodotus leads us to a majestic and, I would argue, morally based worldview, what sets his *History* apart from other works, both ancient and modern, is his powerful evocation of just what human beings are capable of believing, and how deeply they do indeed believe, for the sake of their own salvation."[14]

Cicero. Marcus Tullius Cicero (106–43 BCE), ancient Rome's greatest statesman and orator, lived in the last century BCE when the Roman Republic was breaking down and the Roman Empire rising. Cicero was a proponent of the republic, and opposed both the dictatorship Rome was becoming under Julius Caesar and the democracy it threatened to become if civil war broke out (he once called democracy "the worst of all forms of government").[15]

Cicero saw law as the cement that held a just state together. He wrote,

> The function of a state official, as you know, is to govern, and to issue orders that are just and advantageous and in keeping with the laws. Indeed, it can truly be said that an official is the speaking law, and the law is a non-speaking official. Besides, government is something supremely in accordance with the prescriptions of justice and with nature; by which I mean that it is supremely in accordance with the law. For, without government, no household can exist at all, and no community, and no nation, and not the human race itself, or the world of nature, or for that matter the entire universe.[16]

To be an effective statesman in Rome, it was essential that one be an effective orator. The people had to be "moved," and Cicero may have been Rome's finest orator (and among their most influential politicians).

The good leader, Cicero said, "needs to have a complete understanding of the highest principles of justice, because without such understanding, it is not within anyone's power to be just at all."

To Cicero, a just set of laws, embedded in a mixed or balanced constitution—one that included elements of a monarchy, oligarchy, and democracy—kept this balance.[17]

Cicero believed the best form of government was one that divided power among three different segments of society: the one (monarch), the few (aristocrats), and the many (the people). If an appropriate balance among these three entities could be achieved, this "mixed government" would prove best. This concept would, over time, evolve and morph into what we today refer to as checks and balances and the separation of powers.[18]

When Brutus and Cassius conspired to assassinate Caesar, Cicero, who was sympathetic to the cause, was not called upon to join the conspiracy. The end result of the killing of Caesar was the death of the republic and the emergence of imperial Rome. Cicero had lost.

Plutarch. One of the most important figures in classical studies is Plutarch (45–125 CE). He wrote a series of parallel lives of Greek and Roman leaders, was a chief source of several of Shakespeare's plays, and in the founding era of the United States, the only work more frequently cited than Plutarch was the Bible.

Born just after the time of Christ, Plutarch came from a small village in Greece. He concentrated his writing on great men of action who shaped history. Courage, good judgment, and moral character were seen as the keys to success. To Plutarch, the type of government mattered less than the quality, character, and soul of the individual leader. He thus saw politics—and history—in very personal terms.

His parallel lives pair off a Greek with a Roman: Theseus and Romulus, Solon and Poplicola, Pericles and Fabius, Anthony and Demetrius, Alcibiades and Coriolanus, Caesar and Alexander, Brutus and Dion. He wrote of great warriors such as Achilles, Agamemnon, Odysseus, and Alexander; great statesmen such as Pericles, Solon, and Philip of Macedonia; great thinkers like Socrates, Plato, and Aristotle; and influential artists and writers such as Homer, Herodotus, Sophocles, and Thucydides.

Plutarch helps us understand what motivates leaders. His cases may be seen as object lessons in the good and bad, strengths and weaknesses, wisdom and foolishness of leadership, of what is to be avoided and what should be emulated.

From Plutarch we can draw many lessons, and although history does not provide us with many clear answers, it does help us raise the right questions, heed the warnings of the past, recognize the limits of power, and learn from the successes as well as the failures of those who came before us. We neither need to reinvent the wheel nor make the same mistakes twice. The paradoxical nature of the uses of history was summed up by Aldous Huxley who once noted, "The charm of history and its enigmatic lesson consist in the fact that, from age to age, nothing changes and yet everything is completely different."[19]

We are tempted all too often to use history not to learn from it, but, as A. J. P. Taylor reminds us, to prop up our prejudices. Plutarch compels us to take a cold, hard look at these cases of leadership, good and bad, effective and ineffective, desirable and undesirable.[20]

In Pericles (495–429 BCE), we see a leader of extraordinary accomplishment, who makes one fatal mistake that leads to disaster. Pericles was a leader of skill, high morals, and high purpose. A man of "majestic bearing" and high intellect, he decided to attach himself to the people's party. He governed for the aristocracy as he spoke to and for the people—a difficult balancing act.

His fatal flaw is that he allowed Athens to engage in the Peloponnesian War, a war that was unnecessary (today we would call it a *war of choice* not a *war of necessity*) and led to the destruction of Athens. His ambitions exceeded his abilities, and after Pericles, Athenian democracy began a steady decline.

In Nicias (470–413 BCE), we see a leader, cautious in the extreme, reluctant to act even when all the evidence calls for action. In Alcibiades (450–404 BCE), we see a self-centered, arrogant yet charming, even beautiful figure (Plutarch refers to his "beauty" and "physical perfection"). Yet with all his positive attributes there was also a deep insecurity, an insatiable need to prove himself, and a demonic hunger to defeat others.

Arrogant and spoiled, he had an appetite for life that led to excesses. Yet he was also a skilled orator and respected horse breeder. As he rose in public life, his private life descended into debauchery. He was contemptuous of the law and thumbed his nose at convention.

He became a traitor to Athens and the city condemned him. He saw himself as above the city and in the end renounced Athens and went to side with its enemy Sparta, where he was welcomed. He served Sparta well. Until, that is, King Agis left town and Alcibiades seduced the king's wife, Timaea (generally not a good idea). Timaea became pregnant by Alcibiades.

Sparta and Athens engaged in a war on the seas; and King Agis, still smarting from Alcibiades' seduction of his wife, succeeded in getting the city to condemn Alcibiades to death. Alcibiades got wind of this and abandoned the Spartan cause.

Playing one power off another was a dangerous game. Alcibiades eventually went back to help the Athenians. Yet he was initially distrusted and kept his distance. Ironically, he later came to the aid of Athens and is treated as a hero. Plutarch writes: "If ever a man was destroyed by his own high reputation it was Alcibiades."[21] He kept reinventing himself and in the end died under mysterious circumstances.

To Plutarch, Alexander was a leader both born and made. Born the son of a king, Alexander was groomed for greatness (with Aristotle as one of his several personal tutors).[22] Alexander was self-confident (asked if he intended to run in the Olympic Games, he said he would, if he "might have kings to run with"), intelligent (he was able to train a famously wild horse that his father's best trainers failed to tame when he noticed that the horse was spooked by his own shadow), well taught (by Aristotle), given fulsome encouragement (his father announced that "Macedonia is too small for you; seek out a larger empire worthier of you"), curious (he often engaged in questioning of leaders), jealous and envious, and visionary (he dreamed expansionist, imperial, and inspirational dreams).

In ten years, between the ages of twenty-two and thirty-two, Alexander the Great ruled over at least half the known world. He built an empire.

For Plutarch, leadership mattered, and it could be taught, studied, and learned. Great men made history (both good and bad), and he saw virtually everything in personal terms—what mattered is what people, powerful leaders, did. Technology was unimportant, social and political movements were of little significance, and ideas mattered little. All revolved around the cult of leadership.

We now turn to Plutarch's Roman leaders. Coriolanus (490 BCE), about whom you will read more in our discussion of William Shakespeare, was a masterful military leader. He possessed all the skills necessary to govern effectively—except, importantly, for his arrogance and contempt for the people. When Coriolanus put himself before the people to rise in the political arena, he refused to "pander" to the people. His pride prevented him from submitting himself before the people who were to select the leadership. Coriolanus would do no such thing. His "total *disdain* and contempt for his audience"[23] precluded him from leadership. So arrogant was he that the people banished him.

Coriolanus sought his revenge by siding with Rome's enemy, the Volscians; but that, too, ended in disaster, and Coriolanus tragically ended his public life.

Brutus (85–42 BCE), the honorable but misguided defender of the republic against the imperial ambitions of Julius Caesar, is a complex and contradictory figure. He wanted to save Rome from an emerging tyrant yet his actions led to the destruction of the republic and the rise of the empire.

Brutus tried to live a life of balance. His goal was to give selflessly in support of a greater good: the republic. When that was threatened by the rise of Caesar, Brutus was persuaded to act. Yet, in killing Caesar, a civil war ensued, and in its aftermath, a dictatorship controlled Rome as an empire emerged. Brutus's good intentions led to unwanted and unintended consequences.

An honorable man, guided by high principles, Brutus nonetheless lost all, including his life, when the complexity of events overwhelmed the simple if noble dictates of his vision.

Another of Plutarch's studies deals with Plato (428–347 BCE). A critic of democracy, Plato argued that only the "wisest" in society could become leaders as the training of a leader was taxing and difficult. Although democracy is the litmus test of political legitimacy today, it was not always so. The great Peloponnesian War nearly shattered the democratic idea with several oligarchic or right-wing putsches temporarily eclipsing rule of the many in Athens. But in Plato's day, although the Athenian democracy had its critics, it would be foreign enemies, not domestic foes, that would overthrow it. It remains true, however, that in this period, serious thinkers from Socrates to Plato found democracy deeply flawed as a basis of government. Who in his right mind would advocate mob rule or the rule of the unwashed rabble? In a democracy, leaders would pander to the masses. No, only the "best" in society should govern.

Few could match Plato in antidemocratic sentiment. He had personal as well as philosophical reasons for disliking democracy; after all, his mentor Socrates was condemned to death by "the mob" of common citizens. Accused of corrupting the minds of Athens' youth, the majority of a five-hundred-citizen jury found him guilty. This soured Plato on "the people."

He saw the crowd becoming a mob, prone to inflamed passions and irrational exuberance. To please the people, not necessarily do what was right, was the goal of the leaders in Athenian democracy. Plato saw little room for true statesmanship in a world where politicians merely fed the appetites of the masses.

His disdain for democracy drove Plato to offer a competing paradigm, found in *The Republic.* And Plato had a specific vision for effective leadership: the *Philosopher-King.*

As Plato wrote,

> Until philosophers are kings, or the kings and princes of this world have the spirit and power of philosophy, and political greatness and wisdom meet in one, and those commoner natures who pursue either to the exclusion of the other are compelled to stand aside, cities will never have rest from their evils,—no, nor the human race, as I believe,—and then only will this our State have a possibility of life and behold the light of day.

Plato feared leadership by amateurs or commoners. He saw leadership as a specialized capacity that one could learn. Of course, it took a lifetime devoted to learning this craft. Leadership is specialized knowledge, and Plato demonstrates this by way of a simple metaphor:

> The sailors are quarreling over the control of the helm.... They do not understand that the genuine navigator can only make himself fit to command a ship by studying the seasons of the year, sky, stars, and winds, and all that belongs to his craft; and they have no idea that, along with the science of navigation, it is possible for him to gain, by instruction or practice, the skill to keep control of the helm whether some of them like it or not. If a ship were managed in that way, would not those on board be likely to call the expert in navigation a mere stargazer, who spent his time in idle talk and was useless to them?[24]

Should the most popular person become the leader? The tallest? The most handsome? The most athletic? The smartest? No, only the person well trained in the art and science of leadership—only the most qualified to perform the task—should lead.

Only a Philosopher-King is qualified to govern. Of course, all men are susceptible to corruption, so what distinguishes Plato's Philosopher-King from others? His ruler, Plato answers, can enjoy neither private property nor the joys of family life. He studies philosophy, knows justice, and acts justly. He is *trained* in the arts of leadership. The Philosopher-King studies math, geometry, and dialectics; he must do extensive public service in military and/or administrative capacities; he must take up the life of the philosopher, then may eventually govern the polity.[25] The key components of Plato's leadership model might be summed up as:

- Leadership is a solitary, individualized activity.
- As long as the ruler is concerned with the common good, citizens are expected to follow.
- A benevolent tyrant is preferable to rule by the masses.
- Only after extensive specialized training might one be qualified to lead.
- The leader's job is not to please the people but to do the right thing.
- Only a philosopher could lead justly.

Impractical perhaps, Plato nonetheless describes for us both the potential dangers of democratic leadership and the specialized training and temperament he believed were essential to govern effectively.

In a democracy, leaders would likely pander to and mislead the masses. In Plato's scheme, we are still left with one of the most fundamental questions of political leadership, asked by the Roman poet and social critic Juvenal: *who shall guard the guardians*?

The premise on which Plato bases his analysis is open to question. Plato insists that leaders need expert knowledge that can best be attained through training and education. Thinkers like Plato and his teacher Socrates, as well as many who study modern leadership, insist that, yes, leadership can be taught. But is good *judgment* more important than good *training*? Are common sense, a curious nature, a tough personal constitution, intelligence, a natural skepticism, a burning hunger for knowledge, a good evaluation of talent, and a sense of timing more important than specialized training? Can one teach common sense? Judgment? Leaders need subtle personal skills and a robust emotional and contextual intelligence as well as training and experience. Plato's insistence on a type of benevolent dictatorship of the philosophically trained has surface appeal, yet may fall short when it meets the harsh reality of politics in practice.

In *The Republic,* Plato offers his alternative to rule by the people. The goal was to govern wisely, justly, and virtuously; and only a properly trained Philosopher-King could know justice and act justly. The soul of the Philosopher-King will be well ordered and governed by reason and knowledge,[26] or so Plato would have us believe. In any event, Philosopher-Kings there have never been, and doubtless will never be, except in the Platonic imagination.

If Plato gave us the compelling if far too ambitious idea of a Philosopher-King, his student Aristotle gave us an equally difficult yet more attainable (and hopeful) image of the leader practicing *phronesis* as servant to the interests of the community.

Born in 384 BCE in the Greek city of Macedonia, Aristotle studied in the Athenian Academy under Plato until he was thirty-seven. When Plato died, Aristotle assumed he was the likely choice to replace his mentor as head of the Academy, yet that post went to one of his friends. Aristotle, it seems, was thought a bit too arrogant to head the Academy. He left Athens and returned to Macedonia where he became, as mentioned earlier, the tutor to Alexander (the Great), guiding the future leader's education from his thirteenth to sixteenth years.

Aristotle may have also been bypassed for the leadership of the Academy because he was an open critic of Plato's concept of a Philosopher-King. "It is not merely unnecessary," he wrote, "for a king to become a philosopher, it even may be a disadvantage."[27]

At the age of fifty, Aristotle returned to Athens where he was once again rejected by the Academy, this time because his goal—to have the Academy adopt a more pragmatic, realistic, and scientific approach to learning—struck the faculty of the Academy as wrongheaded. So Aristotle started his own academy, the Lyceum, which would later become the model for education in the Western world.

Aristotle pursued a more scientific approach to learning. He is "remembered today as a polymath and organizer of knowledge ... who introduced a structure of logical thought and laid the groundwork for empirical science in the centuries to come."[28]

Although it would be impossible to reduce Aristotle's views down to a few salient points,[29] it is possible to focus on his views of leadership to discern some of his thoughts on what constituted good leadership.[30] Aristotle sought "the golden mean," a type of prudent pursuit of self and community interests. Humans were both individual and political (by this he meant community-oriented) animals. Individuals, through the practice of good acts, developed good (persistent) habits. This applied both to individual behavior and to communal goals and acts.

True happiness and harmony were reached when each individual found his intended purpose and developed it to the fullest. This was the pursuit of virtue and excellence.

We do not pursue virtue and excellence merely for self-gain. As we are also political animals, we need communion in civil society. We need others. Our fulfillment takes place not in isolation but in the good life *and* the good community.

And what role does leadership play in this process? Aristotle sees the ideal, soul-filled leader as practicing *phronesis*.

In terms of leadership, Aristotle's contribution has been enormous. He rejected the dominant view of his time that cast the world in either/or terms (good versus bad), and developed a more nuanced approach that posited a "golden mean" or middle ground as the ideal. His goal of achieving balance struck some as too moderate, yet Aristotle saw this as a more realistic approach. After all, we are neither pure saints nor impure sinners. We are human, imperfect, yet capable of reason and growth. We cannot create perfect leaders or perfect institutions, but we can become better. Human nature makes us prone to mistakes; reason offers some prospect for improvement. No utopian, Aristotle offers us a difficult path that promises little yet offers a modicum of hope.

His chief works, *Politics* and *Nicomachean Ethics,* use empirical observation as their starting points and build his philosophy around the belief that the primary distinguishing characteristic of human beings is the ability to reason. More advanced humans develop their reasoning abilities and thus have a greater chance to achieve happiness as they search for "the good life."

To Aristotle, life is about the journey, or the process of seeking higher forms of rationality as we attempt to find and achieve the good life.[31] It is, as Thomas Jefferson would point out over two thousand years later in the Declaration of Independence, "the pursuit of happiness" or the journey that matters most. The end result—happiness—comes from the activity of contemplation of higher-order values and living a life in accordance with those virtues that help us maximize our potential to achieve *Eudaimonia*—those needs rooted in human nature that lead to growth. Growth toward our best selves is what leads to happiness. It is self-actualization, a learned process of development toward a morally sound goal, or the pursuit of excellence. This pursuit to Aristotle means individual development and engagement in the affairs of one's community. The highest form of excellence is to attain it, then create conditions for others to grow and develop—that is leadership.

An individual leader who pursued excellence and paved the way for others to engage in that pursuit gave to the community, helped it achieve its potential, enriched and empowered others.

Good leaders are both effective *and* virtuous. They achieve excellence by balance, by practicing the golden mean. The best leaders are those who are skilled at achieving a moral end for themselves and for their communities. Aristotle called this *phronesis.*

Aristotle, as noted, tried to guide the enlightened statesperson toward effective leadership and stewardship in his discussion of *phronesis. Phronesis* means knowledge put into appropriate action for a good cause. It is reason and good judgment, sound logic as applied to a complex world, recognizing the limits and possibilities at hand, and deciding on a constructive course of action that is most likely to lead to a morally and politically good result. The verb *phronein* suggests "intelligent awareness," and the noun *phronesis* means "practical prudence, or sound deliberation resulting in correct suppositions about a good end." Wisdom, prudence, good judgment, morally appropriate ends—these are the factors that bring *phronesis* to light. It is moral discernment applied to complex human affairs, prudence in action, goal maximization directed toward socially good ends, the effort to convert morally and socially sound ideals into policy—and it is what defines good leadership.

Phronesis goes beyond mere prudence; it is prudent judgment directed into action to achieve a good result. It is *judgment* and *action*. In this way, *phronesis* is the art of the statesperson and an explicit recognition of the moral and pragmatic dimensions of effective action. The leader who possesses the skills to govern effectively has competence, judgment, and a sense of justice. This person has the necessary skills to govern effectively and the ethical compass to govern wisely. It is—or should be—the goal of the leader.

Aristotle had his eye on the great Athenian lawgiver Pericles as a model of *phronesis*. To Aristotle, Pericles had the ability to see what was good and to further translate that vision into feasible policies designed to achieve those worthy and attainable goals (the Peloponnesian War notwithstanding). Pericles served the public interest even as he shaped it. He sought justice in an unjust world, and had the skill and insight to translate his vision into policy. If you are looking for presidents to fit this model, look to George Washington, Abraham Lincoln, and Franklin D. Roosevelt. Most of the time they did the right things, for the right reasons, toward the right ends.

The Athenian Theater

A vibrant democracy will have a vibrant political culture. In ancient Athens, the theater was the source not merely for entertainment but was also a communal outlet for political expression and community building. The dramas, satires, and comedies of Sophocles, Euripides, Aristophanes, Aeschylus, and others drew huge crowds and were much discussed in Athens. In fact, the ancient Greeks called dramatists *didaskalos*, meaning "teacher" or "guide."

Aristophanes, born in 446 BCE, is probably the best known of the Greek playwrights. Known as the "Father of Comedy," he had the ability to mock and ridicule convention, which was unsurpassed on the stage. Aristophanes survived the Peloponnesian War, revolutions, and democratic revivals.

Such works as *The Wasps*, *The Frogs*, *Lysistrata*, *The Clouds*, and others skewered contemporary society, holding a mirror up to the hypocrisy and shallowness of the politics of the day. In *Lysistrata*, Aristophanes' most famous play, we find the women of the whole region joining forces to end the Peloponnesian War by withholding sex from their husbands until they stop making war on each other. This play empowering women was radical and controversial in its day. *The Clouds* mocks the intellectual pretensions of Athenian society, with an especially devastating caricature of the now iconic Socrates. And *The Wasps* pokes fun at King Creon as well as the law courts of Athens.

The Greek playwright *Sophocles* (496–406 BCE) demonstrated a different method of commenting on leadership: jarring humor and dramatic tragedy.

Sophocles is best known for his classic works *Ajax, Oedipus the King,* and *Antigone. Ajax* is the tragedy of a leader unable to adjust to changing times. Ajax's pride overshadows his judgment, leading to tragedy. He rises so high that his fall is all the more tragic.

Sophocles is considered the greatest playwright of Athens' golden age of theater. He wrote over one hundred and twenty plays, yet only a handful have survived. *Oedipus the King* is considered his greatest work. A master tale of psychoanalysis, *Oedipus* is the story of the hero who unwittingly kills his father and marries his mother, all to escape the fate he unknowingly walks right into. It shows us how the most careful plans of leaders can go awry.

> *Oedipus:* How great is the envy roused by wealth, by kingship, by the subtle skill that triumphs over others in life's hard struggle! Creon, who has been for years my trusted friend, has stealthily crept in upon me anxious to seize my power, the unsought gift the city freely gave me. Anxious to overthrow me, he has bribed this scheming mountebank, this fraud, this trickster, blind in his art and in everything but money! Your art of prophecy! When did you say nothing, when you might have saved the city? Yet her puzzle could not be solved by the first passer-by. A prophet's skill was needed, and you proved that you had no such skill, either in birds or any other means the gods have given. But I came, I, the ignorant Oedipus, and silenced her. I had no birds to help me. I used my brains. And it is I you now are trying to destroy in the hope of standing close beside Creon's throne. You will regret this zeal of yours to purify the land, you and your fellow-plotter. You seem old; otherwise you would pay for your presumption.
>
> *Creon:* No. You would see, if you thought the manner through as I have done. Consider. Who would choose kingship and all the terrors that go with it, if, with the same power, he could sleep in peace? I have no longing for a royal title rather than royal freedom. No, not I, nor any moderate man. Now I fear nothing. Every request I make of you is granted, and yet as king I should have many duties that went against the grain. Then how could rule be sweeter than untroubled influence? I have not lost my mind. I want no honors except the ones that bring me solid good. Now all men welcome me and wish me joy. Now all your suitors ask to speak with me, knowing they cannot otherwise succeed. Why should I throw away a life like this for a king's life? No one is treacherous who knows his own best interests. To conspire with other men, or to be false myself, is not my nature. Put me to

the test. First, go to Delphi. Ask if I told the truth about the oracle. Then if you find I have had dealings with Tiresias, kill me. My voice will echo yours in passing sentence. But base your verdict upon something more than mere suspicion. Great injustice comes from random judgments that bad men are good and good men bad. To throw away a friend is, in effect, to throw away your life, the prize you treasure most. All this, in time, will become clear to you, for time alone proves a man's honesty, but wickedness can be discovered in a single day.

Chorus: Sir, that is good advice, if one is prudent. Hasty decisions always lead to danger.

Oedipus: When a conspiracy is quick in forming, I must move quickly to retaliate. If I sat still and let my enemy act, I would lose everything that he would gain.

Creon: So then, my banishment is what you want?

Oedipus: No, not your banishment. Your execution.

Creon: I think you are mad.

Oedipus: I can protect myself.

Creon: You should protect me also.

Oedipus: You? A traitor?

Creon: Suppose you are wrong?

Oedipus: I am the King. I rule.

In *Antigone,* one of the most beloved and most performed plays of all time, we find a strong-willed woman, Antigone, who refuses to give in to earthly authority when the law, as interpreted by the nervous, accidental, new king Creon, forbids her to properly bury her dead brother. This play illustrates the competing claims of the state versus individual conscience, or civil versus natural law. It also vividly depicts the great price a leader pays for an unwillingness, or inability, to listen.

These plays demonstrate how art and politics mix. They hold society up to an often unflattering mirror and show us—warts and all—in ways we usually find disturbing; so it is that playwrights often have disturbing the peace as one of their primary goals.

Playwrights also speak to the vanity and arrogance, hubris and shortsightedness, as well as the wisdom and insights of leaders. They show us that leaders are usually less in control of events than they assume, more prone to pride and conceit than they are willing to admit, and more shortsighted than is healthy.

The Bible

Although not a text devoted to leadership, the Bible, especially the Old Testament, contains countless stories about leaders, good and bad, and the New Testament offers a vision of leadership deeply at odds with our conventional wisdom.[32]

In the book of Deuteronomy, from the Old Testament, we are given a portrait of what a good ruler is:

> And when the king has been established, he will not increase the number of his horses, nor will he lead the people back to Egypt with the aid of his numerous horsemen. He will not have several wives who would distract his attention, nor huge quantities of silver and gold. But after he has taken the throne of his kingdom, he will write out for himself another copy of the law in a book, borrowing the original from the priests of the tribe of Levi; and he shall have it with him all the days of his life so as to learn to fear the Lord his god, and to guard his words and ceremonies which have been laid down in the law. And let him not lift his heart in pride over his brothers, nor turn aside to the left hand or the right, so that he and his sons may reign for a long time over Israel.

Here, the Hebrew king is enjoined to learn the law and not act as a superior to the people. Conversely, in Ezekiel (Proverbs 28:15), we find a description of the tyrants as princes who are "like wolves savaging their prey to the shedding of blood." The tyrant is not a shepherd guarding his flock, but a wolf who crushes them. *Solomon* says, "A wicked prince over a wretched people is a roaring lion and a ravaging bear" (Proverbs 29:2). Elsewhere, he warns, "when the wicked assume princely power, the people groan" (Proverbs 28:28). And when God is offended by the transgressions of the Israelites, he threatens them with the following (Isaiah 3:4): "I will give them children to be their princes, and girlish weaklings shall rule over them."

The Old Testament offers numerous leadership lessons and examples. We learn of *Abraham,* a transformational leader who has vision, charisma, self-confidence, courage, humility, adaptability, and a sense of justice—all valuable traits in great leaders.[33] We see *King David* of Israel, another charismatic leader, made famous for slaying Goliath. He unites the tribes of Israel. Yet David marries often, and this causes problems. As he centralizes power, his son *Absalom* leads a revolt against his father. Absalom goes straight to Jerusalem, the heart of his father's empire, forcing David to abandon his prized city. On the run, David reverts to his old skills and fights a guerilla war against Absalom.

David is capable but morally flawed. In the book of Samuel (11:1) it is written: "And it came to pass ... that David ... saw a woman (Bathsheba), who was beautiful to look upon." Lamentably, she is already married to Uriah, the commander of David's army. David, coveting Bathsheba, comes up with a sinister plan to get rid of Uriah; he sends him on a suicide military mission, knowing Uriah will never return. Indeed, Uriah is killed, and David marries Bathsheba, who bears him a son, Solomon.[34] David maintains power and names Solomon his successor.

Solomon's prayer to the Lord is to "give me wisdom to rule your people," and even today, we associate Solomon with wisdom and fairness. Where David is charismatic, Solomon is solemn. And yet, his meticulous, pondering style serves to institutionalize as well as stabilize Israel, and Solomon's wisdom becomes legendary.

Theologian Martin Buber warned that the analysis of leaders in the Bible results in counterintuitive results, such as the weak and humble (e.g., Moses) being chosen for leadership positions, the willingness of these leaders to serve a higher calling, and the recognition of failures alongside successes.[35] Thus, the use of the Bible to discern leadership lessons may be complicated.

One of the most compelling of the leadership stories from the Bible is the case of *Moses.* He lived around 1300 BCE, at the time of Jewish enslavement in Egypt, and is today an important figure in several major religions, including Judaism, Christianity, Islam, and others.

Moses is recruited by God to lead the Israelites out of bondage in the famous "burning bush" incident from the book of Exodus. God reveals Himself to Moses as a burning bush to tell Moses of his task. "Who am I, that I should go to Pharaoh, and that I should bring the children of Israel out of Egypt?" asks Moses (Exodus 3:11). He later appeals to God, confessing that "I am slow of speech and slow of tongue" (4:10). His is not a false modesty, and yet Moses is already an activist and rebel, having killed at least one Egyptian slave master who had beaten one of Moses's relatives. Moses believes in the cause but is ambivalent about being chosen as its leader.[36]

Moses accepts the responsibility and goes to Pharaoh with the plea, "Let my people go" (Exodus 8:21). The Pharaoh refuses and God unleashes ten plagues on Egypt, after which Moses leads the Hebrews out of Egypt and across the Red Sea.

Wandering in the desert for forty years, Moses faces stiff opposition and understandably has difficulty keeping his people together. At one point, he climbs Mount Sinai and returns with a new set of laws for the Israelites, the *Ten Commandments.*

Finally, Moses leads his people to their homeland, but he is not allowed to enter the promised land with the people for whom he did so much.[37]

Moses was a leader, a visionary, a nation builder, lawgiver, judge, founding father, and prophet. He was also goal focused, tireless, and determined. In James MacGregor Burns's term, Moses was a *transformational leader.* He was also an adaptive, flexible leader. As Michael Keren writes, "In the many years he leads the Exodus, no exceptional strategies are used by Moses. Like other leaders, he argues, negotiates, fights, prays, kills, schemes, legislates, aligns in coalitions, uses magic, exercises power, etc. What, then, distinguishes his strategies...? It is a set of principles accompanying the strategies."[38] These principles guide his way.

From the Old Testament, we get enduring narrations of warrior kings struggling to lead during troubling times. They often resort to violence and power to accomplish their goals. In the New Testament, an entirely different model of leadership is offered: the life and teachings of Jesus Christ.

Evaluating Jesus as a leader is complicated by the fact that although he was clearly a leader, his goal was not to establish a kingdom on earth, but to establish a moral code that leads not to happiness on earth, but to eternal salvation. An ambitious agenda.

What were the prime characteristics of Jesus as a leader? He had: a compelling vision; attracted committed followers; performed impressive feats (miracles); was persuasive, even charismatic; challenged a corrupt status quo; demonstrated great moral courage; set an excellent example; had unimpeachable character; appealed to a populist or mass audience; was an embracing, empowering leader; started a mass movement; tirelessly promoted a distinct set of ideas and ideals; and sacrificed for his cause.

Jesus was, in many respects, an unlikely leader. The Israelites expected their promised savior to be a warrior king who would conquer the enemies of Israel. Jesus came from humble roots and, by the age of thirty when his public life began, had neither performed truly heroic deeds nor distinguished himself from his peers. He seemed ordinary.

Yet he would do extraordinary things. The story of Jesus Christ is too well-known to repeat here. We are interested in his qualities and actions as a leader. What characteristics did Jesus demonstrate?

Ability to Convey His Message: Central to Christ's magnetic leadership was his message. That message was disappointing to some (there would be no earthly kingdom for the Israelites), but to others, it was powerful, personal, hopeful, and transforming (eternal life). A small sampling of some of the key elements that comprise the message of "the good news" will suffice:

- In everything do to others as you would have them do to you.[39]
- You have heard that it was said, "You shall love your neighbor and hate your enemy." But I say to you, love your enemies and pray for those who persecute you.[40]
- You have heard that it was said, "An eye for an eye and a tooth for a tooth." But I say to you, do not resist an evildoer. But if anyone strikes you on the right cheek, turn the other also.[41]
- Blessed are the peacemakers: for they shall be called the children of God.[42]

Jesus displayed a wide range of skills that enhanced his leadership abilities. And yet, he also had to overcome shortcomings.

Experience: Could anyone have been *less* well prepared for leadership than Jesus Christ? He was woefully unprepared to assume such a key leadership role.

And yet, this lack of relevant experience did not prevent Jesus from offering himself up as a leader.

Ability to Communicate: Jesus was an excellent communicator. His persuasive skills and ability of self-dramatization attracted followers. Jesus often spoke in parables, stories designed to bring his points to life. These parables helped him reach a wide audience, similar to the way Abraham Lincoln would use stories and humor to reach his audience.

Ability to Focus on Goals: Jesus was on a mission and never lost sight of where he was going. His focus on a goal was one of his chief leadership assets. As Warren Bennis reminds us, "The leader has a clear idea of what he wants to do."[43]

Ability to Inspire/Charisma: Both Jesus and his message touched people. He became a focal point of emotion and attention. His person and his message were magnetic. Jesus quickly became an iconic figure (a "Che" figure before there was a Che Guevara).

Clear Principles: Jesus stood for powerful, clear principles. Love, justice, a preference for the poor and dispossessed, and peace were significant parts of his principled message and leadership.

The Makeup of a Rebel, Agitator, Revolutionary: Jesus came to turn the world upside down. He terrified the authorities, threatened the comfortable, and challenged the status quo. Jesus was a troublemaker; he came to disrupt, even upend, the status quo. That is one of the main reasons the authorities had to dispose of him.

The Mission of a Selfless Servant: Jesus's leadership emphasized giving of himself (after all, he sacrificed his life to his cause) and serving his people. His mission was not to elevate and glorify himself but to serve and save his flock. In a way similar to George Washington, who willingly gave up power and office, by giving, he received; by being selfless, he became more attractive and popular. He was humble, and that helped make him grand. As Jesus said, "For everyone who makes himself great will be humbled, and everyone who humbles himself will be made great" (Luke 14:11).

A Certain Trumpet: Jesus was not hesitant, ambiguous, or uncertain. He sounded a clear message that he repeated consistently and forcefully. There was never any doubt regarding his message or the conviction with which he pursued it.

The Makeup of a Countercultural Critic: Jesus was an oppositional leader. He challenged the orthodoxy of his age. Even in the Jewish community—his community—he came as a change agent, undermining the leading authorities of his own faith.

A Call to Teaching: Jesus was a master teacher. It was one of the most fundamental aspects of his leadership. He came to show us and to teach us a new way of being. All great leaders are teachers, and Jesus's ability to help us see anew allowed his message to be understood by his flock. As Jesus said, "You call me

Teacher and Lord—and you are right, for that is what I am. So if I, your Lord and Teacher, have washed your feet, you also ought to wash one another's feet. For I have set you an example, that you also should do as I have done to you" (John 13:13–15).

The Makeup of a Visionary: Jesus had a clear, compelling, hopeful vision for the future: eternal salvation. He inspired his followers with this vision.

The Ability to Empower Others: The leadership of Jesus was designed to create other leaders. He empowered his followers—especially his apostles—to take up the leadership challenge and go forth to preach and cultivate a following.

The Quality to Lead by Example: Jesus led by example, whether by washing the feet of his apostles or turning the other cheek. He lived the life of his words and vision. This example was a model others might emulate, similar to the Tao model of leadership.[44] As Jesus said, "I am the good shepherd. The good shepherd lays down his life for the sheep" (John 10:11).

The Ability to Fulfill Individual and Group Needs: Jesus was concerned with both individual and group needs. He offered people what they hungered for: hope, meaning, salvation. He also offered community, a community of brethren who joined in the celebration of faith.

Tirelessness: Jesus devoted himself to his cause with energy and focus. He was tireless in his drive to spread the word. His stamina and hard work paid dividends and served as an example to his disciples.

The Ability to Recruit Leaders: What was it about Jesus that got men to drop their nets and follow him? Jesus recruited leaders—apostles—who would take over after he was gone and continue to pursue his vision.

Put all of this together, and one can see how and why Jesus was a leader. The person, the message, the connection to people, and the ability to communicate a vision and allowed him to become a successful and iconic leader.

Jesus's message of hope, leading to salvation, was a powerful vision that attracted a multitude of willing followers, and although his message may at times be lost in the organized yet often stumbling and imperfect human church and modern-day ministry, it remains a powerful and compelling message.

Conclusion

As noted earlier, the major narrative from early classics was that history was made or shaped by larger-than-life heroes acting on the big stage.

We turn next, jumping ahead, to celebrated sixteenth-century classics.

Chapter Five
What the Classics Teach Us

Machiavelli to Shakespeare

> There is nothing more difficult to carry out, nor more doubtful of success, nor more dangerous to handle than to initiate a new order of things.
>
> —***Machiavelli***[1]

The Renaissance World

Jumping from the classical and biblical eras to the Renaissance requires a leap of intellectual gymnastics, as the ancient Greek world sought a balance between the individual and society, and the world of the Bible sought obedience to a moral code. In the Renaissance the individual was paramount, transcending the community. It was an age of grand individual self-exploration and self-expression where creativity as well as greed was elevated to near-sacred dimensions. How is one to govern, or lead, such a public?

Beginning in the fourteenth century in Italy, the Renaissance celebrated the individual at the expense of the community. Rather than promoting a balanced integration of self and state, the Renaissance sought to free the individual from the chains of society. Only through free choice and pursuit of individual interests could humans be both free and fulfilled. This era saw the development of great art, significant writings, and a new relationship between man and community.

The Renaissance was followed by the Industrial Revolution. If the ancients sought a balanced union between self and society, and the Renaissance promoted the elevation of the individual over society, industrialism sought to subsume the individual into the machine of the large industrial organization. The organization mattered more, the individual mattered less.

Out of the classical period and the emergence of Christianity, an era of one-man rule emerged throughout most of the Western world. Buoyed by a link to the divine, rulers were able to establish a fiction known as the divine right of kings wherein the king was seen as the legitimate power on earth based on the will of God. As long as the king could persuade most people to accept this fiction, he ruled on solid ground. To defy the king was blasphemy.

How is it possible to promote good government in such an era? The great thinkers, following Plato, argued that one must "teach justice" and that the king must "act justly." Good soulcraft led to good statecraft. And yet, if that was the goal, it was markedly unsuccessful in getting the ruler to behave in a manner consistently well suited to the long-term interests of the people. Many rulers acted on self-interest, greed, ambition, impulse. In practice, teaching justice proved an insufficient tool, a blunt instrument in efforts to produce good government in an absolutist state.

The realist Niccolò Machiavelli (1469–1527) had no such optimistic view. In *The Prince,* he jettisons this hopelessly optimistic view and compels us to come to grips with the reality that the pursuit of justice is not what motivates leaders. Their real goal is power. In divorcing soulcraft from statecraft, Machiavelli caused a backlash, attracting the condemnation of the church and the scorn of philosophers as well as practitioners.

Although much of what Machiavelli wrote and referred to was contemporary, there was also a pronounced classical bent to his work and thoughts. Leaders of ancient Greece and Rome—Alexander the Great, Nabis the Spartan, Caesar, and Scipio Africanus—provide the exemplary material illustrating his key principles, making clear the connection between classical past and Renaissance present. Not only did Machiavelli shockingly reveal the nature of politics, his ideas have greatly influenced those of later political thinkers as well.

If the classical era failed to fully account for the greed and ambition of rulers, or if it embraced too optimistic a view of the ability of teaching justice to control the grosser manifestations of abuse by princes, it did provide us with many of the central questions on which leadership studies are based today. If the classical era failed us in one way, we should not forget that centered in the classical age are the roots and seeds of democracy, republicanism, participation, "consent of the governed," and constitutionalism.

As the adage has it, societies have followed the Golden Rule: whoever has the gold makes the rules. The few govern and take from the many. In the classical age, the most important social distinction was free and unfree. Most stoically accepted their lot in life, an attitude that Christianity left unchanged. Even those who, for example, saw slavery as unjust and inhumane seldom imagined something different. Plato, in *The Republic,* even went as far as to suggest that the guardians should perpetuate the myth that those who took no direct role in governing should be content with their place and role in society. That changed with the Renaissance.

Thomas Aquinas

Born to great wealth, Thomas Aquinas (1225–1274) was drawn to the life of the mind, and became an influential philosopher and theologian. Aquinas tried to merge Aristotle's philosophy with Christian theology, the classical with the biblical. His major work *Summa Theologica* remains one of the most valued books in the canon.

Aquinas grew up in a world of monarchies, and that, plus his devotion to the church and its hierarchical rule, informs his philosophy. And yet the practice of more democratic and participatory decision making that characterized his religious order, the Dominicans, led him to tilt toward a more democratic sensibility. This led Aquinas, like Cicero and others before him, to embrace a mixed form of government.

Aquinas called for a constitutional monarchy. This system was designed to enable man to achieve happiness through a virtuous life. The merging of political with religious life was a common feature of this age and was designed to help man find God's purpose for us on earth. Later Erasmus, in *The Education of a Christian Prince,* would pick up where Aquinas left off and directly apply Christian virtue to the life of the prince, insisting that only when the prince led a highly moral life could a just society emerge.

Where Aquinas focuses on the king he does so assuming the presence of Christian virtue and assuming that humans *needed* a king (on earth, as in heaven) as part of a natural order. The king was needed to give direction to society. "Human beings," he wrote in *On Law, Morality, and Politics,* "need something that directs them to their end"—the end being a moral and Christian life. As Solomon said in Proverbs 11:14, "The people will be destroyed if there is no ruler." The king compelled people to Christian beliefs, and thus, the life of the king on earth was to guide his people to eternal life in heaven. This incestuous merging of faith and politics may sound onerous in our age, but at that time, such sentiments were the norm, not the exception. The king was on earth to do God's work and lead his flock to salvation, to government, and to a good life.

Machiavelli and the Birth of the Modern

Niccolò Machiavelli, Florentine diplomat turned author, has a bad reputation. Is that reputation justified? The name alone sends shivers down the spine. To be called a Machiavellian is to be referred to as an opportunistic, manipulative dirty dealer, someone in league with the devil. Today, five hundred years later, he still evokes images of cunning and evil, an amalgam of a Mao, the Godfather, Tony Soprano, and the Terminator.

Bertrand Russell called *The Prince* (1513) "a handbook for gangsters." The Roman Catholic Church placed both *The Prince* and the *Discourses* on its index of banned books, the *Index Librorum Prohibitorum*. Woodrow Wilson said of *The Prince,* "It recognizes no morality but a sham morality meant for deceit, no honor even among thieves and of a thievish sort, no force but physical force, no intellectual power but cunning, no disgrace but failure, no crime but stupidity." Most contemporaries still view Machiavelli with horror as an advocate of dishonesty and cruelty. Does he deserve such harsh sobriquets?

If Machiavelli's *Prince* was publicly condemned, it was privately read. Cardinal Richelieu read it several times; Napoleon consulted it repeatedly; President John Adams kept a copy by his bedside. Voltaire helped Prussian king Frederick the Great write a broadside against *The Prince* entitled *Anti-Machiavel.* Frederick was, however, not at all shy about employing Machiavelli's methods—when thought to be necessary.

In short, everyone read *The Prince,* from the Founding Fathers in America, to modern corporate chiefs, to Adolf Hitler. It is the most widely read book on leadership strategy and tactics.

If *The Prince* is Machiavelli's treatise on power politics, his *Discourses on Livy* (written in 1519) is a plea for the development of republican government in Italy. So who is the real Machiavelli—messiah of power politics, or champion of republicanism—and what has he contributed to our understanding of leadership? (He wrote other books as well, including a lesser-known classic, *The Art of War* [1521], which we will discuss in Chapter 9.)

Perhaps Machiavelli's principal "crime" in *The Prince* was to defy convention and present a stark portrait of the naked use of power divorced from Christian ethics. *The Prince* was seen as an attack on the classical as well as the Christian tenets of political thought. He argued that such high-minded advice, although sounding nice, was simply wrong. He subverted the conventional wisdom. Before Machiavelli, statecraft was intimately connected to soulcraft: a good man would make a good prince. Thus, from Plato's Philosopher-King to Erasmus's Christian prince, the ruler was taught to know justice and act justly. The teaching of virtue was the check and balance guiding the behavior of the prince. At least that was the idea.

Machiavelli thought this was bunk. As noted, he divorced statecraft from soulcraft and focused on the former. Machiavelli was concerned with *how* leaders behaved, not how they *ought* to behave. As he wrote in Chapter XV (*The Prince*):

> But because I want to write what will be useful to anyone who understands, it seems to me better to concentrate on what really happens rather than on theories or

> speculations. For many have imagined republics and principalities that have never been seen or known to exist. However, how men live is so different from how they should live that a ruler who does not do what is generally done, but persists in doing what ought to be done, will undermine his power rather than maintain it. If a ruler who wants always to act honorably is surrounded by many unscrupulous men his downfall is inevitable. Therefore, a ruler who wishes to maintain his power must be prepared to act immorally when this becomes necessary.

These excerpts from *The Prince* telegraph his pragmatic and blunt realism:

- "A prince, particularly a new prince, cannot afford to cultivate attributes for which men are considered good. In order to maintain the state, a prince will often be compelled to work against what is merciful, loyal, humane, upright, and scrupulous."
- "A wise ruler cannot and should not keep his word when it would be to his disadvantage."
- "Men must be either flattered or eliminated, because a man will readily avenge a slight grievance, but not one that is truly severe."
- "How one lives and how one ought to live are so far apart that he who spurns what is actually done for what ought to be done will achieve ruin rather than his own preservation."

Delivering a stiff dose of realism was Machiavelli's goal. In advising the Prince, he offered "good advice" rather than advice on "how to be good." He had a jaundiced view of human nature, seeing ambition and the hunger for power as trumping personal morality. Machiavelli sought a rational understanding of how princes actually behaved, thereby affording him the opportunity to advise the Prince in ways to gain and use power wisely in the real world.

Machiavelli's goal was not to justify evil. He merely described *how* leaders behaved. And in the brutal world of power politics, to survive and to thrive, one had to know how the game was played, and what it took to win. At times, fighting fire with fire (tit for tat) made political sense. Machiavelli did not advise the Prince to do evil; he merely suggested that under certain conditions it might be "necessary" to do so. He argued that the Prince must be able "not to depart from good where possible, but to know how to enter into evil, when forced by necessity."[2]

The Prince argues that these ingredients lead to success: *virtù*, *fortuna*, and *occasione*. By *virtù* he does not mean virtue as goodness but ability, skill, intelligence, boldness, decisiveness, and a disciplined sense of power. *Virtù* for Machiavelli was largely a military quality providing inner strength and force of will needed to be effective in adverse or challenging circumstances. *Fortuna* means "fate and fortune," or "luck." Some are blessed with good luck, others are not.

Napoleon used to say, "Find me a lucky general!" *Occasione* means "opportunity and the proper reading of context or situation." When *virtù, fortuna,* and *occasione* were aligned, effective leadership was likely. Only *virtù* was under the control of the Prince. When *virtù* and prudence (*prudenza*) could be artfully combined, the Prince could serve the common good.

And what are the chief components of individual *virtù*? The effective leader was capable of being (at the right time) generous or cruel, faithless and compassionate, faithful and frivolous, affable and selfish, religious and unbelieving, caring and haughty, rapacious and miserly. In short, the effective leader could be many different things depending on what he needed to be at any particular time. Effective leaders were smart, flexible, and adaptable. In today's vocabulary, they knew how to combine hard and soft power strategies so they could govern smartly.

The Machiavellian leader was able to "style-flex," fitting his dance to the music being played. He could accurately assess the situation (*occasione*), fit his style of leadership to the needs of the situation (*virtù*), and if lucky (*fortuna*), emerge victorious. Yet, for Machiavelli, who understood the paradoxes of power, even the right decision at the right time could lead to failure if *fortuna* did not favor the leader. Such are the vagaries of leadership in a complex world. As he put it, "And so it is with Fortune, who displays her might where there is no organized strength to resist her, and directs her onset where she knows that there is neither barrier nor embankment to confine her." The most a leader can do is to construct some barriers or embankments to channel or try to engineer fortune.

Nowhere does Machiavelli call for the exercise of cunning for its own sake. That would be dysfunctional. The occasional use of cunning, however, may be necessary to preserve power. It is only wise to use cunning when it is absolutely necessary to do so.

At times, in order to be effective, leaders had to be ruthless and cynical. To be ruthless and cynical on a day-to-day basis would make one a cruel autocrat. No, one employs these tactics only when they are necessary. To do otherwise would be unwise. A cold, political calculation of what must be done precedes all action. If being a saint serves one's interests, by all means, play the saint. But on occasion an amoral or immoral act may be required. The leader must be prepared to be good "or not good" as the situation demands. At times, the Prince must play the fox who can "recognize traps," while at other times he must be the lion who can "frighten wolves." Thus, the Prince must resemble the centaur of mythology—half man, half beast. At times mean, at times smart. As Machiavelli notes in Chapter XVIII: "Everyone knows how praiseworthy it is for a ruler to keep his promises and live uprightly and not by trickery. Nevertheless, experience shows that in our times the rulers who have done great things are those who have set little store by keeping their word, being skillful rather in cunningly confusing men; they have got the better of those who have relied on being trustworthy."

The job of the Prince was to win; and if, at the end of the day, a few moral corners were cut, so be it. History forgives the winners; it condemns the losers. Does he then recommend that the Prince be immoral? No. Machiavelli is not concerned with conventional morality. He is interested in success. And as theologian Reinhold Niebuhr perceptively noted, those who place too great a stock in idealism may take the moral pretensions of others as fact, sometimes blinding them to the complex web of motivations, justifications, rationalizations of which we are capable. In this way, we may be fooled.[3] Machiavelli enjoins the leader to face each situation with skepticism. Humans are capable of high, as well as low, acts.

Machiavelli did not invent the ideas associated with Machiavellianism. His ideas had already been practiced by leaders for centuries. He did, however, have the nerve to openly defy religious niceties and write about a stark, and to some brutal, reality.

To Machiavelli, the ideal way to gain control was to acquire power through honorable means. This allowed one to have both power and glory. Yet, in a harsh world, such high-mindedness is not always possible. Thus, the next best method was to gain power by whatever means necessary. Here one acquired power, but not glory. To Machiavelli, the worst offense was to misuse or squander power or opportunity. Such foolishness led, and rightly so, to failure and defeat.

In this way, Machiavelli directs the Prince to use power wisely and well, brutally where absolutely necessary (and only when necessary), and always to be conscious of his status. The skillful pursuit and use of power is Machiavelli's goal.

True, Machiavelli's *Prince* seems more concerned with pursuing power than justice, something Plato, Aristotle, and the ancients would find objectionable; yet there is nothing in *The Prince* that argues against the promotion of justice. It is merely that to achieve a good end—and to Machiavelli, the good end ultimately sought was a peaceful, unified, and republican Italy (worthy goals, indeed)—the Prince must be in command, in control, and powerful. If Machiavelli does not explicitly link power to principle in *The Prince,* he does so more clearly in the *Discourses.*

Also, Machiavelli does not ask for a moral escape clause for the leader. He does not argue that evil is not evil. He merely notes that if your adversary is using evil tactics, you would likely lose if you remained morally pure.

Machiavelli and the Thorny Question of Power

Machiavelli raised the question not previously discussed in polite company: how does one get and use *power*? It is the DNA, the building block and foundation of leadership. And Machiavelli forced us to confront power in its raw and subtle forms.

And yet, there are important differences between *leadership* and *power.*

The words *leadership* and *power* are often used interchangeably. Yet, the two words mean different things. As we have pointed out, leadership deals with *influence*; power is about *command.* Leaders inspire and persuade; power wielders demand compliance. Leaders induce followership; power holders compel or enforce acceptance. Office holders have some power merely by virtue of occupying an office. Leaders must *earn* followership. Leadership is a process of influence wherein the leader helps propel the group toward the attainment of some mutually desirable good. Power is the ability to command or force compliance in an area of recognized authority.

In his classic *Leadership,* Burns suggested that leadership takes place when "persons with certain motives and purposes mobilize, in competition or conflict with others, institutional, political, psychological, and other resources so as to arouse, engage, and satisfy the motives of followers.... Leadership is exercised in a condition of conflict or competition in which leaders contend in appeal to the motive bases of potential followers."[4]

The *American Heritage Dictionary* defines *leader* as "one that leads," a not particularly useful definition. This same dictionary defines *lead* as "to show the way," a more apt definition. Leaders show the way. They may or may not be office holders. Martin Luther King Jr. held no political office, yet he showed us the way. The dictionary also defines *lead* as "to guide," again an apt definition. Leaders guide us. And they do much more. They set a vision, move the machinery of the organization behind the achievement of that vision, mobilize supporters, recruit others to their cause, organize, direct, set strategy, educate, coach, persuade, influence, and set goals.

Power is often *positional*; that is, it attaches to a particular office or position, and is dependent on one's occupying that office in order to be powerful. General Norman Schwarzkopf, who ably commanded the coalition forces in the first Persian Gulf war, noted after leaving the military, "Seven months ago I could give a single command and 541,000 people would immediately obey it. Today I can't get a plumber to come to my house."

But power is also *personal*; that is, it attaches to the skills and attributes of the individual. The position *and* the person—the former suggests *power,* the latter suggests *leadership.*

All great leaders have a finely tuned *power sense*; that is, they are focused on the accumulation and uses of power. They know what power is, how to get it, and how to use it; they know how to play one interest off another; they know how to attract attention and mobilize people and situations to their advantage. They are often ambitious, self-centered, and power conscious.

"Power," said Henry Adams, "is poison." And as Lord Acton reminded us, "Power corrupts. Absolute power corrupts absolutely." All true. Yet, power is a major resource for getting things done.

Shakespeare's Leadership Insights

The world's greatest playwright, William Shakespeare (1546–1616), was one of the most insightful and astute students of human nature and human behavior in all its manifest forms, and he has much to teach us about power, politics, and leadership. Shakespeare lays before us the good, the bad, and the ugly of politics and power and the precarious nature of the human condition. His many insights into leadership and the use and abuse of power by tyrants and kings give us instructive images of powers and principle.

We see Shakespeare not only as an excellent source of drama, but also as someone who compels us to reflect deeply on leadership. For Shakespeare asks the perennial questions, explores the pressures and possibilities, confronts the good and bad in us and in leaders, and squarely confronts the dilemmas and paradoxes of authority, position, and leadership. His grasp of human nature made him as much of a psychologist as a playwright. And his ability to see vice and virtue made him a leadership moralist of the first order.

Over twenty of his plays deal explicitly with politics and leadership, especially his histories and tragedies. Leadership succession, grasping the reins of power, rulership, the uses and abuses of power, manipulation and deceit, authority, flattery, and themes of the rule of law reverberate in his classic works.

We may never know with certainty what Shakespeare's political convictions were. Given the demands of drama, he gives to his characters words he may or may not personally endorse, yet he offers them for dramatic purposes. We know that Shakespeare wrote in an age of upheaval, when the doctrine of the divine right of kings was receding and demands for more representative and popular forms of power were only just beginning in England and elsewhere.

Most educated people in Shakespeare's time believed in the appropriateness of hierarchical order. This order was being challenged, and fears of approaching anarchy were real. The Elizabethan doctrine of order and obedience to the king was much in vogue in Shakespeare's age; and to a significant, although not complete degree, his plays reflect adherence to this principle.

Although clearly no democrat, the extent to which Shakespeare embraced a hierarchical model of society and politics is unclear. In some of his plays, the ruler clearly has a responsibility to govern with the interests of society and the people in mind.

Hierarchy, to Shakespeare, represented the true order of nature. In his age, to live according to nature was to live in accordance with God's will; and if the king ruled in the name of God, one had an obligation to obey. As God ruled over us, so too must a king be God's temporal voice on earth. Elizabethan historian Sir John Hayward sums up this view: "As one God ruleth the world, one master the family ... so it seemeth no less natural that one state should be governed by one commander."[5] This concept finds its way into *Richard II* when King Richard reminds the audience, "The breath of worldly men cannot depose the deputy elected by the Lord."

If Shakespeare accepts the legitimacy of a hierarchical order, he is nonetheless concerned that the king rule justly and effectively. His good kings consult widely; they are open and willing to brook criticism. Rulers who are arrogant and haughty fail of their own weaknesses. Shakespeare did not question monarchy—he was, after all, a man of his age. But he did question the ruling strategies and behavior of many of the kings.

If Shakespeare accepts the legitimacy of monarchy, he clearly does not give his monarchs a free pass. Tyranny is derided, as only "good" rulers claim Shakespeare's approval. He was also wary of the state as a censor, and he knew all too well the brutalities and hypocrisy that characterized leadership. "When Shakespeare thought of the state," Harold Bloom writes, "he remembered first that it had murdered Christopher Marlowe, tortured and broken Thomas Kyd, and branded the unbreakable Ben Jonson" (some of Shakespeare's contemporaries).[6]

Macbeth deals with kingship, *The Tempest* with power, *Julius Caesar* with individual glory and the battle for a republic versus empire, *Cymbeline* with war and peace, *Measure for Measure* with the rule of law and hypocrisy, *Henry V* with what it takes to be a leader, *Hamlet* with decision making, and *Richard III* with how power is exercised and abused.[7]

Shakespeare's leading characters work within different regimes of power. How each one performs—the choices made—determines his own fortunes and also the fortunes of the state. Leaders make choices, good and bad. When their choices are designed for self-promotion, they often fail; when their choices are made rashly, they often fail; when they decide based on poor or faulty information, they usually fail; when they are too self-absorbed and develop narcissistically big egos, they usually fail. It is in the choosing that Shakespeare's politics and his morality play out. Fate may play a role, but human intervention—choice—matters most. Therefore, leaders matter.

Shakespeare's view of politics was shaped in part by the age in which he lived. He lived in an age of momentous change, violence, fear, and strain. England was experiencing cataclysmic changes and decisive social pressures. Religious warfare, the rise of nationalism, and foreign wars characterized the era. Out of this chaos and violence, Shakespeare seemed to admire the politics of *order*. In this, he was somewhat conservative in his politics.

In Shakespeare's day, society was rigidly divided along class lines, and wealth was unevenly distributed. Roughly 80 percent of the English people lived in small, rural communities. In his age, rulers mattered. Although society was beginning to reject the notion that the king ruled by divine right, democratic practice was still far in the future. Societies depended largely on the quality of leadership provided by the king. Like most of his contemporaries, Shakespeare was unable to envision a country governed by the people as a viable option.

Shakespeare's suspicion of democracy is evident in *Julius Caesar* and in *Coriolanus.* Shakespeare saw the common man as fickle, irrational, and prone to manipulation. For example, people fell in love with Caesar and welcomed his autocratic rule; this invited tyranny. Equally weak is the foundation on which republican rule is built. When the republic collapses and Caesar is killed, a new brand of tyranny is unleashed—the tyranny of the mob.

As Shakespeare valued order, he believed order came from good leadership. What can we say of his views on what constituted good leadership? Shakespeare's focus on individual agency reinforces the conception not only that leadership matters but also that leaders are virtually all that matters. This leader-centric view helps shape public and elite opinion and supports the leader-as-hero (or villain) lineage that dominates conventional thinking.

What, to Shakespeare, constitutes good and bad leadership? Military leaders do not fare well in the world of William Shakespeare. Macbeth, Othello, Titus Andronicus, Henry Bolingbroke, and Coriolanus all come off as too quick to act, too cynical, hardened, and harsh.

Greed, ambition, and swollen egos play a large part in Shakespeare's view of human motivation, lead most often to catastrophe, and are presented as dysfunctional and counterproductive. Shakespeare may not have questioned the legitimacy of the monarchy, yet he cautioned against excess. In attempting to define the ideal prince, Shakespeare would have been familiar with the arguments of Erasmus (*The Education of a Christian Prince,* 1603) as well as Machiavelli. Shakespeare may have modeled his good princes on Erasmus, although his villains display a Machiavellian wickedness even Machiavelli would have condemned (as not strategically useful),[8] going so far as to refer to one cad as "that notorious Machiavel!"[9] In fact, what makes Shakespeare's villains so delicious is their level of self-awareness of their crass acts. Richard III turns to his audience to persuade and enlighten them, enlisting us in his self-justifications. Shakespeare's flawed characters take morality seriously, especially as they violate conventional morals in favor of self-serving expediency.

The stability of the state depends on the ability of the prince. As Hamlet's friend, Rosencrantz, reminds us:

> The single and peculiar life is bound
> With all the strength and armour of the mind
> To keep itself from noyance; but much more
> That spirit upon whole weal depends and rests
> The lives of many. The cease of majesty

> Dies not alone, but like a gulf doth draw
> What's near it with it. It is a massy wheel.
> Fix'd on the summit of the highest mount,
> To whole huge spokes ten thousand lesser things
> Are mortis'd and adjoin'd; which when it falls,
> Each small annexment, petty consequence,
> Attends the bois'trous ruin. Never alone
> Did the king sigh, but with a general groan.[10]

Coriolanus. As noted, Shakespeare was no friend to democracy. He admired strong, smart, prudent leaders who had a clear grasp of reality and were able to apply wise policies to the tumult of politics. And yet, in his era, the voice of the people was welling up and making demands on the political elites. It was a conflict Shakespeare found troubling. Chaos, confusion, and conflict threatened the order and stability he so valued.

The case of Coriolanus[11] illustrates the conflict and Shakespeare's misgivings about the appetites of the rabble. Caius Martius Coriolanus, a fourth-century BCE Roman general, is a heroic and successful warrior. Much honored and highly decorated, Coriolanus knows how to win battles. Yet, his utter disdain for the common man and his contempt for "the people" leads to his downfall. As Plutarch (from whom Shakespeare takes the story) notes, Coriolanus has an impatient and choleric personality and a disdain for the people that is so powerful he loses all legitimacy.[12] To rise in Rome meant, in part, that one had to have a mass following. Coriolanus sought the position of consul, yet he refused to place himself before the public for approval. Coriolanus was unwilling to submit his clearly superior nature to such humiliation as appealing to the people. To Coriolanus, his integrity was at stake: "Would you have me false to my nature? Rather say I play the man I am." But Coriolanus's integrity is seen by the people as arrogance and false pride. Even when Coriolanus submits in a small way, donning his "gown of humility" wherein he reveals his war wounds gained in the service of Rome, he does so with such obvious contempt that it backfires; and Sicinius, one of the people's tribunes, enjoins them to "forget not with what contempt he wore the humble weed, how in his suit he scorned you."

His unwillingness to appeal to the will of the masses doubtless developed because of his swollen ego and sense of entitlement. This led to the people's turning on the hero, and he is accused of treason. Coriolanus decides to leave Rome and joins Tullus Aufidius, the leader of the Volscians and enemies of Rome. Coriolanus leads the army headed for Rome. Some patricians in Rome try to dissuade Coriolanus but he is undeterred. Finally, his mother Volumnia lies down in her son's path and pleads with him.

Coriolanus reluctantly gives in to his mother's plea. Yet this too ends in tragedy as the Volscians accuse him of treason and have him killed.

How could so accomplished a military leader end up such a tragic failure? His military leadership and his courage, skill, and strategic brilliance on the battlefield were widely recognized. Yet, he was unable to adapt to the different demands posed by public or civic leadership. Those qualities or attributes that so aided him as a general proved dysfunctional in the new setting of the public arena.

Coriolanus is a man accustomed to wielding power, to getting his way. His self-confidence and understandable pride led to arrogance and overconfidence. The world was to adapt *to him,* not he to the world.[13]

Coriolanus just doesn't "get it." In today's understanding, he lacked "emotional intelligence." He sees no need to bare himself before the people. Are not his talents manifest and obvious? Is that not enough? No, in the context of civic leadership, it is not enough.

Context is an important feature of leadership. The demands of military leadership are dramatically different from civic leadership. The skills of one arena do not always translate to the other. Coriolanus does not recognize this and thus does not adapt his approach to the demands of the new context.

Coriolanus saw such adaptation (wrongly) as a betrayal of his integrity. And because he is blinded by pride, he ends up betraying Rome. So self-absorbed is he in his own world (trapped by his successes) that he ends up not recognizing that his betrayal of Rome is the ultimate act of duplicity. It demonstrates that he did not truly possess the virtues necessary for leadership.

In his plays, Shakespeare repeatedly deals with power and its impact on those who have it and use it. Coriolanus seems to have the potential for effective leadership, and yet he fails to adapt altogether to the new and challenging contexts of the civic arena, and he tragically self-destructs.

Othello. Shakespeare's *Othello* is a tragedy about how easily we can be misled.[14] Othello, the "Moor of Venice," like Coriolanus, is a supremely successful military leader; and yet, so wise and successful a commander falls victim to a jealous rival's trickery with tragic repercussions.

The play opens with military officer Iago complaining to his compatriot Roderigo, a Venetian gentleman, that his commander Othello has passed him over and given a sought-after promotion to Lieutenant Cassio. Iago vows revenge for this slight.

In the meantime, the Duke of Venice asks Othello to sail to Cyprus to prevent a Turkish invasion of Venice. The duke, seeing that his daughter Desdemona and

Othello are deeply in love, allows the two to embark on this voyage together. As they reach Cyprus, the Turkish threat has receded.

Iago goads Cassio to get drunk and get into a fight. For this, Othello strips Cassio of his promotion, much to the enjoyment of Iago. But his revenge is not enough. Iago next sets his sights on Othello.

His plan is to make Othello believe his new bride, Desdemona, is unfaithful. As Iago coaxes Cassio to approach Desdemona and have her plead with Othello to reinstate him to his former post, Iago tries to persuade Othello that Cassio is having an affair with Desdemona.

Mad with jealousy, and blindly trusting Iago, Othello gives the promotion to Iago and enlists his aid in a plan to kill both Cassio and Desdemona.

Othello approaches his sleeping wife, wakes her, and accuses her of adultery. While she protests, Othello smothers her. Emilia interrupts and Desdemona is revived, protesting that she is innocent. Desdemona dies, and as the truth of the situation emerges, Othello sees that Iago is behind it all. He tries to kill Iago, but Iago escapes, only to later be captured. Othello admits to his error and commits suicide.

Why was Othello so easily manipulated by Iago? In his defense, Othello did demand "proof" from Iago.

Yet, the "evidence" provided was circumstantial and flimsy. Why did Othello fall for it? Iago makes a good case for his claim; yet, with the stakes so high, why did not Othello probe deeper, demand more, check his assumptions? Othello lets himself be manipulated. In this, Othello reminds people of a more recent episode: George W. Bush in the lead-up to the war in Iraq when Bush allowed himself to believe things that were not true. Othello, and Bush, allowed themselves to be deceived; in fact, they were compliant in their own deceit. Both should have known better. Leaders are understandably guided by emotions, yet they also have a responsibility to get as much valid information as possible. And they have a responsibility not to lie to their constituents.[15]

Othello's suspicions became self-fulfilling prophecies. His self-doubt fed by jealousy (the "green-eyed monster") makes him irrational and ill equipped to make the important decision he has to face. He becomes the victim of his emotions, not the master of them. And once he starts down that tragic road, he serves as an enabler of his own destruction.

Richard III. For political intrigue and sinister behavior, it would be hard to top Richard III, Shakespeare's physically and morally deformed tragic king. Richard, the hunchback Duke of Gloucester, who conspires to become King

Richard III via a web of intrigue and a string of horrible acts, is one of Shakespeare's most compelling as well as offputting figures. So vile, so sinister, is he that we are drawn to him like glue, fascinated by his vile behavior, yet intrigued by his rise, then fall. To get to the top, he kills enemies, relatives, his wife, and most of his "friends."

The monstrous Richard, misshapen and wallowing in self-pity as he systematically destroys all claimants to the throne, delights in his evil. He is blissfully, intoxicatingly evil, and as with a car wreck, we know we shouldn't look, yet we can't turn away. The self-anointed villain may be a monster, yet he is a fascinating monster.

Richard III is a play about grabbing power by evil means. The plot is merely a device for Richard to hatch his villainous schemes.

Hungry for power, ambitious beyond words, Richard signals his intentions in the opening—self-pitying—lines of the play. He is back from the war, where his family, the Yorks, have won the throne. War gave direction to Richard's ambitions. Now, with peace at hand, a new regime, a political age, has arisen, one in which Richard's traits and abilities are a liability. He contrasts war and politics:

> Now all of my family's troubles have come to a glorious end, thanks to my brother, King Edward IV. All the clouds that threatened the York family have vanished and turned to sunshine. Now we wear the wreaths of victory on our heads. We've taken off our armor and weapons and hung them up as decorations. Instead of hearing trumpets call us to battle, we dance at parties. We get to wear easy smiles on our faces rather than the grim expressions of war. Instead of charging towards our enemies on armored horses, we dance for our ladies in their chambers, accompanied by sexy songs on the lute. But I'm not made to be a seducer, or to make faces at myself in the mirror. I was badly made and don't have the looks to strut my stuff in front of pretty sluts. I've been cheated of a nice body and face, or even normal proportions. I am deformed, spit out from my mother's womb prematurely and so badly formed that dogs bark at me as I limp by them. I'm left with nothing to do in this weak, idle peacetime, unless I want to look at my lumpy shadow in the sun and sing about *that*. (Act 1, Scene 1)

"But I'm not made to be a seducer," he laments. His physical deformities ("I was badly made") leave him, he argues, with no other option for satisfying his ambitions than to turn to evil. "Since I can't amuse myself by being a lover, I've decided to become a villain." And what a villain!

Richard's rise to power is swift and remarkable. In a few months he wipes out virtually every rival and has taken the throne. Once in power, he must deal with the consequences of his actions. Interested only in gaining power, once he achieves his goal he knows not how to govern. He acknowledges no limits on his authority, and although he is decisive, he lacks legitimacy and the skills of a consensus builder. He is unable to adjust to the needs of governing. All he knows is force, or "hard power"; he is unable to use the gentle guiding hand to lead. He justifies his continued resort to force by arguing that his "kingdom stands on brittle glass"; yet it is his own actions that have made it thus.

Richard goes too far and it backfires on him. He was well suited to grab for power but ill suited to use it.

Is Richard III, as some critics suggest, a "Machiavellian" leader? His cynical pursuit of power leads some to see him as a prototypical Machiavellian. But would Machiavelli really endorse such wholesale (and at times unnecessary) human slaughter? Probably not. More likely, Machiavelli would see Richard III as a psychopathically driven figure who is almost guaranteed to self-destruct. Richard gains power but can't use power; he misreads and misjudges many people and situations, and is driven to excess by his self-loathing. Richard is not a wise or prudent pursuer of power. He is a madman.

A more apt analogy may be that Richard III of Shakespeare resembles another Richard, President Richard Nixon. As Richard III resented those around him who were without his deformities, so too did Nixon loathe various establishment elites, the Harvard educated, the rich and wellborn, the handsome and athletic (especially the Kennedys). Richard's physical deformities led to moral deformities, just as Nixon's negative sense of self and inner demons led to his justification of immoral and illegal acts.[16] Malicious, hungry for power, bitter about his physical shortcomings, Richard descends into his own personal prison, as Nixon descended deeper into isolation until his moral and personal weaknesses—like those of Richard III—brought him down. Richard III and Richard Nixon enter the heart of darkness and end up destroyed.[17]

Julius Caesar. If *Macbeth* shows us the high price of unbridled ambition, *Julius Caesar* shows us how ambition, crossed by jealousy, in a republic on the verge of empire, can lead to chaos and civil war.

Julius Caesar returns to Rome, triumphant after a victory in battle. The Roman Republic is teetering and strong leaders grab for power. No one is better positioned to take control than Caesar. The rise of a strong man threatens to destroy the republic. And yet Caesar is popular, capable, charming, larger than life, ambitious, and ready to take power. Empire or republic? Rule by one strong hand or by representatives of the people?

Several senators, especially Caius Cassius (who is envious of Caesar's rise) and Marcus Brutus (who earnestly wishes to preserve the republic), are suspicious of Caesar and his motives. They fear he will become emperor. They plot to assassinate Caesar, who is warned to "beware the ides [15th] of March."

Caesar's wife, Calpurnia, fearing for her husband's safety, begs him not to go to the Senate; but in the end, Caesar refuses to heed the warnings, surrendering instead to flattery and appeals to his ego. Caesar goes to the Senate where Brutus and his conspirators kill him.

Mark Antony, a longtime Caesar ally, who was not part of the plot, is allowed to speak at Caesar's funeral. He has his own agenda, to stir, not calm, the masses; he successfully manipulates the people with deft rhetorical maneuvers. This is the famous "Friends, Romans, countrymen, lend me your ears" speech. Do read it on your own, and if you can, watch Marlon Brando's memorable award-winning film version of the Antony speech.

Mark Antony's speech stirs the people and a civil war ensues. Brutus, Cassius, and the "Republicans" lose; Antony and Octavius (who later takes control of Rome as Caesar Augustus) are triumphant.

Caesar was a military genius yet he is portrayed here as a demagogue—vain, imperious, and arrogant. He was a man bent on the pursuit of power. He was also highly accomplished. His individual aims clashed with the demands of the republic. Yet Cassius was no better. Only Brutus seems torn between betraying Caesar and preserving the republic. In the end, he strikes the deadly blow against Caesar, and his actions contribute to the demise of republican Rome. In the end, everyone loses.

Oh, how toxic the blind pursuit of power can be. Was this Caesar's blind spot? How could someone so smart, so successful, so experienced, so capable walk into his own destruction, eyes wide open? Caesar even goes so far as to tell Mark Antony early in the play that Cassius is "dangerous ... very dangerous." Why fall so easily into his trap? Why does he not prepare for the danger he knows Cassius poses? He enters the Senate without bodyguards, without an escape plan, and against the pleas of his wife and the warnings of danger from the soothsayer. Caesar was blinded by his own selfish ambitions. With the republic crumbling around him, he saw himself as the imperial savior, as an emerging god about to rise to the heights. Mere mortals, or so Caesar thought, do not conquer a god.

Yet Shakespeare, probably a monarchist at heart, concerned with preserving order, does not support just any form of monarchy. He, too, sees the dangers inherent in unbridled ambition, greed, arrogance, and the blind pursuit of power. In *Julius Caesar,* the "monarch"-in-waiting is killed and the civil war ends, producing Augustus as emperor.

With all his manifest skills and talents, the strutting Caesar lacked both self-knowledge and political knowledge. In fact, all the major characters fail to know themselves or know the world. Only Brutus—confused and torn apart from within—displays the human depths and possibilities that tragically also end in his death.

Through *Caesar,* Shakespeare examines the drive for power and glory and its impact on personal conscience. Brutus is torn between loyalty to Caesar and loyalty to an ideal, the republic. In the end, he chooses the republic, yet all ends in tragedy.

Shakespeare wrote at a time of upheaval and social unrest in England. In 1558, Elizabeth came to the throne amid rebellion and chaos. There were several attempts on her life. By 1599, she was old and in decline. With no direct heir to Elizabeth, the possibility of a protracted civil war over control of the state seemed likely. It is in this context that Shakespeare—who valued order—wrote *Julius Caesar.* This is less a play about some distant historical figure than a play that speaks to the fears as well as the hopes of Shakespeare's own age. And the play, of course, also raises significant concerns about the role of the people and their clamoring for heroic savior leaders.

Elizabeth was a flexible, effective leader, who at times compromised her beliefs for the greater good. By contrast, Mary Tudor had been rigid and unyielding. She governed in strict accordance with her religious convictions. Shakespeare hungers for an effective leader: one who can balance a personal drive for power with the skill and flexibility needed to govern effectively. Caesar is too arrogant, Cassius too ambitious, Brutus too internally torn. It is in Brutus we see Shakespeare's central point that a good man's private beliefs may clash with political necessity. Mary Tudor's strong beliefs led to disaster; Brutus's well-intentioned act also led to disaster. Where are the wise, prudent leaders who ***know themselves*** and ***know politics***?

Shakespeare prefers the wise exercise of power over the pursuit of pure virtue or power. In this he seems a bit of a Machiavellian. Virtuous behavior may at times be impolitic. Wisdom, skill, and prudent judgment trump goodness and virtue.[18]

When Caesar dies, chaos and civil war ensue. A vacuum is created and, at first, chaos fills that vacuum. In the end, Brutus's valued republic crumbles and an emperor emerges.

Henry V. Shakespeare's tragedies are the tales of kings making what often seem to be avoidable mistakes. Shakespeare's flawed kings ought to know better yet do not see or cannot bring themselves to act prudently in a complex political arena. They overreach, overstep, hesitate too long, or can't seem to match policy to situation.

In *Henry IV, Parts I and II,* and *Henry V,* Shakespeare shows us the other side of leadership—how to prepare to assume and use power with skill.

Shakespeare gives us a clear picture of not only what makes for a good leader but how one can self-consciously work to become a good leader.

In *Henry IV, Parts I and II,* we find Hal (later Henry V), the son of the king, a fun-loving cad who seems ill prepared to assume the throne. But there is method to Hal's madness, as he tells his cronies:

I know you all, and will a while uphold
The unyoked humor of your idleness.
Yet herein will I imitate the sun,
Who doth permit the base contagious clouds,
To smother up his beauty from the world,
That, when he please again to be himself,
Being wanted, he may be more wond'red at
. . .
By so much shall I falsify men's hopes;
And, like bright metal on a sullen ground,
My reformation, glitt'ring o'er my fault
Shall show more goodly and attract more eyes
Than that which hath no foil to set it off.
I'll so offend to make offense a skill,
Redeeming time when men think least I will. (Act 1, Scene 2)

Falstaff, Hal's fun-loving companion, a lecher and thief, teaches the would-be king about life and the concerns of the common man. Hal's political education is good preparation for the day when he assumes the throne. But the king is worried about his rascal son. Warwick, however, assures the king:

The prince but studies his companions
Like a strange tongue, wherein to gain the language
. . .
The prince will in the perfectness of time
Cast off his followers, and their memory
Shall as a pattern or a measure live,
By which his grace must mete the lives of others,
Turning past evils to advantages. (Act 4, Scene 4)

Hal lives the high life in the court and the low life of a scoundrel. He is a complex and complete being. His experiences enrich and educate him, prepare him for the responsibilities of state. And when he becomes king, Hal, now Henry V, repudiates his old friend Falstaff, saying, "I know you not, old man.... Presume not that I am the thing I was."

And indeed, he is not the man he was. Henry is wiser for his past experiences. He has learned from his youthful indiscretions and is rich with experience and knowledge. He knows how all elements of the kingdom work and how his people think. Henry has tasted life at all levels and is now prepared to rule.

What lesson can we draw from Shakespeare's Henry V? Shakespeare warns us not to expect perfection in our rulers. Kings and presidents, like us, are human beings and are prone to the same drives, fears, and passions that make up human nature. We humans are complex, even contradictory, beings. We are motivated by a variety of factors, some noble, others base. And we all make mistakes. Some, like Hal, learn from their pasts; others, like Lear, do not. Better the ruler who has sinned and learned the lesson than the would-be leader who refuses to recognize and learn from life's hardships and travails.

Shakespeare would probably also tell us to live life fully. Life is a learning process, and the good ruler, like the good person, is one who knows fully life's richness—the good and the bad. Clearly, we should choose the good, but "not so fast," Shakespeare might warn us; know life, then decide.

Leaders are asked to be many things: moral leaders, wartime leaders, high priests, and occasional sinners. The things we expect of our leaders are complex and often contradictory. We want our leaders to be of the highest character, yet there are times when—especially in dealing with foreign adversaries—we require them to be manipulative and deceptive, if not worse. Would a Mother Teresa make a good national leader? Although she would serve as an excellent role model for individual behavior, would she, could she, stand up to the sometimes harsh world of politics and power?

As discussed in Chapter 1, we place paradoxical demands on our leaders. That being the case, we should not be surprised that on occasion, they behave in ways ill suited to life in the priesthood. Our search for the good leader should not be the search for perfection, but for the fully human person who knows good and evil, strives to bring about the good, attempts to bring out "the better angels" in all of us, knowing full well that at times he or she may have to make morally questionable decisions, life-and-death choices. Leadership is no place for the faint hearted. It is a place where the high and low arts of politics are practiced. At its best, it produces an Abraham Lincoln and a Franklin D. Roosevelt, leaders who knew what was right, attempted to steer the ship of state in that direction, and on occasion behaved in ways that were not totally virtuous.[19]

Henry V is a multidimensional man. He knows himself, knows his world, knows how to appeal to the people, and knows politics. He is prepared to govern (although there remains doubt about his true motives for going to war, as well as his treatment of French prisoners, but these are for another story).

Conclusion

Our survey here forced us to hydroplane over richly divergent writings and ideas. The overarching lessons from this survey are the following.

First, historically, some versions of the *Great Man/Great Leader* theory have, until contemporary times, been a dominant paradigm of leadership. Second, and related, the hunger for *Heroic Leadership* is persistent yet troubling over time.

Third, *Antidemocratic* sentiments, which have characterized most of history, have shaped the demand for strong/heroic leadership. It is only in recent decades that the demands for democratic and more consultative and collaborative leadership have been viable. It is also only in recent times that effective leaders are urged to call upon both masculine and feminine strengths. As Bruce Miroff notes, even today the typical political leader is preoccupied and nurtured in the conventions of masculinity, "but for the politician who would also be a democratic character it is necessary to transcend the conventional American dichotomy of gender qualities." Above and beyond Machiavellian maneuvers and *virtù,* the democratic leader of tomorrow, Miroff suggests, "must also develop the capacity for empathy and care and be skilled in the process of empowerment."[20] And there are exceptions to the conventional classic models. Thus the leadership of Jesus Christ and of the Zen models (and the Gandhi and Mandela experiences as well) illustrates that one size and one style do not fit all.

We turn next to classical writings that shaped constitutional and representative government.

Chapter Six
What the Classics Teach Us

The Rise of Constitutional Democracy

> It would be a dangerous delusion were a confidence in the men of our choice to silence our fears for the safety of our rights ... confidence is everywhere the parent of despotism—free government is founded in jealousy, and not in confidence; it is jealousy and not confidence which prescribes limited constitutions, to bind down those whom we are obliged to trust with power.... In questions of power, then, let no more be heard of confidence in man, but bind him down from mischief by the chains of the Constitution.
>
> —*Thomas Jefferson*[1]

If the classical era failed to grasp or take full account of the greed and ambition of rulers or embraced too optimistic a view of the ability of teaching justice to control the grosser manifestations of abuse by leaders, it did provide many of the principles on which leadership is based today. If the classical era failed us in one way, we should not forget that centered in the classical age are the roots and seeds of democracy, republicanism, participation, "the people" and constitutionalism, and the leadership challenges that would emerge along with them.

By the 1700s, dramatic changes in our conception of leadership challenged the old order. These changes affected first the political world but would later spread to the business world and the culture as well. As the ancient regime collapsed and the myth of the divine right of kings crumbled, a new orthodoxy began to emerge. In England, challenges to the authority of the king led to the English Civil War (1642), the beheading of Charles I,[2] and the emergence of a rule-of-law regime.[3] Later in the century, with the Glorious Revolution (1688), England started its transformation from rule by a king to rule by parliament. The gradual death of the divine right of kings led to the evolutionary birth of the rights of the people and constitutional democracy.[4]

Of course, not everyone was optimistic about this transformation. Remember Shakespeare's fears. Lacking divine authority meant that rulers were forced to gain the *consent* of the people. Their authority was thus always on shaky and shifting ground. The people might give their consent and later might take it away. Subjects became citizens. Rulers were forced to become leaders. Power was replaced with persuasion. Command was transformed into consent. And force shifted to influence. Rulers were no longer commanders; they had to become *leaders*.

If the foundation of this new brand of rulership rested on shaky ground, it gave birth to a new force: the will of the people. How did this transformation take place and what were its implications for the development of democratic and republican forms of leadership?

Grasping for Authority

Thomas Hobbes. The age of the divine right of kings was fading, eclipsed by the rise of more democratic sensibilities. Yet, the old order did not die quietly. In fact, it put up a fierce battle for its life. In seventeenth-century England, nascent democratic forces challenged the old order, resulting in a bloody civil war, chaos, and violence. Writing in the midst of this chaos and confusion, Thomas Hobbes (1588–1679), in his 1640 work *The Elements of Laws, Natural and Politic,* calls for the rise of an absolute sovereign to restore order and ensure stability. Anti-royalist feelings were so high in England, however, that Hobbes had to flee his homeland for the safety of life abroad.

And yet he did not give up on his quest for strong central leadership. In 1651, he published *Leviathan,* where he vigorously advocates an absolutist sovereignty. To justify such strong central authority, Hobbes takes us back to the state of nature, before governments were created. In this state, man's true nature was unchecked, and self-interest and violence predominated. Chaos and conflict, a world of "war of everyone against everyone" existed. Here, life was "solitary, poor, nasty, brutish, and short." Hobbes essentially agreed with Machiavelli that people are self-centered and motivated by desires, appetites, and passions. But he believed that through the establishment of a strong state, and with the end of anarchy, a moral order could come into being that would encourage civil and moral behavior.

To escape this chaos, humans banded together, forming a political union. They would agree, entering into a social contract, to give up their rights to a strong central authority in exchange for order, stability, and protection. Hobbes believed the only force that could bring about this much desired order was a Leviathan.[5] Note, however, that he explicitly rejects the previously traditional theories of the divine right of kings: that royalty was somehow designated and legitimized by God. No, in *Leviathan,* Hobbes suggests that political legitimacy comes only from the people, from those who understand the necessary trade-off of safety and security in exchange for personal liberties and protection.

John Locke. The English philosopher John Locke (1632–1704), building and improving upon Hobbes, had a profound impact on the framers of the U.S. Constitution. His most famous work, *Two Treatises of Government* (1689), was a masterpiece of Enlightenment thinking that promoted a brand of classical republican government under a social contract.

Locke wrote as the era of the divine right of kings was coming to an end. That divine right was based on the belief God had selected the king to rule on earth. To defy the king was to defy God.

Yet, as the divine right of kings began to erode, new, more representative or democratic aspirations replaced it, and the ground on which the new leader's authority rested was brittle and unsure. The old ruler relied on the will of God to gain consent. The new (democratic) leader would have to persuade the public to follow, gain its consent, and win over the populace. And the people were under no obligation to follow. Followership had to be earned.

Locke saw humans as capable of exercising reason. This made republican or constitutional government possible. He also promoted a concept of individual rights as found in the state of nature. Government—strictly limited government—could intrude only with the consent of the citizens through the social contract. Locke also promoted toleration of differences, believing that only those things that endangered others should be suppressed.

Locke emphasized the need for leaders and government to protect private property. But he also understood that too much centralization of power in any one institution can be dangerous. Thus the need for multiple branches with separate responsibilities.

Locke believed that the legislature is the supreme power, yet, drawing the useful distinction between those who make laws and those who execute them, Locke noted the legislature would not always be in session, and laws could not anticipate every contingency. Thus, in separating the legislative power from the executive power, the executive—who presumably would always be available—may be called upon to act in the absence of clear legislative direction.

And although Locke believed in the rule of law, arguing that "whenever law ends, Tyranny begins," he was also an advocate of the leader in certain emergencies who exercises what he called prerogative powers.[6]

By "prerogative," Locke meant that laws could not account for every possible contingency. Therefore, some executive discretion or prerogative was a necessary ingredient of good government. Prerogative might be especially necessary in a crisis where the executive could act in the absence of law, or at times, even against it. This sweeping and unchecked executive power was alarming to rule-of-law advocates, but Locke saw no other method of governing in a complex world.

Jean-Jacques Rousseau. Rousseau (1712–1778) believed that "man is naturally good"; it was by institution and society "that men become wicked." Taking on Augustine (man is born with original sin) and Hobbes (man is selfish and violent), Rousseau with his benign view of human nature developed a *social contract* view that aimed at restoring humans to the natural harmony that was in our nature before we were corrupted by society.

In *Of the Social Contract,* Rousseau calls for a balance between freedom and obedience. His ideal was some form of populist local direct democracy similar to the government of Geneva (where he grew up), in which the people would assemble, reaffirm their bond of connection to one another and to the common good, make laws, evaluate the performance of the executive, and empower the government to act in their name and on their behalf. This created a "general will" that empowered effective governance.

In Chapter 11 in *Of the Social Contract,* Rousseau allows for a quasi-dictatorial government to meet the threat of a crisis: "In these rare and obvious cases, public security is provided for by a special act which entrusts its responsibility to the most worthy." This is legitimized as the proper exercise of the general will to meet the demands of crisis.

Charles-Louis Montesquieu. Charles-Louis de Secondat, Baron Montesquieu (1689–1755), French Enlightenment philosopher, is credited with bringing the concept of the separation of powers to the modern world. In *The Spirit of the Laws* (1748), Montesquieu argues that virtually all states, regardless of how they are organized, are prone to abuse and corruption. As he wrote, "When the legislature and executive powers are united in the same person, or in the same body of magistrates, there can be no liberty."

The remedy was to separate the three key functions of government—legislative, executive, and judicial—and create three separate bodies to assume these powers. By separating powers, the threat of abuse and corruption would presumably be lessened.

Montesquieu's views influenced the American framers, who, with their jaundiced view of human nature and fear of despotism, saw the separation of powers as a structural means of preventing tyranny. Of course, this also inhibited the freedom of the leader to act, but that was Montesquieu's goal, as it also was for the framers. Separation of powers made despotism less likely, yet it also made leadership more difficult.

Edmund Burke. Amid the American and French revolutions, the status quo was being attacked and, where possible, destroyed. A new democratic, egalitarian ethos was replacing the old hierarchical order. The divine right of kings was being replaced by the divine right of the people. The voice of the people, *vox populi,* was replacing *vox Dei.*

This created an entirely new and different basis for legitimacy and authority. Decisions were no longer handed down from on high; they had to percolate up from the will—or at least consent—of the people. Democratic republics, condemned by most of the great thinkers from Plato to at least the young Alexander Hamilton, were becoming a promising model for political organization; because of this, our notions of leadership also began to change.

The consent of the governed was now required if government actions were to be legitimate. Would-be leaders now had to persuade citizens (not subjects) to support new initiatives. The people could not be compelled; they had to be led. Leaders had lost considerable power to decide on their own; rather than command, they had to lead, and lead an often reluctant populace.

Burke (1729–1797), often considered one of the fathers of modern conservatism, worried, like Plato before him, about the potential for the people to be guided by excess and passion. He promoted a more organic view of politics in which tried-and-true practices should be honored. After all, if they had been in use for an extended period of time, the people found utility in such methods.

Although no slave to the status quo, Burke nonetheless respected past practices and was reluctant to make too many changes too quickly. Burke believed in the value of traditions that had developed over years of experience. In the Americas, and later in France, the public began to embrace universal principles, such as unalienable rights and "truths" that could not be questioned.

Burke was suspicious of such absolutist universal truths. Each society developed practices and habits that worked for them, and the search for "truths" and absolutes only led to excesses. To Burke, the excesses of the French Revolution were dystopian warnings against the emerging embrace of universalist democracy. His book *Reflections on the Revolution in France* remains one of the classic works of conservative thought.

What brand of leadership did Burke espouse? In general, a managerial or facilitating style was best suited to a conservative regime. Leaders effectively and efficiently managed public business and, where change was necessary, facilitated such change. There was little room for bold, heroic leadership—except in crisis or war.

Charles Darwin. Darwin (1809–1882) had a profound impact on the way we view politics and—although indirectly—leadership. Darwin, at age twenty-two, set off on a cruise aboard the HMS *Beagle,* which sailed to several locations in South America and elsewhere. While on this voyage, the young naturalist developed the theory that all species evolved over time from common ancestors via natural selection. Evolutionary theory revolutionized science.

His book *The Origin of the Species* (1859) forever changed the way we view evolution. It had political applications as well. Social Darwinism posited the view that "the fittest survived" by a process of natural selection. When this view was combined with those of Herbert Spencer (1820–1903), it took on a conservative, even reactionary, motif, serving as justification for all sorts of inequalities and injustices (such as slavery). Although Darwin disavowed the more draconian interpretations of his work, the damage had already been done. It was Spencer who coined the phrase "survival of the fittest." Yet Darwin did not support so simplistic a view. To Darwin, the key was *survival of the most adaptable,* not necessarily the fittest. A strong tree may break in a stiff wind, yet a tree that bends—that is adaptable and flexible—survives.

To Darwin, *adaptability* and *flexibility* were the keys to the success of a species. They are also the keys to effective *leadership.* Leaders who are rigid, even if strong, might more easily break. Life and politics require adaptability, flexibility, the ability to match style to circumstances. The fittest sometimes lose; the more adaptable often win.

Henry David Thoreau. As a counterforce to the industrial and organizational forces emerging in society, Thoreau (1817–1862) offered a less-is-more alternative. Thoreau urged us to go back to basics, to "simplify, simply." His classic essay *Walden, or, Life in the Woods* was a celebration of the simple life and a precursor of an idea later made popular: "small is beautiful." Thoreau distrusted large, impersonal organizations—corporate or political. He feared they would overwhelm and gobble up the individual. In his essay "Civil Disobedience," he charted a course for individual action when confronting the large organization, placing the individual above the organization.

Leaders who are sensitive to the pressures and forces at work in large, complex organizations can sometimes find ways to honor individualism and make room for the outsider and rebel. Outsiders often see us better than we see ourselves. A wise leader is open to the voice of the constructive critic.

Alexis de Tocqueville. The observant French political thinker Tocqueville (1805–1859) served as such a critic for the United States. Tocqueville traveled the country and published *Democracy in America* (1835 and 1840). It tells of the rise of political and social equality in the United States and the emergence of the new democratic republic. He wrote in what doubtless was an overstatement that "Americans are so enamored of equality that they would rather be equal in slavery than unequal in freedom."

Tocqueville expressed concern that liberty might be subordinated to egalitarian tendencies, yet he was impressed by the rise of interest groups and associations of all types. In contrast to the aristocratic world of Europe, the United States was where hard work and money making were cherished, and where common men could rise to challenge the aristocracy—even join it.

Tocqueville portrayed an independent common man who through association (groups) joined in common cause with others to form allegiances to the polity. He also saw personal ambition in both its positive and negative terms. The old aristocratic arrangement brought stability and order to the system; the new democratic order of the Jacksonian era was susceptible to ambition and greed. And yet, if equality were truly the highest value, would this undermine the healthy amount of ambition necessary for democratic leadership? To Tocqueville, the greater danger of democratic leadership would not be the rise of the tyrant but the rise of the trivial. If equality was the highest value, then those who were truly superior would not be allowed to lead.

Republican Leadership

As the old order was receding and a new, more democratic order was rising, a nation was being invented: the United States of America. The creators of the U.S. Constitution met in Philadelphia in the hot summer of 1787. Seventy-four delegates were chosen by the states; however, only fifty-five attended the convention held in the State House (now Independence Hall), in the room where more than a decade earlier, many of the same men met to sign the Declaration of Independence.

Noticeable for their absence were some of the strongest advocates for a more direct form of democracy: Thomas Paine, Thomas Jefferson (who was in Paris), John Adams (in England), and Patrick Henry (who refused to go; fuming, he "smelt a rat"). Those in attendance were among the wealthiest, most respected, most educated, and most influential in the states. Indeed, one historian joked that, as a group, they were notably "well bred, well read, well fed and well-wed."

The problem the delegates faced was that the Articles of Confederation created too weak a central government. Under the Articles, the national government could not pay the war debt to foreign nations (especially France) or to U.S. citizens, could not regulate commerce or create a stable national currency, and could not levy taxes to establish a viable military (needed to protect national security, expand westward, and, increasingly, to protect private property from threats of growing debtor revolts). In addition, the Articles contained no executive office for the new nation. At the state level, local democracy did not appear to be working well.

There developed a broad consensus that the federal government had to be strengthened, but beyond that there was little agreement. The Revolutionary War had been fought by the average citizen, who in general was committed to the democratic and egalitarian principles found in Thomas Paine's *Common Sense* and Jefferson's Declaration of Independence. But after the Revolution, a "new" voice came to the political forefront: the propertied class. They essentially wanted a government to protect private property, develop an infrastructure to promote commerce, and protect their political and economic interests. However, if financial motivations animated these men, patriotic and good government goals also moved them. These were not one-dimensional figures but complex, even paradoxical men, informed by what was best, as well as basest, in human nature.

The framers' goal was not to create a pure democracy but to encourage collaboration and establish order under a republican form of government.

The framers faced a peculiar problem: how to establish order, protect property, and promote commerce while giving "the people" enough say in the new government to make it acceptable to emerging democratic aspirations. It was a tough balancing act. The framers feared direct democracy as much as the people feared a renewed monarchy. Most of the delegates to the Constitutional Convention opposed direct democracy (some called it "mobocracy"). Although "democracy" is a more revered term today, the word had largely negative connotations during the time of the convention. Delegate Elbridge Gerry called it "the worst of all political evils." He added, "The evils that we experience flow from the excess of democracy." Similarly, Roger Sherman warned, "The people ... should have as little to do as may be about the government." William Livingston argued that "the people have ever been and ever will be unfit to retain the exercise of power in their own hands." And delegate John Dickinson, warning of what might happen if the poor had real political clout, advocated property qualifications for voting because they are "a necessary defense against the dangerous influence of those multitudes without property and without principle, with which our country, like all others, will in time abound."

But others, even if they were suspicious of direct democracy, recognized the political reality they were facing. George Mason warned the convention, "Notwithstanding the oppression and injustice experienced among us from democracy, the genius of the people must be consulted." James Madison agreed: "It seems indispensable that the mass of citizens should not be without a voice in making the laws which they are to obey, and in choosing the magistrates who are to administer them."

James Madison, a chief architect of the new Constitution, feared a government with too much power was a dangerous government. Yet, a government too weak would surely collapse. He thus opted for an enhanced federal government. As a keen and discerning student of history, he believed human nature drove men (at this time, only men were allowed to enter the public arena) to pursue self-interest. Therefore, a system designed to have "ambition checked by ambition" set within rather strict limits was the main hope to establish a stable government that granted the citizen some rights, yet did not endanger liberty. Realizing that "enlightened statesmen" would not always guide the nation, Madison embraced a checks-and-balances system of separate but overlapping and shared powers. Madison's goal to have a government with controlled and limited powers is clearly evident. He said, in *Federalist 51,* "You must first enable the government to control the governed; and in the next place oblige it to control itself."

Madison, like most of the founders, feared government in the hands of the people. Yet, like Locke and Montesquieu before him, he also feared putting too much power in the hands of a single leader. Therefore, the Madisonian model called for both protections against mass democracy and limits on governmental power. This is not to say that the founders wanted a weak or ineffective government; had that been their goal, they would have kept the Articles of Confederation. But they did not want a government that could too easily act. The Madisonian theory of government necessitates political agreement building, coalition building, and cooperation on the one hand; checks, vetoes, and balances on the other. The twin aspirations were enabling an effective state and controlling an accountable state.[7]

A rough balance was sought between *governmental power* and *individual liberty.* The government had to be strong enough to act but restrained enough not to threaten liberty. By separating powers, forcing institutions to share these powers, and limiting powers via the rule of law, the framers hoped both to allow power (ambition) to counter power and to limit the opportunities for power to be abused. As Madison wrote in *Federalist 10,* "Enlightened statesmen will not always be at the helm"; power, in order to be safely exercised, had to be fragmented and dispersed. Madison's goal was to establish a *constitutional republic.*

The framers intentionally created uncertainty regarding who would hold power in the United States. A complex system of separated branches sharing powers created a constitutional mechanism that prohibits one branch from exercising too much power on its own. Opportunities to check power abound; opportunities to exercise power are limited. The fluidity and fragmentation of power create a situation in which "the government" is controlled not by a single person or at one place or by one party but by different people in different places (if it exists at all) sometimes seeking different ends.[8]

Checks and Balances and Separation of Powers: We often think of checks and balances and separation of powers as going together. Actually, they are often at odds with one another. Separating power gives each branch its own sphere of power, yet checks and balances require a sharing of powers so that one branch may block, or check, another. Separate or blended? Both, actually. And as the separation and blending are not always clearly defined, political battles among the three branches often occur.

Interaction, cooperation, and synchronization of the branches are required if the government is to legitimately act. If one branch strongly objects, it may check or veto the others. There is thus a conservative bias toward negative power in the Constitution. It is easier to block, to preserve the status quo, than to initiate change. Leadership is thus circumscribed.

For Madison, separation and checks work to balance power. In *Federalist 48,* he writes that "unless these departments [the three branches] be so far connected and blended [that does not sound like "separation"] as to give to each a constitutional control over the others [checks], the degree of separation ... essential to free government ... can never in practice be duly maintained [balanced]." The centrality of separate institutions sharing powers to the goal of good government is paramount for Madison, as he notes in *Federalist 48* that concentrating powers "in the same hands is precisely his definition of despotic government." Madison's goal is to reach a type of Newtonian equilibrium or balance among the branches.

If power could be separated, if the primary functions of government could be shared, if one branch could check another, tyranny might be prevented. A separation-of-powers system created three distinct, yet interconnected, branches of government: legislative, executive, and judicial. They would be separated in primary function but needed to be connected in the development of policy. No one branch fully controlled another. If one branch encroached into the territory of another, it was in the self-interest of that wronged branch to vigorously defend its power.

Thus, it is no accident that in the United States, political or governmental leadership is often hard to exercise. Sometimes it even seems that the deck is stacked against presidential leadership. In the absence of crises, the presidency is dealt a relatively weak power hand. How each president plays the hand he is dealt and how he uses his skills and opportunities go a long way in determining the success or failure of his administration. But *skill is not enough.* A variety of built-in roadblocks create an immunity system against leadership in all but the most extraordinary of times (i.e., crisis).

The power resources at a president's disposal, the complex and deliberative process of separation-of-power politics, the protectionist tendencies of the system, demand overload, and a host of other impediments make it especially difficult to galvanize the machinery of government into action. In terms of power resources, the presidency is sometimes, depending on the context, anemic. And yet, at least nowadays, the public expects, even *demands,* that the presidents provide direction for the government. Demands may be high, yet the authority and powers to meet these expectations are limited. Everywhere presidents turn (with the notable exceptions of crises and some areas of foreign policy), they face an array of brakes in their path. If presidents are to succeed, they must find a way to either gain collaboration from the other elements of the separated government or else try to impose their will on the system.

As a focus of national attention, the presidency often is, in John Kennedy's words, the "vital center" of American government.[9] But in *power* terms (the ability to get people to do something they wouldn't otherwise do), the presidency is only a *part* of the interconnected system of government; a part that must *share power* with other actors in the system.

Encasing the president is a web of restraints, a network of checks, which bind him and limit his power. Lyndon Johnson expressed the frustrations of office to his successor, Richard Nixon, thus: "Before you get to be president you think you can do anything. You think you're the most powerful leader since God. But when you get in the tall chair, as you're gonna find out, Mr. President, you can't count on people. You'll find your hands tied and people cussin' you. The office is kinda like the little country boy who found the hoochie-koochie show at the carnival, once he'd paid his dime and got inside the tent: It ain't exactly as it was advertised."[10]

The framers of the U.S. Constitution created—intentionally—an "antileadership" system of government. Although on the surface this may sound bizarre, upon reflection, it is clear that their primary goal—rather than to provide for an especially efficient system—was to create a government that would protect liberty. Governmental power was a paradoxical challenge: simultaneously a necessity and always a potential nemesis.

Essentially, the framers wanted to counteract two fears: the fear of the *mob* (democracy, or mobocracy) and the fear of the *monarchy* (centralized, tyrannical, executive power). In fact, the menacing image of England's King George III—against whom the colonists rebelled and whom Thomas Paine called "the Royal Brute of Britain"—served the framers as a powerful reminder of the dangers of a strong executive. Thus, to contain power, they set up an executive office that was constitutionally rather *weak* (Congress clearly had—on paper at least—most of the power), dependent on the *rule of law,* with a *separation of powers* in order to ensure a system of *checks and balances.*

The Paradox of Democratic Leadership

It is time to make *connections,* just as leaders must do. We need to make the connection between leadership and democracy.

Elsewhere we note how many of the great thinkers who influenced the modern world expressed strongly antidemocratic sentiments. From the philosophical musings of Plato, to the biographies of Plutarch, to the plays of Shakespeare, and to the paintings of Ensor, many of the greatest and most influential thinkers and artists were suspicious of, if not outright hostile to, democracy.

Today, we live in an age of constitutional democracy and democratic celebration. Most of today's political systems claim to be democracies, and democracy is the standard by which we judge nations. Democracy has become a "universal truth" to which virtually all pledge their allegiance. To utter democratic doubts is to be seen as an outsider or "retro." How things have turned around. Three hundred years ago, democracy was a problematic concept, at best. Today, democratic constitutionalism is almost universally applauded, or certainly held up as at least an ideal.

The demand for greater popular participation and influence was not restricted solely to the political arena. As demands for popular political democracy grew, the demand for inclusion and power was felt across the culture in unions, universities, and even in corporate boardrooms. Democracy was not only a way of empowering government, it was also a cultural phenomenon that impacted virtually every aspect of our lives.

This begs the question: is there such a thing as "democratic leadership," or are the two words mutually exclusive if not contradictory? Can any system of government exist without leadership? For those who believe in the superiority of democracy over other forms of government, a way must be found to reconcile these two seemingly warring concepts into a sustainable compatibility.

The tension between the need for leadership and the demands of democracy was reinforced by British historian James Bryce, who reminded us that "perhaps no form of government needs great leaders so much as democracy."[11] But what kind of leadership? The strong, forceful direction of a powerful, heroic leader, or the gentle guiding hand of a teacher? Emiliano Zapata warns us that "strong leaders make a weak people," but can the people come together and accomplish their goals with weak leadership?

As Arthur M. Schlesinger Jr. suggests, "The American democracy has readily resorted in practice to the very leadership it had disclaimed in theory. An adequate democratic theory must recognize that democracy is not self-executing: that leadership is not the enemy of self-government but the means of making it work; that followers have their own stern obligation, which is to keep leaders within rigorous constitutional bounds; and that Caesarism is more often produced by the failure of feeble governments than by the success of energetic ones."[12]

Paradoxes notwithstanding, is there a style of leadership compatible with political democracy? Although a tension will always exist between leadership and democracy, there are ways to bring the two into a creative tension: providing a role for empowering leadership that also encourages democratic debate and participation among the citizenry.

Just as Abraham Lincoln gave us a succinct, eloquent definition of democracy as "government of the people, by the people, and for the people,"[13] so too did another of our leaders give us an eloquent, even simple definition of democratic leadership. Thomas Jefferson believed the primary duties of a leader in a democracy were "*to inform the minds of the people, and to follow their will.*"[14]

One can see two key concepts contained in Jefferson's brief definition: *inform minds* and *follow the people's will.* Informing the minds of the people speaks to the role of leader as educator. In a democracy, the leader has a responsibility to educate, enlighten, and inform the people. He or she must identify problems and mobilize the people to act. By informing or educating the citizenry, the leader also engages in a dialogue, the ultimate goal of which is to involve both leader and citizen in the process of developing a vision, grounded in the values of the nation, that will animate future action.

The leader's task in a democracy is to look ahead, see problems, focus the public's attention on the work that must be done, provide alternative courses of action, chart a path for the future, and move the nation in support of his or her ideas. The leader must attempt to mobilize the public around a vision and secure a consensus on the proper way to proceed.

The second component of Jefferson's definition, "to follow their will," suggests that after educating and involving the people, the leader must ultimately heed the will of the people. Several commentators have noted the distinction between the whim of the people (temporary and changing) and the will of the people (deeply held truths that speak to the nation's highest aspirations). The leader's job is to inform, educate, and persuade the public to embrace and work for a vision that taps into the deeper truths and higher purposes of the will of the people. Yet whatever their judgment, the leader must serve the people and ultimately follow their direction. This leaves some room for a "profiles in courage" type of leadership, yet how much is unclear.

In a constitutional democracy, following the will of the people is generally essential. Any leader who for long pursues policies contrary to the expressed wishes of the people will be accused of the democratic cardinal sin: defying the will of the people. Thus, to be a leader requires doing all one can to bring about informed judgments by the people. Then, the leader must *serve* the people. This form of democratic accountability calls for the leader to play an important role, yet it relies upon the people to make aspirational judgments.

The best leadership, in Bruce Miroff's words, "not only serves people's interests but furthers their democratic dignity as well."[15] Thus, Thomas Jefferson's vision of a democratic leadership that informs the public, then follows its will, is designed to elevate both leader and citizen. Such a form of leadership is difficult, time consuming, and fraught with challenges. But it is a style of leadership that encourages strong citizens for a strong democracy. Democratic leaders both lead and follow. Yet they are neither pied pipers nor puppets.

America's dream of a government by the people is about the most exacting venture a nation can undertake. Exhilarating, difficult, and demanding, the burden falls not just upon a select few, but on a large number of us if we would make democracy work.

The challenge is to find:

- Better ways for the individual to participate in government and politics and see that participation counts;
- Better ways to make government open, responsive, transparent, and accountable;
- Better ways to make government serve common interests rather than the narrow interests of those who can afford high-priced lobbyists.

It is important to recall that most of our framers were—apart from their belief in national defense—skeptical of strong, centralized, national leadership institutions and equally skeptical, even hostile to, notions of popular democracy. They had fought their war of independence in large part to get away from monarchy, royal governors, and unresponsive hierarchical leadership. Democracy was regarded as a precarious, dangerous, and unworkable doctrine. The very term *democracy,* we are often reminded, appears neither in the Declaration of Independence nor in the U.S. Constitution.

A system of constitutional democracy implies a government in which ultimate political authority or consent is vested in the people. The aspirations of a constitutional democracy are lofty; they celebrate the individual, personal liberty, equal political rights, and they are based on the noble premise that the people can be shapers of their own destiny, that the people can make moral judgments and practical decisions in their communities. They imply, as well, a search for fairness and virtue in humanity's pursuit of improved ways of building social institutions and ordering human relations.

Warring Concepts

Still, in many respects, leadership—the process whereby an individual or a few select individuals are in a position to provide the vision and make things happen—is at odds with much of what is implicit, if not explicit, in notions of democracy. These have been warring concepts, just as freedom and authority have long been antagonists. The challenge, for those who care about their nation and the dreams of constitutional democracy, is to seek ways to reconcile these concepts—leadership and democracy. Whether we like it or not, any democracy will stand or fall on the quality of leaders as well as on the quality of citizens.

Throughout history, governments have been, in practice, not of and by the masses, but of and by the elites. At least in large-scale societies the question is not whether elites will exist and be important, but whether elites will govern on behalf of the many or on behalf of the few, most especially themselves.

Intellectuals and even average citizens are inevitably skeptical, if not cynical, toward the leaders of the nation-state. This is because leaders have done vast harm as well as served with noble motivations in the cause of liberating ends. Leaders, in a real sense, have to be mistrusted. None are ever infallible, and unquestioning subservience to those who wield public power corrupts the human spirit.

A gap exists between what we think of as the typical politician and the ideal statesperson. This gap exists in part because of unrealistic expectations. We want elected officials to be perfect and they are not. We want them to have all the answers and they do not. Politicians, like all individuals, live in the real world where perfection may be a goal; but compromises, approximations, negotiated settlements, and personal ambition are necessary.

Much of the criticism and skepticism about political and societal leaders is healthy. Evil leaders are all too real—past and present. The evidence of the past is compelling that leaders have it in their power to destroy civilization, corrupt societies, and abuse and repress the rights and freedom of their people. Thus, the reality remains that we may love our country and even love our ideals of constitutionalism, yet we rarely love our government and least of all "our politicians," who are generally viewed as overly opportunistic with swollen egos.

An Engagement among Equals

We believe there can be an alternative form of leadership. This is the view that leadership can be of an enabling, facilitative kind. Leadership, reconceptualized as an engagement among citizens, as a collegial collaboration, can empower and liberate people.

Democratic leadership at its best recognizes the fundamental—unexpressed as well as felt—wants and needs of potential followers, encourages followers to a fuller consciousness of their higher needs, and helps convert the resulting hopes and aspirations into practical demands on leaders. A democratic leader consults and listens and engages with followers so as to bring them to heightened political awareness and activity, and in the process enables many of these participating followers to become leaders in their own right. The desired leader in a democracy moves away from hierarchical commands and traditional leader-follower relations and instead helps inspire and mobilize others—citizens, contributors, participants—to undertake common problem-solving tasks.

The challenge of reconciling leadership and democracy is part definitional, part attitudinal, and part behavioral. We have long held a view of leaders that is hierarchical, male, and upon which followers, like subjects or slaves, are dependent. That conception is antithetical to democratic aspirations. The word *followers* is negative and demeaning and ought, if possible, to be discarded or at least gently modified. John W. Gardner once suggested *constituents* as a preferred word. For a nation of subservient followers can never be a democratic one. A democratic nation requires educated, skeptical, caring, engaged, and contentious citizen leaders—citizens who are willing to lead as well as follow, who are willing to point the way as often as they are persuaded in one way or another, and who prize the spirit of liberty and free speech that animates our Bill of Rights.

More than any other form of government, democracy requires a peculiar blend of faith in the people and skepticism of them. It requires a faith concerning the common human enterprise; a belief that if the people are informed and caring, they can be trusted with their own self-government; and an optimism that when things begin to go wrong, the people can be relied on to set them right. Plainly, however, a robust, healthy skepticism is needed as well. Democracy requires us to question leaders and never to trust any group with too much power. We may prize majority rule, but we also have to be skeptical enough to regularly debate whether the majority is right.

Democracy Demands Competing Leaders

Conceived this way, democratic politics is a forum or arena for excellence and responsibility whereby, acting together, citizens become free. Politics in this sense is not a necessary evil but a realistic good, transcending the domains of narrow interests and power in the conventional sense, and providing citizens with opportunities to achieve a sustained educational process in which to seek agreement about the common good and the proper ordering of liberties.

Democracy is never self-activating. It needs competing leaders who have a sense of the past and who are willing to share their competing conceptions of the public interest. Political leaders—both elected and unelected—are those who are bold enough to step forward in the midst of endless controversies. This requires ambition and assertiveness, leadership traits we sometimes undervalue.

The American people will never be completely satisfied with their politicians, nor should they be. The ideal politician is a fiction because the ideal politician would be able to please absolutely everyone and make conflicts disappear. Such a person could only exist within a small community of like-minded people. But liberties invite diversity and, therefore, conflict. Hence, politicians as well as the people they represent will invariably have different, contending ideas about what is best for the nation.

Effective political leadership involves motivating people to create change when desirable, to uphold the status quo when necessary, and to serve shared common aspirations whenever possible. All kinds of leadership—intellectual, educational, entrepreneurial, cultural, as well as political—are necessary to make a diverse system live up to the ideals of the democratic creed.

An indispensable quality of future citizen leaders is breadth—the quality of mind and the capacity to relate disparate "facts" to a plausible theory, to fashion tactics that are part of a strategy, to act today in ways that are consistent with an informed understanding of the future. This kind of societal leadership discovers enough common interest across the region, class, religion, race, gender, and age cohorts to order and regulate the affairs of a great society. Constitutional democracies need leaders who will enlighten and exalt the mind and enlarge, empower, and unlock the forces for good.

Freedom and obligation go together. Liberty *and* duty go together. The answer lies not in producing a few larger-than-life leaders. The answer lies in educating a nation of citizen leaders who, regardless of their professional and private concerns, will devote at least some of their time to making our constitutional system work.

We shall know we are making progress not when we discover or produce a handful of charismatic, heroic Mount Rushmore leaders, but when we can boast we are a nation no longer in need of such larger-than-life great leaders because we have become a nation of citizens who believe that people can make a difference and every person should regularly try.

Conclusion

Over time, the divine right of kings gave way to a new myth: the divine right of the people, or democracy. The ground beneath the king's authority collapsed and was replaced by a secular legitimacy based on the will or consent of the people. In this new age, people had to be persuaded to follow, or they believed that the "elected" leaders were to follow *their* will. The grounds of authority and legitimacy were weakened. If it was good to be the king, it was exceedingly difficult to be president or prime minister.

To understand the difficulty of governing in an age of mass democracy, stripped of the lubricating assistance of divine power, we turn to the beautiful

Getty Museum in Los Angeles. Perched on a hill overlooking the city on one side and the Pacific on the other, the Getty is a gorgeous venue for art and culture.

One of its most prized paintings—James Ensor's *Christ's Entry into Brussels in 1889* (1888)—holds special interest for students of leadership. Believed to be the first "expressionist" painting, Ensor's work is mad, magnificent, complex, confusing, anarchistic, and beautiful. Rich and colorful, it depicts Christ's entry into the city, but in a way that is unorthodox, even shocking to our sensibilities.

Picture in your mind's eye what a painting entitled *Christ's Entry into Brussels* should look like. Most people would imagine that a painting with such a title should show Christ, with a halo, sitting atop a donkey. Christ would be the center of attention, with adoring followers lining the streets, bowing in respect, laying palm leaves across his path.

However, in Ensor's dystopian version, Christ is barely visible. Amid a garish, cluttered, colorful anarchy of people and puppets, one has to squint hard to find Christ, who is lost in the crowd. There are clowns, a marching band, costumed characters, masked figures, self-important officials, skeletons, and clerics. From the pompous to the pitiful, it is a mad cacophony of the leering mob. To Ensor, it is democracy.

This painting is relevant to our understanding of leadership because Ensor's allegorical work portrays the dilemma of leadership in a mass democracy. Rather than deferring to Christ, the mob barely pays attention to him. There are too many distractions, too many entertaining diversions to pay attention to, not to mention defer to, this leader of the Christian movement. There is a party going on; do not bother the crowd with the boredom of authority. If the choice is party or piety, let the parade begin!

In this world, Christ is not the center of attention, not the recipient of worshipful respect; this Christ must compete with the entertaining party of the human parade. The anarchy of fun trumps the discipline of worship. Self-indulgence trumps hierarchy; individualism trumps obedience; party trumps followership. As leadership and management scholar James O'Toole muses:

> Ensor understood that social chaos would soon arise from the secular democracy then aborning in Europe. A hundred years ago, he foresaw the seeds of the tradition-destroying trend that would eventually germinate and produce, among countless other cultural horrors, seventy-six channels of cable television. The painting forces the viewer to think about the unprecedented obstacles to effective leadership in a world that has grown, in the subsequent century, even more turbulent than Ensor's frenetic Brussels street scene.... Ensor saw that henceforth leaders would face the challenge of having to lead without the traditional powers of station, sanction, or threat of suppression. Instead, like Christ, leaders would have to appeal to the minds and hearts of their followers.

> Ensor causes us to wonder how anyone could lead from the middle of an inattentive crowd of individualists, each a political and social equal, and every last one bent on demonstrating that fact. Though people have always resisted efforts to bring about changes, even those in their own self-interest, Ensor suggests that modern times would be characterized by widespread resistance to being led at all.[16]

The emergence of large-scale constitutional democracy as a new social and political paradigm, and new notions about the consent of the people, challenged authority and legitimacy. No longer would subjects automatically follow; citizens now had to be persuaded. They could choose to follow or not; they might give to a leader their authority and power, or not. Followership was no longer automatic but had to be earned.

And in a world of mass consumerism, those wishing to lead seem to have little to offer by way of inducement. Why follow the leader when the carnival is going in the other direction? Why sacrifice for the cause when our comrades offer intoxication? Why give to the community when we can further our own pockets? Thus, instead of kings commanding, in the new world elected office holders had to "lead."

Commanding was easier than persuading. But democracies are not like that—and herein rests the difficulty of leading in a world where the deference, hierarchy, authority, and legitimacy of the old order have evaporated, and a new grand experiment of constitutional democracy requires something called *the consent of the governed.*

Leadership in a democracy is considerably different from ruling in a command-based system. Although the analogy is stretched a bit, the difference might be likened to the distinction between being an elected political leader—a president, for example—and being the head of a large corporation. Although there is an overlap in demands and skills that are a part of each job, being president of the United States is also quite a different job from heading a corporation. Presidents are required to do more leading; corporate heads have greater command authority (though not as great as once was the case). Presidents must elicit support; corporate heads can often assume support. Presidents face a separation of powers; in a corporation there is a fusion of powers. Presidents also face the reality that multiple, often competing goals guide the state's general mission (community, efficiency, equality, liberty, prosperity, and national security—to name a few). Leaders of corporations usually have a more defined and agreed-upon set of goals.

In sum, the birth of constitutional democracy has made it harder for leaders to lead. Yet, has it also tamed leadership and made it more responsible, representative, accountable? And if today we hunger for more efficient leadership, is that compatible with the goals of controlling the state and democratizing our politics and culture?

It has, at least to some extent, "tamed the prince," and made leadership somewhat more responsive, representative, and responsible. Still, we are often frustrated with our leaders and leadership institutions. We yearn for even more accountability, yet, at the same time, yearn too for more efficiency and effectiveness. In recent times, too, we yearn for political leaders who can somehow magically transcend politics, transcend regionalism, and transcend all the polarizing forces that are prompted by our much beloved diversity and liberty. Controlling the state and democratizing our politics—at the same time—challenge us still.

We turn in the next chapters to deconstructing what business, politics, the military, and the entertainment industry teach us about leadership and its paradoxes.

Chapter Seven
What Business Teaches Us about Leadership

> Today's successful business leaders will be those who are most flexible of mind. An ability to embrace new ideas, routinely challenge old ones, and live with paradox will be the effective leader's premier trait. Further, the challenge is for a lifetime. New truths will not emerge easily. Leaders have to guide the ship while simultaneously putting everything up for grabs, which is itself a fundamental paradox.
>
> —*Tom Peters*[1]

What do business executives learn from experience? And what do we learn from management "gurus" about the strategies or habits of effective leadership?

This chapter discusses what we learn about leadership from business executives and business researchers. Be warned that although there is a growing body of conventional wisdom about fundamental leadership ideas, there are plenty of contrarian notions as well.

One of us served for thirteen years as a college president and both of us have served as directors, board members, or trustees for about two dozen organizations—ranging from a New York Stock Exchange–listed company to a food bank—as well as professional, educational, and philanthropic organizations. We too have learned from successes as well as mistakes.

This chapter builds on our personal experiences, yet it especially synthesizes, selectively, from dozens of CEO memoirs and "the best works" findings of management analysts.

Another cautionary note. Most books written by retired business executives are self-indulgent and often rather pedestrian. Yet there are exceptions. Alfred Sloan's writings on his years at General Motors and Chester Barnard's rigorous reflections of what he learned at New Jersey Bell long ago set an instructive standard.

More recent reflections from Max De Pree, Andy Grove, Paul Hawken, Jan Carlzon, Louis Lundberg, Sam Walton, David Packard, Michael Dell, Kay Graham, Lou Gerstner, Carl Sewell, Ray Anderson, Bill George, and Jack Welch are worth a careful reading. So also, the writings of Peter Drucker, Warren Bennis, Michael Porter, Jim Collins, Manfred Kets de Vries, Tom Peters, Rosabeth Moss Kanter, John Kotter, and their peers yield countless insights. What follows are central leadership themes that are regularly emphasized by these practitioners and consultants intermixed with our own ideas.

We discuss ideas that have worked for effective executives in a variety of settings. But just as no size fits all, so too many of these leadership ideas are better suited for certain kinds of organizations or for certain phases in an organization's maturation than others. The central themes are as follows:

- Being disciplined, mature, and passionate
- The ability to manage paradoxes
- Being optimistic and brutally realistic at the same time
- Balancing humility with relentless focus and determination
- Constantly learning from customers, colleagues, competitors, and mistakes
- Being effective at hiring and firing
- Shaping organizational culture; developing adaptive strategies for coping with change and opportunities
- Providing for strategic central direction yet flattening the pyramid, decentralizing, delegating, and fighting needless hierarchy

Personal Discipline, Maturity, and Passion

"Be yourself; everyone else is already taken" is a wonderful adage. Leaders are expected to be themselves as well as to develop a sophisticated self-awareness that allows them to understand their strengths and weaknesses.

Precisely because strong leaders also have strong weaknesses, they must work at developing their strengths and mitigating their weaknesses as much as possible, for the crucible of leadership magnifies both—especially the weaknesses.

One of the oldest proverbs in management is that leaders can lead others only after they have successfully organized and disciplined themselves. Simply put, the most challenging person to lead is often oneself.

Every organization yearns for the perfect leader, one who balances a sense of humility and sensitivity to others with the ambition, drive, and tenacity needed to be a stalwart achiever. Similarly, organizations search for leaders who can lead by example yet understand the art of delegating. In short, we yearn for qualities of bearing, tact, judgment, character, integrity, agility, warmth, decisiveness, tenacity, adaptability, and passion, as well as experience rarely found in any one person.

Leadership and management gurus have famously generated long lists of traits, habits, and adaptive skills in an attempt to define what makes for creative leadership. But, as scholars at the Center for Creative Leadership several years ago concluded: "It seems obvious that no one, the talented executive included, can possess all of these skills. As we came to realize, executives, like the rest of us, are a patchwork of strengths *and* weaknesses."[2]

Shakespeare urges, "To thine own self be true." But psychologists have long warned that people with the drive to excel, to achieve, to earn high office and fame are very often those whose narcissism or raging demons may bring out the worst in them and prove costly for their colleagues. Sophocles, Shakespeare, and Ibsen, among many others, have made us laugh and cry as we read their plays about leaders who have near-pathological egotism, pride, and cunning.

President Richard Nixon, a sometimes gifted politician and diplomat, had inner demons he never fully understood and certainly never conquered. Aides recount how his insecurity, resentment, and inner prejudices poured forth with harmful results. "He set up teams inside the White House to pursue his enemies in national security, real and perceived, and those teams eventually focused their efforts on electoral politics," writes former Nixon aide David Gergen.[3] Eventually, crimes occurred and his whole administration collapsed. Writes Gergen, Nixon "became the architect of his own demise—a prime example of a man who had all the makings for the presidency but failed because he never developed what it took inside himself."[4]

Ego management is essential. It is said of Abraham Lincoln, for example, that he was almost always able to put past hurts or insults behind him and avoid letting wounds fester. He somehow found balance in long rides around Washington as well as in frequenting local theaters for plays. (He attended, by one count, nearly one hundred such shows during his four-year presidency.) Richard Nixon, in contrast to Lincoln, was a resentment collector.

Political scientist Fred Greenstein warns, we should beware any presidential contender who lacks emotional intelligence. He writes that Nixon's anger and suspiciousness were of Shakespearean proportions. He faults Lyndon Johnson's "vesuvial" mood swings, Jimmy Carter's rigidity, and Bill Clinton's deficient personal discipline.

"It has been argued that the tortured psyche of a Nixon," Greenstein muses, "is a precondition of political creativity." But Greenstein rejects this interpretation, saying, "Great political ability does sometimes derive from troubled emotions, but the former does not justify the latter in the custodian of the most destructive military arsenal in human experience."[5] The need for emotional and social intelligence is as greatly valued in the private as in the public sector.

Chief executives of large corporations find themselves as virtual celebrities and sometimes even as rock stars on large stages on which they can grow or they can swell. And it is the swelling of the ego and the lack of personal discipline and maturity that are too often the downfall of corporate titans.

One of the great paradoxes of effective leadership, as noted, is that transformational leaders invariably are self-centered, ambitious, and have a certain level of narcissism. No one ever accused Henry Ford, Jack Welch, or Steve Jobs of being self-effacing. They were bold and driven. Complex organizations often need a narcissistic personality for the passion, fearlessness, and daring to break new ground. Most of the cunning and narcissism will be forgiven if the leader in question can put them in service of achieving great goals. That was the case with Steve Jobs.[6]

The scholar and erstwhile Canadian political leader Michael Ignatieff says we need to live fearlessly in our fearful world. Yes, fear can be a great teacher. But leaders have to stand up to fear, take its measure, and refuse to let it shape and define their lives or their organizations. "Living fearlessly means taking risks, taking gambles," writes Ignatieff. It "means refusing to take no for an answer when you believe the answer should or could be yes."[7]

Talented, productive narcissists have the audacity of hope and the guts to push through necessary reforms, reorganizations, and even transformations. But as management analyst Michael Maccoby suggests, narcissists can also be poor listeners, insensitive to their colleagues, and their faults tend to become even more pronounced as they become more successful.[8]

Maccoby cautions, however, that there are productive narcissists like Jack Welch at GE, Bill Gates at Microsoft, and Herb Kelleher, "the flamboyant self-promoter who built Southwest Airlines. These leaders," writes Maccoby, "have developed disciplined management by partnering with operational managers who implement their strategy."[9]

A few former chief executive officers, as we discussed earlier, call for leaders to be conventional servant leaders and emphasize that humility, empathy, and modesty should be the hallmark of all would-be leaders. Yet the more conventional verdict is that leaders also have to be supremely self-confident. Here again, however, what is desired is a strong ego, not a swollen ego.

Leadership scholar Manfred Kets de Vries says that a leader's central responsibilities involve a psychological paradox—at one level leaders appeal to their followers' natural capacities yet their message also deals with complex nuance and the unconscious. In this second sense leaders are "masters in the use of disguise, seduction and manipulation."[10]

Narcissism, like Janus, has two faces. Some self-love is necessary for survival. "On the other hand," writes Kets de Vries, "too great a preoccupation with the self—can become self-destructive."[11]

Part of the challenge of developing personal self-mastery is understanding how one uses time. Management guru Peter Drucker preaches that effective executives must "know thy time" and ruthlessly eliminate time-wasting activities.

An executive's job is, it is often said, a series of interruptions interrupted by yet more interruptions. Studies find business leaders spend nearly 50 percent of their time in meetings. Yet Peter Drucker urges, "Meetings should never be allowed to become the main demand on an executive's time. Too many meetings always bespeak poor structure of jobs and the wrong organizational components."[12]

Although Drucker discourages the misuse of meetings, most executives nonetheless say meetings are indispensable to the effectiveness of healthy organizations. The challenge is to make them efficient and effective and to ensure they do not waste time. Effective meetings need a clear purpose, an agenda, preassigned homework, and a skillful chair. The disciplined executive must be a creative architect of committees and their operations, and must have incredible patience in ensuring that minority or contrarian points of view get the respect they deserve. Andrew Grove, a co-founder of Intel, has several useful suggestions about making meetings effective in *High Output Management*.[13]

Virtually all the writings by former chief executives and leadership consultants agree leaders must have palpable passion and a contagious commitment to their organizations' mission. Just as no one likes working for a pessimist, few people would be inspired to reach their peak performance levels for a leader who is indifferent or ambivalent about the importance of what needs to be done. Management scholar Warren Bennis writes that people want to be engaged in meaningful undertakings, they regularly need to be reminded of the significance of the enterprise, and they need affirmation that what they do matters.[14]

There is an oft-told parable that at least partially captures this point. It involves two stonecutters who are chipping square blocks out of granite. A visitor to their quarry asks what they are doing. The first stonecutter, sour and seemingly unmotivated, mumbles, "I'm cutting this damn stone into a block." The second stonecutter, with visible pride in his work, replies, "I'm on this team that's building a cathedral."

The lesson here is that "a worker who can envision the whole cathedral and who has been given responsibility for constructing his own portion of it is far more satisfied and productive than the worker who sees only the granite before him. A true leader is one who designs the cathedral and then shares the vision [and passion] that inspires others to build it."[15]

Effective leaders are physically and intellectually fit. This involves personal strategies for self-renewal. Self-renewing people realize they are always in a process of becoming, and they know the really important challenges are never completed. The process is similar to the mountain climber's refrain that "we didn't conquer the mountain; we conquered ourselves." Self-renewing individuals view the world as an incomparable classroom and life as an incomparable teacher. They understand that wanting to win is seldom as important as preparing to compete, and they learn to free themselves from the prison of self-preoccupation and immediate gratification. John W. Gardner's classic essay on self-renewal reminds us of the crucial need to cultivate our inner strength and to establish emotional, moral, and spiritual ties beyond ourselves.[16]

A Creative Ability to Manage Paradoxes

A paradox, as we discussed in Chapter One, is a statement that seems contradictory or even unbelievable yet may actually be true. Balancing the challenges and the paradoxes of each day is what leadership is all about. Most leaders readily acknowledge that their leadership experiences were "loaded" with paradoxes.

Leaders have to manage for short- as well as long-term results. They have to be cheerleaders for their organizations' teams as well as be ruthless in firing ineffective members of their organizations. They have to be supremely self-confident yet able to admit mistakes.

Management consultant Tom Peters devotes a chapter in one of his many best-selling books to outlining paradoxes executives have to embrace. A central paradox for him is that leaders must foster internal stability as a means of encouraging the pursuit of inevitable and constant change. In other words, they must preserve the enterprise's core yet turn it into an experimenting, learning, adapting, and change-seeking organization. "Promote those who deal best with paradox," Peters also urges. "If the ability to deal with these paradoxes is the key to success, then we should promote at all levels those who show the greatest facility in doing so."[17]

"Every great group has a strong leader. This is one of the paradoxes of creative collaboration," write Warren Bennis and Patricia Ward Biederman. On the one hand, creative organizations are made up of people with exceptional talent who work together as equals. "Yet, in virtually every one there is one person who acts as maestro, organizing the genius of the others. He or she is a pragmatic dreamer, a person with an original but attainable vision."[18] Thus another paradox: how to provide the stewardship of liberating one's colleagues yet do so in as nonhierarchical a way as possible.

Change in higher education is often resisted by alumni who believe that their rose-tinted memories of their beloved college days, perceived and imagined, should be what their college remains. Alumni "see their Alma Mater through a rosy haze that gets thicker with the years," said Robert Maynard Hutchins of the University of Chicago. "They do not know what the college was really like. They do not want to know what it is like now. They want to imagine that it is like what they think it was like in their time."[19] And since alumni comprise a majority of the trustees and major donors, they can often play a paradoxically restraining role in a college's otherwise earnest disposition to innovate, adapt, and modernize.

Jim Collins and Jerry I. Porras, in *Built to Last: Successful Habits of Visionary Companies,* write that effective companies learn to accept paradox. They have to understand contrarian ideas and figure out creative ways of integrating or at least balancing them. Collins and Porras contend corporations must reject the tyranny of "either/or." Organizations can have change *and* stability, be conservative *and* bold, can invest for the future *as well as* focus on the short term. They can be values driven *and* profit driven. It's not about achieving "mere balance" or going half and half. "A visionary company doesn't seek balance between short term *and* long term. A visionary company doesn't simply balance between idealism and profitability; it seeks to be highly idealistic *and* highly profitable," say Collins and Porras. "In short, a highly visionary company doesn't want to blend yin and yang into a gray indistinguishable circle that is neither highly yin nor highly yang; it aims to be distinctly yin *and* yang—both at the same time, all the time."[20]

In a subsequent study Collins reports that good companies that transformed themselves into great corporations invariably had leaders who *paradoxically* maintained an unwavering faith in the determination to excel at what they were doing yet had the discipline to face whatever brutal realities they confronted.[21]

Still another regularly articulated corporate leadership lesson is that high-performance organizations are led, not managed. As discussed earlier, this is an oversimplification. Such organizations need plenty of creative managers as well as passionate leaders. Still, effective companies typically are led by individuals who are passionate about success. "Great CEOs roll up their sleeves and tackle problems personally. They don't hide behind staff," writes former IBM chairman Lou Gerstner Jr. "They never simply preside over the work of others. They are visible every day with customers, suppliers, and business partners."[22]

Every great chief executive officer he knew, Gerstner adds, was passionate about winning. They wanted to win every day and hated losing. They insistently demanded new strategies or corrections so their companies could excel.

Passion, he writes, is never a substitute for good analytical thinking or effective execution. "Rather, it is the electricity that courses through a well-made machine that makes it run, makes it hum, makes it want to run harder and better."[23]

Most experts agree that passionate leadership can provide a positive edge in any complex organization. But, like most things, excessive or over-the-top passion can paralyze. Relentless passion can sometimes lead to mindless commitment and rigid loyalties to a set way of doing things. It can also breed groupthink and cultish communities.

Business executives Max De Pree, Robert Greenleaf, and Bill George, all with extensive corporate leadership experience, caution against an overreliance on heroic, passionate, "shooting star" leaders and business saviors. They emphasize the crucial role of followers and the need for sustained communities created less by the passion of a top leader than by the significance and meaning of the work being done.[24]

A central paradox that needs to be confronted here is that although leadership invariably involves passion, commitment, and ferocious resolve, such behavior has to be exercised cautiously so as to avoid an overly president-centric or overly president-dependent enterprise.

Can successful leadership in business translate into successful leadership in the world of politics? Sometimes, yet it is best not to assume that success in one endeavor leads to success in another.

In business, the goals are clear: return on investment and expanding the market. In politics, the goal is often a point of contention. Should we seek liberty? Justice? Security? Equality? Should we heavily tax the rich in order to help the poor? Should we strive for a bigger or smaller government? Politics is about deciding what to do and *how* to do it. Politics is more about choice and persuasion. Politics is contested territory for societal norms and values. It is the process we use to arrive at collective decisions. Thus, the worlds of business and politics are distinct domains, and the skills and methods necessary for success are often different.

Being Optimistic and Realistic at the Same Time

Effective leaders, paradoxically, have to be optimists who work hard at becoming better informed. American presidents are sometimes described as the nation's "First Optimist" or our "Optimist in Chief." They are expected to radiate confidence and affirm our better instincts, our hopes, and our expectations that the future will bring even more opportunities than the past.

Both sunny Ronald Reagan and hopeful Barack Obama campaigned for the White House vaguely calling for hope and change more than they ever spelled out specific policy changes. In doing this they were following FDR's famous slogan, "The only thing we have to fear is fear itself." Friends of Ronald Reagan liked to say that "he cured America of its self-doubt." Reagan aides say he believed optimism was a "force multiplier." "We can do it—we're Americans" was a typical Reaganism.

Part of leadership in nearly every organization is symbolic as well as physical—it involves projecting vitality, stamina, pride, and style as well as passion in the larger enterprise. This is what General Patton did in World War II, what

Richard Branson did in his various Virgin enterprises, what Steve Jobs did for Apple, and what Martin Luther King Jr. did for the civil rights movement.

The best leaders are able to hit the "sweet spot" between optimism and realism as Lincoln tried to do as commander in chief during the Civil War.[25] A leader who only wears rose-colored glasses, who only accentuates the positive and fails to acknowledge waste, ineffectiveness, or scandal, quickly loses the respect of colleagues. Needed are tough-minded and pragmatic optimists who acknowledge the possibilities yet appreciate the challenges and realities, who can balance hope with realism.

An American president or a private sector leader who oversells a new venture, or who fails to plan prudent financing of a military action or a new acquisition, risks major backlash. This happened to George W. Bush with much of his decision making on the Iraq War. His reasons for going to war proved unfounded and his planning for nation building proved inadequate.[26]

Here again, effective executives rarely have a choice. They have to be confident and optimistic, yet their optimism has to be shaped by more than mere blind faith, cheerleading, or gut instincts. Leaders have to seek out data, evidence, and rational analysis of the probabilities of desired alternative actions. They must ask tough counterfactual questions. They constantly ask of the advice they are offered: What if the opposite course would be better? Might plan B be more prudent than plan A? The best executives form inner circles and multiple-advocacy procedures that tease out the pitfalls or misconceptions about proposed actions. In the end, leaders have to be optimistic, intuitive, and "possibilitarians" yet not at the expense of the data.

Many institutions of higher education have invited problems and even the firing of presidents when they failed to balance sweeping and audacious building campaigns with adequate programs to finance highly expensive goals. In the arms race of wanting to keep up with rival institutions, there is nearly always the temptation to start this new program, build these new buildings, add these sports or activities, and on and on; but all such aspirations invariably have a price tag. One of the inherent afflictions of being a CEO is the disposition to embrace and cheerlead on behalf of multiple bold initiatives. Yet executives also need to selectively prune or terminate existing programs to provide funding for new ones.

Bold, new programs may be needed. Yet how to finance them requires a leader's attention just as much if not more than their planning.

Thus the challenge for most leaders is to project self-confidence and behave fearlessly even in uncertain times, yet do so with as much information and intelligence as they can generate. That said, nearly every executive knows that key decisions frequently need to be made with imperfect information. Leaders often have to act, especially in crises, with perhaps only 60–70 percent of the information they ideally would like to have. A leader who waits until all the information is available has almost always waited too long. That's just the nature of leadership.

Balancing Humility with Relentless Focus and Determination

This idea has already been touched on. Yet its importance merits at least a few examples.

General George S. Patton and National Football League coach Vince Lombardi were legendary for their fierce resolve and for occasionally losing their tempers with associates. No one questioned their will to win. No one ever questioned that they were leaders.

Lombardi was often overwhelmed by his inability to control his anger. "At one time or other he was rude and inconsiderate to his family, his staff, his players, the media—almost everyone he met!" writes Lombardi's biographer. "Success and fame swelled his ego."[27]

An army general in war or an NFL coach obsessed with winning can under certain circumstances get away with arrogance and fear-driven leadership. To conflate what political theorist Niccolò Machiavelli argued, in such times, some leaders are both feared and loved.

But fear seldom is the best way to encourage productivity and human cooperation in the long run. People yearn to be treated with respect and as colleagues. Emerson once warned us that "what you are speaks so loudly I cannot hear what you are saying." So, too, the bully quickly loses our loyalty. Former Bank of America chairman Louis Lundborg spoke for most business leaders when he wrote that a leader is someone "others will follow willingly and voluntarily. That rules out tyrants, bullies, autocrats, and all others who use coercive power to impose their will on others."[28]

Most talented executives understand that they must treat fellow workers the way they themselves would like to be treated. "Generosity of time and talent is essential for effective leadership. So is magnanimity, which involves the practice of forgiveness," writes retired major general Perry M. Smith. "Some leaders have a terrible time forgiving associates who have fouled things up! Good leaders are willing to pardon those who make honest mistakes!"[29]

Humility and collegiality are great, but they have to be joined by a relentless focus on results. Members of virtually every kind of organization want efficiency and especially effectiveness. They want to win the war, win the game, produce the pioneering product, and in short, make a difference, make history.

Effective executives have a mission that matters, one that is clear, compelling, and purposeful. That mission has to have "buy-in" from an organization's participants. It has to speak to mutual aspirations and shared goals. A chief executive officer has to be the chief articulator, chief motivator, and chief visionary constantly trumpeting the company's purpose.

Constantly Learning from Customers, Colleagues, Competitors, and Mistakes

"Success," joked Winston Churchill, "is going from failure to failure with great enthusiasm." It is said of Thomas Edison, similarly, that his invention of the lightbulb was the result of his willingness to learn from a thousand mistakes until he figured out what would work. Leaders are lifelong learners, constantly viewing mistakes as experience. They embrace the axiom that a mistake is not so much a mistake as it is an opportunity to improve the organization. They try new things, learn new skills, reach out to new people and new ideas. They have an openness and wonder, are willing to accept failure, learn from it, then move on. They don't dwell on mistakes, their own or their associates'; they transcend them, adapt, and improvise as best they can with whatever hand is dealt them.

As Bill Gates once said, "Success is a lousy teacher." How true. We are all human and humans make mistakes. The test is how we deal with failure and what we learn from it.[30]

Inventors and creators fail far more often than they succeed. The mark of real success is persistence and drive. If the great inventors had given up after a few failures, we might still be in the Dark Ages.

No one likes to fail, but we all fail, often. The key is: What can we learn from failure? Do we profit by it or become paralyzed by it? Does it spark a new line of thought or relegate us to self-defeat? Does it make us shrink from battles or inspire us to seek an alternate route? Does it push us to grow or to accept less? Abraham Lincoln lost more elections than he won; George Washington lost more battles than he won; Winston Churchill failed more than he succeeded.

"Try again, fail again, fail better," Samuel Beckett encouraged. In truly successful people, failure is the gateway to greatness—ironic, isn't it? In her classic work *The March of Folly,* historian Barbara W. Tuchman looks at the human folly of trying to govern:

> A phenomenon noticeable throughout history regardless of place or period is the pursuit by governments of policies contrary to their own interests. Mankind, it seems, makes a poorer performance of government than of almost any other human activity. In this sphere, wisdom, which may be defined as the exercise of judgment acting on experience, common sense and available information, is less operative and more frustrated than it should be. Why do holders of high office so

often act contrary to the way reason points and enlightened self-interest suggests? Why does intelligent mental process seem so often not to function?[31]

The pursuit of folly often seems to characterize the exercise of governing, something Tuchman characterized as "wooden-headedness" or "assessing a situation in terms of preconceived fixed notions while ignoring or rejecting any contrary signs." It is acting according to wish while not allowing oneself to be educated by the facts.[32]

Samuel Coleridge speculated, "If men could learn from history, what lessons it might teach us!" We are so often blinded by emotion, belief, or ideology that we fail to see and fail to learn. "But," Coleridge noted, "passion and party blind our eyes, and the light which experience gives us is a lantern on the stern which shines only on the waves behind us." How can we bring wisdom, experience, judgment, and facts to bear on our decisions? We seem committed to repeating and building on our errors, not correcting them. Machiavelli's *Prince,* as discussed earlier, is in many ways a guide of what *not* to do. To Machiavelli, the greatest danger is for the prince to be guided by emotion and not by reason. He tries to assist the prince in making choices in a complex world. His concern is that the Prince will be guided by his desires rather than reason, wisdom, or facts.

What do we do when we make a blunder, when the wound from which we suffer is self-inflicted? There is a tendency to run and hide, blame the problem on someone else, or deny, deny, deny and cover up, cover up, cover up. Leaders avoid this human temptation. When a mistake or blunder happens, they tell it all, tell it early, tell it first, tell it themselves.

How ought a leader to deal with failure? The formula is simple and applies to leaders and citizens alike.

- Acknowledging the failure.
- Owning up to it, correcting it, not letting it happen again.
- Examining what one did to contribute to it.
- Thinking about what one *should* have done and why it didn't happen
- Figuring out what lessons can be derived about oneself and the situation
- Putting those lessons into one's memory bank.

If you make a mistake, admit it, and admit it fully and immediately. Take full responsibility right away. When George W. Bush blundered in the federal response to Hurricane Katrina, his first reaction was to blame everyone but himself. Then he issued the generic "mistakes were made" statement. A week or so later, when he finally took responsibility for his failures, it was too little, too late. His adversaries were handed an opportunity to make him look insensitive and out of touch. The Bush administration was put into an unwinnable position as the members tried to undo the damage done by the president. But as they scrambled, they only further dug a hole for the beleaguered president. The effective executive avoids this trap. Effective executives as well as politicians do as John F. Kennedy did after the Bay of Pigs fiasco: take full and immediate responsibility, try to learn from their mistakes, and move on. If leaders take responsibility, most people will understand, appreciate their honesty, and forgive them. If they cover up, they will be—and they deserve to be—hammered.

Leaders acknowledge mistakes, apologize for them, and then set about fixing them. Businessman Paul Hawken puts the best face on it when he writes, "A mistake is not a mistake. It is a chance to improve the company."[33] His point is that mistakes, whether in one's own business or others, can often lead to better products, improving services, newer ideas, and more satisfied customers.

Of course it is always best to "do it right the first time." But mistakes happen. And they happen in every industry, every profession.

One of the partners of Goldman Sachs, the noted investment banking firm, was indicted for insider trading a few years ago. The firm did what most firms do: it defended the partner—indeed spent tens of millions of dollars (which, of course, most firms don't have) in the partner's defense.

But once the partner was convicted, Goldman Sachs realized its reputation was at stake and it went to considerable lengths to implement a "zero defects" system that would prevent similar breakdowns. "They had lawyers and accountants go through the operations procedures used by every business at the firm looking for any holes in the system. Although it is virtually impossible, they attempted to put in place infallible systems that would eliminate the possibility of impropriety whether deliberate or accidental," writes Lisa Endlich. "As an outgrowth of this episode, the firm has state-of-the-art compliance procedures."[34] Goldman would have more than its share of other problems, financially and politically, during the great recession of 2008–2009, yet it regularly bounced back.

"Don't try to perfume a pig," writes Michael Dell. "You never want to fake it and you never want to make something appear better than it really is."[35]

Just as quality is remembered long after the price is forgotten, corporate screwups or malfunctioning products can lose customers for life. That's why embracing mistakes and errors and quickly addressing the underlying problems are essential in any organization.

"All leaders, great and little known, make mistakes. It is a part of life. Great inventors and innovators had more failures than successes. You only truly fail when you give up. Persistence counts."[36]

If you don't make mistakes, you probably aren't taking serious risks. Leaders take calculated risks. And across the long careers of all leaders one finds the path littered with mistakes. And yet, leaders recover from mistakes, learn from them, and move forward. They don't let mistakes defeat them.

"A business is not defined by the company's name, statutes, or articles of incorporation," writes management legend Peter Drucker. "It is defined by the want the customer satisfies when he or she buys a product or a service. To satisfy the customer is the mission and purpose of every business."[37]

The upscale clothier Stanley Marcus was raised by a demanding father who held that "there is never a good *sale* for Neiman-Marcus unless it's a good *buy* for the customer."[38] Similarly, no advertisement is as powerful as the satisfied customer.

An instructive memoir by a successful entrepreneur is Dallas car dealer Carl Sewell's *Customers for Life: How to Turn That One-Time Buyer into a Lifetime Customer.* He may overstate his case yet he claims that customers will tell you how to provide good service. "If you give customers a chance to talk, and if you're willing to listen, they'll tell you exactly what's important to them."[39]

This is how Sewell learned. People want their phone calls answered by the second ring. They want companies to do what they say they are going to do and to "do it right the first time." If there is a mistake, they want an apology and they want the problem fixed. They don't want their time wasted. They want top quality and are willing to come back time and again if they are treated as lifelong customers, not just as solo drive-by visitors. Sewell also learned that you don't charge for an extra service, such as fixing a flat or loaning people a new car when theirs is being repaired. "If it is something a friend would do for another friend, don't charge. Don't worry, you'll more than make up the money in future business."[40]

Sewell and similar effective entrepreneurs "under promise and over deliver," understand what customers appreciate, nurture employees to be "service superstars," and create an organizational culture and distinctive competencies that allow their companies to excel.

Effective executives understand that everyone in their organizations needs to be a customer service representative, and that everyone, most especially on the front lines, needs the authority, power, and encouragement to fix problems and satisfy customers. This is the lesson of successful retailers like Nordstrom, L.L.Bean, and Les Schwab Tires (a Northwest franchise).

Customers, to be sure, are not necessarily always right; yet customers are quick to judge companies on how they perform in those "moments of truth" that often define a company's professionalism, authenticity, and agility. The Disney corporation preached this credo to its staff or "cast members" and educated them to treat every visitor as a guest with a capital "G."

The best companies learn to "flatten the pyramid," that is, to move authority as much as possible to frontline employees who regularly deal with customers. This isn't always easy to achieve. Yet "if you can flatten your own pyramids you will be creating a far more powerful and resilient organization that not only serves customers better but also unleashes the hidden energy within your employees," writes former SAS airline executive Jan Carlzon. "The results can be absolutely astounding."[41]

One of Lou Gerstner's first initiatives when he was brought in from outside IBM in 1993 to revive that iconic corporation was to launch Operation Bear Hug. He mandated that fifty top executives from his senior management team visit hundreds of their biggest customers in his first few months. These executives were to listen to customers and assess what was working and where they had complaints. "Bear Hug became a first step in IBM's cultural change. It was an important way for me to emphasize that we were going to build a company from the outside in and that the customer was going to drive everything we did in the company."[42]

A word of caution here: just as politicians shouldn't slavishly follow and act upon temporary public opinion polls, so also leaders need to know when and when not to follow customer advice. Henry Ford famously noted that had he only listened to his customers he would have merely built a better horse and buggy. Steve Jobs implied that he was a better judge of what was good for his customers: "It's not the consumers' job to know what they want." Similarly, college leaders who listen only to their alumni's version of what the college should be can be misled by visions of what alums sometimes mistakenly believe their college was like, shaped by heavy doses of nostalgia.

Customers get shaped by what is familiar, and thus, especially in the field of technology, don't appreciate new products that can come about from new breakthroughs. Customers can be the inspiration for innovation yet this does not mean they are always right. "The literal voice of the customer," Anthony Ulwick writes, "sidetracks the innovation process because customers are not qualified to know what solutions are best—that is the job of the organization."[43] So the lesson is to listen and consult customers regularly, yet be prepared to innovate on their behalf.[44]

Effective companies regularly learn from their own employees. Employees are often the best source of ideas for cost-saving initiatives, for new ventures that will add to the bottom line, and for ways to better serve customers. In some ways a company is only as good as the inventiveness and imagination of its stalwart employees.

This is why it is important to try to give as many employees as possible an economic or at least a psychological stake in any organization. Stakeholders invariably have an enhanced incentive to achieve both efficiencies and effectiveness.

There is an instructive story about some young Enterprise Rent-A-Car employees. When the September 11, 2001, terrorist attacks occurred, hundreds of travelers were stranded at airports. At Washington, DC's Reagan airport, most car rental agencies closed down. Enterprise stayed open and was swamped.

What did a young staffer do in a situation like this? A relatively new employee was inspired to stand up on the counter and say: "Folks, let me explain what we've got going on here. I've got 100 cars and there are a lot more of you than I have cars. So here's what we'll do. I've got a gentleman up here going to Atlanta. How many of you are going to Atlanta or in that direction?" And he continued to match up people going in similar directions. And when this was nearly done two young employees, obviously acting completely on their own, drove one of the remaining stranded travelers all the way to South Carolina in their own personal car.[45]

This Enterprise Rent-A-Car story is a good example of a follower assuming a leadership role. The company leaders apparently created a culture that allowed relatively junior employees to feel empowered to do what they did. In any event both the company and the young employees deserve credit.

Jack Welch, when he ran GE, placed great emphasis on turning the company into a continual learning company, learning across divisions, learning from talented people in the company, and learning from other effective organizations. He was proud that surveys indicated that nearly 90 percent of GE employees believed their ideas mattered.

Welch joked that creative borrowing, swiping, or plagiarizing was not only legitimate but even crucial to his notion of a learning culture. You always have to be alert to new ideas, new best practices. "It is a badge of courage if I learn from Larry Bossidy, the CEO of Allied Signal, or Motorola or somewhere else. It used to be a badge of weakness. Rank isn't important. Title isn't important. It's the idea that wins. And that's the big deal."[46]

Steve Jobs and his early Apple team borrowed ideas from an array of other companies, most notably from a Xerox think tank in Palo Alto that had done pioneering basic research on personal computers but didn't have the idea of developing them for a mass market.

One of the best strategies is listening to the customers and turning the best ones into teachers. Michael Dell writes that he spent as much as 40 percent of his time with customers, especially listening to what they liked or disliked about his and his competitor's products. People sometimes responded to him by saying, "Wow—that's a lot of time to spend with customers," to which he responded, "I thought that was my job."[47]

The need for leadership is greater when times change and uncertainties increase. Fear of making mistakes or fear of underestimating technological or social disruptions is wholly appropriate. The brilliant Intel executive Andy Grove said he constantly worried about his competitors and about finding his way through uncharted waters. "Now, nobody will ring a bell to call your attention to the fact that you are entering into major transitions or industrial turbulence."[48]

That's why executives need to develop an outsider's intellectual objectivity. And that's why they need to worry and listen to appropriate fears. "Fear of competition, fear of bankruptcy, fear of being wrong and fear of losing can all be powerful motivators," says Grove. "It is fear that gives me the will to listen to Cassandras when all I want to do is cry out, 'Enough already, the sky isn't falling,' and go home."[49]

Hiring and Firing

Every business executive learns, often the hard way, that effective hiring is one of the most important of the leadership arts. Putting the right people in the right positions in the right way is a crucial part of implementing a vision.

Many executives say half the problems in any organization come from faulty hiring. Firing people is costly and disruptive and usually indicates poor judgment by senior management. "The best way to avoid firing people," writes Paul Hawken, "is to hire well in the first place."[50] And hiring well in the first place takes much more time and creativity than are usually devoted to it.

The first rule of hiring is to hire the person, not the position. Is he or she a good person, with good instincts, good values, good judgment? Will he or she enjoy colleagues and customers, and vice versa? The lesson everyone learns is, hire less for a specific position than for a candidate's potential to grow, develop, and become a star. Effective executives hire people with the long term in mind. "We're not bringing them in to do a job. We're inviting them to join the company. If it's a great match, their jobs are likely to change many, many times as we segment the business, and as we focus more heavily on some areas rather than others," says Michael Dell. "If you hire people with the potential to grow far beyond their current position, you build depth and additional capacity into your organization."[51]

Best-selling management author Jim Collins popularized the saying that the first responsibility for business executives is to get the right people on the bus and the wrong people off the bus—even before deciding where the bus is headed. In effect, he says, "first who ... and then what." "The key point ... is not just the idea of getting the right people on the team. The key point is that 'who' questions come before 'what'—before vision, before strategy, before organization structure, before tactics. First who, then what—as rigorous discipline, consistently applied."[52]

Collins and other business analysts also emphasize that executives who have doubt about a candidate shouldn't hire, they should keep looking. Here is one area where it pays to be thorough and deliberate. "Errors of judgment in other business areas can be costly, but can be survived if the batting average—the ratio of good to bad judgment—is high," wrote former Bank of America chairman Louis B. Lundborg. "But a mistake in the picking of an executive can be devastating."[53]

Job candidates should be asked a lot of questions, including the following:

- What are they especially proud of?
- What do they consider their biggest failure?
- What are their most cherished values?
- Why should they be hired? How can they convince us they have the fight and spirit to excel at our company?
- What are the toughest problems they've solved, and how did they do so?
- When was the last time they changed their minds about an important matter?
- What is the biggest mistake they've made, and what did they learn from it?
- What do they want to learn to do?
- Who are their heroes and why?
- What are their long-term personal and professional goals?
- How would they describe their character, integrity, authenticity, and past experiences concerning safety and caring?
- How would they describe their passion, stamina, intellectual firepower, and emotional intelligence?
- How have they earned, and how will they earn, the respect of colleagues, customers, subordinates, and peers?

One executive recommends watching prospects over a social dinner. How carefully do they behave? Are they good conversationalists? Do they have breadth? Are they smart and savvy? How well will they understand and embrace what our organization is all about and what we are trying to accomplish? Will they be continual learners? How have they bounced back from failure and tragedy? Do they enjoy people, challenges, and life? Another executive bluntly warns never to hire any self-centered jerks. Even pass up the "smart jerks." Life is too short for putting up with jerks and losers. He invokes one of Warren Buffett's acquisition rules: one should never acquire a company unless one likes and respects the people and unless one is going to enjoy working with the people.[54]

As any National Basketball Association coach will affirm, one of a coach's greatest responsibilities is putting the right "matchups" on the floor. Matchups and team building go hand in hand.

Every executive wants all-stars and likely Hall of Famers. Yet most organizations have to settle for a few people of high potential along with a number of "projects" and role players. The challenge for the effective executive is not to change human nature or human beings. "Rather, as the Bible tells us in the Parable of the Talents," writes Peter Drucker, "the task is to multiply performance capacity of the whole by putting to use whatever strength, whatever health, whatever aspiration there is in individuals."[55]

Creative and even brilliant hiring is only the beginning. A new recruit needs first-class mentoring and training. Even the most talented new hires will fail to grow and become star contributors unless they are given clear expectations, are allowed to learn from their mistakes, and are given the appropriate orientation and feedback that will allow them to develop.

New recruits must understand the mission and the vision of their organization. New recruits also have to be given responsibilities and learn about the joys of competition, success, and accomplishment. Creative feedback is as essential as constant reinvestment in skill development and leadership. Few companies do this well, though some, like IBM, W. L. Gore and Associates, and Google, have worked hard at creating a performance culture that takes these essentials into account.

Most workers and managers at all levels crave thanks, praise, and opportunities to excel. Orientation, training, and feedback programs must be designed with these human realities in mind. Mistakes will always be noticed, but breakthroughs and exceptional contributions deserve more notice and celebration. All organizations need to learn to honor and reward success.

Firing people is one of the hardest responsibilities an executive has to do. "Anyone who enjoys doing it shouldn't be on the payroll, and neither should anyone who can't do it," writes former GE chairman Jack Welch.[56]

Welch was criticized for terminating thousands of GE employees and earned the nickname "Neutron Jack," a tag he hated. But he hated bureaucracy, waste, and coming in second to business rivals even more.

Welch's business philosophy was that GE would hire talented people and then provide them superb training and development and ample opportunities for personal and professional growth. He rejected the notion of guaranteed lifetime employment. "Any organization that thinks it can guarantee job security is going down a dead end," says Welch. "Only satisfied customers can give people job security. Not companies."[57]

Executives learn they shouldn't be afraid of removing people when things don't work out. Younger executives invariably wait too long before firing incompetent employees. The lesson learned is: don't hesitate to let dysfunctional employees go.[58] As one CEO friend of ours puts it, "It is never too soon to fire someone," by which he means that when you begin to feel someone needs to be fired, now is probably the time to do it.

Peter Drucker says it is the duty of an executive to ruthlessly remove anyone, especially managers, who constantly fail to perform at the highest levels. "To let such a man stay on corrupts the others. It is grossly unfair to the whole organization. It is grossly unfair to his subordinates who are deprived by their superior's inadequacy of opportunities for achievement and recognition. Above all, it is senseless cruelty to the man himself."[59]

The people who are inadequate or misfits in an organization, Drucker adds, generally know they are a drag on their colleagues and the organization. They need to be liberated so they can find a more realistic and less oppressive job situation. Some of these organizational misfits, if they find their proper niche, may excel. Yet not all organizations are right for all people at all times in their careers.

"A deserved firing is not only the right thing to do, but it also sets the tone that there are certain standards of performance and ethics to be met," writes Perry Smith. Thus, a central responsibility for an executive is "to fire the individuals who, after proper counseling, fail to live up to the organization's standards."[60]

In sum, hiring the right people and terminating the wrong people and doing both of these in creative and compassionate ways are key leadership responsibilities. Leaders should never rush to hire. They should never neglect training, coaching, mentoring, and the constant need to fire people up. Yet they should not be afraid to remove the people who lack the will to compete, win, and contribute.

Shaping Organizational Culture and Adapting Strategies for Dealing with Change and New Opportunities

Every organization develops its own and usually distinctive culture. We use the term *culture* here to refer to shared values, assumptions, and aspirations as well as the spirit of pride and flexibility in an organization. One can often tell within a few minutes of visiting a company, college, or even a restaurant whether employees enjoy their work, whether they take pride or some form of partial "ownership" in their organization.

An organization's culture can be a liberating and empowering asset, yet it can also be a decided liability. Paradoxically, an organization's culture can provide a competitive edge or can stifle needed change and innovation. An organization's culture can be set up like Google, W. L. Gore, Whole Foods, Sears, or the U.S. Postal Service. Culture matters.

Some organizations have a clearly hierarchical culture. Thus, the U.S. Marines as well as the Mafia have a decision-making system of command and control. Leadership is expected. Followers know who is in charge and are expected to carry out instructions, or else.

Other organizations are more egalitarian or certainly more fluid and ambidextrous. At W. L. Gore, the maker of innovative chemical and clothing products, there are few if any titles, no organizational chart, and as few management layers as possible. Core operating units are small, self-managing teams motivated by two simple goals: to make money and have fun. If a plant gets up to 200 employees, Gore builds another one rather than expanding the original one. Why? To keep things simple, lean, and personal.

Executives and management consultants insist that getting the culture right is a top priority. Every organization has to create its own culture and encourage one that serves its particular mission. Thus it is nearly impossible to outline the ideal culture that is "right" for every organization.

Yet here are a number of principles that executives have learned over the past two generations. Obviously, many are as much about aspirations as about distinct achievements. Most organizations want members who:

- Take pride in the mission
- Have a sense of urgency about the work to be done
- Have a passion for their work
- Understand the way in which they are contributing to both their organization's success and society
- Recognize that although it is okay to make mistakes, they have to quickly learn from them
- Promote teamwork, collaboration, and trust
- Understand the importance of stopping to fix broken processes
- Understand the critical importance of honesty, integrity, and ethical considerations
- Are a good match of skill to task
- Understand customer needs, the competitive market, and the need to capitalize on comparative advantages
- Understand the importance of using good judgment in all situations
- Understand the importance of eliminating waste and inefficiencies
- Understand that high quality and continual innovation are everyone's responsibility
- Celebrate breakthroughs at all levels of the organization and encourage the joy and fun of solving problems, serving customers, and doing good
- Recognize the crucial importance of both personal renewal and organizational renewal strategies, all aimed at fostering agile, nimble, and adaptive flexibility
- Fight unnecessary bureaucracy and standard operating procedures that create bloat and kill spark

Yes, this is an ambitious list of cultural aspirations. And it is clearly the case that changing or modifying organizational culture in large corporations, large universities, or governments is exacting. Some conditions that provide leverage for change include crises, leadership turnover, and strategic inflection or tipping points that force an organization to overhaul how it does its work.

Harvard Business School's Rosabeth Moss Kanter looked closely at the corporate culture of several highly esteemed international "vanguard" companies. In companies such as IBM, Procter & Gamble, Brazil's Banco Real, and South Korea's Shinhan

Financial Group, she found that a commitment to continual innovation combined with corporate commitment to public service projects forged resilient corporate cultures. Profitability and societal problem solving can be compatible and mutually reinforcing goals. "[These] vanguard companies and the humanistic values-based model they exhibit offer hope for solving problems in a troubled world, especially if aligned behind an agenda that reflects the areas that people in general care about. Vanguard companies survive and flourish under difficult conditions by building profitable, sustainable enterprises that also keep their eye on their role in society."[61]

Successful companies sometimes fail after a while. Often it is because disruptive or new technologies or more innovative competitors devastate their market share. Companies like Polaroid, Wang, Kodak, and Digital Equipment went under for some of these reasons. Other companies such as Lehman Brothers and Washington Mutual became overextended in risk taking and mismanaged their assets. Still others developed a culture of greed, deception, and duplicity that led to their implosion. The Enron case is sadly illustrative.

It is fascinating to note how some of America's largest corporations managed to recast or reframe their corporate cultures. IBM is a prime example; Proctor & Gamble is another. Ford Motor Company is struggling to do that today.

IBM's legendary founder Thomas J. Watson promoted a distinctive and disciplined culture. A few critics likened it to a cult. Watson was a self-made success story, and he preached the virtues of hard work, ethical behavior, and respect for individuals. He also promoted deep-seated loyalty among his employees and initiated company songs and a formal dress code (dark suits and white shirts). He inspired IBM golf courses and a variety of remarkable team- and community-building cultural activities. IBMers were bright, highly trained, loyal, and for a long while highly successful.

But IBM became outmaneuvered by new, innovative challengers like Microsoft, Apple, Amazon, and e-businesses that transformed the marketplace. The Watson-inspired culture doubtless had served IBM well; yet by the early 1990s, it was clear IBM needed a reinvigorated organizational culture that would make it competitive again.

Fortunately for IBM, Lou Gerstner and some of his successors managed to tackle the old IBM culture head-on and reinvent a more nimble, competitive IBM. "Changing the attitude and behavior of hundreds of thousands of people is very, very hard to accomplish," writes Gerstner. "Business schools don't teach you how to do it. You can't lead the revolution from the splendid isolation of corporate headquarters. You can't simply give a couple of speeches or write a new credo for the company and declare that the new culture has taken hold. You can't mandate it, can't engineer it."[62]

Gerstner knew, however, that for IBM to be competitive it needed to change, and its culture especially needed to change. He changed the rigid dress code rules. He fired large numbers of employees. And he shook up the IBM business model, transforming it to become what he called a "high-performance culture," where everyone is a self-starter and everyone would be passionate about quality and winning. Gerstner came to see that the company's culture wasn't merely just one aspect of the game; "it is the game."

His greatest ally, he admits, was IBM's own precipitous collapse. He leveraged that and won widespread support from his board, investors, and most senior managers.

As part of his efforts to turn IBM around, Gerstner needed a new marketplace-based mission, a new compass for IBM's operating practice, and a defining focus of its new culture. In his own words, he proclaimed e-business as IBM's new "moon shot." This would be the galvanizing or overarching objective. "We infused it into everything—not just our advertising, product planning, research agendas, and customer meetings, but throughout our communications and operations—from my e-mails, broadcasts, and town hall visits to the way in which we measured our internal transformation."[63] In short, it helped him reshape the corporate culture and provide a major driver for organizational renewal.

Many of the technology company start-ups in the 1970s, 1980s, and 1990s demonstrated how organizational culture could help contribute to organizational productivity and innovation.

In their early days, both Microsoft and Google were viewed as "hot" places to work, and they attracted incredibly smart young people to work on cutting-edge technologies. Part of the fun was that the Microsoft and Google campuses were designed according to an almost counter-IBM, counter–General Motors, or counter–Procter & Gamble model. The model was more like the extension of a Stanford University where people could play volleyball, bring their dogs, dress as they liked, and in general have fun as they worked on teams with like-minded young professionals.

This is how the chef at Google summed up lunch and festivities such as regular TGIFs at the Googleplex: "My goal every day was to create the illusion you were not at work but on some type of cruise or resort, through the cuisine, décor, entertainment, and the extra things we did."[64]

Google recruited people who wanted to not only make money but also make the world a better place and have fun at the same time. Its Web site of the Top 10 Reasons to Work at Google included these four:

- Life is beautiful. Being a part of something that matters and working on products in which you can believe are remarkably fulfilling.
- Appreciation is the best motivator, so we've created a fun and inspiring workplace. You'll be glad to be a part of it, including on-site doctor and dentist, massage and yoga, professional development opportunity.

- Work and play are not mutually exclusive. It is possible to code and pass the puck at the same time.
- There is such a thing as a free lunch after all. In fact we have them every day: healthy, yummy, and made with love.[65]

Successful companies go to considerable lengths to create distinctive cultures—cultures that encourage pride, meaning, fellowship, and that special hum, flow, or X factor that helps them attract and retain talent and achieve peak performances. There is now a good-sized library about "The HP Way," "The GE Way," and how companies can become exceptional, vanguard companies.[66]

One final note about organizational cultures: executives have to figure out how to promote loyalty and teamwork and a culture of fellowship and fun without turning their organizations into cults. Google, W. L. Gore, and other "most admired places to work" figured that out.

IBM, Proctor & Gamble, Walmart, some of the auto companies, and maybe even Nordstrom developed, at various stages, a cultlike culture. Visionary or vanguard companies must have distinctive and empowering cultures yet not degenerate into cults. Collins and Porras wrestle with this dilemma in their best-selling study *Built to Last.*

One of their case studies is about how Nordstrom department stores developed a series of cultlike practices that apparently worked well for them. Nordstrom's careful recruiting, orientation, customer-driven ethic, and spirit instilled "an intense sense of loyalty" and influenced employees to achieve consistency and high levels of both customer and employee satisfaction. Somehow Nordstrom did it, say Collins and Porras, without becoming an actual cult.[67]

Executives have also learned the vital importance of designing quick-to-change, adaptive organizations. What Andy Grove of Intel once called "strategic inflection points" or what others call disruptive technologies are part of the challenges and opportunities contemporary executives have to prepare for.

Over the past generation the reality of a borderless and global economy, the transformation of the Internet, the rise of the Chinese and Indian economies, and the reality of terrorism, pandemics, and global recessions have forced organizational leaders in every sector to emphasize the imperative of strategies for coping with change and looking for opportunities that disruptive challenges provide. That's what Gerstner tried to do for IBM and what Lee Scott tried to do for Walmart (he was the CEO who helped reframe Walmart as a leading green corporation).

Fear is okay, says Grove. "Fear of competition, fear of bankruptcy, fear of being wrong, fear of losing can all be powerful motivators."[68] The lesson for companies is not to become a prisoner of their past or the organizational culture that may have served them well in prior times. Some of the most rigid organizations today, it needs to be remembered, started out as innovative and entrepreneurial start-ups. But they boxed themselves into a corner and failed.

Organizations have to reinvent themselves and have programs for personal and organizational renewal that encourage relentless innovation.[69] Ambidextrous organizations realize that innovation, change, and the ability to adapt are their bloodlines. A sense of urgency is needed as well, and this spirit not only has to be created, and created well, but may have to be re-created again and again. John P. Kotter suggests that "with a culture of urgency, people deeply value the capacity to grab new opportunities, avoid new hazards, and continually find ways to win. Behaviors that are the norm include being constantly alert, focusing externally, moving fast, stopping low-value-added activities that absorb time and effort, relentlessly pushing for change when it is needed, and providing the leadership to produce smart change no matter where you are in the hierarchy."[70]

Sometimes the paradoxical character of an effective corporation defies easy understanding. Take the paradox of the late Steve Jobs, for example. What he and his colleagues at Apple did was revolutionary in terms of inventing and sharing instruments that helped liberate people and added enormous freedom and convenience to their lives. But at his peak, Steve Jobs was often an authoritarian and his highly secretive, tightly controlled corporation seemed as though it was designed primarily to execute Jobs's vision, or visions.

Jobs was known for having a mercurial management style, for his habit of berating employees, and for being combative and even abusive in describing rival corporations like Adobe, Amazon, Google, IBM, and Microsoft. He apparently liked being a rebel, but a rebel with visions of "insanely" (a favorite word of his) valuable and tasteful new products. Jobs and his company were walking paradoxes (Jobs's heroes included Gandhi as well as David Packard and Bill Hewlett, Bob Dylan, and Walt Disney)—and it is perhaps because of these multiple contradictions and tensions that a series of ingenious products emerged.

The effective executive, in sum, creates adaptive, nimble organizations rich with purpose, meaning, and with a fierce commitment and sense of urgency to innovate.

Providing for Strategic Central Direction yet Flattening the Pyramid, Decentralizing, and Creatively Delegating

One of the most enduring challenges in every organization is deciding when and what to centralize and when and what to decentralize. Every executive in all but the smallest organizations learns that a chief executive officer can't run the organization.

Delegation is not only a necessity; it is the best way to empower one's colleagues so (a) they can better serve their staffs, (b) they can better serve their customers, and (c) they can develop their own abilities as future senior leaders in the organization.

Top executives still need to manage the vision and dreams. They cannot delegate the overall effectiveness of their organization. Yet they can hardly micromanage all the decisions and implementation operations needed to run a complex organization. "The CEO's greatest influence shifts from direct to indirect means—articulating and communicating a clear, easily understood strategy; institutionalizing rigorous structures and processes to guide, inform, and reward; and setting values and tone," writes Harvard Business School's Michael E. Porter and colleagues. "Equally important is selecting and managing the right senior management team to share the burden of running the company."[71]

Alfred P. Sloan Jr., an MIT-trained engineer who served for twenty-three years as CEO of General Motors, writes that one of his greatest challenges in the early years of GM was how they could exercise effective control over the whole sprawling corporation in a way consistent with the decentralized and divisional structure of GM. "We never ceased to attack this paradox."[72]

Sloan and other executives insist that the temptation to centralize all decision making needs to be resisted. The genius soloist will very often be more talented than an orchestra's conductor, yet the soloist will rarely understand the large number of things that have to be harmoniously blended.[73]

Effective leadership invariably rests on a reconciliation of decentralization and centralization. "From decentralization we get initiative, responsibility, development of personnel, decisions close to the facts, flexibility—in short, all the qualities necessary for an organization to adapt to new conditions," writes Sloan. "From coordination we get efficiencies and economies."[74]

Decentralizing, delegating, and flattening the hierarchical pyramid can all help increase morale and encourage trust, responsibility, and empowerment of frontline associates. Yet there is a limit to how much decentralization can be achieved.

"In any institution," writes Peter Drucker, "there has to be a final authority, that is, a 'boss'—someone who can make the final decisions and who can expect them to be obeyed."[75] Drucker may overstate the point yet says all the talk about the "end of hierarchy" is, in his words, "blatant nonsense." "The unquestioning acceptance of [hierarchy] by everyone in the organization is the only hope in a crisis."[76]

Drucker at the same time insists that it is a sound structural principle to have as few management layers as possible. Drucker, like Sloan, preaches the middle way, recognizing that teamwork and decentralization are the key for many tasks although hierarchy might be needed for different tasks.

As noted earlier, one of the useful case studies of decentralizing decision-making authority or "flattening the pyramid" is SAS airlines executive Jan Carlzon's personal memoir, *Moments of Truth*. "People sometimes equate delegating responsibility with abdicating one's own influence. But that's hardly the case," writes Carlzon. "Actually, the middle manager's role is indispensable in the smooth functioning of a decentralized organization."[77]

Objectives and vision are still largely provided by those in a central office. Middle managers have to break these down into more precise objectives for frontline people to implement. At this point middle managers have to artfully switch from being administrators to serving as support for frontline people. This requires rigorous planning and the development of coaching, mentoring, and educating abilities for middle managers.

Carlzon found that empowered frontline workers who truly understand the vision or big picture and were given the responsibility of making independent judgments as situations arose worked with newfound confidence.[78]

Longtime management consultant Ken Blanchard says nothing is wrong with having the conventional hierarchy for certain tasks, such as defining and defending core values and vision. "The paradox is that the pyramid has to be right side up or upside down depending on the task."[79] Blanchard echoes Carlzon by insisting that effective executives learn to care less about defending traditional hierarchy than turning their organizational pyramids upside down to ensure customers get served and visions get implemented.

Who is at the top of the upside-down organization? The customer-contact people. Who is *really* at the top? The customers. Who is at the bottom? Top management. When you turn a pyramid upside down philosophically, you work for your people. "In a traditional pyramid, the boss is always responsible and the subordinates are supposed to be responsive to the boss. When you turn the pyramid upside down, these roles are reversed. The people become responsible, and the job of management is to be responsive to them. . . . If you work for your people, your purpose as a leader is to help them accomplish goals."[80]

The biggest challenge for all executives is how to find the right balance. Direction is important. But delegation and decentralization are equally important. Getting feedback is crucial. Leaders need to stay engaged yet learn to discipline the normal temptation to control or even complete what has been delegated to others.

Conclusion

Business leadership is fraught with paradoxes, and learning to juggle, manage, or master paradox is essential. Leaders should be optimistic yet embrace the brutal realities. They should seek simplicity, yet distrust it. They should learn from their customers, yet realize the consumers don't always understand the future. They should be humble yet fight boldly for results. They should get the wrong people out of their organizations yet not rush during the hiring process. Finally, they should centralize when needed, yet flatten the pyramid when possible.

Culture is key. Teamwork is key. So also are focus, passion, energy, tenacity, and flexibility. Leaders should be allergic to unnecessary hierarchy. They should be persistent yet only selectively bullheaded. They should hire good people and then keep them, hiring for the long term, not just for the current season. They should view mistakes as a great chance to learn and improve things. They should use both mistakes and customers as teachers and be intuitive, imaginative and risk taking, but not at the expense of facts and reality.

Such are the lessons executives regularly learn. These are not unlike the lessons we learn from the classics and from republics and empires over the long stride of history. And we learn some of these lessons too from politics and the military.

An old saw has it that a wise man was asked where he gained his wisdom. The wise one said he gained it, of course, "from experience." And just how, the questioner persisted, did he gain all his experience? It's simple, the wise man offered: "Experience comes from making a lot of mistakes and then learning from them." It's even more convenient, of course, if one can mainly learn from other people's mistakes.

Chapter Eight
What Politics Teaches Us about Leadership

> The student of politics will not make a beginning till he has realised that in this art there are antinomies [contradictions or paradoxes] everywhere, and that it is no shame to a politician, or to the man who writes about him, if the opinions he utters are often in conflict one with another.
>
> —***Frederick Scott Oliver***[1]

Politician bashing is an old pastime everywhere. "If you can't say anything nice about a candidate," according to one adage, "by God, let's hear it!" "Next to kidnappers," wrote the legendary journalist H. L. Mencken, "politicians seem to be the most unpopular men in this great republic. Nobody ever really trusts them. Whatever they do is commonly ascribed to ignoble motives."[2]

There are, of course, countless hardworking, dedicated people in public life; yet we read a lot about Governor Shakedown, Congressman Kickback, Senator Flip-Flop, Assemblyman "Pay to Play," Mayor Hypocrite, and about liars, cheats, and other rascals and rogues. Honest law-abiding politicians rarely make the news. It's the ones who have been indicted and convicted that we're more likely to hear about.

Such regularly heard comments as "Oh, that's just politics," "It's all politics, you know," or "What we really need today are leaders not politicians" imply things somehow would be much improved if we could simply do away with politics and politicians. In America, the outsider and citizen leader are iconic; professional politicians, our nemesis.

There is a widespread feeling that politics changes, if not corrupts, those who win office. Thus, nearly 60 percent of the public told the Harris Poll a few years ago that "most politicians would take a bribe if they could get away with it." People believe fat-cat donors have too much influence and that politicians once in office forget about ordinary citizens. They're "mostly bought and paid for" is a common view.

But, as discussed in earlier chapters, political philosophers such as Machiavelli, Hobbes, and Locke, as well as political realities, persuasively argue that governmental compacts are and can be a positive necessity.

There is no option for "not having a government" or "for not having politics and politicians." Factions and partisan divisions are a reality in every society. Politics is the art of accommodating the diversity and variety of interests and building durable coalitions to solve public problems.

One of the most enduring leadership paradoxes in America is that we yearn for "leaders" not politicians, but it is the politicians who can get elected who earn the opportunity to lead our governments. We want great leaders who somehow transcend politics. We easily forget that Lincoln, Franklin D. Roosevelt, and Truman were politicians. To be a political leader, whether elected or unelected, requires political savvy, political instincts, and a certain amount of political courage.

This is where politicians come in. Politicians, when effective, work out acceptable compromises that in effect prevent us from shooting at one another. It is in their mediating role that politicians are indispensable.

Yet politicians are also the visible symbol of governments, and governments have power and can be a coercive as well as a liberating force in our lives. Thus, politicians provide us with an ever-present scapegoat target for anything we dislike about government—such as taxes, regulation, licensing, bureaucracies, and especially any restrictions on our liberty.

This chapter seeks to answer two basic questions: What is politics? What are the leadership lessons that both politicians and we learn from politics?

What Is Politics?

Politics, like leadership, means different things to different people. And like leadership, it can be hard to define.

Politics is a process and a covenantal set of rules whereby civilized societies try to resolve differences without resorting to violence. Politics and our political processes—elections and governments—are the indispensable instruments through which we try to achieve our shared purposes. Political leadership enables us to create civil communities of shared interests and aspirations.

Politics is also about power or influence, getting it, stabilizing it, and using it to manage and mitigate societal conflict. It assumes there will always be diverse and contending interests—self-interests, group interests, ethnic interests, religious interests, economic and nation-state interests. Politics is the process of mediating among clashing interests. Politics is the process of bargaining over the rules and regulations (and constitutions) that make it possible for us to get along with one another despite differing and sometimes conflicting interests.

To study political power is to analyze the changes of how things of value are distributed in a society. Illustrative values are safety, income, opportunity, and deference. Politics as a field is the study of who gets those values, when and how. "Since a few members of any community at a given time have the most of each value," wrote Harold Lasswell, "a diagram of the pattern of distribution of any value resembles a pyramid. The few who get the most of any value are the *élite*; the rest are the rank and file. An elite preserves its ascendancy by manipulating symbols, controlling supplies, and applying violence."[3]

Machiavelli taught that the first law for any political system or government is ensuring reasonable stability, order, and national (or in his case city-state) security. Abraham Lincoln added that "the legitimate object of government is to do for the people what needs to be done, but which they cannot by individual effort, do at all, or do so well, for themselves."

Politicians, whatever we may think of their flaws, are essential for the effective running of a government, especially one like ours whose Madisonian system of fragmented powers, separate branches, and intricate federalism arrangements necessitate politicians to act as social architects mediating among factions, building coalitions, and negotiating sensible compromises among and within branches of government—all in an effort to produce acceptable laws, policies, and actions.

Politics is rarely about achieving Socratic or Platonic justice, and more routinely about trying to bring about—with imperfect leaders and imperfect governmental institutions—balance, social harmony, possible progress, and the achievable and desirable for as many people as possible. It is often more a "game" of inches, incrementalism, and adjustment than a case of decisive or majestic "victories."

It is seldom tidy or pretty, yet elected officials (politicians)—in the engine room of state—are the necessary horse traders, coalition builders, and agreement makers we temporarily hire to help us transcend anarchy and violence and to keep a diverse, pluralistic society going.

Politics Is about Power and Purpose

Politics is about power—acquiring it, enhancing it, and carefully using it for personal as well as public interest ends. Power is the possession of resources that can influence desired behavior. It is pretty hard to lead if you do not have a certain amount of power. Power is a relationship and depends on context and situations. As emphasized earlier, holding a position or having a title is not the same as leading. Physical might and weaponry are classic sources of power. Information can convey or enable power. Money can be a power resource. Charisma and judgment come into play as well. Sometimes power is a matter of strength, coercion, and command, but in everyday political life it is usually a matter of consulting, collaborating, and bargaining with others.

It is helpful to distinguish *hard power* from *soft power*. Harvard political scientist Joseph S. Nye Jr. suggests:

> Police power, financial power, and the ability to hire and fire are examples of tangible *hard* power that can be used to get others to change their position. Hard power rests on inducements (carrots) and threats (sticks). But sometimes one can get the outcomes one wants by setting the agenda and attracting others without threat or payment. This is *soft* power: getting the outcomes one wants by attracting others rather than manipulating their material incentives. It co-opts people rather than coerces them.[4]

It is sometimes tempting to say power deals with command and force, and leadership deals with persuasion and collaboration. This is too simplistic. There are many kinds of power, the power of the effective coalition building that leads to positive policy results as well as the power of having the best bombs.[5]

"Power is the capital in which politicians deal," writes former mayor and Montana legislative leader Daniel Kemmis. He likens politicians to power entrepreneurs. "Like any entrepreneur, their job is to watch for opportunities to increase their capital, and like other entrepreneurs those opportunities are almost always accompanied by risk." Politicians make bets all the time, hoping to enrich their power, hoping to maximize chances of getting reelected and enhancing their bargaining power. Says Kemmis, "This constant round of risking, reaping, and reinvesting power is a fundamental dimension of the art of politics."[6]

One of the reasons people hate politics is that they view politicians as having power over them and they understandably fear the possible or real manipulation that can result. The power games and the political maneuvering and horse trading seem distasteful to those unfamiliar with politics.

But, as Machiavelli emphasized, political leadership and having a stable, secure state require that power be centered in an individual or a few people. Controlling these people, keeping them accountable, and making sure they serve desired public purposes are what constitutionalism is all about.

Some political scientists warn that purely self-interested, power-maximizing politicians love power and the fruits of office so much that they single-mindedly work and behave in such a way as to win reelection. Thus they become preoccupied with helping big donors and primarily serve those interests back home who can help them stay in office. They probably also avoid controversies and trade their votes in ways that will be productive in raising funds or earning reciprocity on bills that can enhance their reputation.

There are plenty of elected officials who behave this way. But there are others, in contrast, who care deeply about issues and behave in ways that serve the common interest sometimes at the expense of their own political survival. John F. Kennedy's classic *Profiles in Courage* discusses several U.S. senators who exemplified this ethic.[7]

Politics Is about Interests

We learned from Machiavelli, Hobbes, and others that *people are naturally self-centered and are primarily motivated by their appetites, interests, needs, wants, and passions.* We all have family, neighborhood, and ethnic loyalties. In addition to self-interests, there are group interests, religious interests, economic sector interests, and, at the nation-state level, national interests.

The first law of politics is to understand these human interests and aspirations and how they can be in some cases moderated, and in others, served. And in a system that believes in majority rule *and* minority rights, the enduring challenge is how to reconcile the variety of and sometimes contending self-interests that make up the larger community.

Here is how Tip O'Neill, Speaker of the House of Representatives, put it:

> A politician learns that if a constituent calls about a problem, even if it's a street light out, you don't tell them to call City Hall. *You call City Hall.*
>
> Members of the House learn this quicker than anyone else because they only have a two-year term. They learn that if you don't pay attention to the voters you soon will find yourself right back with them.
>
> I tell them to pay attention to their backyard and take care of their folks. Get home often and report to their constituents. Keep them informed and you will find they will like and respect you and allow you to be a "national" Congressman and vote for things that are good for the country but may not have direct impact on your district.[8]

We all have personal interests, such as having a safe neighborhood and good schools, reducing environmental pollution, and much more. We want, and even insist, that politicians act on behalf of our interests. This means that they have to listen to us; consult with us; and fight to achieve public safety, quality schools, and our other priority interests.

This is true at the national level as well as at the state and local levels. A leader in Congress is only as good as how well he or she understands colleagues' and constituents' interests. Lyndon B. Johnson was a master of knowing his fellow senators and especially the key interests of their states.

Former Minnesota governor Jesse Ventura tells the story of why he got into politics. Simply put, he believed his mayor and city council didn't understand or care about his neighborhood's interests. Ventura thought the incumbents were not only uncaring but mere putty in the hands of developers. So he ran for mayor and trounced a long-term entrenched incumbent. It was primarily a case of his and his neighbors' interests being ignored.

We expect politicians to be representative, to share our interests, to protect and promote our interests. But, and this is a familiar leadership paradox, we also want them to educate us about both our local and our national interests. Sometimes these collide. Many a southern Democrat in the mid-twentieth century favored civil rights legislation but had persistent and powerful local interests who favored segregated schools and businesses.

This was not just a southern issue. It was the strongly held view of politicians in such places as South Boston that to each community belonged its own way of life and, particularly, its own neighborhood schools. This was in part racism, yet it was also local self-interest—the right of every community to its own schools.

That politics is about self-interests reminds us of the now famous Tip O'Neill aphorism that "all politics is local." What Speaker O'Neill meant was that politicians must deal with both *retail* and *wholesale* politics. O'Neill warned his colleagues that they shouldn't forget the people who sent them. And they should never offend or forget their bread-and-butter interests. There is a transactional aspect of politics that recognizes that political power is very much a quid pro quo equation. Former O'Neill aide Chris Matthews explains: "If you want to understand how a politician behaves, look at what affects him at home back where his voters are. Politicians use the same hard-nosed approach in dealing with one another: if you want to hurt someone, hit him where it matters to him the most, in his own backyard."[9]

Most legislators know who elected them and they know they can be readily replaced. They also know that nobody in political life is indispensable. Term limits for presidents and many state and local officials now guarantee this.

But the larger truth here is that virtually all politicians calculate their initiatives and their votes in large part on what people back home will think of their behavior. That's what we get when we design a representative system with frequent elections, especially in an age when television and the Internet cover most of what takes place in politics.

However, as discussed in Chapter One, we paradoxically want leaders to represent us and at the same time educate us, inform us, teach us, and bring out the best in us. This remains one of the great riddles in American political life: leaders should act in our self-interest *yet also* act on behalf of what will be best for us, our children, and grandchildren, not just tomorrow but in the decades to come.

Politicians Nominate Themselves

Most politicians nominate themselves for elective office and are motivated by a combination of policy concerns, civic patriotism, and personal ambition. Candidates for public office succeed in large part because they care about people and know how to talk on their own behalf as well as on behalf of their friends and neighborhoods. Most politicians, well before they get elected, become political entrepreneurs, joining groups, assuming minor leadership responsibilities, and helping out on other people's campaigns. One of the traditional ways of paying one's dues is helping to run someone else's campaign or working on the staff of an elected official. Thousands of assistant district attorneys, to cite one example, have gone on to run for the DA position or similar county and state positions. The colorful story of Providence's mayor Buddy Cianci is one illustration.[10]

Willie Brown, the legendary mayor of San Francisco and state legislative leader, got his start by protesting real estate racism in his hometown. In the process he won attention from local Democratic officials who both wanted to support him and get him involved in politics. It didn't take much for them and others to get him to run for office. He ran but he lost a close election. But he learned enough to run again two years later, this time successfully.[11]

Most candidates instigate their own candidacies by going to a lot of meetings, taking a few stands, and presenting themselves as a plausible possibility for some office. It's not unlike a sport. They get some of the equipment, go out and begin to play at whatever entry level they can join, and learn to play, practicing and learning the rules of the game. Perhaps they take some lessons or go to a summer camp. But initially everyone is an apprentice, a learner, and a mere beginner.

The skills candidates have to learn are rather simple. They have to get people to adopt them and like them. They have to ask for money and support. One of the first laws of politics is that "if you don't have enough confidence in yourself to ask for money, you don't belong in politics." And they have to be willing to spend huge amounts of time learning the skills, tactics, and strategies of the craft. Journalist Alan Ehrenhalt sums it up in *The United States of Ambition*:

> The skills that work in American politics at this point in history are those of entrepreneurship. At all levels of the political system, from local boards and councils up to and including the presidency, it is unusual for parties to nominate

> people. People nominate themselves as candidates. That is, they offer themselves as candidates, raise money, organize campaigns, create their own publicity, and make decisions in their own behalf. If they are not willing to do that work for themselves, they are not (except in very few parts of the country) going to find any political party structure to do it for them.[12]

Why do people run? It's rarely for one reason. It's usually some combination of intellectual, emotional, and psychological reasons. Sometimes it is a case of their friends urging them to do so. Often it is because would-be candidates think they could do a better job than the aging, entrenched, or incompetent incumbent. Then, too, the fascination and allure of power, politics, and civic patriotism play a role.

A friend of ours once ran unsuccessfully for Congress. He says being an intern in the U.S. Congress and being impressed with the powers and especially the opportunities for doing good and making things happen were his motivation. He also was frank in acknowledging that patriotic symbolism was a motive too.

> Anyone who has seen Jimmy Stewart in *Mr. Smith Goes to Washington* knows why I ran for Congress. Jefferson Smith arrives by train at Union Station. He sees the Capitol dome and is drawn toward it. He is oblivious to all around him, lost in the history and symbolism of Washington. That scene may well be the corniest of all the trite statements movie makers have made about blind patriotism. But in a real sense, the aura of Washington, the sense of history, the call of patriotism draw many into the political arena.[13]

People who become politicians invariably say they wanted to "give something back" to their great city, state, or nation. They seldom say they yearned to be in the limelight and they liked the semi-celebrity aura of being on the political stage. Ronald Reagan, reflecting on his youthful years as a lifeguard, mused, "It was like a stage." He said of his elevated lifeguard's chair, "Everyone had to look up at me," and he pursued professions in which he would continue to be on stage.

Politics demands long hours and hard work and comes with a variety of hardships, privacy loss, and pain. Yet it is "the fun of having a box in the theater that never closes . . . it is also the work of being an actor in that theater, and having many roles in the same play," writes former Massachusetts legislative leader Billy Bulger.[14]

Elsewhere in this book we have speculated that narcissism and the need for attention and affirmation play at least a partial role in encouraging individuals to pursue and exercise leadership activities. If anything, this role is probably greater in politics than in most other professions. This is hard to quantify. Yet we only have to watch politicians on every stage of the national political theater.

Hollywood snobs sometimes quip that politics is merely show business for ugly people. But sarcastic though this remark may be, politics is a stage, a platform; and just as on Broadway or in Hollywood, we can witness majestic performances and also see pathetic flops.

Politicians Run Scared

Politics is an unsentimental and often risky, brutally pragmatic business. Today's ally can be tomorrow's foe. Public surveys of voters in recent years indicated that 70 percent or more of likely voters think incumbent members of Congress should be replaced. "Fire them!" "Throw the bums out!" That's surely enough to make politicians nervous about their tenure.

All elected officials are mindful of friends who were defeated in recent elections. They know, too, that there are plenty of potential rivals in their own as well as the opposition party who would love to replace them at the first opportunity.

"One of the little secrets politicians rarely share is that most of them don't dislike their opponents in the other party nearly so much as their allies in their own party," writes journalist Jon Margolis. "In this country most congressional districts and even some states are pretty safely in the hands of one party. So for lots of Congressmen, state legislators, city aldermen, county commissioners or clerks of the works, the only real opponents are the ones they have to face in primaries. Ambition is more likely to be thwarted by an intraparty foe."[15]

Incumbent defeats by one's own party "friends" are rather common. Democratic governor Endicott Peabody was defeated by his own lieutenant governor in the 1964 Massachusetts gubernatorial primary. Republican mayor John Lindsay of New York City was knocked out by Republican state senator John Marchi in a 1969 Republican primary fight. Democratic challenger Lloyd Bentsen defeated a Democratic incumbent U.S. senator in Texas in 1970. Conservative Republican U.S. senator Bob Bennett from Utah was defeated in the Utah Republican state convention in 2010—by a fellow Republican who was farther to his political right. The list is long and the lesson for incumbents is a compelling one.

Winning a landslide election the last time is no guarantee in politics of success in the next election. Lyndon B. Johnson in 1964 and Richard M. Nixon in 1972 won landslide victories. Yet LBJ suffered devastating losses in his midterm election of 1966 and was forced to withdraw from seeking reelection in 1968. And Nixon was booted out of office a couple of years after his 1972 landslide.

All politicians understand and probably even have an exaggerated view of their political vulnerability. This explains why most elected officials constantly claim credit for programs, especially monies and projects going to their districts. And it explains a certain amount of posturing on issues that the politicians may not be all that interested in or that have no chance of passing—but will please certain constituents back home.[16]

No matter how hard politicians work, they dread the often-asked question "What have you done for me lately?" Thus politicians spend a lot of time trying to help constituents. They also do a lot of fence mending and try to win over people back home who may have once been rivals or political enemies.

Politicians know how fickle and unforgiving constituents can be. Politicians also know they need all the allies they can get. They know that yesterday's foe may be tomorrow's needed ally. As Providence mayor Buddy Cianci once put it, "Be careful how you act. The toe you stepped on yesterday may be connected to the ass you have to kiss today."[17]

Politics Can Get Rough

Politics has never been for the faint of heart. The American Revolution cost at least 25,000 American lives. The Civil War cost over 600,000 lives. Some even call politics a blood sport, with the fateful (for Hamilton) 1804 duel between former vice president Aaron Burr and former treasury secretary Alexander Hamilton being an iconic early example.

Politics, to its practitioners, is a rough-and-tumble as well as unsentimental business. It's a profession where they have to be thick-skinned and learn not to take things too personally. It's also a profession where they can just as easily be stabbed in the front as in the back.

Politics puts politicians in a goldfish bowl. As one politician complained, "You can't go to the bathroom without being observed." A politician's privacy is regularly invaded and diminishes the higher the office held.

Marriages are often a casualty. Politicians, several writers suggest, are obsessed with their careers, starved for publicity and attention, and often crippled by insecurity. "A politician ought to be born a foundling and remain a bachelor," quipped the loyal and highly tolerant Lady Bird Johnson, wife of LBJ.[18]

Politics is tough on marriages and tough on the children of politicians. But, most of all, politics is tough on politicians. Their hours are long, their tenure is always in doubt, and they regularly get hammered by the opposition party, the press, the comedians, and the intellectuals. Candidates are forever begging for campaign contributions. And many of their campaign events, such as candidate forums, can be boring beyond belief.

Once in office, politicians have to live with high expectations yet painfully slow legislative and bureaucratic processes. Our checks-and-balances system makes it hard for leadership breakthroughs unless there is considerable consensus, including interbranch consensus.

Then there are the physical pain and the violence. We've assassinated nearly 10 percent of our presidents, and several others, including Ford and Reagan, were shot at. Death threats are not uncommon, including even for members of the federal judiciary.

We've sent dozens of congressmen and governors to jail and forced many others, such as Governors Eliot Spitzer, Rod Blagojevich, and James McGreevey, to leave office prematurely. Both President Nixon and Vice President Spiro Agnew were forced out of office.

The whole history of politicians who speak out, rebel, or stick their necks out is strewn with brutal retaliations—Socrates, Caesar, Joan of Arc, Lincoln, Huey Long, JFK, RFK, MLK, San Francisco city supervisor Harvey Milk, and countless others. It's a tough, rough, demanding business, and the stakes are much higher than in comparable professions.

Politics Changes People

Politics changes people, often amplifying personal strengths and weaknesses and, at the very least, encourages a sense of inflated self-importance if not arrogance. Power has certain aphrodisiacal qualities. Even an unsuccessful candidate for Congress can write, "I also had a taste of the aphrodisiacal appeal of power. Others' lives revolved around mine. Others cared what I said, what I did. They looked after my schedule, drove me from place to place, provided for my every need. Someone was always at my beck and call to do whatever I said needed to be done." A reflective Sandy Maisel adds that "I found that appalling at first, but I quickly became used to it. In the final analysis I found that to be frightening. I am not that important; I have seen too many politicians who feel that they are. I came away from the campaign uncertain that I could resist the temptations.... If I was unable to resist that temptation as a candidate, how much easier would it be for me to submit as an office holder?"[19]

Countless political careers have crashed because politicians' greed, lust, and narcissism got the best of them. The examples of Illinois governor Rod Blagojevich, U.S. senator John Edwards, and Providence mayor Buddy Cianci are just three of the more colorful examples in recent years.[20]

Politicians have to have uncommon drive. They have to take risks. They have to have contagious self-confidence, and they have to have an uncanny ability to attract campaign volunteers, colleagues, and backers. All this requires ambition and a sense of urgency. The healthy politician needs a strong internal compass and a certain amount of humility to keep all of this in perspective.

Lyndon B. Johnson had all the necessary drive and ambition to excel in politics. But, after a while, especially in the White House, his humility was sometimes in short supply. A legendary, if perhaps apocryphal, story has a young military officer guiding LBJ to his helicopter during the Vietnam years. "Mr. President, this one here is your helicopter." To which Johnson allegedly replied, "Son, they're all my helicopters." This unseemly possessiveness was unfortunately part of the consuming and narcissistic aspect of LBJ's sense of entitlement. Nixon was another president whose personal insecurities altered his judgment and ultimately ended his political career.

There is an aphorism about the endless parade of promising, ambitious, young politicians who come to Washington, DC. Old-timers have a saying that "some of them grow, most of them just swell." It is often a deformed sense of entitlement that causes the swelling and the ensuing swollen egos.

A candid Willie Brown writes that "if you are an attractive person in public life, you're going to have lots of opportunities to have fascinating relationships with women or men." And he continues, "A spicy social life usually can add to your panache. In San Francisco, the city's hostesses treat me as a star guest because I add flavor to the evening.... When I walk into a party or public dinner or other social gathering, instantly all the attention is focused on me. Everybody wants to BS with me." Brown adds, "Well, there is something in power that motivates people, women and men, to be more interested in you than they would be otherwise. You can clearly see that in people's behavior towards you when you have power ... power is indeed an aphrodisiac."[21]

This doesn't mean politicians are any different from athletes, professional entertainers, or business leaders. It's just that they often live lives on a larger and more scrutinized stage and that, because many of them do exercise political influence and power over other people, they are both targets for criticism and jokes and the focus of a lot of attention.

A veteran political operative who specialized in opposition research for a series of Republican campaigns has a slightly inelegant yet probably apt way to summarize this: "I learned fast that politicians of both parties are about equal—roughly one-third good folks, one-third assholes, and one-third somewhere in between (which is probably the same, or close to the same breakdown in other walks of life)."[22]

A subsidiary lesson here is that, whether we like it or not, politicians have to be ambitious, assertive self-publicists—traits we may undervalue. There is a misguided notion that politics should be all about service and high principles. But personal ambition in politics is a necessary lubricant that sparks the desire to excel. It motivates the problem-solving politician just as it motivates the talented cyclist, scientist, or composer.

It is the politician's willingness to run, go public, beg for support, serve, and respond, within reason, to our interests (often narrow self-interests) that is the indispensable link in making democracy work. A cardinal principle of constitutional democracy holds that those who exercise power and make the laws win the right to do so only by winning public election.

Ideas, Words, and Timing Matter

Candidates usually campaign on a handful of issues that are of current interest. But they often have only a superficial understanding of budgets and the one hundred and one complex policy matters they will have to deal with. Politicians privately confide that "our knowledge is a mile wide yet only an inch deep."

Once elected, politicians are constantly engaged in "cram courses" to stay abreast of issues. Said one rookie California state legislator: "I confess, before I became a legislator, I always knew I had the answer to every question. Since I've been here, I've come to realize that there are no easy answers, sometimes no answers at all. It's because we all have our own interests."[23]

Politicians, like all leaders, have to have ideas, have to contribute substance to ongoing explorations of how problems get solved. Here is how former U.S. senator Bill Bradley from New Jersey viewed it:

> By the end of my first Congress, in 1980, it had become clear to me that success in the Senate was a function of substance, procedure, and personality. The senators who had an impact and got other senators to listen to them had to know what they were talking about. . . . These were all senators who commanded respect because of the knowledge they possessed. They were influential because they had full control of substance.[24]

Although ideas are important, timing is also something politicians have to master. The effective elected politician needs to understand that, most of the time, he can't hurry history, and in Garry Wills's words, "the useful politician is never a man in advance of his time."[25]

Politicians learn to pick their fights wisely, and they learn that silence or vagueness can frequently be the best response. Politicians learn, usually the hard way, that what they do not say does not later need to be explained. They learn, too, that—especially in politics—they get only one reputation. Virginia governor George Allen probably lost a U.S. Senate seat in Virginia for a regrettable ethnic slur that doomed his candidacy in 2006.

Former Republican Speaker of the House of Representatives Newt Gingrich wrote a chapter in a memoir entitled "Learn to Keep Your Mouth Shut." One of his "Lessons Learned the Hard Way" is that reporters and political opponents can exploit unguarded or risky commentary. After one heated fight with Bill Clinton, Gingrich writes, "It would take me two painful years to learn that 'no comment' was very often the best thing to say. Reporters, after all, have the right to ask any questions they want to.... But we have no obligation to answer. 'No comment' beats a self-destructive comment every time."[26]

Politicians learn, to their regret, that lies, exaggerations, and hypocrisy can be costly. "A lie," Winston Churchill once said, "gets halfway around the world before the truth has a chance to get its pants on."[27]

Several Republican lawmakers who had preached family values, abstinence education, and opposed same-sex marriage were later found engaging in compromising and hypocritical behavior. This led one Republican political consultant to write that "the most bitter pill for me to swallow was something I knew subconsciously but refused to admit for many years: that Democrats are not even close to Republicans when it comes to personal hypocrisy."[28]

Journalist and former political insider Chris Matthews suggests silence can be a strategic political weapon. He quotes approvingly Senator Ed Muskie's rule that politicians "should only talk when it improves the silence." Matthews adds, "Real power on Capitol Hill is wielded by men who know that silence can be a sharper tool than rhetoric and that noise is rarely tantamount to action.... There are two businesses conducted on green felt tables [on Capitol Hill]: pool-sharking and lawmaking."[29]

Here again we see paradoxes. We want to hear the truth and we want political leaders with courage. But politics is often about timing. And most politicians learn to heed the aphorism "If you don't stick your neck out, you are less likely to get it chopped off." And they also learn what is humorously called *the politician's prayer*: "O Lord, give us the wisdom to utter gentle and tender words ... for tomorrow we may have to eat them."

Politics Is a Team Sport

Politicians may nominate themselves, but they don't get far unless they can surround themselves with campaign managers, campaign strategists, and a number of others who can compensate for their inevitable weaknesses and limited time. The much-studied presidential campaigns of John F. Kennedy, Ronald Reagan, and Barack Obama are case studies of recruiting staffs and volunteers who could do the fundraising, fieldwork, issue research, and tedious job of winning delegates across the country. These candidates began recruiting, networking, and making friends years earlier as they worked their way up from local and state politics.

But, whatever the political level, a key leadership lesson to learn is how to work with all kinds of people and especially to learn how to disagree without becoming disagreeable.

Politicians as different as Barry Goldwater and Hubert Humphrey, Ted Kennedy and Orrin Hatch, or Ronald Reagan and Speaker Tip O'Neill could really go at each other on their policy disagreements, yet it rarely spilled over to personal animosity. Indeed, Barry Goldwater writes in his memoir that "I was to learn that integrity and fairness wear no party label. Hubert Humphrey, with whom I disagree across the entire political spectrum, was one of the most honorable men I have met in my life." Goldwater adds that "the day of Humphrey's funeral I was barely able to walk because of an operation, but I would not have stayed home even if I had to crawl. Hubert was a clean fighter."[30]

Effective politicians learn to listen to their colleagues across the partisan divide. They learn that no individual and no party have all the answers. They learn, too, that the art of creative collaboration and compromise is indispensable to policy-making progress. This is amply born out in hundreds of case studies of major public policy advances—a few obvious examples being civil rights legislation, the Marshall Plan, higher education legislation, and major environmental protection public policies.[31]

Perhaps the most trenchant complaint against politicians is that they are wheeler-dealers, fixers, or mere brokers. Thus, they get depicted as opportunists lacking fixed and consistent principles. They appear willing to sell out to the highest bidder, wily operatives always seeking the best deal.

This is usually an unfair rap. Yet a core of truth remains. Most politicians—to get where they are and to enhance the likelihood of staying in office—are entrepreneurial as well as transactional brokers. They are understandably juggling their own interests, their district's interests, and their perceived understanding of the national interest.

Moreover our system, as previously discussed, has so much built-in conflict, is so adversarial in nature, is purposely designed to have so many representatives of competing and ever-warring constituencies, and has so many checks and balances that brokering, compromising, artful negotiating, and "smoothing over" are not only needed but are indispensable to agreement building, getting to yes, getting things done.

This doesn't mean that everything should be done in a bipartisan manner. Partisanship can be healthy. Healthy partisanship is a check on unhealthy or unwise legislating. And partisan debates can elevate the quality of debate over confirmations and in investigations. Just as judicial dissents often provide important points that deserve further consideration, partisanship is sometimes an invaluable way legislators protect their institution's prerogatives.

But compromise is at the heart of democratic politics in any constitutional system. Bargaining and compromise are to politics what imagination is to poetry, what precision and rigorous testing are to physics, and what sun and adequate water are to gardening.

A politician who isn't an effective team builder, alliance maker, and coalition builder is unlikely to be an effective political leader. "The hardest part of leadership is compromise," says former Speaker Tip O'Neill. "People often think when you compromise, you are compromising your morals or your principles. That's not what political compromise is. Political compromise is deferring your idea so a majority can be reached."[32]

Business writer Charles Handy adds that most of the time it is interests, not principles, that get compromised. "Most of the dilemmas that we face in this time of confusion are not the straightforward ones of compromise between right and wrong ... but the more complicated dilemmas of right and right.... Most compromise in life ... is not about our principles, but our interests. No compromises means no allies, and no progress."[33]

Another hard lesson all politicians learn is how to say no to their friends. They can't be in favor of everything. Politics involves hard choices, not just between good and bad ideas, but also between good and good ideas. Also, facts matter. Effective politicians occasionally have to tell their friends that "they are entitled to their own opinions but not to their own facts."

Media Power Is Political Power

"The press," said Richard Nixon, "is the enemy." Nixon may have exaggerated. But politicians learn that everything they say and do is on the record. Political careers "can be more easily broken than made by the press."[34]

The media, for their part, are justifiably cautious or even distrusting of politicians. They know that politicians are clever, sometimes too clever, in trying to get credit, favorable publicity, and endorsements. Veteran reporters learn that "there are few straight pitches in politics, mostly curves and sliders," and thus they act accordingly.

One politician whose career may have been damaged, if not broken, by the media was former Minnesota governor Jesse Ventura. He was colorful, iconoclastic, and a self-described maverick. The media loved his personal narrative. He had been a Navy Seal, a popular wrestler for World Wrestling Entertainment, appeared in several Hollywood movies, and took on both Republicans and Democrats to get elected as an independent. "I quickly became even more popular behind the microphone than I was on the mat, but I was no less outrageous," said Ventura. He was loved by some, hated by others, but was proud that "they all know who I am."

But his picking fights regularly with the state and national press was ill-advised. As he himself admits, he became their "whipping-boy-of-choice." His verdict on the media: "There are a few honorable exceptions, but for the most part, they're corrupt, shameless, and irresponsible as hell."[35]

Politicians need media attention to help further their careers and their agenda. But politicians often engage in excessive spinning and claiming too much credit for either past or future initiatives.

Seasoned politicians learn to use the media. They know little or nothing is off limits, that their every blemish or weakness will likely be targeted by the press. Politicians live in a world of negative television ads where opponents characterize them in harsh ways. Politicians know they have to refute such charges and that the media often love the back-and-forth of negative charges. Effective politicians learn to leave no false accusation unanswered. They also learn, sadly, that negative campaigns work—and that it usually takes three positive ads to help refute one negative character slam.

Former U.S. senator Alan K. Simpson, a Republican from Wyoming, enjoyed favorable media coverage at several stages of his career. He was also blessed with a clever sense of wit and great storytelling ability.

He tells of one of his friends warning him in his early days in the Senate: "They love you. But watch out." One day, his friend said, "They're going to say, 'He's been getting away with murder and now we're going to cut him down to size.'" Simpson says his time did in fact come. Indeed, in retirement he wrote a book criticizing media biases, excesses, and manipulation. He is especially critical of what he calls the "hunting mentality" of the media, their relentless search for the dark side of politics and deal making. Simpson admits he manipulated the media on occasion but he fears this media arrogance and manipulation have gotten way out of line. Here is his lament:

> I'm not saying reporters should be cheerleaders. I'm not asking them to sell their journalistic souls to curry favor. I'm not suggesting they surrender their independence. I'm simply saying that they ought to help show an increasingly cynical, saddened, and disappointed American public what's right about this magnificent country.... None of us can build up America while all around us are tearing it down. Boy, now, the media have trained their microscopes on every local blemish, picked every state pimple, and scratched the scab off every national sore, to the point where our beautiful country is barely recognizable.[36]

Money Is the Mother's Milk of Politics

Politicians may nominate themselves, but they quickly learn that the second priority in any campaign is asking people to donate money to fuel the campaign. Spending in campaigns at all levels of politics is crucial in gaining name recognition and recruiting the best staff.

Incumbents are usually already better known than challengers. And incumbents almost always have a built-in advantage when it comes to raising money. Special interests and political action committees want access and they reward incumbents who give it. They'll reward challengers, too, yet only if the challengers have a serious chance of winning.

Politicians learn to ask large numbers of people—including a lot of people they don't know—to contribute large sums for their races. Most people in politics dread this part of the process. They know donations make them at least psychologically in debt to people who make them. And it is not uncommon for many groups to ask candidates to fill out questionnaires as to how they will vote on key issues of great concern to those groups.

Campaigns are expensive because television ads are expensive, field staff operations are expensive, and phone banks and travel can add up as well.

Generally speaking, the candidates with the best war chests win. Personal wealth also is a factor. Members of the U.S. Senate, for example, have been disproportionally wealthy compared to their challengers, not to mention average Americans. The widely publicized spending by Nelson and Jay Rockefeller, the Kennedys, New York mayor Michael Bloomberg, New Jersey governor Jon Corzine, and former eBay executive Meg Whitman are just the tip of the iceberg. Bloomberg, for example, spent over $100 million of his own wealth to get reelected as New York City mayor in 2009. Corzine spent over $60 million, mostly his own money, to win the governorship in New Jersey. The 2008 Obama campaign for the White House cost more than $1 billion.

The 2008 Obama campaign ran on several idealistic issues, but it deliberately rejected federal funds for the general election that year because it knew that its phenomenal Internet fundraising machine would raise far more funds and outgun Obama's rival John McCain. The Obama campaign marshaled its money carefully and spent lavishly in battleground states.

Lyndon Johnson's rise to majority leader in the U.S. Senate is closely correlated with his ability to raise a lot of money, usually from Texas gas and oil friends or similar deep-pocket allies. His biographers report he could always find an extra several thousand dollars to help a colleague who was in a contested race back home. Eventually, Johnson had plenty of IOUs to cash in as he competed for Senate leadership positions.[37]

The process of raising large sums of money is a compromising if not corrupting one. It is the reason why many people refuse to enter the profession, or retire from it early. Hubert Humphrey, a reform mayor of Minneapolis, an unusually creative U.S. senator and a two-time loser of presidential elections, learned firsthand on multiple occasions how important campaign contributions are. He lost to John F. Kennedy in two critical 1960 presidential primaries when the Kennedy family wealth overwhelmed him.

Humphrey sums up the harsh realities of fundraising this way:

> Campaign financing is a curse. It's the most disgusting, demeaning, disenchanting, debilitating experience of a politician's life. It stinks. It's lousy. I just can't tell you how much I hate it. I've had to break off in the middle of trying to make

> a decent, honorable campaign and go up to somebody's parlor or to a room and say "Gentlemen, and ladies, I'm desperate, you've got to help me."
> ... And you see people—a lot of them you don't want to see. And they look at you, and you sit there and you talk to them and tell them what you're for and you need help and, out of the twenty-five who have gathered, four will contribute. And most likely one of them is in trouble and is somebody you shouldn't have had a contribution from.[38]

Bribery and kickback scandals in Louisiana, New Jersey, Illinois, and New York, as well as Republican lobbyist Jack Abramoff's conviction, are a warning to all politicians and a commentary on the fine line between a contribution and illegal activity. The constant need for fundraising in this age of the "permanent campaign" is the dark underbelly of American politics.

Politicians who decide to retire voluntarily say that one of the reasons was that they feared the constant fundraising was making them into someone they could no longer respect.[39] The challenge for all candidates is how to win without proving they are unworthy of winning.

The Separation-of-Brain-and-State Factor

Politicians not only clash with factions in their own and rival parties, and with the press, but they are also regularly subjected to sharp criticism and rebuke from intellectuals. So much so that there is often a veritable separation of brain and state. An intellectual is a person who enjoys ideas and values, thinks about them, talks about them, worries about them, breaks them down, and builds them back up in different recombinations. In a larger sense, intellectuals connect ideas in order to build models and theories about the meaning of life, the universe, truth, beauty, and justice.

An intellectual is also, in part, a philosopher, a lover of truth and knowledge, someone interested in ideas for the love of wisdom. Intellectuals question conventional assumptions and view things in the longer, higher, and wider sense of "truth" and "justice." Philosophers also regularly assign themselves the responsibility to speak truth to power, expose lies, fight, or at least disdain political and social orthodoxy.

Intellectuals commonly disparage many of the required practices of politics: compromise, pragmatism, bargaining, cunning, manipulation, and the endless squabbling and deliberation that make up politics. Shakespeare set the tone with his epithet of the "scurvy politician" in *King Lear* (Act 4, Scene 6) and again in *Hamlet* (Act 5, Scene 1)—"A politician ... one that would circumvent God."[40] Henry Adams wrote that nobody in politics could be trusted, and he contemptuously satirized the American politician in *Democracy: An American Novel.*[41] Henry David Thoreau wrote that what is called politics "is comparatively so superficial and inhuman, that, practically, I have never fairly recognized it concerns me at all."[42]

The poet Shelley self-servingly claimed that "poets are the unacknowledged legislators of the world."[43] "Writers legislate the interior world, they tell us the secret meanings of places and things as well as our morally immense human secrets," writes E. L. Doctorow. "We writers may be unacknowledged as legislators, but the politicians hold no lifetime office as we do, they rise and fall and their works crumble, and as it turns out, the truth is more likely to inhere in literature."[44] At their best, intellectual critics are a shadow or opposition government. The task of the artist and writer, in Solzhenitsyn's words, is to sense more keenly than other citizens the harmony and beauty of the world, and the outrage man and his governments have done to it, and poignantly let people know.

The world of prophets, poets, and philosophers is often at odds with that of political practitioners. The pursuit of new ideas, new ideals, and knowledge for its own sake invariably brings the intellectual into personal and professional conflict with the political mainstream. Politicians for their part typically dismiss academics and poets as unrealistic theorists preoccupied, if not obsessed, with the world as it should or might be and largely ignorant of the world as it is.

Yes, like everyone else, intellectuals can be vain, corruptible, and sometimes misguided. But ideas matter. Ideas are powerful regardless of whether they are right or wrong.

Thus, a partial separation of brain and state inevitably persists. Politicians prize loyalty, gradualism, and realism. Artists and philosophers prize detachment, skepticism, idealism, truth, and courage, and are averse if not allergic to pragmatism and compromise.

Politicians as well as the public need the ideas that intellectuals, inventors, and experts generate. So also intellectuals and specialists of every kind need politicians who provide the indispensable brokerage function of defining public purpose and pragmatically mobilizing people and resources to address public policy problems.

A politician can be an intellectual yet this is seldom the case. An intellectual can on occasion participate actively in the public arena, yet this is usually a temporary activity. But a healthy constitutional society needs both a vital intellectual community and as many "public intellectuals" or "public policy intellectuals" as possible, as well as vital and conscientious professional politicians. This is yet another of the checks and balances in modern society, and it is all part of the broadly dispersed leadership that characterizes our times.

Politicians Regularly Learn That Ours Is a System of Broadly Dispersed Leadership

Innovative policy leadership seldom originates from those in high elected offices. The same is true in most states and businesses. Ideas and calls for change come from all kinds of places and, not uncommonly, from unlikely places.

New ideas come from experiments in states, cities, or other nations, from research breakthroughs, from think-tank research, from enterprising legislators and their committee staffs who are always on the prowl for new measures, from interest groups, from political and grassroots social movements, from rebels and mavericks, and sometimes from the young (think Google, Facebook, and Teach for America).

Elected officials and their aides are agents who consciously serve pluralities and majorities. They have fought to win elections by appealing in broad terms to as many groups and sectors as possible. Candidates for the White House and other high offices view their campaigns more as strategic fights to win broad-based support and less as occasions to spell out in any great detail the vital policy initiatives needed in the next decade. In a sense, too, we never know what problems elected leaders will have to face specifically; thus we elect leaders who seem competent and trustworthy and let them deal with policy dilemmas as the situation demands.

Breakthrough ideas, as noted, seldom come from the top of the establishment. "No sophisticated student of contemporary American policy making," writes Nelson Polsby, "believes that policies normally spring fully formed from the overtaxed brow of the President or even from his immediate entourage."[45]

Major policy change often takes place over a lengthy period, and sometimes it seems as though the White House is the last to learn about the pending change. This is in part because we have created a presidency that is necessarily a brokerage institution: it waits for other groups, individuals, and institutions to take the lead. The White House responds to ideas and suggestions for change, yet usually not until such ideas or proposals have gathered substantial support; civil rights, health insurance reform, gay rights, and climate change regulations are examples.

Does this mean presidents and similar national leaders are followers more than they are leaders? Ironically, this is often the case. This is not to say they can't offer or exercise leadership. Presidents exercise leadership in emergency situations (although not all of them do so decisively or prudently) and often in secretive diplomatic and national security initiatives. Presidents can also assist those who advocate policy innovation. By their tone and example they can nurture, or dampen, a national debate and in doing so can often expand or contract public support for an idea whose time has yet to come.

There have been presidents who have surprised people by their tenacious advocacy of pet causes: Theodore Roosevelt's preserving national forests or Reagan's infatuation with the Strategic Defense System. Still, most of the time presidents are cautious. They respond to national yearnings and movements; they rarely invent initiatives. They fear being in advance of their time. They are preoccupied with appearing prudent, practical, sensible, and effective. Hence they act upon ideas for which they can gain congressional passage, public support, or bureaucratic compliance. In effect they spend political capital and use their personal leverage at the margins, to lift a cause over the threshold of acceptability, yet mainly when it is almost there.

Presidents Cleveland, Harrison, and McKinley, for example, were clearly not leaders of the grand women's suffrage movement of their day. Presidents from Hoover to Kennedy were hardly civil rights leaders. Policy leadership and incubation are always going on throughout the nation, often in activist and vigorous ways.[46]

Lincoln is a somewhat harder case. Yet Lincoln's prudence rather than boldness and his political dissembling rather than intellectual or moral leadership are well documented. Even his African American admirer, Frederick Douglass, portrays Lincoln as at best a reluctant mediator between the inflamed insurrectionists and the impatient, demanding abolitionists.

> He was preeminently the white man's President, entirely devoted to the welfare of white men. He was ready and willing at any time during the first years of his administration to deny, postpone, and sacrifice the rights of humanity in the colored people to promote the welfare of the white people of this country....
>
> Our faith in him was often taxed and strained to the utmost.... When he tarried long in the mountain; when he strangely told us that we were the cause of the war; when he still more strangely told us that we were to leave the land in which we were born; when he refused to employ our arms in defense of the Union.[47]

Douglass, who in many ways was the Martin Luther King Jr. of his day, was enormously frustrated by the way Lincoln groveled before the foul curse of slavery. Yet Douglass appreciated that the often lonely and melancholy Lincoln was constantly assailed by slaveholders, by abolitionists, by people wanting peace at any price, by those who wanted a more ruthless prosecution of the war, by those who wanted it to be a war of abolition, by those upset when it became a war of abolition, and on and on. "He was often wounded in the house of his friends," Douglass observed. "Reproaches came thick and fast upon him from within and from without, and from opposite quarters."[48]

Significant changes in national policies as a rule come between elections. There are exceptions, but most social, educational, and domestic political breakthroughs are nurtured by policy activists or professional experts at the neighborhood, city, and statewide levels long before they attract solid backing from state and national leaders. This is as true for issues of policy approaches advanced by the political right as by the political left.

Thus, the suffragettes won support around the country in places as unlikely as Wyoming and Colorado before succeeding at the national level. The same has been true for abolitionists, civil rights reformers, consumer and environmental protection advocates, and property tax reformers.

Presidents and other national leaders are pragmatists, cautious and ever fearful of rocking the boat or going outside the traditional boundaries on most policy issues.

Top elected officials have critically important roles to play. They can lead and their leadership makes a difference. But they rarely provide the kind of cutting-edge idea leadership that prophets, poets, rebels, and movement organizers can and do provide. Nor should they. A movement or reform should pass the trial stages at lower levels before national implementation.

A Framework for Understanding the Many Stages and Roles of Political Leadership[49]

Policy ideas usually go through a series of stages prior to their gaining acceptance by top elected officials. To borrow a metaphor from the theater, policy change typically requires leadership in at least three distinct phases. In Act I, policy ideas are formulated; in Act II, they are spread and support for them is mobilized; in Act III, power brokers modify the ideas and gradually intervene to oversee their enactment and implementation.

Russian playwright Anton Chekhov once suggested that playgoers should watch for the gun on the wall in Act I. If there is a gun on the wall in Act I, he predicted, it is highly likely to go off in Act III. This metaphorical warning is

Table 8.1 Illustrative Roles and Jobs of Act I, II, and III Leaders

Act I	Act II	Act III
Agitators, disrupters	Consciousness raisers	Power brokers
Rebels, dissidents	Coalition builders	Office holders
Crowd gatherers	Alliance educators	Elected officials
Inventors, idea people	Lobbyists, mobilizers	Government advisers
Policy prophets	Policy advocates	Policy announcers
Movement founders	Movement organizers	Political party leaders

similarly apt for students of political and policy leadership. For we are usually insufficiently attentive to what goes on in the "off Broadway" phases of policy evolution. The storybook myths of heroic or failed presidential leadership too often focus on Act III leaders and assume, wrongly, that Act III leaders perform just about all the leadership that occurs. Such oversimplification is misleading and wrong.

Innovative discoveries in a whole variety of fields often come from the edge, or fringes, of a particular field rather than emerging from the mainstream. Virtually all organizations, and most nation-states, begin with an infusion of new ideas and ideals; but as they gradually progress from Act I to Act III status, they rigidify and become less open to new ideas or innovations. When this happens the breakthroughs are more likely to come from outside the orthodox leadership and conventional paradigms of the day.

"It is precisely the ability to perceive change when most of one's contemporaries are still unable to do so that would enable a leader to take advantage of new opportunities as soon as they arise," writes economist Albert Hirschman. In such situations, a leader often appears to create such opportunities single-handedly.[50]

In the American Revolutionary period, it was people like Sam Adams, Patrick Henry, and Tom Paine who saw need for change, agitated, and rebelled in classic Act I behavior. They gathered crowds, gave impassioned addresses, and stirred things up as they performed the indispensable catalyst role in igniting the Revolutionary movement.

Yet, the talents needed in Act I activities are different from those required for implementing the cause, or governing, or staying in office and protecting the gains later on. Agitation and mobilization necessarily give way to leaders of the struggle (in the Revolution's case, to the Washingtons and Jeffersons) and to those who build the foundations for the new order, exemplified by the work of Alexander Hamilton, John Adams, and James Madison.

Act I Leadership

Some historians have suggested what might be called a "crank" theory of political change, suggesting it is the cranks and disrupters on the fringes who come up with the novel ideas or inventions that elude the mainstream experts. The cranks or rebels, working on the edge of a field, do not have the boundary constraints leaders in the mainstream have. Since they are not burdened with the "conventional wisdom" of the day, they are less biased against new, different, or revolutionary ideas. Those who view new evidence through old paradigms are less likely to understand the true nature or implications of changing conditions.

Also, since they are not inhibited by the same paradigms as the experts, they see things insiders do not see.[51]

The process of inventing new paradigms and the cycle of new discoveries and their acceptance by the mainstream relates closely to the theory of Act I, II, and III leaders and the way in which innovations, policy change, and major political shifts are brought into operation.

Act I leaders are dreamers, visionaries, rebels, heretics, and creative catalysts who initiate, invent, and innovate. They rarely hold public office. They are the people who question the status quo and reject prevailing paradigms. Often it is simply the discovery that "hey, we don't have to accept things as they are; we can do it our way." They have an outsider approach and can see what is fresh or valuable in the things others take for granted. Act I types, precisely because they do not have responsibilities of running large-scale systems, are measurably less inhibited in taking risks. They are blessed with the flexibility to reason, to explore, to question, to protest, and possibly to discover new ideas and thereby provide the basis for new movements.

Living or existing on the edge, Act I types do not have to adhere to the constraints of the orthodox establishment. Act I people often exist, at least initially, in leaderless groups. They promote visions that challenge prevailing norms. Yet having these iconoclastic visions accepted by the mainstream depends to varying degrees on whether Act II leaders will emerge, with quite different skills, to lobby and build movements that will advocate and advance the ideas introduced by the Act I types.

Act I rebels are continually struggling to make our society live up to its ideals of freedom, social justice, or productivity. They often do what the rest of us would like to do but seldom dare to do. The rebels fight not only for the relief of fellow citizens but also for integrity and authenticity. These Act I types appeal, usually with passion, to our moral ideals and point out the inconsistencies between our ideals and our practices.

In the case of the nineteenth-century civil rights movement, Act I leaders were angry abolitionists and insurrectionists who believed everyone should immediately be granted equal rights under the law, regardless of their race. Thomas Paine, William Lloyd Garrison, Nat Turner, and John Brown were not concerned about majority public opinion. They believed they knew what was right and this was what mattered. "He was not one to be affected by the opinion others had of him," Charles Madison writes of Garrison. "He pursued his destined course with an inflexible will that made him, like the prophets of old, the scourge and conscience of his generation."[52] Garrison saw himself as a renouncer of lies and a restorer of truth.

In the case of the environmental movement, Act I leadership is illustrated in the writings of the late Edward Abbey, especially in his novel *The Monkey*

Wrench Gang (1975). Abbey became a cult figure for radical environmentalists who believed we should keep things the way they used to be. This meant fighting development on most fronts. Walt Whitman's aphorism "Resist much, obey little" became their motto. The idea of "monkey wrenching" was to blow up Glen Canyon Dam, a structure Abbey believed ruined a wonderfully pristine stretch of the Colorado River's most scenic canyons. "He had the soul of a true believer and the stinger of a scorpion in defending a natural, free, unmanaged, unmanhandled wilderness of his chosen country," wrote Wallace Stegner in a letter read at Abbey's memorial. "He was a red-hot moment in the conscience of the country, and I suspect the half-life of his intransigence will turn out to be comparable to that of uranium."[53]

Abbey's writings have inspired eco-minded terrorists to blow up John Deere tractors at development sites, place steel spikes in redwood trees to prevent sawing them, and dynamite dam projects.

The earliest suffragettes, who voted when it was illegal and submitted to arrest and jail terms, were also activists in Act I.[54] The early activities of Howard Jarvis in the 1960s before he became known as the father of the California Proposition 13 tax revolt measure illustrate yet another Act I example.[55] The populist organizers of coal miners in the 1880s qualify as well, as does Cindy Sheehan, an outraged mother of a U.S. soldier killed in Iraq who led vigils against President George W. Bush in protest of that war. The iconic Che Guevara served as an Act I "soldier" in at least a handful of Latin American countries. Father Dan Berrigan performed in Act I in his early protests of the Vietnam War. Tea Party activists and the Occupy Wall Street activists who call themselves the "99 percenters" like to see theirs as authentic, grassroots, leaderless resistance movements.[56]

In case after case, Act I types become defiant and reject the way things are. They dream dreams of how things might be. They are outsiders and willingly take risks in order to protest the status quo and share their visions of change. They transform themselves into voices of protest. They adopt the role of agitator, crusader, populist, or rebel in defiance of an order they refuse to accept. They are hell-bent on stirring things up in hopes of unlocking new possibilities.

Just as most entrepreneurial business start-ups fail and just as most new inventions fail to be turned into successful products, so also not every Act I leader or cause succeeds or deserves to succeed. To say that major breakthroughs often come from the fringes is not to say that every crank is right and should "win." Cranks and prophets of all sorts also work on behalf of radical causes that often are, and deserve to be, lost causes. "Most daring new ideas are foolish or dangerous and appropriately rejected or ignored," says Stanford University's James G. March. "So while it may be true that great geniuses are usually heretics, heretics are rarely great geniuses."[57]

Note, too, that Act I leaders often pay dearly for being in advance of their times. Countless civil rights leaders from Nat Turner and John Brown to Malcolm X were lynched, executed, or assassinated. And for every Solzhenitsyn there were thousands of others, talented and untalented, who were left behind to rot in Soviet prison camps. The celebrated American physician Jack Kevorkian, champion of physician-assisted suicide, spent nearly a decade in prison. Others have paid the price of ostracism and rejection by their families and communities as payment for their agitations. Act I leaders often operate in ways that the majority considers reckless. However much we may later grow to admire what these visionaries have done, most of us gladly assign ourselves much more conventional, conservative, and comfortable roles and responsibilities.

Still, many social, economic, and political breakthroughs have welled up from Act I policy prophets before they get attention in the more publicized and more "accepted" Act II stage of policy leadership evolution. A final note on Act I types. Some of these Act I activists and their friends mistakenly consider themselves "leaderless" groups, but this is because they wrongly equate leadership with formal authority, office holding, and fancy titles. Leaders emerge in every act.

Act II Leadership

The handiwork and legacy of the Act I types, or some modified version of them, are typically picked up in Act II by mobilizers, organizers, lobbyists, activist researchers, and educators with an interest in policy. Act II people are Susan B. Anthony, Martin Luther King Jr., and U2's Bono. They and countless lesser-known individuals like them are the alliance builders who bring pressure on the elected legislators and political establishments of their day.

Their goals are seldom accomplished in short periods. Such efforts usually span years, decades, and sometimes generations. Act II leaders seek to educate the public and to raise consciousness by demonstrating the validity of an idea, no matter how long it will take.

Popular writers occasionally perform some aspects of the Act II role. Thus, Harriet Beecher Stowe's *Uncle Tom's Cabin* aroused and rallied the abolitionist cause just as it educated and focused the public's consciousness on the racism of her day. Rachel Carson's eloquent *Silent Spring* likewise educated thousands of activist citizens who in turn would mobilize, lobby, and protest in the ranks of the environmental movement. Similarly, in different ways, the writings of Milton Friedman and Ralph Nader helped to spur on tax reformers and proconsumer activists in the 1960s, '70s, and '80s.

Act II leaders seldom run for political office; they seek to change the thinking of both officials and electorates. They understand what a veteran member of Congress once told us: "Don't rely on Congress to start anything." And they know the truth, too, that most elected officials are preoccupied with getting reelected and listening attentively to their past and prospective campaign contributors.[58]

Understanding that few bold measures begin at the top, Act II leaders know that few Act III people have original ideas. This is in large part due to the structure of American politics and the incentive system that rewards caution and low-risk behavior. The power of the Act II types lies in their ability to swell the ranks, and they do this by arousing people and convincing them of the validity of their visions.

They are intermediaries who, though not exactly part of the mainstream, are nonetheless savvy enough about the ways of the establishment to win converts to their cause. They can translate fresh approaches and new values into at least tentative propositions that will be entertained if not entirely embraced by top power brokers.

The Act II leader is the coalition builder, the one who takes the ideas or innovations of the Act I types, sees their potential, and attempts to make them into a viable force, a movement. The Act II leader is, in a sense, the mobilizer or coalition builder, the one who takes the inventor's (or crank's) discovery from the workbench to the workplace and attempts to market it to the society at large.

In the case of the American Revolution, it took military leaders like George Washington and public relations alliance-building geniuses like Thomas Jefferson to put the revolutionary spirit of the disorganized Act I types into a galvanized, strategic movement that could rally the new states and mobilize them in battle.

In the case of the civil rights movement, it would take a legion of people like Frederick Douglass, Thurgood Marshall, Rosa Parks, Ella Baker, Martin Luther King Jr., Andrew Young, John Lewis, and others to build and sustain a nationwide civil rights movement that eventually would win multiple legislative and court victories in the 1950s.[59]

There have been plenty of conservative or libertarian populists on the Right who served in the Act II tradition. Russell Kirk, William Buckley and his *National Review,* anti-ERA leader Phyllis Schlafly, moral majority organizer Jerry Falwell, and Focus on the Family leader James Dobson have crusaded, agitated, educated, and organized on behalf of conservative principles and platforms.

Act II types often defy facile Left and Right labels. Huey Long and Father Charles Coughlin, the famed radio priest of the 1930s, were on the Left, Right, and center depending on the issue.[60] Candy Lightner, who founded Mothers Against Drunk Driving, illustrates another type of Act II activist organizer. Her thirteen-year-old daughter, Cari, was killed by a drunken driver on a quiet street near Sacramento as she walked to a school carnival. Lightner was told by a highway patrol officer that it was doubtful that the driver who killed her daughter would spend any time in jail. "That was just the way the system worked," he said. Lightner was so furious she decided to organize. She became, in her own words, an "angry, raging mother" who stormed her state capitol with picket signs. She later helped build MADD into an organization with hundreds of chapters around the world.[61]

Rock star Bono of the Irish band U2 became an indefatigable consciousness raiser for debt relief and financial aid for struggling African countries. He relished the role of being an agitator and coalition-building lobbyist on behalf of the impoverished Africans. And he was unusually effective in using his celebrity status to lecture and exhort Tony Blair, Bill Clinton, George Bush, Barack Obama, and their cabinet heads to take up his issue.[62]

The Roosevelt (FDR) and Kennedy presidencies are often criticized for becoming conventional power brokers and for succumbing to the traditional practices of Act III office holders rather than serving as bold innovators challenging the established orthodoxies of the day. The disappointment is generally one of yearning for Act I– and Act II–style leadership from an Act III office.[63]

If Act I types are rebels and revolutionaries, Act II types are best characterized as evolutionaries. Act III types are pragmatic power brokers and incremental fixers.

Act III Leadership

Act III leaders, the epitome and very symbol of the mainstream establishment, take the once-radical ideas of Act I leaders, now softened, refined, and modified as well as vigorously championed by those in Act II, and refashion those ideas in politically achievable and acceptable ways.

Political leaders in Act III strike the bargains and gauge public and legislative sentiment for what is doable. Possessing insider skills, status, and credibility, they formulate new approaches that can be merged with existing policies and standard operating procedures. "We nudge it along. This is the real world. Things are complex," a high-ranking national party operative told us.[64]

Act III people are either elected officials or hold high appointive, advisory positions. They regularly operate under the glare of public attention. Consequently, Act III leaders are highly sensitive, perhaps too sensitive, to what the public thinks and wants. Act III types are poll readers and know that on a certain range of issues they must follow public opinion more than they can mold it.

Act III leaders spend considerable time trying to understand their followers. This, as Garry Wills points out, "is the time-consuming aspect of leadership." And it helps explain why great thinkers and artists are rarely the leaders of others.[65]

Officials performing in Act III typically talk about their responsibility and accountability to those who elected them. They view themselves as agents, as delegates, as coordinators on behalf of the larger public; and they translate their responsibility to their constituents as an incentive to be cautious. This is in marked contrast to Act I types who feel responsibility primarily to their conscience, to principles, and to the truth.

Act III leaders must balance and reconcile competing claims about how best to serve the public interest. They become preoccupied, too, with what is doable and with the pragmatic adjustments they believe the system needs.

Act III types typically view Act I and II types as adversaries, and as irresponsible. "Who elected them?" they ask. Paradoxically, the heavy set of expectations on Act III leaders to act responsibly and to serve the public places constraints on them as agents of innovation. Moreover, Act III people live in a world where they rarely have the time and energy to think about fresh ideas. They react to events. They respond to crises, movements, and the urgencies they find in their "in baskets." As one top Obama strategist put it, "In Washington, D.C. election day is every day. Every day officials move up or down in various rankings."[66]

The most serious charge against many of the Act III types is that they are simply horse traders, bargainers, or fixers. They are often pictured as unprincipled, moving in whatever direction the wind is blowing, as opportunists willing to sell out to the highest bidder in money or votes. This charge is overstated yet a core truth remains. The American political system, in common with most democracies, has so much built-in conflict, so many representatives of competing or warring constituencies, so much tension between liberty and equality, between community and efficiency, between individualism and fairness, and so many checks and balances that higher-level adjustment and compromise are essential.

Political office holders are invariably criticized for not providing leadership for all scenes, acts, or seasons. On the other hand, a more realistic appreciation of how leadership works in a constitutional democracy should lead to an understanding that most highly visible elected officials necessarily operate predominantly in the mid–Act II to late Act III range. They are, far more than we appreciate, dependent on both their dependents and timing. They are necessarily dependent on other types of leaders to generate the inventions and the movements that help a nation renew itself.

Act III leaders may strike us as unprincipled when, for reasons of political survival, they claim they must refrain from taking sides on controversial issues until it becomes clear to them that they will lose more votes by straddling the fence or being labeled indecisive than they will lose by taking a stand. Thus most Act III types, in their efforts to avoid risk, regularly look and act as if they are presiders rather than leaders.

Leadership, as performed by the Act III leader, is interpretation. Such a leader continually reads the common pulse. An Act III leader's attention is fixed more on relationships with constituents than on grand ideas or ideals.

Leadership in America is broadly dispersed and much of the leadership we need—on many occasions—is not leadership from the top, but adversarial, movement, group, and entrepreneurial grassroots leadership from outside governmental and other establishment organizations. FDR and Lincoln both knew this. Lincoln, for example, very much understood that his Act III leadership was informed, inspired, and enhanced in many, many ways by the abolitionists and by "leaders" like Harriet Beecher Stowe and Frederick Douglass.

Those who look for charismatic leaders should appreciate that charisma, when found, is more likely found in Act I and Act II. Gandhi, Martin Luther King Jr., and Mandela are examples of the appeal. Complex institutions and charisma are often incompatible. To be sure, there can be theater and drama surrounding celebrity—personalities such as JFK, Margaret Thatcher, or Ronald Reagan. Still, most United Nations chiefs, presidents, and other leaders in developed nations are prototypical Act III office holders. Jimmy Carter and George H. W. Bush are prime examples.

Act I leaders come in all varieties, but they are sometimes introverted and highly intuitive in their dispositions. Act II types are a mixed collection of introverts and extroverts, yet lean more in the extrovert direction. Act III leaders are extroverts and pragmatists—typically preoccupied with their relationships, images, and consensus.

Act I leaders reject the conventional ends and means or practical goals and methods of the day. They are, like Socrates and Joan of Arc, willing to die for their beliefs. Act II types accept most of the ends but reject existing means. They are more moderate in their taking of risks; they may be willing to fail yet seldom want to put their life on the line. Act III leaders, in contrast, accept both the ends and means of the existing order. Further, they are risk averse and are constantly concerned about losing power, losing office, and losing face.

All of us have Act I, II, and III impulses (and capabilities) from time to time. We generally accentuate patterns that fit into one of the acts. The Reverend Jesse Jackson over his career performed in all acts, although we commonly label him an Act II star. He performed Act I functions when he was an outspoken young lieutenant in the Chicago civil rights movement, served as an Act II organizer of Operation Push, and had brushes with Act III in 1984 and again in 1988 when he sought the Democratic Party's nomination for president. He had to broaden his coalition, sometimes calling it the Rainbow Coalition, however, as he sought higher office, which required him to moderate, tone down, and redefine his formerly radical appeal. Nelson Mandela, as discussed earlier, was a rare and notable leader in all three acts.

Examples discussed here are almost exclusively from government and politics, yet the Act I, II, and III process also takes place in businesses and nonprofit organizations. Some business leaders are terrific at founding an organization but become too restless or disruptive once their company becomes well established. Bill Gates at Microsoft moved somewhat gracefully through all three business stages. His partner, Paul Allen, left early in Act II. The now-legendary Steve Jobs flourished in Act I but was literally forced out of his own company in Act II, and remarkably came back in Act III to reinvent and reenergize a dysfunctional Apple. He admitted that innovators are not necessarily the best people to run large corporations.[67]

Garry Wills aptly suggests that our disapproval of Act III politicians "is misguided when it focuses on the political operator's hedging or hesitating ways." Washington, Lincoln, and FDR all obfuscated, hesitated, and compromised—and they were all devious. What seems lacking nowadays, says Wills, "is not the skills of the operator but the goal toward which those skills should, all the while, be working."[68]

Until politicians can supply an important and valid sense of mission for their skills, these skills, such as they are, "will look cheap and cheapening. It is time to rescue the good name of politics, not by renouncing the dubious means that politicians have always used, but by coming up with ends that make the means worth using."[69]

Thus, leadership in the broad sense of the term rarely happens conclusively in any one act. Important political and policy leadership is the result of activities that emerge over the course of a multistage process. Visible, popular "Meet the Press" leaders are dependent, more than they and perhaps any of us realize, on Act I and II types for ideas and new initiatives. Yet Act I and II types also depend on presidents, governors, mayors, and other Act III leaders to bring about the brokered agreements that permit breakthroughs in legislation, court decisions, or executive actions. Although we understandably yearn for heroic leaders to challenge injustice and the inevitabilities of history, leaders—especially in Act III positions—will primarily be pragmatists balancing the appeals and ideals of contending constituencies.

Transforming leadership in a democracy rarely comes from a single person or a single institution. There are countless faces of leadership in modern-day societies. Leadership is dispersed, and leaders in a constitutional democracy are dependent on colleagues and other leaders to help shape, develop, and implement the policy changes a society needs.

Political leadership—the capacity to inspire and mobilize masses of constituents—is always a public transaction played out in at least three acts. It is a shared performance in which Act I and Act II leadership is needed to make Act III possible. Those who favor progress yet are impatient with political agitation are people "who want crops without plowing up the ground ... and they want rain without thunder and lightning."[70]

Conclusion

Political leadership is among the hardest professions. It takes ambition, drive, courage, patience, self-sacrifice, and a lot of understanding of how people working through imperfect institutions can try to make good things happen.

Elected politicians frustrate us. They move cautiously. And partisanship and polarization often make even small steps seem contentious. Elected officials see little benefit in long-term solutions when their next election is a short-term consideration. That's why Act I and Act II unelected politicians have such an important role to play—to focus on what's important for all of us in the longer term.

We are tough on politicians who don't speak clearly and assertively as to what should be done. But this is what Lincoln did throughout the election of 1860. He kept his options open. Same with FDR in 1932.

We also need to appreciate that politicians occasionally need to and should change their minds. Circumstances change. Politicians learn and grow. Compromises need to be brokered. Thank goodness, for example, that Lincoln changed his position on how to deal with slavery. And that FDR changed his mind on the need to go to war in the early 1940s. And that LBJ grew to accept full civil rights for black Americans. And that Richard Nixon changed his views on dealing with China, and that Reagan changed some of his early views of the Soviet Union.

There are so many lessons politics teaches us about leadership, yet one of the most important is that we need all kinds of politicians, elected and nonelected, the cautious as well as the dreamy agents of reform; and we need them to perform in a whole variety of roles and acts that help make up the larger theater of politics we affectionately call constitutional democracy. Context, culture, and institutions matter, yet so also politicians in all acts and in every scene can matter, sometimes a lot.

Chapter Nine
What the Military Teaches Us about Leadership

> War is a matter of vital importance to the State, the province of life or death, the road to survival or ruin. It is mandatory that it be studied thoroughly.
>
> —*Sun Tzu, Chinese general*[1]

War has been a constant of the human condition since the beginning of recorded history. Civilization, democracy, and modernity haven't made much difference. Out of the last 3,500 years, according to one account, fewer than 300 years have been without a war somewhere on the planet.[2]

The study of leadership is inescapably connected to the study of wartime strategy and tactics, and to those who have commanded in battle. In perhaps no other human endeavor is leadership valued and developed more conscientiously than in the military. Military academies, war colleges, and defense universities view themselves as leadership as well as military training schools. Today's military devotes enormous energy and resources to leadership education, on the assumption that much, if not most, about leadership can be learned.[3]

In this chapter, we will focus on a few noted theorists who have written on the art and the reality of war; on several larger-than-life commanders; on three military leadership paradoxes; and on the accumulated, yet not necessarily unified, lessons that war and military leaders teach us.

We turn to four classical writers on the history of war: the Chinese general Sun Tzu (544–496 BCE), the Greek historian Thucydides (460–395 BCE), the Florentine diplomat and philosopher Niccolò Machiavelli (1469–1527), and finally, the nineteenth-century Prussian general Carl von Clausewitz (1780–1831).

Legendary Writings on the Art of War and Military Leadership

Sun Tzu: *The Art of War*

This fascinating 6,000-word manual of military preparation, strategy, and warfare is one of the world's most widely read treatises on the art of war and strategy. It was written, or so most people believe, by the Chinese general Sun Wu, who was later awarded the honorary title of Tzu (meaning "master") in recognition of his expertise and valued contributions.

His thirteen chapters distill his military insights into almost poetic maxims, doubtless influenced by a deep belief in reason and the iconic writings of Confucius. Some of Sun Tzu's injunctions strike us today as quaint. Thus, the military leader, he says, should be "serene and inscrutable." And those who do not know the position of the mountains, forests, passes, and marshes will be unable to move effectively over the terrain. Or his analogy that the strategy of proper positioning can learn from the path water takes: "moving water evades heights and hastens through lowlands.... Water follows the territory and systematically flows; the strategy follows the opponent and systematically triumphs."

Many of Sun Tzu's ideas, however, have a remarkable ring of currency, and can be found in one form or another in the writings of contemporary authors such as Peter Drucker, Tom Peters, and Jim Collins and in courses at West Point and the Naval War College. Thus, knowing oneself and self-discipline are vital. "Know the enemy and know yourself and victory is never in doubt ... [yet] when you are ignorant of the enemy but know yourself, your chances of winning or losing are equal. If ignorant of both your enemy and yourself, you are certain to be in peril in every battle." "Invincibility," Sun Tzu notes, "depends on one's self, while the vulnerability of the enemy depends on him. One has, therefore, to do all one can to ensure the first by cleverness, reason, preparation and good organization."[4]

Like Thucydides, Machiavelli, and Clausewitz who would follow, Sun Tzu is explicit on the subject of discipline. Soldiers, he says, must be kept under control by means of iron discipline. "This is the certain road to victory." And in the training of soldiers, commanders must be strict and consistent enforcers.

Sun Tzu urges his readers to capitalize on the power of paradox. Subtlety and surprise are vital. So also are deception, counterintelligence, and skilled use of illusion. "Those who have supreme skill use *strategy* to bend others without coming to conflict" and "take paths that are unexpected, and attack locations that are unprotected."

Those who know when to fight and when not to fight will be victorious, he writes. "In battle, there are not more than two methods of attack: the direct and the indirect." But, he adds, "these two in combination give rise to an endless series of maneuvers."

All warfare, he writes, is based on deception. The commander's job is to outwit and outmaneuver the enemy. A great military leader, says Sun Tzu, prepares in such a way and engages in indirect strategic approaches so that victory is achieved before the first sword is drawn.

Tactical paradox, Sun Tzu points out, is the ability to project to the enemy a contradictory view of one's position and plans. Thus:

> When capable, feign incapacity / When active, inactivity / When near, make it appear that you are far away / When far away, that you are near / Offer the enemy a bait to lure him; feign disorder and strike him / When he concentrates, prepare against him / When he is strong, avoid him / Anger his generals and confuse him / Pretend inferiority and encourage his arrogance / Keep him under a strain and wear him down / When he is unprepared, sally out when he does not expect you.[5]

And Sun Tzu celebrates mobility, surprise, flexibility, and swiftness:

> Hence, during swiftness, be like the wind / During stillness, be like the forest / During aggression, be like fire / During immobility, be like a mountain / Be as unknowable as the dark / Move like a thunderbolt.[6]

One need only remember the terms *blitzkrieg* and *shock and awe* to see Sun Tzu's ideas as still present in contemporary war strategy.

Sun Tzu recommends that defeated enemies be treated humanely in order to lessen the likelihood of future hostilities. He warns against attacks on cities and against protracted wars. He calls on commanders to earn the trust and confidence of their soldiers. If they can forge a bond with their soldiers, as if the soldiers were their sons, then together they can march effectively.

Sun Tzu telegraphed many of the leadership narratives still taught today. We know that Napoleon, Mao Zedong, and Vietnamese generals Vo Nguyen Giap and Ho Chi Minh carefully studied Sun Tzu. We know, too, that Sun Tzu's status in contemporary China remains very high and that some analysts credit him with inspiring various forms of "soft power."[7] Leadership, in sum, is courage, discipline, reliability, preparation, inspiration, and the strategic use of intelligence, paradox, deception, and surprise.

Thucydides and His *History of the Peloponnesian War*

Thucydides was born in the Athens area to an aristocratic and wealthy family. (His family owned gold mines in Thrace, and probably had ties to the royal family there.) He grew up in the golden age of Pericles, when Athens was producing so many contributions to the arts and sciences. A thriving city-state, with notable sea power and flourishing trade, Pericles' Athens was a grand experiment in democracy—at least for its property-owning and established male citizens.

But Athens was also ambitious to exert its influence and control over other islands and cities in the Aegean and Mediterranean region. Perhaps Athens wanted more grain or more trading partners. Or perhaps Athens simply wanted more power and glory.

Thucydides grew up observing Athens in all its glory and ambition. He became a citizen and, perhaps in his early thirties, a general in the Athenian military. Sent to command a fleet to aid an Athenian-controlled city on the north Aegean, he was (perhaps not his own fault) unsuccessful. A Spartan commander beat him there and forced the city to surrender. Thucydides had arrived too late and failed to protect the city.

Athens punished unsuccessful officers. It is unclear whether Thucydides was sentenced to death or merely banished in exile. In any event, he fled to Thrace, where his family had roots, and lived for the next twenty years in comfortable exile. There he wrote a brilliant history of the Peloponnesian War, the twenty-seven-year conflict between Athens and Sparta (431–404 BCE) that resulted in Athens's ignominious defeat.

Thucydides' ambitious goal was to explain why Athens and Sparta fought, what motivated them, and how the mighty Athens came to ruinous defeat after its misguided and poorly led Sicilian campaign. Along the way, he provides a remarkably detached and objective analysis of political and military leadership.

He made clear to his readers that his work was less aimed at his contemporaries than intended as a work with insights and lessons "for all time." Thucydides wrote because he believed what brought about this war and subsequently the end of Athenian democracy was full of lessons for later generations. He was right.

He did extensive interviewing. He personally knew many of the Athenian leaders. He gathered documents (such as they were in those days), and he traveled to many of the regions, probably including Sicily, soon after the Athenian defeat there.

Historian Edith Hamilton believes Thucydides accurately pinpoints the underlying reason wars are fought. "The motive power was greed, that strange passion for power and possession which no power and no possession satisfy. Power, Thucydides wrote, or its equivalent, wealth, created the desire for more power, more wealth." She continues:

> The Athenians and the Spartans fought for one reason only—because they were powerful, and therefore were compelled to seek more power.... The war had nothing to do with differences in ideas or with considerations of right or wrong.

> Is democracy right and the rule of the few over the many wrong? To Thucydides the question would seem an evasion of the issue. There was no right power. Power, whoever wielded it, was evil, the corrupter of men.[8]

Thucydides' history ends six or seven years before the war ends, perhaps because he died before he was able to complete it or perhaps some of his writing disappeared. Still, his analysis of effective and ineffective leadership is striking. He plainly admires Pericles and gives credit to both Spartan and Athenian military leaders and their strategies where they are effective. But he is also highly critical of men like Alcibiades who misled Athens and failed in military strategy.

The most important contribution Thucydides makes is his realistic view about the motives and the machinations of those involved in this protracted war. He is widely regarded today as the father of objective history as well as the father of realpolitik, an interpretive school of international relations based on hard-nosed politics. He dissects the realities of power and force and gets to the heart of hypocrisy and immorality in war. His rich narrative of how the Athenians coerced the little island of Melos to submit to their authority is illustrative.

The Melians wanted to remain neutral between Athens and Sparta. Athens found this unacceptable and rejected any request for justice, fairness, or compassion. The Athenians basically said: do what we say, or else! "Right, as the world goes, is only in question between equals in power, while the strong do what they can and the weak suffer what they must." Athens, home of democracy and enlightenment, captured the little island of Melos, killed the men, and enslaved the rest of the populace.

Thucydides also writes of the foolhardy Athenian expedition to Syracuse, where the once mighty naval power of Athens was slowly but surely humiliated in devastating defeat. He shares insight after insight about the perils of divided leadership, the lessons of inadequate military preparation, and the vulnerability of a democracy at war without competent and effective political leadership at home.

Implicitly, Thucydides is a precursor to Machiavelli who wrote many centuries later. For despite his praise of Pericles and his celebration of Pericles' funeral oration (describing the virtues and glories of Athens), for Thucydides, man is incurably power seeking, and this—and related hubris or selfishness—often lies at the heart of all human relations and is the cause of war.

Echoing Sun Tzu, Thucydides writes that the strength of an army lies in strict discipline and undeviating obedience to its officers. The more militaristic and hierarchical Sparta had these values engrained in its culture. The more democratic and individualistic Athens did not; and as the war dragged on, Athenians became more divided, more contentious, and less unified.

Thucydides' *History* captures the brutality of war and the consequences it has on people, politics, and the fate of the polity. Thucydides dissects the ways political and military leadership are intertwined and dependent on each other. It has become a bible for American neoconservatives and continues to shape the study of war, military leadership, and the temptations of imperial reach. Thucydides set out to write a work that "would last forever" and thus far it has.[9]

Machiavelli: *The Art of War*

Niccolò Machiavelli, the famous Florentine, is best known for *The Prince* and to a lesser extent for *Discourses (on the First Ten Books of Titus Livius)*, which is a defense of the principles of republican government.

His *Art of War* may be less famous but it deserves attention, for it was in some ways the first *modern* classic on military science.

Machiavelli was never a general and had no military training. But much of the fourteen years when he served Florence as a senior official were devoted to military and defense matters. He wrote state papers on military policy and had a career-long preoccupation with overseeing military operations, planning, fortifications, and with helping to recruit conscripts, mercenaries, and regular militia. Indeed, he often found himself in the middle of his poorly funded government and its quarrelsome generals.

He was an astute scholar of Roman and Greek history, especially Roman history. *The Art of War* (1521) pulls together what he considered the best practices of the ancients along with his own understanding of political-military requirements. Significant portions of *The Prince* are also devoted to military matters, such as how to act in captured territories, the role of mercenaries, fortresses, and so on. Indeed, in *The Prince*, he suggests that the study of war should be the top priority for a prince. A prince, he says, should consider the occasional peace as merely a breathing time between wars, a chance to train and plan for the next military involvement.

Machiavelli's ideal commander, as outlined in *The Art of War*, is capable of constantly improvising novel tactics and strategies to deceive and overpower an enemy. "War for him is war, a no-holds-barred contest," writes political scientist Neal Wood. "Victory is the aim to which all other considerations on the battlefield must be subordinated. Behavior toward the enemy is not subject to common moral considerations. Every type of trickery and violence is legitimate when used against the enemy."[10]

Machiavelli was not as scientific as later Prussian analysts would become. He was probably too admiring of the Roman military successes. And some of the military ventures he advised proved disastrous, although his government's eventual strategic reconquest of Pisa was a success. In any event, later commanders, like Frederick the Great and Napoleon, turned to Machiavelli as a military thinker of broad and instructive principles. Machiavelli's ideas are both explicitly and implicitly found in much of Clausewitz's writings on military leadership.

Here are his central prescriptions:

- Leadership is the key to victory; the ability to exact willing and devoted obedience is the test of leadership.
- A military operation must be secretly and meticulously planned upon the best intelligence that can be collected about the enemy and the terrain.
- A clearly defined and rationally devised strategy requires the choice of techniques for implementation that are adequate for the prevailing conditions and that are flexible enough to be changed with changing conditions.
- The initial blow should be delivered with rapidity and energy at the decisive moment, in as economic and concentrated a fashion possible, and at the enemy's weakest point.
- Throughout the operation, the advantages of surprise and deception must be fully exploited.
- Of all social organizations, an army requires the greatest precision and the greatest discipline.
- The ideal general should be a cool, rational, calculating individual with enormous self-discipline. He cannot fail to use force and deception when necessary ... but must never lust for blood or relish cruelty for its own sake.[11]

The Art of War is written as a dialogue among friends discussing war and its requirements, a device that Plato and many of the ancients had used.

Here are additional precepts from *The Art of War*:

- "Never come to an engagement until you have inspired your men with the courage and see them in good order and eager to fight, nor hazard a battle until they seem confident of victory."[12]
- "But what most commonly keeps an army united is the reputation of the general, that is, of his courage and good conduct; without them, neither high birth nor any sort of authority is sufficient."[13]
- "Good commanders never come to an engagement unless they are compelled to by absolute necessity, or occasion calls for it."[14]

Machiavelli devotes attention to various formations, to the role of bridges and rivers, to various military tricks, to the proper mix of infantry and cavalry, and even to the best musical instruments useful to instill courage and martial spirit.

Machiavelli's philosophy, evident in *The Art of War* and most of his other writings, is to provide for order and prevent anarchy. He eschews abstractions such as Philosopher-Kings and the idea of the "City of God." His philosophy is grounded in the psychology of men, their appetites, and their ambitions. He acknowledges the important role luck or fortune plays, but he believes in preparations and strategy as a counter to the unfolding of impersonal forces.

Machiavelli biographer Miles J. Unger cautions:

> But for all his passion on the subject, *The Art of War* has held up less well than his other major works. Despite his years organizing and provisioning the citizen militias of Florence, Machiavelli was not a professional military man, and many of his prescriptions are impractical or counterproductive. His disdain for the artillery and for engineering, as well as his preference for infantry over cavalry, derive from his study of Roman history but have little to do with the realities of Renaissance warfare, where cannon and musket were changing the dynamics of battle.[15]

The larger importance of Machiavelli's work is that in his day, as in ours, security was fundamental to the establishment of political order. A concern for military strength and military preparedness had to be the top priority for those who tried to govern. Machiavelli's belief in a military remedy for the ills of his city-state and for Italy does not provide all the answers for governance, yet the enduring connection of military and political leadership is a reality and one that Machiavelli understood.

Carl von Clausewitz: *On War*

Carl von Clausewitz (1780–1831) was the son of a retired Prussian military officer. He joined the army when he was twelve years old and spent the rest of his life as a soldier, commander, adviser, and general. He also wrote about the philosophy of war and military leadership. Indeed, his work *On War* has probably been the most widely read and debated treatise about war.

He lived in an uncommonly war-saturated period. The American Revolution against the British was going on when he was born. The French Revolution took place in his youth. The multiyear and multistage Napoleonic Wars, which he became directly engaged in, dominated his soldier years.

He was in several battles fighting against Napoleon, after one of which he was a prisoner of war for a year in France. Later he would help the combined forces of Prussia, Russia, Britain, and others defeat Napoleon during the Waterloo Campaign of 1815.

Clausewitz in many ways admired Napoleon the soldier but never Napoleon the imperialist and dictator. Clausewitz devoted most of his time between wars trying to reform Prussian military training.

He graduated from the leading military academy in his country and became a fascinating combination of fighter, theorist, reformer, and adviser. He combined ideas from his own battlefield experiences, from studying Napoleon, and from previous works such as Machiavelli's.

Clausewitz believed that having talented and courageous leaders was crucial to winning wars. He believed such leadership could be encouraged and cultivated but not necessarily taught. He stressed the essential unpredictable elements in war, saying war is a perpetual conflict with the unexpected.

Like Sun Tzu and Machiavelli before him, Clausewitz emphasized the crucial role of surprise: "It is the most important element of victory. Napoleon, Frederick II, Gustavus Adolphus, Caesar, Hannibal, and Alexander owe the brightest rays of fame to their swiftness."[16]

He also believed in the most rigorous training programs, saying that those troops who have been pushed the most, with extreme exertion and great privations, would be the hardiest and most advantaged in actual battles with their enemy.[17]

Clausewitz insists that personal courage is the first requirement of military leaders: both the courage to face personal danger and the courage to accept personal responsibility. He celebrates tenacity, firmness, strength of character, and speculates that of all the passions that can inspire the military officer in battle none "is so powerful and so constant as the longing for honor and renown." He understands that patriotism and vengeance play a role, "but they are no substitute for a thirst for fame and honor."[18]

He also favors quick, intuitive judgment and determination as more necessary than a reflective or intellectual mind.

His wide-ranging work treats the nature of war, theories and strategies of war, the need for great energy and decisive commitments of force at critical stages of a battle, the need for extensive war planning, and much more. He talks about both the importance and the severe limits of intelligence. He offers interesting distinctions between limited and absolute wars. He discusses the advantages and superiority of defensive war yet knows well that the defenders don't necessarily win.

He understands the role of nationalism and the need for civilian as well as military mobilization if a nation is serious about winning.

Clausewitz had worked closely with top Prussian and Russian political leaders and was even involved in treaty negotiations during the Napoleonic Wars. Thus, he brings to his understanding of war the realities that war and politics are inevitably interconnected. He understands that every age has its own kind of war, its own peculiar political preconceptions and aspirations.

He writes that "war is nothing more than the continuation of politics by other means." This has become a much-debated observation. But what he probably means is that war commences when peace negotiations fail, and that war is the darker, more brutal side of politics, but it is still politics—the process of bargaining as well as fighting over who gets what, when, and how.

Clausewitz seems to appreciate that there can be no purely military solution to military conflicts. And he is aware, too, of the dialectical nature of war and politics. "War, he famously proposed, was a 'remarkable trinity,' whose essential elements—primordial violence and passion, the 'free play' of chance and creativity on the battlefield, and intelligent political purpose—could never be fixed in any arbitrary relationship."[19]

War should be subordinate to political goals and regulations, yet Clausewitz knows this is always an uneasy and imperfect principle. Daniel Moran interprets Clausewitz as claiming:

> War always threatened to escape its political restraints, and often did succeed in modifying the course of policy to some extent. The violence of war and the rationality of politics [to Clausewitz] were thus theoretical opposites whose real existence was nevertheless marked not by mutual repulsion or exclusion, but by intense and continuous interaction.[20]

Clausewitz, like his predecessors, didn't get everything right. He may have been overly mesmerized by Napoleon and many of his strategies. And some of his notions of military genius are rather vague and sometimes opaque. But he hoped he was writing both a philosophical and useful work that would be of continuing value. Nearly two hundred years later, military leaders may struggle with *On War*, but they cannot and do not ignore it.[21]

Legendary Military Leaders

Space limits us here to focus on only a handful of legendary commanders. We look next at these military leaders and their battles (we will treat General George S. Patton in Chapter 10).

- Alexander the Great
- Julius Caesar
- Joan of Arc
- Napoleon Bonaparte
- U. S. Grant
- Erwin Rommel
- George S. Patton

Alexander the Great. Having a father (King Philip II of Macedonia) who was a militarily powerful and successful king and having a whole series of imported tutors, including Aristotle for at least three years, gave Alexander a head start on leadership. But so many others who have been born to power and wealth squandered their lives away. What made Alexander such a legend?

Alexander (356–323 BCE) was a talented horseman, was physically powerful, and had a charismatic bearing. Schooled in the art of war by his militarily talented father, Alexander commanded his first military expedition at the age of sixteen. Within two years, he won the Battle of Chaeronea, giving Macedonia control of most of Greece. But Alexander hungered for more—Asia Minor, then Persia.

When his father was killed, Alexander took full command of the army of Macedonia. He was twenty years old. Alexander's army consisted of pikemen who wielded the *sarissa*, a spear twice the length of the enemy's weapons. He also controlled light infantry that was highly mobile and a trained cavalry that gave Alexander the opportunity to strike hard and fast.

Alexander assembled an army of thousands and marched through Asia Minor. He was challenged by Persian naval power. Having virtually no navy of his own, Alexander engaged in a back-end maneuver, attacking the Persian port cities from land and destroying their link to land, thereby neutralizing Persia's naval advantage.

Encountering little resistance along this route into Asia Minor, Alexander marched his troops to the Granicus River (in modern-day Turkey), where he met the forces of Memnon of Rhodes. Outnumbered by the Persians and their Greek mercenaries, Alexander managed to cross the river undetected and launch a surprise attack. It was a stunning victory and allowed Alexander to march his army farther southward.

When Alexander reached Issus (the Syria of today), he was met by the main forces of the Persian army, led by King Darius III. Again Alexander was outnumbered, this time perhaps by three or four to one. Yet, Alexander went on the attack. Early efforts to breach the Persian defenses failed. All seemed lost until, in a bold move, Alexander rode to the head of his troops and made a concentrated assault directly at King Darius. The cavalry broke the Persian defenses, and Darius—along with his troops—quickly retreated, leaving (we may assume, mistakenly) the king's wife, mother, and children behind.

In victory, Alexander, who might have sought brutal recriminations, gave the Persians the opportunity to join his army and continue the conquests. He continued to move forward, through what is today Israel, through Gaza, and into Egypt where he founded the city of Alexandria in 332 BCE.

After visiting Egyptian temples, Alexander began, it is alleged, to believe in his own divine destiny, seeing himself as a god. The next year, Alexander rejoined his march of conquest, crossing the Tigris and Euphrates rivers (Iraq), capturing the Persian capital Persepolis.

In his five-year expedition, Alexander conquered all of Asia Minor and Persia, creating the largest empire in history. But Alexander's ambitions kept growing.

He invaded Afghanistan, moved east to central Asia, then into northern India. In eight long years, Alexander had never lost a battle and had conquered much of the then-known world. He had, however, been injured on a number of occasions. His injuries and his heavy drinking, as well as continually stressful campaigns, must have taken a toll on him.

His battle-weary troops longed to return home and, in essence, mutinied. Alexander reluctantly relented. But he never made it home. On the journey back to Macedonia, Alexander fell ill and died in Babylon in 323 BCE, still in his early thirties. Within a year or two, his empire collapsed.

What made Alexander such a successful military commander, and why is he still idolized today?

We are told he revolutionized military tactics and strategy. He introduced maneuver warfare into battle, creatively integrating cavalry and infantry into more coherent and mobile attack forces.

He mastered the art of inspiring loyalty and inspiring bravery. Much of this was done by his leadership by example, by his being right in the middle of battle, by sharing in much of the hardship and sacrifice, and by sharing with his men the benefits and booty of their success.

He was exceptionally brave and had a fearlessness that continues to be celebrated by military historians. Noted military historian John Keegan admired both Alexander's military wizardry and his undaunted resolve. He had ferocious energy that, along with his physical and intellectual gifts, transformed him into a passionate warrior, writes Keegan. He had an unblinking courage. "Alexander was brave with the bravery of the man who disbelieves his own mortality. He had a sort of godlike certainty in his survival whatever risk he chose to run."[22]

He was revered by his troops and feared by his enemies. This was apparently due to the fact that he was successful and that he demonstrated a brutal ruthlessness that instilled fear. He was also smart politically, knowing how to delegate political authority, knowing how to honor his colleagues, knowing how to recruit, and, presumably, train his new troops.

He also developed a charisma and a messianic image of Homeric proportions. He could allegedly trace his ancestry, on his maternal side, back to Achilles, the famed heroic Greek fighter in Homer's *Iliad*. Alexander saw himself as a latter-day Achilles who wanted to excel and transcend both his father's and Achilles' military prowess.

Everyone agrees that Alexander was ambitious, vain, theatrical, daring, and an insatiable explorer. His thirst for victory, for conquering, and for glory inspired his relentless commitments. Doubtless his troops were inspired not just by Alexander but also by the extensive and enriching looting that came with victories.

Critics call him a professional thug and killer who had a dark, compulsive addiction to killing. Some view him as a variation on being a noble or perhaps not so noble savage.

Still, most military historians continue to celebrate the feats of Alexander. "His achievements were indeed superhuman," writes Robin Lane Fox, "and their style was long invoked and imitated by his successor-generals. Even in his lifetime, Greek admirers and hopeful flatterers gave him honours equal to those of the gods."[23]

What does the legend of Alexander teach us? It teaches us a lot about bravery, fearlessness, loyalty, total commitment, and the role of intensity, leadership by example, battlefield inspiration, and expansive vision. It also teaches us about the brutal realities of war, the assassinations, the pillage, and all the darker, toxic realities of war. It raises major questions about overreaching and the dire consequences for his nation and its fragile empire, especially after the charismatic leader is gone.

The Macedonian hegemony crumbled soon after the thirty-two-year-old Alexander passed away. Was this a precursor of what would befall Rome, Napoleon, the various empires of Spain, Britain, the Soviet Union, and others? His story raises questions, too, about the inevitable interconnections of political and military objectives, of political and military leadership.

In the end, the legend of Alexander is an idealized version of leaders and followers and of organizations motivated by honor, fame, glory, and victory. We might be able to overlook the brutality, pain, and savagery of war and celebrate fearlessness, bravery, and the capacious vision of someone wanting to unify the world and to reach for the audacious, unimaginable goal of controlling the world. His ambition, in his day, may be similar to some of our ambitions, such as sending men to the moon, conquering space, or more altruistically, wiping out malaria, poverty, and inequality. We are, in many ways, ceaselessly in search of heroic leaders who will do great deeds and dare to do the impossible.

Julius Caesar: The Roman Republic (509–49 BCE) began with the defeat of the Etruscans and stretched for nearly five hundred years. In that time, Rome expanded its power and reach, and eventually the republic morphed into an empire. Julius Caesar (100–44 BCE) would become Rome's first emperor.

Caesar devoted his early public career to politics, and used family connections, charm, guile, and skillful bureaucratic maneuvering to quickly rise in republican Rome. But the republic was unstable and Caesar saw an opening to exploit. In his forties, he was elected consul (an important executive position), and he used that office as a springboard to advance both his personal and his political power. He began to grab power from the Roman Senate and, with each new power grab, elevated himself higher and higher.

In 59 BCE, Caesar, Pompey, and Crassus conspired to form a triumvirate, essentially carving up Roman territory into three sections, with Caesar controlling Gaul (northern Italy, southern France, and parts of the Adriatic). In addition to Gaul, Caesar took command of four Roman legions (about twenty thousand men).

Caesar wasted no time in expanding his territory. He led his army on a seven-year conquest, moving north and taking control of the rest of France, Belgium, most of Germany, Holland, and Switzerland.

Caesar's troops were invariably outnumbered. But Caesar developed a strategy to go after each territory piece by piece, grabbing a region here and a valley there. Caesar believed—rightly it turned out—that although he was outnumbered, his adversaries would not unite against him. Therefore, he was able to win a series of smaller wars that in the end meant a massive victory.

According to Plutarch, Caesar subdued three hundred tribes, conquered or took over at least eight hundred cities, and may have killed a million men. He was, Roman historians agree, the most important soldier, commander, and leader of men in history up to that point.

Describing his style of military leadership (in the third person), Caesar wrote:

> The situation was critical and as no reserves were available, Caesar seized a shield from a soldier in the rear and made his way to the front line. He addressed each centurion by name and shouted encouragement to the rest of the troops, ordering them to push forward and open out their ranks so they could use their swords more easily. His coming gave them fresh heart and hope. Each man wanted to do his best under the eyes of his commander despite the peril.[24]

After conquering Gaul, Caesar took Germany, then crossed the English Channel and invaded Britain. He was the conquering hero, and his fame spread throughout the Roman sphere of influence. His rising fame and popularity raised alarm bells with Pompey and Crassus, as well as the Roman Senate. Fearing Caesar's next step, the Senate (49 BCE) ordered Caesar to return to Rome and return to the lifestyle of a private citizen. Of course, Caesar would have none of this. He marched his forces toward Rome, crossed the Rubicon River, and a civil war ensued.

It took Caesar barely two months to take control of Italy and send Pompey and the Senate into exile (Crassus had died on a military mission in what is now Syria). Rome was his.

But Pompey was still on the loose, and Caesar pursued him to Greece where in the Battle of Pharsalus (48 BCE), Caesar, vastly outnumbered, took personal command of his troops to destroy Pompey's army. Caesar chased Pompey to Egypt where assassins killed him. Caesar continued to march into Egypt where he destroyed what remained of Pompey's army, and where he would meet Cleopatra and destroy her adversary King Pharnaces of Pontus (47 BCE). In trumpeting his victory, Caesar famously said, "*Veni, vidi, vici*" (I came, I saw, I conquered).

Not finished, Caesar later led forces into North Africa and Spain (45 BCE). When he returned to Rome as the conquering hero, he was made dictator for life.

Less than a year later in 44 BCE, Caesar fell to assassins (the description and intrigue involved in this form the basis for Shakespeare's majestic play *Julius Caesar*). If Caesar fell, his empire endured, lasting roughly another five hundred years.

Caesar, Rome's most successful and illustrious general, fought at least fifty pitched battles. He was charismatic and earned almost fanatical loyalty from his troops. He was a rigorous trainer yet generous with promotions and praise. He was said to know his officers by name and was famous for addressing his soldiers as "comrades." He took big risks, encountered a few setbacks, but invariably won his battles. Caesar was also a talented writer, and his *Commentaries* on his military operations in Gaul and in the great Roman civil war were widely admired and later studied by notable generals such as Napoleon.

Joan of Arc: Born to a tenant farm family in Domremy, France, Joan (1412–1431), at the age of thirteen, began to hear voices, later believed to be several saints. These voices told Joan of her mission to help free her country. Joan did not publicly discuss these strange voices until 1429. Still a teenager, she approached a captain in the local militia with her story, asking him to escort her to meet with the future king Charles VII.

Charles, who had been denied the crown via the Treaty of Troyes (1420), had been attempting futilely to claim the throne through military means. When he met Joan, he was understandably suspicious, yet ordered church leaders to investigate. Church officials confirmed her claims, and the dithering, wishy-washy Charles was rather mesmerized by Joan's self-confidence and focus. Charles outfitted her with a small military force that would accompany her to Orléans.

In May of 1429, Joan led her ill-equipped army in a number of attacks against the English, and the English withdrew from Orléans. Joan was catapulted to heroic stature in France. The "little girl" who heard "voices from God" lifted French spirits and her inspiration apparently carried her unlikely army to multiple victories.

After Orléans, Joan led her army to Rheims, thereby preparing safe passage for Charles, who was to be crowned king. In Rheims, Joan pressed the newly crowned king to go to Paris and attack the British occupiers. Charles hesitated. Eventually he relented, allowing Joan to lead his "coronation army" to Paris in hopes of liberating the city and driving the British from France.

In Paris, the British defeated Joan's army, and she retreated. Six months later, Joan returned with a small army and battled with British allies in Compiègne, where she again met with defeat. Here she was taken prisoner, then taken to Paris for trial.

The trial (1431) was allegedly a mockery of justice. She was charged with practicing witchcraft, a charge that was changed midtrial to heresy. Then, she was accused of refusing to allow the church to further investigate her "voices," and she was also accused of wearing men's clothes. In fact, she had become a threatening figure, both to church leaders and to the military. She was a loner who literally marched to her own "voices" and thus was antiauthoritarian and antiestablishment.

Joan was taken to a courtyard and told that she would be executed if she did not confess to her crimes. After initially admitting to "crimes and errors," she recanted and again donned men's clothes. Joan was declared a "relapsed heretic" and was burned at the stake in Rouen. She was twenty at the time of her execution.

Her life ended but her influence continued. Joan's example inspired members of the French army to form guerrilla brigades in her memory and resume attacks against their foes. After five years of battle, the French drove the English out of Paris.

Joan of Arc was not a tactical genius, nor was she an innovative military strategist. And yet her legendary courage and tenacity changed the course of the Hundred Years' War. Her leadership moved hearts and minds in battle; she led the soldiers at the front. Wounded twice, she nonetheless resumed the lead of her army. Joan was among the most enigmatic military leaders in history, yet in her day she was a bit like Latin America's iconic Ernesto "Che" Guevara in that she may have led more by inspiration than military inventiveness or military genius. In any event she is still widely venerated as a patron saint in modern-day France. Perhaps because of her lower-class status, she became a rallying symbol once again during the French Revolution, which was fought in large part on behalf of the poor. As noted in a previous chapter, playwright George Bernard Shaw's *Saint Joan* embellishes her story, as do several movies.

Napoleon Bonaparte: Born to a Corsican Italian family in 1769, Napoleon attended military school in France while a teenager. At sixteen he graduated from the military academy in Paris and sought a military commission.

Napoleon became an active Jacobin during the French Revolution (1789) and also began his rise in the military. As a participant in the siege against British forces at Toulon, Napoleon achieved acclaim when, although suffering from a bayonet wound, he took command of the French artillery and helped his side to victory.

Eventually, Napoleon was given command of the French army in Italy. He followed victory with victory, personally leading a bayonet charge against the Austrian army in Lodi for which his loyal and admiring troops nicknamed him "the little Corporal."

Napoleon continued to lead his French troops through Italy until he controlled both Italy and Austria. Hailed a conquering hero in France, he continued with his ambitious, power-seeking military exploits, returning to France in time to join the revolt against the ruling Directory (1799). The coup was successful, and Napoleon was made first consul, the head of the new French government. In 1802, he rewrote the French constitution, making himself "consul for life." In 1804, he declared himself emperor.

Such hubris and naked power grabs usually stir up fierce opposition, but Napoleon capitalized on fast-moving events. In 1803, Britain and France were again at war. In 1805, Napoleon began a masterful campaign in which he moved quickly and attacked viciously. He defeated the Austrians, then an Austro-Russian force, then the Prussians. A result of these impressive victories was the Treaty of Tilsit, which divided most of continental Europe between France and Russia.

Napoleon did not rest. He refocused on the ongoing war with Britain ("a nation of shopkeepers," he called the English) and seized Portugal (1807). Stymied in his effort to conquer Spain, he turned his attention to Russia and in 1812 invaded it. While winning much of the war on the ground, Napoleon saw a brutal Russian winter do in much of his army. Napoleon returned to France with but a fragment of his once mighty army.

In 1813, the combined forces of Britain, Prussia, Russia, and Sweden attacked France. Napoleon quickly rebuilt his depleted army, but he suffered a series of debilitating defeats. He abdicated power in 1814 and was banished to the Mediterranean island of Alba.

But Alba could not contain the still-ambitious Bonaparte. In 1815, he escaped the island and made his way back to France. The French forces, sent to arrest Napoleon, instead joined forces with him. He began to build another army, went on the attack, and began to achieve victories in battle. But in June of 1815, he met his "Waterloo" as Napoleon's army was defeated by Britain's talented Duke of Wellington and Prussia's Gebhard von Blücher. Napoleon surrendered and was exiled to the British-controlled island of St. Helena. He died there a year later, aged fifty-one.

What made Napoleon's success in battle? He was not a particularly innovative strategist, but he was flexible and adaptive. He quickly adjusted to battlefield conditions and changed tactics accordingly. He was also a master of morale building, using his personal charisma and demonstrated bravery to rally troops behind him. He preferred speed, maneuverability, and a type of "shock-and-awe" approach to battles. Flexibility was achieved by organizing each of his divisions into smaller corps, each of which could be mobile and act quickly, independently, and aggressively. Where most generals sought rigid control over their troops, Napoleon had more interest in quickness, decisiveness, and surprise, and allowed for more flexibility in order to better take advantage of opportunities that arose. He would carefully plan each battle, but he also recognized that in the fog of war, constant adjustments had to be made. Napoleon also understood the old paradox that it is soldiers who win battles even if generals usually get the credit for victory. But he knew full well that it is always the artful blend of troops and commander that is required.

U. S. Grant: Born to a tanner who was mayor of a small town in Ohio, Grant (1822–1885) won an appointment to West Point as a teenager. His academic record at West Point was modest. But he became a splendid horseman, winning the outstanding equestrian prize in his senior year at the academy.

He saw a lot of military action in the Mexican War, won respect for his courage, and earned promotions. But he seemed dissatisfied with his assignments after the war. Rumor had it that his excessive drinking may have led to his being forced out of the military. He returned to civilian life and was largely unsuccessful in various local business enterprises.

Duty called, however, when the Civil War broke out in 1861. He raised and trained Illinois volunteers; and because of his graduation from West Point and his Mexican War record, he soon moved up from being an obscure colonel to service as a brigadier general in the western front of the Civil War.

He didn't enjoy initial success, but his victory at Fort Donelson, Tennessee, won national attention. He began to earn a reputation as a clearheaded strategist and a ruthless battle commander. He also became a master of logistics, using railroads and rivers to transport his supplies and troops. He mastered the use of written dispatches through the telegraph to share orders, gain intelligence, and expand his capacity to command. He also generally mastered the complex geography on the southwestern battlefields.

What really catapulted Grant in the national news was his 1863 success in capturing the city of Vicksburg. With that triumph came the control of the mighty Mississippi River.

Grant's personal style was understated and almost unheroic. He often rode alone on horseback. He surrounded himself with friends from Illinois who were not especially trained as military men. He was also somewhat of a loner with less of a consultative style than effective leaders usually have.

But his commitment to fight and win set him apart from virtually every other Civil War general. Grant's view was that the army needed generals who concentrated on what they were going to do to the enemy, not what the enemy was going to do to them. He early on developed an "unconditional surrender" policy of dealing with the Confederates, a policy that Lincoln grew to share and adopt. His was a ruthless commitment to completely subjugate the South and its economic life.

Grant would occasionally get in trouble for bouts of drinking. Indeed he faced calls for dismissal. Lincoln overlooked this, saying, "I need this man, he fights," and "What I want is generals who will fight battles and win victories." Grant did this.

In early 1864, Lincoln, after getting Grant to acknowledge he would not run against him in the November 1864 elections, promoted Grant to be his top commanding general and arranged for Congress to appoint him as lieutenant general, the first and only person so designated since General George Washington had held that rank in the American Revolution.

Grant and Lincoln worked well together. Grant shared Lincoln's policy of arming black Americans, and at the end of the war, these blacks comprised about 10 percent of the army. Grant and Lincoln differed, sometimes sharply, on other matters. Lincoln's oversight of the conduct of the war is much debated, but it is clear he became much engaged. He visited battlefields eleven times, spending at least fifty days with the troops. And despite his reputation for humanity and humility, he willingly encouraged Grant's brutal approach to total war.[25]

In the end Grant was up against the South's Robert E. Lee, the quintessential Virginia gentleman but also a brilliant military tactician and an impressive operational leader. Grant, at a cost of tens of thousands of men, doggedly pursued Lee in his spring 1864 campaign with a relentless series of attacks that eventually left General Lee no time to catch his breath or escape.

Grant hated the human toll this war took. He also hated military celebrations and parades. He was not much of a speaker and in fact rarely addressed his troops. But he became the hero the Union was looking for, and he eventually would be elected president of the United States (1869–1877) despite his general aversion to politics and political fanfare. His presidency, in contrast to his role as a military commander, was not a success.

Erwin Rommel: Rommel was designated the "Desert Fox" because of his brilliant leadership of German forces in North Africa during World War II. Rommel (1891–1944) was an innovative, inspiring commander whose professionalism and honor led him to clash with Adolf Hitler, and in the end, led to his betrayal of the führer.

Born in Heidenheim, Germany, in 1891, Rommel attended Danzig Infantry School and in 1912 was commissioned as a lieutenant in the German army. In World War I, he fought on the western front, and was awarded an Iron Cross.

After the war, Rommel continued to advance in the army and, in 1937, published a book on military tactics entitled *Infantry Attacks.* The book impressed Adolf Hitler, and the führer appointed Rommel as commander of headquarters. Rommel was later attached to Hitler's staff, where he learned the newly emerging blitzkrieg tactics being employed by the German army.

Rommel sought and was given his own command and, in 1940, took control of the Seventh Panzer Division. That year Rommel's division was part of the invasion of France. Rommel's troops moved fast and struck hard. They were mobile and flexible and relied on the quick strike. During the campaign, Rommel developed a set of attack tactics that he would master through the course of his military career. He used surprise and firepower to overcome the enemy. He used tanks to breach the enemy lines. But if any one word characterized Rommel's approach, it would be *speed.*

His success in France led to a promotion to general, and Hitler sent Rommel to North Africa to command the new Deutsches Afrika Korps. In that post, he drove the British Eighth Army out of Libya, advancing with his troops, leading from the front. He loved being at the front of the action, believing that by gaining immediate, firsthand knowledge he could better calculate battle tactics. He commanded from the front, yet kept his distance from his men. His biographies praise him as one of the last great cavalry captains.[26]

Rommel went to considerable efforts to look the part of the great general, with a medal-draped, tailored uniform and tanker goggles sitting just so on his forehead. Rommel apparently oozed generalship. His style, speedy panzer tactics, success on the battlefield, and catchy nickname "Desert Fox" led to celebrity status and international fame. Even Winston Churchill called him "a great general."

Rommel's army continued to sweep across North Africa. But dwindling supplies and the arrival of technologically superior U.S. troops proved too much for the outmanned German army. Hitler ordered Rommel to fight to the last man, but instead Rommel surrendered his army to the Allies.

Although angered that Rommel disobeyed a direct order, Hitler realized he needed the skilled general, ordering his return to Germany just prior to the surrender. Rommel was sent to France to prepare for the much-anticipated allied invasion. But Hitler rejected Rommel's advice on defending French territory; and Operation Overlord, July 15, 1944, better known as the D-day invasion, led to a fateful defeat for Germany. Wounded when a British plane strafed his staff car, Rommel returned to Germany to recover. Although not a direct participant, Rommel knew of the July plot to kill Hitler; and when the plot failed, Rommel was, rightly or wrongly, considered one of the conspirators.

Aware that Rommel would be an ongoing threat or possible rival, on October 14, 1944, Hitler sent two generals to Rommel's home where he was given a choice: suicide with a state funeral and the guarantee of his family's safety, or a public trial for treason. He would, of course, have been found guilty and executed, and his family would have been punished and lost his pension and related benefits. Rommel chose suicide.

George S. Patton: Patton was Exhibit A of twentieth-century larger-than-life commanders. He was the most effective U.S. commander in World War II. Never known for his tact or diplomatic skills, he was a fighter's fighter and remembered for his "lead me, follow me, or get out of my way" mantra. We treat him at length in the middle of Chapter 10.

Paradoxes of Military Leadership

The great writers on war, from Sun Tzu to Clausewitz and beyond, all appreciated the paradoxical nature of war. Even Clausewitz's central thesis is paradoxical—that the main aim of war is peace and that many aspects of peace and war coexist simultaneously and continually.

"Military professionals," write Paparone and Crupi, "need to become proficient at considering simultaneous, multiple, and opposite perspectives in order to make sense of the inherent complexities of warfare."[27]

There are leadership paradoxes in every professional sector, and they are often slight variants of those found in other sectors. Space permits us here to highlight just three military-related paradoxes.

Paradox I	All officers are leaders except when followers choose not to follow, and officers actually gain authority by sharing it or giving some of it away.
Paradox II	The principle of civilian control over the military is sacred in constitutional democracies, yet this doesn't prevent many generals from believing war is too important to be left to political leaders, and vice versa.
Paradox III	The role of obedience, discipline, and faithfully carrying out the orders of superiors is explicit in the military, yet not every order should be carried out.

We will now examine these three paradoxes in more detail.

I. "All officers are leaders" is an oft-mentioned official military view, yet research shows that those who occupy leadership positions only become leaders when followers, or troops, choose to cooperate and follow them. Paradoxically, leaders gain authority by sharing it.

The hope is that only leaders get to become officers. But leadership effectiveness, as we have emphasized throughout, is defined largely by followers and context. Thus the old military proverb: "If you think you're leading but no one is following, you're only taking a hike."

Colonel Christopher R. Paparone, writing in the *Military Review*, reminds us that the long-dominant military paradigm was a Eurocentric, white male–centered style; was characterized by hierarchical command and control; and was typically illustrated by the metaphor of a pyramid with the "Great Man" or Alexander/Caesar/Napoleon atop the structure.

But, as Paparone writes, traditional notions of top-down hierarchical leadership are less and less relevant in today's hyperturbulent and hyperinterconnected military-political environment. "Hyperturbulent environments do not wait for change to trickle down the hierarchy. The process of doing things effectively is dynamically nonlinear. If leadership really exists, it is more likely a mutual process between leaders and followers, with followers sometimes becoming leaders."[28]

Thus, just as Clausewitz taught that the fog of war comes with a continual interaction of unexpected and often contradictory events, so also, few set military leadership principles can be rigidly applied in every context.

Writers on military leadership increasingly appreciate that leadership involves leading collaboratively and laterally, not just from the top of some pyramid.

Similarly, military writers appreciate the role that trust, culture, and paradox play in encouraging an organization's effectiveness. "We can reach new ways of framing the problems of paradox through synthesis and dialectical reasoning or by accepting paradox as a normal state of organization," writes Paparone.[29]

Leaders, in the military as elsewhere, accept and embrace paradoxes and try to put them to good use. "Army soldiers and civilians need tools to decipher what those paradoxes are and, if necessary, embrace paradox as the way things are. Instead of seeking a consensual, single model of leadership, the Army should embrace multiple models, even if they seem contradictory."[30]

Military leaders, even though they have been raised in a hierarchical system of command and control, find, in the helpful words of Admiral Jim Stockdale, that they can actually gain authority by giving it away.

Leadership is always a reciprocal interaction. You have to give in order to receive. Natural leadership is never a zero-sum game where one person wins and the other loses. What is given to followers is not something taken from a leader. Both get by giving. This was the majesty and authenticity of the great battlefield commanders discussed earlier.

Retired U.S. Air Force general Perry M. Smith suggests that the creative delegating and sharing of authority with one's subordinates are simultaneously challenging yet liberating. "Decentralization and delegation do not mean that the top leader becomes invisible or disengaged; they signify that the hand on the tiller is a light one.... It is important to realize that micromanagement—the compulsive inclination to get personally involved in an infinite number of unimportant details—is seldom productive for leaders.[31]

II. **The principle of civilian control over the military is sacred in constitutional democracies, yet political and military matters are hard to disentangle. Some generals may believe that war is too important to be left to political leaders, and vice versa.**

American presidents together with the Congress are charged by the U.S. Constitution with providing for the common defense. They must raise the troops, finance, and in general, supervise the military. Further, a president is assigned the duty to serve as commander in chief of the military when it is "called into the actual service of the United States." Now, of course, that means all the time since we have long had a permanent military and indeed have over five hundred bases of one kind or another in at least sixty countries around the world.

The idea of civilian control is to make national security and defense matters subordinate to the larger purposes of the nation. The explicit purpose of the military is to defend a nation, not to define it. The irony here, or perhaps yet another paradox, is that the nation creates a military that is expert at violence in order to protect the nation, yet we want safeguards against that same military for our own security and protection.

So the people's elected representative is the military commander in chief. Military officers have freedom of speech; yet to ensure the principle of civilian supremacy, commissioned offers who disobey a president or who even use "contemptuous words" against a president can be subject to punishment, including being relieved of command.

When the legendary General Douglas MacArthur challenged President Harry Truman's overall policy directions during the Korean War, MacArthur was famously forced to resign. MacArthur had overplayed his hand, apparently believing he could obey only presidential orders he liked but could use the media to help him get the ones he disliked changed. The next year the five-star general would deliver the keynote address at the Republican national convention.

When a general made rude and critical remarks against President Bill Clinton in the 1990s, that general was fined and forced to retire. Similarly, when highly regarded general Stanley McChrystal, the top commander in Afghanistan, embarrassed the Obama White House, not once but twice, he was removed from his post in Kabul.

Leaders like Lincoln, FDR, and Churchill prod, challenge, and try to give strategic direction to the military. Members of Congress also get involved, especially in promoting weapons development, the location of facilities, troop levels, and even whether or not we become involved in war.

Lincoln clashed with Union general George B. McClellan because Lincoln believed McClellan lacked the killer instinct and had let too many opportunities slip through his fingers. So strained were relations between Lincoln and his top general that at one point in 1862 Lincoln quipped, "If General McClellan isn't going to use his army, I'd like to borrow it for a time." McClellan was experienced, talented, handsome, and popular with his troops, who had prematurely dubbed him "Young Napoleon." But Lincoln replaced him. McClellan responded by entering politics and running against Lincoln in the 1864 presidential election.

Military historian Eliot Cohen praises the Lincoln experience: "It was Lincoln's understanding of the interplay of war and politics, no less than his ability to absorb military detail and to read human character, that made him the greatest of American war generals." Cohen adds: "Lincoln educated his generals about the purpose of war and then reminded them of its fundamental political characteristics. He had not merely to create a strategic approach to the war, but to insist that the generals adhere to it."[32]

"You show me a general in Washington who ain't political," Colin Powell once said, "and I will show you a guy who ain't gonna get promoted again, and probably should not be a general in the first place."[33]

Politics and military matters, as Clausewitz pointed out, are difficult to disentangle. Military leaders, at all levels, have their own political views. They usually repress them, at least publicly. Although some senior officers, like the celebrated admiral Hyman Rickover, have a way of letting friendly members of Congress know their policy views.

Retired officers frequently make their political views known. At least a dozen American presidents were former military leaders. Several presidential wannabes, including MacArthur, Colin Powell, and Wesley Clark, encouraged presidential boomlets.

Chairman of the Joint Chiefs of Staff Admiral William Crowe, shortly after he retired, strongly endorsed Bill Clinton's presidential bid for the White House in 1992.

After he retired from serving under President George W. Bush and Defense Secretary Donald Rumsfeld, former chairman of the Joint Chiefs of Staff Hugh Shelton refuted their decision to go to war in Iraq by writing that the idea that the United States was in any way militarily threatened by Iraq "was utter bullshit and every one of them knew it or should have known it."[34]

Useful lessons and revisionist thinking are shared by savvy and insightful former military officers. The writings of Andrew J. Bacevich, Bing West, H. R. McMaster, and Howard Wasdin are illustrative. They might not match Thucydides but they are worth reading, especially as they share military perspectives on political leadership during wartime.[35]

Other examples of the interplay of politics and the military in recent years have been the controversy of the former "Don't Ask, Don't Tell" policy and former defense secretary Rumsfeld's clash with the military over his reform efforts to move toward a lighter, more technologically driven military.

Presidents, more than anyone else, have to be able to balance politics and military matters; they have to help promote as well as fire top officers. They have to understand the harsh realities and the limits of war. And just as much as the generals, they not only have to master the lessons of Sun Tzu, Thucydides, Machiavelli, and Clausewitz, but they also have to understand the changing nature of war, the changing role of military power, and the economic and political reality that America cannot be both an empire and a republic.[36]

III. The role of obedience, discipline, and faithfully and professionally carrying out the orders of a military superior is explicit, yet not every order should be carried out.

The paradox here is that those in the military have to conduct themselves as military professionals yet at the same time do the morally right thing and uphold the best values of their nation.

This is what the *U.S. Army Field Manual 22-100* says:

> Army leaders must set high standards, lead by example, do what is legally and morally right, and influence other people to do the same. They must establish and sustain a climate that ensures people are treated with dignity and respect and create an environment in which people are challenged and motivated to be all they can be.

Ethical questions arise in every war. Hitler's extermination campaigns against the Jews and other minorities are forever in our memories. Stalin butchered even more people. Early European settlers in America acted against the Native Americans in wholly unacceptable ways. People still debate and deplore the Civil War scorched-earth marches of Sherman and Grant. In Vietnam, the infamous 1968 My Lai massacre by American troops needlessly killed at least a few hundred unarmed civilians. This horrendous and unethical slaughter of civilians prompted outrage around the world and led to intensified opposition to the war in the United States just as it intensified commitment by the North Vietnamese. Three U.S. servicemen, we are told, tried to stop this mindless massacre; not only were they ignored but they were later denounced by some U.S. congressmen and other "patriots." Second Lieutenant William Calley, a platoon leader, said he was just following orders. He alone was convicted but given a light sentence. Years later he apologized and said, "There is not a day that goes by that I do not feel remorse for what happened that day in My Lai.... I feel remorse for the Vietnamese who were killed, for their families, for the American soldiers involved and their families. I am very sorry."

The army was accused of covering this up. And, as in the Abu Ghraib torture and prisoner abuse scandal in Iraq and similar instances, blame was spread around yet those at the top were not held accountable.

Colin Powell, later to become a leading army general and secretary of state, was in Vietnam when the My Lai massacre took place. He says he saw incredible bravery by our troops in Vietnam and found it difficult to criticize soldiers for unethical behavior. He did tell a biographer, however, that "the absence of unit cohesion and the erosion of standards for leadership and training ... had been directly [in Powell's view] responsible for the breakdown in morale, discipline and professional judgment that had allowed My Lai to happen."[37]

But Powell pointedly blamed the higher-ups in Washington, DC, for failures in Vietnam, saying that this war effort suffered because it was poorly conceived, conducted, and explained by America's leaders. To Powell's credit, when he became a higher-up, he tried hard, not always successfully, not to have U.S. troops sent into combat unless the mission was clear and adequate forces were provided.

Not every order can or should be followed. General Dwight Eisenhower once said: "I need officers who know what orders to disobey." Moreover, obedience—even in the military—is never guaranteed. Sometimes this is due to changing circumstances. Sometimes it will endanger too many troops and be wholly counterproductive. The best of leaders try to talk their superiors out of imprudent or immoral directives. But there are toxic leaders in the military just as in every profession.[38]

Most top military leaders stress that "whatever the cost, do what is right." In explaining why he believed some orders can be wrong and need to be contested or disobeyed, General Matthew B. Ridgway wrote that in any action "you must balance the inevitable cost in lives against the objectives you seek to attain. Unless the results to be expected can reasonably justify the estimated loss of life the action involves, then for my part I want none of it."[39]

Top military leaders also understand that soldiers have rights. General Bruce Clarke, an outstanding combat commander in World War II, made this helpful list of "What Soldiers Have a Right to Expect from Leaders":

1. Honest, just, and fair treatment
2. Consideration due them as mature, professional soldiers
3. Personal interest taken in them as individuals
4. Loyalty
5. Shielding from harassment from "higher up"
6. The best in leadership
7. That their needs be anticipated and provided for
8. All the comforts and privileges practicable
9. To be kept oriented and told the "reason why"
10. A well-thought-out program of training, work and recreation
11. Clear-cut and positive decisions and orders which are not constantly changing.[40]

In Search of the Ideal Military Leader

Every service and every military wants to educate its trainees to become leaders. The belief is that most of what comprises military leadership can be taught or learned.[41]

Leadership in war is one of the most exacting jobs possible. An old maxim holds that an army cannot be administered, it has to be led.

It may get overstated yet the military has so often repeated it and taught it that military educators insist that it is *the leader, the commander, the general* who is the indispensable causal agent in success on the battlefield. "Man for man one division is just as good as another," said General Omar Bradley. "They vary only in the skill and leadership of their commanders."[42]

Napoleon made the same point, that the personality and character of the general are indispensable. "The personality of the general is indispensable. He is the head, he is the all of the Army. The Gauls were not conquered by Roman legions, but by Caesar.... It was not the Macedonian phalanx which penetrated to India, but Alexander.... Prussia was not defeated for seven years against the three most formidable European powers by Prussian soldiers, but by Frederick the Great."[43]

Their message is that top leadership matters. But we know, too, that leaders up and down the chain of command matter—as does, as always, the context.

Jefferson Davis and Robert E. Lee had military credentials superior to those of Abraham Lincoln and his top commander, but experience and credentials don't always make the difference.

The United States had superiority in just about every conceivable way when it fought in Vietnam; yet it lost that war, with 58,000 soldiers killed and 300,000 wounded.

The Vietnam loss was blamed on a lot of people—Lyndon Johnson, Secretary of Defense Robert McNamara, senior military leaders at the Pentagon or in the field. A lot of blame was directed at political as well as military leaders who failed to provide clear objectives and an all-out commitment to win that war. One much decorated Vietnam vet speculated that "for too long there have been no courageous leaders at the top" to match the courage of the troops we had on the ground. "For too long we have had a leadership vacuum at the top. A government composed more of managers than leaders, managers who are afraid to tackle the tough problems."[44]

Generals matter. Political leaders matter. Troops matter. Context matters. Vision and purpose matter too. As we said early in this book, leadership always involves leaders, followers, and context; and military experience regularly confirms this.

In war the stakes are always high. Few things are certain in war save that one side will not win.

As Machiavelli and others have observed, fortune or luck may decide some of our fate; but much also depends on leadership, on calculation, and on the ability to profit from opportunities as well as accidents. This is what military leadership programs focus on. Their leadership training is hard to measure quantitatively, except perhaps in the fields of battle; but it is generally more rigorous, more time consuming, and more expensive than comparable training in business, government, or politics.

America, like any nation, yearns for military leaders who have well-developed qualities of judgment, character, strength, agility, courage, decisiveness, patriotism, inspiration, valor, and tenacity that are seldom found fully developed in any one person. We want the audacity of an Alexander, the undaunted courage of a Washington, the determination of a Grant, the wisdom of a Thucydides, the feel for strategy of a Clausewitz or an Eisenhower, the charisma of a Patton or a MacArthur, and the fierce execution of a Rambo or a Terminator. That's a lot to ask. We expect too much, yet we are understandably unlikely to lower our expectations when the survival of our nation is at stake.

In previous chapters, we have discussed many of the defining qualities associated with effective business and political leaders. The military looks for most of these same qualities.

But there are several specific qualities of leadership that the military emphasizes and tries to nurture and reward in the training of officers. Not everyone champions this or that specific quality, and as the nature of war and military weaponry change, so also the requirements for effective military leadership continue to change.

Before listing several personal qualities and critically important military skills, it is important to emphasize there never has been or can be one perfect ideal. If one pulled together a Hall of Fame of outstanding all-star military officers, one would quickly notice contradictory styles. Some were aloof; others had a great knack of mingling with their troops. Some displayed modesty and humility; others were leaders with huge egos and narcissistic personality disorders. Some were charismatic and looked every inch a Hollywood depiction of a general; others were disheveled and inept at stagecraft and public relations. Some were experts at strategy, others at tactics. All have had at least a few of the flaws associated with being human.

If it is impossible to predict in advance who will be the battlefield all-stars, this has rarely curbed military trainers from making assumptions of what is desirable. Most everyone agrees, for example, that character, courage, fearlessness, resilience, and a savvy understanding of war and team building are indispensable.

Personal qualities:

- Character
- Courage and fearlessness
- Integrity and honesty
- Self-discipline and self-confidence
- Loyalty to colleagues

- Ability to lead by example
- Ability to accept blame, assume responsibility, and have the resilience to bounce back
- Contextual and emotional intelligence, savvy, and judgment
- Strength and endurance
- Ability to build teams and delegate
- Ability to train, mentor, and build morale
- Ability to understand war, diplomacy, and nation building

What follows is a brief commentary on several of these.

Character. Character is the foundation of leadership. An old saying has it that character consists of what one does on the third or fourth try, and what one does in the dark when no one is watching. Character is defined as a reputation for dependability; a temperament for rectitude; and a makeup that combines backbone, fortitude, and ethical integrity.

Character is a habit, is cumulative, and is a striving for exemplary conduct. Here is how General Matthew B. Ridgway viewed character: "Character is the bedrock on which the whole edifice of leadership rests. It is the prime element for which every profession ... searches in evaluating a member of its organization. With it, the full worth of an individual can be developed. Without it—particularly in the military profession—failure in peace, disaster in war, or, at best, mediocrity in both will result."[45]

Courage and Fearlessness. Clausewitz said that because war is the province of danger, courage comes ahead of everything else as the first and most desirable quality of a warrior. Guts, bravery, nerve, daring, and gallantry are especially valued in the military. What is not wanted is cowardice.

Soldiers sometimes talk of physical courage and moral courage. Both are necessary. Others describe "the three o'clock in the morning" courage—the readiness and ability to stand and deliver at any time, anywhere. It is variously described as moral backbone, firmness of spirit, grace and tenacity under pressure, and doing the right thing even when the odds are against you.

Fear and courage are often in a continual struggle on any battlefield. Fear can understandably lead to mental and physical exhaustion. Yet fear, writes Major Mark Gerner, can paradoxically lead to feats of unexpected courage. "An analysis of human behavior in battle should begin with a recognition of fear. The fighting soldier fears death, fears wounds and, if he is part of a well-trained cohesive unit, fears failing his buddies. The caring leader at any level fears that he is not up to an immense task, that he may fail his soldiers or that he may not accomplish a critical mission."[46]

Courage and fearlessness, military educators believe, need to be developed long before battle. This involves company cohesion, the development of trust and respect among colleagues, and especially a two-way trust between the leader and the led.

Integrity and Honesty. No one wants to work with dishonest colleagues, and this only gets amplified in battle situations. Soldiers understandably yearn for principled, frank, truthful, fair, and reliable officers and colleagues.

In the military, special emphasis is placed on unselfishness and on the personal commitment of everyone to everyone else in the unit. Unit cohesiveness, as we will discuss, is crucial. But a commitment to look after one another is very important. "No one gets left behind" is a central precept.

Self-discipline and Self-confidence. Discipline and confidence give strength to the leader and the troops alike. In *The Art of War*, Machiavelli recognized that few men are brave by nature, but training and discipline can prepare an army. "Good order and discipline in any army are more to be depended upon than courage alone." The legendary George Patton held that "perfect discipline" was imperative. If you don't enforce and maintain that, he said, "you are potential murderers." Patton continued: "All human beings have an innate resistance to obedience. Discipline removes this resistance and, by constant repetition, makes obedience habitual and subconscious.... No sane man is unafraid in battle, but discipline produces in him a form of vicarious courage which, with his manhood, makes for victory. Self-respect grows directly from discipline."[47]

Loyalty to Colleagues. Loyalty from the top down is important because, as noted earlier, the very legitimacy of a leader is less conferred by a position, a uniform, or medals than by colleagues and subordinates. Loyalty has to be regularly earned. George Washington and Robert E. Lee, one in victory, the other in defeat, succeeded in winning the loyalty of their men.

Patriotism is not so much protecting the land of our founders or our parents as preserving the blessings of liberty and the American Dream for our children and their children.

Research instructs that in the heat of battle a well-trained, cohesive fighting unit is often more motivated to fight for its combat buddies than for its nation or abstract ideals. This is especially the case, as in America's recent past, when soldiers have been sent to fight in unpopular wars such as in Vietnam, Iraq, and Afghanistan—wars, as General Norman Schwarzkopf suggests, that "strained the trust and affection that must exist between Army and society."[48]

Ability to Lead by Example. This is one of the most discussed military training principles. The central idea is that the leader's fitness, integrity, and competence set the standard. These have to be demonstrated by the leader's sharing in the hardships and day-to-day sacrifices he or she expects the troops to endure. This is indispensable both for morale and productivity.

"He never asked of others what he would not risk himself" is what is said of the legendary generals.

Ability to Accept Blame, Take Responsibility, and Have the Resilience to Bounce Back. Just as in business and politics, the effective commander will make mistakes and suffer setbacks or bad luck. The military trains its future officers to bounce back and have the levelheaded resilience to regroup and to turn mistakes into opportunities.

Resilience implies quickness to recover, durability, toughness, and irrepressibility. George Washington displayed resilience in the American Revolution. As is well known, he lost more battles than he won. Large numbers of his soldiers left him or were victims of various diseases. His troops were poorly equipped and often went without pay and adequate supplies. One of Washington's biographers, David McCullough, celebrates Washington's resilience and his ability to learn from his mistakes:

> He was not a brilliant strategist or tactician, not a gifted orator, not an intellectual. At several crucial moments he had shown marked indecisiveness. He had made serious mistakes in judgment. But experience had been his great teacher from boyhood, and in this his greatest test, he learned steadily from experience. Above all, Washington never forgot what was at stake and he never gave up.[49]

Contextual and Emotional Intelligence, Savvy, and Judgment. Most of the legendary military leaders exemplified judgment, perceptiveness, and common sense. They applied common sense and experience to problems they faced. They knew themselves, their strengths and weaknesses, and they were especially proficient in gathering information and counsel. The best commanders could ascertain the second- and third-order side effects or consequences of a decision, could accurately read contexts, and could still decide and act with confidence.

Clausewitz prescribed that what was needed were generals who were geniuses at the decisive tipping points of a conflict. But as Martin van Creveld observes, "However excellent in principle, this advice is less than useful in practice, the problem consisting precisely in the inability of military (and nonmilitary) institutions to achieve certainty either in producing a steady supply of geniuses or in identifying the decisive points into which, once available, they should be put."[50] Just as in politics or business, leaders need to know their strengths and weaknesses and surround themselves with deputies and advisers who can help them build on their strengths and compensate for their weaknesses.

Counterintelligence is also crucial. "Unskillful generals race to the first trap set before them," wrote Frederick the Great. "This is why a great advantage is drawn from knowledge of your adversary, and when you know his intelligence and character you can use it to play on his weaknesses."[51]

Strength and Endurance. The Department of the Army and all the services, most especially special operations commanders, yearn for pentathletes, people whose athleticism and versatility will allow them to be adaptive in ambiguous and dangerous situations.

The military's wish list aims high and is capacious: leaders who are innovative, adaptive, resilient, mentally and physically agile, self-aware, and empathetic.[52]

Every profession should want people with these qualities but it is certainly understandable that the military tries to recruit and train such people.

The military understands all too well that soldiers will experience physical and mental stress. The goal is to be prepared for it, meet it, and if possible, transcend it. Military proverbs speak to this: victory comes to those who hang in there and outlast the enemy. In case of setbacks, the military teaches, regroup: push on and keep pushing. Success comes to those who have the toughness, tenacity, and stamina to persevere.

Ability to Build Teams and Delegate. Few things are as important in the training of military officers as the crucial way teams have to be built and maintained. Unit cohesion is the building block for successful fighting units. Leadership and unit cohesion are inseparable. Lieutenant Colonel Larry Ingraham makes this point when he writes, "Rank and position are conferred from above, but leadership is confirmed from below. Your selection as an Army leader is evidence the Army has confidence in you, but this is an easy vote. In combat, a silent vote of confidence is taken on every order."[53]

Why are some units highly cohesive and others incohesive? Cohesiveness is achieved by discipline, by clear understanding of mission and responsibilities, by the ethic of unselfishness, by the example set by leaders at all levels, and by much more. If a leader isn't caring and visible and isn't sharing in the hardships of his or her unit, the leader isn't very credible and unit cohesion is likely to be low.

But there is far more to this than just the leadership dimension. Skillful delegation, imaginative decentralization, and proper development of subsidiary leaders are a big part of the challenge.

Ability to Train, Mentor, and Build Morale. A first-rate military leader is always training and mentoring. "In no other profession," Douglas MacArthur said, "are the penalties for employing untrained personnel so appalling or so irrevocable as in the military."[54]

Effective commanders have been trainers, mentors, and builders of morale both by being clear about what is at stake and by letting their troops know they will be with them in battle. (On this latter point, see the speeches by Henry V at the Battle of Agincourt, which we excerpted and discussed at the beginning of Chapter 2, and General Patton's talk to his troops, which we will discuss in Chapter 10 when analyzing the film *Patton*.)

On Patton as a trainer, one of his biographers writes:

> Patton was a trainer. In the States, he first made his mark at senior levels by his successes in developing the Armored Force out of a collection of regiments and battalions. In North Africa, his primary achievement involved compelling the II Corps, from its staff and division commanders down, to begin taking war seriously. In Europe, perhaps the most outstanding characteristic of the 3rd Army's order of battle was the constant accretion of green divisions with everything to learn at all levels: even the cadres were raw, and few commanders had any combat experience in the current war. While all U.S. field armies had the same problem, the 3rd Army's new formations [under Patton] seemed to adjust more quickly and suffer fewer casualties relative to their earlier missions.[55]

Ability to Understand War, Diplomacy, and Nation Building. A broad understanding of war, from the classics we discussed earlier to the histories of Korea, Vietnam, and recent wars against genocide and terrorism, would benefit any modern-day commander.

War is changing and many of today's wars require knowing how to navigate different cultures at the nation-state and neighborhood levels. Military leaders nowadays find themselves "attempting to persuade wary local leaders to share valuable information while simultaneously trying to distinguish friend from foe, balancing the need to protect their troops with the need to build indigenous support for America's regional and global interests."[56]

Today's wars involve dangerous negotiations and a sophisticated understanding of local politics as well as trying to understand the sometimes conflicting messages sent by political leaders in the war region as well as in Washington, DC.[57]

Conclusion

Plato was right when he predicted that "only the dead have seen the end of war."

The need for military leaders will be with us as long as we yearn for security and freedom. Well-trained military leaders will remain a vitally essential part of providing for the common defense and for military preparedness.

Most of the same paradoxes that are seen in civilian life also exist in military life. We want assertive, decisive leaders in the military. We know that many of them will have strong egos and pride and that they must have cunning and a hardness about them. But we also want them to be selfless and dedicated both to winning battles and to constitutionally established values. We want quick, decisive victories, yet, as the world has learned in recent decades, wars can be painstakingly long and sometimes inconclusive. The lessons of Thucydides are a useful reminder of the messiness and ugliness of war and the liabilities of the imperial temptation.

One of the major messages from the study of war and military leadership is that people yearn for military heroes. And just as wars produce winners and losers, they also produce heroes and villains. Examined closely, many of the heroes, in their multifaceted glory, are full of complexity, contradiction, and paradox. Britain's Lawrence of Arabia and America's Douglas MacArthur are just two examples of these paradoxical types.[58]

Thus, as we learned from reviewing the classics, and as we shall learn again in the next chapter's analysis of classic leadership films, there is a romantic fascination with larger-than-life leadership. Thoughtful military educators may teach us about the more nuanced, paradoxical, and collaborative realities of leadership, yet the celebration of the leader hero and the yearning for the heroic seem somehow ingrained in our DNA.

Six of thirteen notable "leadership movies" we discuss in the next chapter treat the challenges military leaders face in wartime.

Chapter Ten
What Hollywood Teaches Us about Leadership

> Movies ... tell us about the political system and how it works, or whether it works—that is, whether it can solve our problems. Usually, they tell us that bad people can mess up the system and good ones can set it right.... They seldom point out fundamental defects in the system, and they rarely suggest that social problems can be solved by collective or communal action.
>
> —*Terry Christensen and Peter J. Haas*[1]

Our views of leadership are shaped by a variety of factors; among them is the impact of popular culture, film in particular. Some of our conceptions of leadership come to us in the form of entertainment. Such entertainment educates as well.

Even so seemingly innocent a movie as *The Wizard of Oz* conveys political and leadership messages. Dorothy and Toto, the Tin Woodman and the Scarecrow, the Cowardly Lion and the Wicked Witch of the West are all magical figures out of one of America's most loved movies. But *The Wizard of Oz* was, and is, more than a mere children's fantasy. As written by Lyman Frank Baum in 1900, *The Wonderful Wizard of Oz* was a political allegory of turn-of-the-century American politics. Written in the waning days of the populist movement of the late 1800s, it is the story of the collapse of populism and the issues that movement has championed.

The allegory begins with the title. *Oz* is the abbreviation for ounce, the standard measure used for gold. Dorothy represents Everyman; the Tin Woodman, the industrial worker; the Scarecrow, the farmer; the Cowardly Lion, William Jennings Bryan; the Wizard, the president; the munchkins, the "little people"; and the Yellow Brick Road, the gold standard.

In the story, Dorothy is swept away from Kansas in a tornado and arrives in a mysterious land inhabited by little people. Her landing kills the Wicked Witch of the East (bankers and capitalists), who "kept the munchkin people in bondage."

In the movie, Dorothy begins her long journey through the Land of Oz wearing ruby slippers, but in the original story Dorothy's magical slippers are silver. Along the way on the yellow brick (gold) road, Dorothy meets the Scarecrow, who is without a brain (the farmer, Baum suggests, doesn't have enough brains to recognize his political interests). Farther down the road, she meets a Tin Man who is "rusted solid" (a reference to the industrial factories shut down during the depression of 1893). The Tin Man's real problem, however, is that he doesn't have a heart (the result of the dehumanizing work in the factory that turned men into machines). Next Dorothy meets the Cowardly Lion, an animal in need of courage (Bryan, with a loud roar but little else). Together they go off to the Emerald City (Washington) in search of what answer the wonderful Wizard of Oz (the president) might give them.

When they finally get to the Emerald City and meet the Wizard, he, like most politicians portrayed by Hollywood, appears to be whatever people wish to see in him. He also plays on their fears. Soon the Wizard is revealed to be a fraud—only a little old man "with a wrinkled face" who admits that he's been "making believe." "I am just a common man," he says. But he is a common man who can rule only by deceiving the people into thinking he is more than he really is.

Yes, the Wizard is a leader, yet he is a leader who bases his authority on illusions. He is also a fraud. He manipulates perceptions, and, in the end, he is exposed. The Wizard is last seen departing the land of Oz in a metaphorically appropriate hot air balloon.

Dorothy is able to return to her home with the aid of her magical ruby (silver) shoes, but upon waking in Kansas, she realizes that they've fallen off, representing the demise of the silver coinage issue in American politics.

Dorothy, the average person, turns out to have a repertoire of leadership skills that, when she has no choice but to lead, allow her to reach her goal (returning to Kansas) and also empower her associates.

In order to understand more about where our popular views of leadership come from, we examine several illustrative films that deal with leadership and look at how it has been portrayed in popular film. We deal here only with Hollywood films.[2]

Films:
1941 *Citizen Kane*
1949 *Twelve O'Clock High*
1952 *High Noon*

1954 *The Caine Mutiny*
1957 *12 Angry Men; Paths of Glory*
1962 *Billy Budd; Lawrence of Arabia*
1970 *Patton*
1979 *Norma Rae*
1982 *Gandhi*
1998 *Primary Colors*
2008 *Milk*

If, as we contend, leadership is a learned art, then so too are our conceptions of leadership learned. One of the sources from which we learn about leadership is Hollywood movies.[3] The films discussed below have helped shape both our understanding and our misconceptions of leadership. These films are valuable, too, because they show the conflicts, challenges, and paradoxes all leaders face.

Citizen Kane, 1941

"Rosebud" . . . Charles Foster Kane's last words. It is the mystery we must unravel.

Kane, based largely on real-life newspaper mogul William Randolph Hearst, is the story of a larger-than-life figure who rises gloriously and falls tragically. It is a classic study of narcissism and failed, dysfunctional leadership. It is as well a parable about the use and misuses of power to gain love.

Kane (played by Orson Welles) is a man of great drive and talent. He inherits a fortune and builds on it, amassing great wealth and power. In the process, he is transformed from an ambitious, driven man with a decidedly deficient emotional intelligence to a greedy monster. He builds then destroys, rises then falls. Kane is an obsessed Ahab who is defeated by his white whale . . . "Rosebud."

Citizen Kane traces the rise and fall of a tragic leader who becomes a failed monomaniac. We initially see a young Kane, brimming with ambition, principle, energy, talent, and a compelling vision.

As a young editor and publisher of a failing newspaper, he halts production late one night to put out a special edition, the headline of which is *Declaration of Principles,* his promise to his readers:

Kane: There's something I've got to get into this paper besides pictures and print. I've got to make the *New York Inquirer* as important to New York as the gas in that light.
Leland: What're you going to do, Charlie?
Kane: Declaration of Principles. Don't smile, Jedediah. Got it all written out: Declaration of Principles.

Bernstein: You don't want to make any promises, Mr. Kane, you don't want to keep.

Kane: These'll be kept. I'll provide the people of this city with a daily paper that will tell all the news honestly. I will also provide them …

Leland: That's the second sentence you started with "I" …

Kane: People are going to know who's responsible. And they're going to get the truth in the *Inquirer* quickly and simply and entertainingly, and no special interests are going to be allowed to interfere with that truth. I'll also provide them with a fighting and tireless champion of their rights as citizens and as human beings.

Yet, while delivering these inspiring words, director Orson Welles has Kane shrouded in dark shadow, implying that there may be more—or less—here than meets the eye. The young Kane fully intends—at that moment—to keep his promise. And yet, the young Kane devolves into an arrogant, narcissistic, selfish brute of a man; and his high-minded principles are mere wind.

Kane begins his journey with good intentions and great energy and skill, yet this gets corrupted as he achieves power and hungers for more. As darker impulses take over, his need to dominate and control leads to closed-mindedness and arrogance, and misstep upon misstep. As his drives become obsessions, including a failed run for governor of New York and a shameless bullying lifestyle, he descends into a world where self-control eludes him and the control of others becomes his mania.

Is Kane a leader or a mere power wielder? Kane starts as a leader yet descends into a tyrant. Early on he persuades, inspires, and wins over followers with his personality, energy, and vision. But as time goes by, Kane changes, and followers no longer willingly give themselves to him. He must bully and command. His is doubtless a case of either narcissistic personality disorder or borderline personality disorder, or both—which result in self-destructive manipulations and grandiose, attention-seeking exhibitionism. We'll leave this to psychiatrists to fathom.

Must power corrupt? It certainly corrupted Charles Foster Kane, but can power be tamed? America's constitutional framers believed that only by separating power and creating separate branches could it be controlled. *Citizen Kane* vividly reminds us, just as does the Willie Stark figure in *All the King's Men,* the Academy Award–winning film version of Robert Penn Warren's classic political novel based on Huey Long, of the dangers of unchecked power.

Analysts have long speculated that Kane's emotional immaturity that led to his undoing comes from his lost childhood, a childhood that abruptly ends when he is suddenly whisked away from a loving mother in rural Colorado to live under a cold, stern Wall Street mentor until he comes into his inherited fortune in his early twenties. Most of that is left to the imagination, but the loss of his boyhood sled "Rosebud" is probably what drives him to excess, and perhaps madness. This symbolizes, we are led to believe, his loss of emotional security, love, and happiness. In the end Kane can buy virtually everything, yet he is never able to buy love.

Twelve O'Clock High, 1949

Set in World War II, *Twelve O'Clock High* has been a staple in leadership training courses for decades. The story focuses on different styles of leadership as applied to a World War II bomber squadron, the 918th Airborne stationed in England. Its mission is to fly dangerous daytime precision bombing raids on Germany. The 918th has been underperforming and suffers from poor morale. Its commander, Colonel Keith Davenport, seems to be part of the problem. His style of command leadership is to be close, supportive, and empathetic with his men—a "soft" leadership style. His men love him and are fiercely loyal to him, yet the combat results are disappointing. The implication is that the soft, "carrot" approach leads to lax performance.

Some housecleaning seems in order, and Davenport is replaced by Brigadier General Frank Savage (Gregory Peck). Savage arrives to find his squadron in disarray. He immediately begins a new and different approach. In sharp contrast to Davenport, Savage is a disciplinarian who practices a brand of tough love that is not well received by his squadron. Savage is strict, demanding, critical, hard. He demands "maximum effort." Where Davenport offers the carrot, Savage applies the stick. The men of the 918th reject Savage and his "hard" style of leadership command, and all of the 918th's pilots apply for a transfer.

Savage is able, however, with help from his adjutant, to delay these transfer applications. The combat missions continue, and over time, Savage's tough methods produce results. Eventually, the pilots come around and recognize that the tough love is for their own good and that of the war effort, and makes them into a much more effective fighting unit. Savage succeeds in instilling discipline, pride, a sense of purpose, and productivity. In challenging and pushing his squadron, Savage has built them into a first-class fighting team.

Yet his impressive, if stern, leadership approach takes its toll on Savage, who suffers a breakdown. Colonel Ben Gateley, toward whom Savage has been a severe critic, steps up and takes over the air command, leading to a successful mission. Savage has helped make Gately a leader, demonstrating that good leaders empower others to lead.

Does tough love (hard leadership) lead to better results than soft leadership? Football coach Vince Lombardi or General Electric's former chairman Jack Welch might agree. And yet, the jury is out on this question. John Wooden of the University of California–Los Angeles and Mike Krzyzewski of Duke University, two of the greatest coaches in college basketball, exercised a softer, more supportive hybrid style, which led to their legendary successes. Similarly, Generals Dwight Eisenhower and David Petraeus, notable contrasts to the hard-driving Generals Douglas MacArthur and George S. Patton, were seemingly more successful.

High Noon, 1952

Will Kane, played by Gary Cooper, is the marshal of Hadleyville, New Mexico Territory. He cleaned up Hadleyville and brought law and order to this rough-and-tumble frontier town. As the movie opens, he has just married Amy (Grace Kelly), an attractive and innocent Quaker pacifist. Kane is about to retire and become a storekeeper in another town.

But Hadleyville learns that outlaw Frank Miller, whom Kane brought to justice, has been released from prison and plans to return to Hadleyville to exact revenge. Three of Miller's thugs await his return and plan to join forces with their leader. The battle lines are drawn.

Marshal Kane, as all good leaders do, explores his options. He can leave town and retire as originally planned, organize a posse and prepare for the fight, or act alone. Kane prudently opts for the second approach.

At a local church service, the sheriff addresses the townspeople. He reminds them of what is at stake and says, "I'm going to need to deputize all the men I can get." But fearful citizens raise concerns about the dangers inherent in such a strategy, with one man shouting, "Hey, this isn't our job. That's what we pay the sheriff for!" Other voices rise to defend the sheriff, with one man saying, "This man made this town safe for our families. Most of us remember when Frank Miller and his gang made it unsafe to leave our homes. Some people even left to seek a safer place to settle. Now that he needs our help, we have to give it to him."

In the end, the voices of fear prevail. There will be no posse to take on Frank Miller and his men. Kane is the man Miller is after, and the townspeople leave Kane alone to deal with him. Frank Miller is set to arrive on the noon train. The consensus of the church gathering, as well as that of others in the town, is that Kane should leave town. The dilemma Kane is faced with is a sense of duty to his old town versus love and personal safety. Duty prevails.

Kane faces the gunmen—alone. He shoots two of Miller's men and he himself is wounded. When Amy, who has boarded an outgoing train, intent on leaving this violence behind her, hears the gunshots, she leaves the train and hurries back to the main street in town. Amy must choose between her deeply held religious beliefs and her new husband ... she shoots the third gunman in the back.

Miller takes Amy hostage and offers Kane a trade: Amy for Kane. Kane agrees. Then Amy fights back, clawing Miller's face. Miller lets Amy go and Kane shoots him.

As the dust settles, the townspeople come out of hiding. They are in awe. Yet Kane contemptuously rips his badge off, throws it in the dirt, and along with his wife, rides out of town.

Will Kane is a man of courage, skill, accomplishment, and integrity. He is admired by a grateful town. He seems every bit the heroic, ideal, and fearless leader. Yet, he is *not* a leader. Leaders have followers, and Kane can't get the townspeople to follow. He is a lone wolf, a heroic lone wolf, but in the end, a man who acts alone (nearly). In spite of an impending crisis, Will Kane is unable to articulate and sell a compelling vision. He is unable to inspire others to follow. He succeeds in his task (killing Miller and his men) but fails as a leader. Good triumphs over evil, yet not because Kane is an effective leader. Still, Kane's example may inspire heroism or civic engagement in those who view this classic—that, at least, is the hope. We learn in *High Noon,* as we did in *To Kill a Mockingbird* (1962), that courage can be a solitary endeavor.

As a historical side note, *High Noon* was made in 1952 amid the Red Scare, the McCarthy era, the anticommunist hysteria, and the Hollywood blacklist. A witch hunt to identify and destroy both Communists and leftists devastated the film industry. Hollywood retreated from making "problem films" and produced sanitized and homogenized films. If one wanted to attack the blacklist, it had to be done indirectly, by allegory. Films like *High Noon* and *Invasion of the Body Snatchers* (1956) were condemnations of the cowardliness of the blacklist and the cowardliness of those who caved in to the pressure and cooperated with the assault on rights in that era. Carl Foreman, the author, as well as the *uncredited* producer, of *High Noon,* was called before the House Un-American Activities Committee (HUAC) to testify under oath and "name names" of Communists in Hollywood. Foreman was considered an "un-cooperative witness" and was later blacklisted, thus not permitted to work in Hollywood.

In this context, *High Noon* is about one man standing up to evil (Miller and his gang in the movie; HUAC and the blacklist in real life). As the townspeople cowered in fear, so too did many in the Hollywood community,[4] who stood by silently as friends and coworkers were (sometimes) unfairly blacklisted.

The Caine Mutiny, 1954

The USS *Caine* is a clunker of a ship. A dilapidated minesweeper, it seems held together by rust and willpower alone. Being assigned to the *Caine* is not a sought-after posting.

The Caine's captain, Lieutenant Commander William De Vriess, is replaced by Philip Frances Queeg (Humphrey Bogart), a strict, by-the-book disciplinarian who has a distinguished record in battle. Almost immediately, Queeg alienates his officers when, in their first meeting, he signals a new and tougher style of command:

> Just another naval officer. I've had seven tough years in the Atlantic, and believe you me, they made the last two mighty interesting. The way those subs ganged up on us, I thought they had it in for me personally.... Anyone who knows me will tell you I'm a book man. I believe everything in it was put in for a purpose. When in doubt, remember on board this ship, we do things by the book. Deviate from the book and you'd better have a half a dozen good reasons. And you'll still get an argument from me. And I don't lose arguments on board my ship. That's, uh, one of the nice things about being captain. I want you to remember one thing. On board my ship, excellent performance is standard. Standard performance is substandard. Substandard performance is not permitted to exist. That—I warn you.

Queeg tells his officers that he wants a smarter-looking, spit-and-polish approach and that he won't tolerate substandard performance. He wants all shirts tucked in, all the men clean shaven, all hair closely cropped. He turns to his second-in-command and says, "There are four ways of doing things on board my ship. The right way, the wrong way, the Navy way, and my way."

Initially, one might draw a comparison between Frank Savage of *Twelve O'Clock High* and Queeg. Both are tough-minded, demanding, and stern. Yet where Savage eventually wins over his men, Queeg antagonizes and loses the respect as well as the support of his men.

Queeg, obsessed with small details, sometimes loses sight of the big picture. A series of avoidable missteps occur, some due to Queeg's obstinance, some to poor seamanship. Queeg calls a meeting with his officers and asks them for cooperation, assistance, and loyalty. "Constructive loyalty" is how Queeg terms it. "A ship," he says, "is like a family. We all have our ideas of right and wrong but we have to pitch in for the good of the family. If there was only some way we could help each other." The officers' response is silence. They do not like their boss and are unwilling to come to his aid.

Tensions and conflicts build until finally Queeg seems to "lose it" over "the strawberries." A quart of strawberries goes missing, and Queeg becomes Ahab-like in his search for the thief. Acting like an obsessed madman, Queeg works out the incident "with perfect geometrical precision." His officers begin to suspect him of paranoia. He seems unstable. What to do?

A short time later, in a raging typhoon, Queeg seems paralyzed in this turbulent "fog of war." The ship's executive officer relieves Queeg of his command on the grounds of mental instability. The officers steer the ship through the crisis, yet two are later charged with mutiny.

The drama shifts from ship to courtroom, where a wily defense attorney, Barry Greenwald, gets Queeg on the stand to testify and presses him unrelentingly. Queeg, under great stress, breaks. The charges of mutiny are dismissed.

At a party celebrating the officers' victory, an intoxicated Greenwald shows up. Ashamed that he destroyed a man who had served his country with honor, Greenwald wondered if the wrong man hadn't been broken.

The Caine Mutiny is a complex and compelling drama that raises more questions than it answers. Yes, Queeg, deficient in social and emotional intelligence, is strange and a bit "off"; yet had the officers come to his aid—as he had asked—might things have turned out dramatically differently? Queeg's belated effort at team building seems too little, too late; yet had he built an effective team and enlisted the help of his officers at the outset, things might have turned out differently.

Leadership is seldom, if ever, the province of one lone individual. Good leaders build teams of leaders. Queeg does not, and probably cannot, do this. His closed, narrow, insecure, perhaps paranoid personality limits his ability to open up, reach out, and make the ship, or any organization, a smooth-running enterprise.

12 Angry Men, 1957

This courtroom drama centers on a jury of twelve men, called upon to decide the guilt or innocence of a young boy from the wrong side of the tracks who is accused of killing his father. Virtually all the action takes place within the jury room on a hot afternoon, as the jurors discuss, deliberate, argue, and ultimately come to agreement.

An initial vote reveals eleven jurors believe the boy to be guilty, with only one (Henry Fonda, juror 8) holding out. It is hot and stuffy in the jury room; the jurors want to decide and go home. Pressure is applied to juror 8, but he wants to discuss the case further. Juror 8 begins to call into question some of the evidence and testimony. He plants seeds of doubt.

Under intense pressure, juror 8 agrees that if another vote is taken and all eleven jurors vote guilty, he will relent and join them. In the next vote, juror 9 does not join the others in voting guilty. An intense, often heated discussion ensues.

One by one, the jurors come around and express doubts about the young boy's guilt, until finally the vote is unanimous, not guilty. The movie *12 Angry Men* is a case study in subtle leadership. Juror 8 is a skilled, subtle, determined leader who demonstrates several key leadership talents: persuasion, good judgment, good timing, evidence-based analysis, consensus building, focused listening skills, emotional intelligence, situational sensitivity, empathy, and the courage to question the accepted wisdom.

His *courage* allows him to stand up alone against eleven determined men. His good judgment compels him to question the *evidence* presented and reach his own conclusion. He is able to slowly and carefully use *evidence* to *persuade* his fellow jurors. His *timing,* knowing when to push and when to hold back, helps him control events. His *empathy* and *emotional intelligence* give him an advantage in dealing with a diverse set of individuals. These skills, plus the fact that he is a good listener, allow him to get a good read on people and the *situation,* and to develop a group *consensus.*

Paths of Glory, 1957

The title of this film comes from a line in the eighteenth-century romantic poet Thomas Gray's *Elegy Written in a Country Churchyard*: "The paths of glory lead but to the grave."

Paths of Glory, a film treatise on injustice and dysfunctional leadership, set in France in 1916 during World War I, is one of the most powerful antiwar films ever made. Inspired by a true story from the Battle of Verdun, it tells the story of military madness and injustice.

In a palatial chateau, surrounded by comforts and luxury, the French high command plot strategy. Corps commander General George Broulard, an evil, scheming, self-centered leader, meets with General Paul Mireau, his snobbish subordinate. "I've come to see you about something big," Broulard tells Mireau, "the taking of a fortified German stronghold known as Ant Hill." It is a suicide mission, doomed to fail from the beginning. Mireau expresses skepticism. "It's out of the question, George. Absolutely out of the question. My division was cut to pieces. What's left of it is in no position to even hold the Ant Hill, let alone take it. I'm sorry, but that's the truth."

But Broulard does not want to hear the truth; he wants a victory that will catapult him in the eyes of his superiors. He appeals to Mireau's vanity. You will be considered a "fighting general," get another star, be a hero. But Mireau demurs.

Mireau: I am responsible for the lives of 8,000 men. What is my ambition against that? What is my reputation in comparison to that? My men come first of all, George. And those men know it, too.

Broulard: I know that they do.

Mireau: You see, George, those men know that I would never let them down.

Broulard: (unimpressed, with a glib reply) That goes without saying.

Mireau: The life of one of those soldiers means more to me than all the stars and decorations and honors in France.

Broulard is persistent and the appeals to Mireau's vanity finally work. "Nothing is beyond these men," he finally says. "Once their fighting spirit is aroused...."

We might just do it!" Delusion becomes self-delusion, and the suicide mission goes forward.

Prior to the assault, a resplendent Mireau visits his troops. The contrast between the immaculate Mireau and the squalor and mud-soaked troops is striking, and Mireau is visibly uncomfortable in the trenches with his warriors.

Mireau visits Colonel Dax (Kirk Douglas), the regimental commander and the man who will be responsible for the attack on Ant Hill. Mireau hesitantly presents the plan of attack to Dax:

> Naturally, men are gonna have to be killed, possibly a lot of them. They'll absorb bullets and shrapnel, and by doing so make it possible for others to get through ... say five percent killed by our own barrage—that's a very generous allowance. Ten percent more again in no man's land, and twenty percent more again into the wire. That leaves sixty-five percent, and the worst part of the job over. Let's say another twenty-five percent in actually taking the Ant Hill—we're still left with a force more than adequate to hold it.

Dax isn't buying what the general is selling. He knows it is a hopeless suicide mission. Mireau appeals to Dax's patriotism, to which Dax responds with the Samuel Johnson quote "Patriotism ... is the last refuge of a scoundrel." Mireau then threatens Dax, informing him he will be relieved from his command, and finally Dax concedes.

Of course, the attack is an utter failure. The first wave is nearly wiped out within a few feet of the trenches. The rest of the men refuse to attack. Eventually, the mission is called off. But Mireau cannot admit his mistake. He blames the failure on the cowardice of the troops and orders three men selected by lot to be executed as an example to the troops. Dax tries valiantly yet in vain to defend his men, but his cause is doomed from the start.

In the final scene, a German woman is brought before the French troops and forced to entertain them with a song. The rowdy French mock her as she sings a German folk tune that is ironically a French song. The mood of the group changes as they realize how little really separates them from their enemy.

Banned in France for twenty years, *Paths of Glory* is a frontal assault on the hypocrisy of military justice, the danger of selfish leadership, the damage done by corrupt and callous leaders, the danger when there is a huge gap between leaders and followers, the destructive capacity of the "politics and fog of war,"[5] and the effects when leaders don't care for the welfare of followers and think only about themselves. Morally bankrupt and self-centered leaders who think only of themselves (leadership as a one-way street), who are willing to sacrifice their men for their own glory, are classic examples of dysfunctional leadership.

Billy Budd, 1962

A novel (by Herman Melville), play, movie, and opera, *Billy Budd* is a classic story of innocence, power, leadership, and good and evil. Melville left the novella unfinished at his death in 1891, and it was not published until 1924.

It is 1797. Young sailor Billy Budd is impressed (forced) to be a crewman on the HMS *Avenger*. Billy is naïve and innocent, and he sees the good in almost everything.

Billy works diligently, helps everyone, and charms his crewmates; and they adore him. Yet he is disliked by John Claggart, the ship's suspicious and creepy master-at-arms. Claggart falsely accuses Billy of conspiracy to mutiny and brings those charges to the ship's captain Edward Vere. As Claggart accuses the young sailor, Billy, enraged and unable to control his emotions or speak in his own defense due to his speech impediment, strikes and accidentally kills Claggart. Vere sadly intones, "Struck dead by an angel of God! Yet the angel must hang!"

Vere convenes a court-martial. The case is confusing, yet Vere's senior officers initially rule it a matter of self-defense and not murder. Still, although not his intent, Billy did kill Claggart, and Vere goes on to issue a guilty verdict. Vere is following military code and believes that to do otherwise—to let Billy go free—would be a sign of weakness, inviting disrespect and mutiny. Although Vere struggles between duty and conscience, in the end duty wins out.

As Billy faces the hangman's noose, he shouts out, "God Bless Captain Vere."

This conflict between good and evil, innocence and worldliness pits the young, handsome, charismatic, and naïve Billy Budd against the hardened, cruel, world-weary, tough-minded, and doubtlessly sadistic Claggart. The difference between the two men is apparent in an earlier exchange after Claggart flogs one of the crewmen.

> **Budd**: It's wrong to flog a man. It's against his being a man.
>
> **Claggart**: The Sea is calm you said. Peaceful. Calm above, but below a world of gliding monsters preying on their fellow murderers, all of them. Only the strongest teeth survive. And who's to tell me it's any different here on board, or yonder on dry land?

Melville sees the alternating forces of good and evil running throughout the human experience. In the world, innocence is corrupted by the harsh demands of existence. Billy's innocence is admirable yet ill suited to the rough-and-tumble of the real world. It blinds Billy who is kind and forgiving. It is society that corrupts, and as Billy cannot adjust to the demands of society, he is destroyed. If good is not prepared to deal with evil, evil will win.

Billy Budd compels us to ask if it is better to be naïve, innocent, and ignorant of life's crueler side, or must we make our peace with the devil and become a bit more hardened, cautious, and worldly? Is there a place for the Billy Budds in this world?

And what does *Billy Budd* tell us about leadership? There are distinctive leadership models represented by three main characters. Billy represents goodness and innocence. His Christ-like ways draw others to him. He is admired, respected, even loved. His purity of spirit wins over the support of the hardened crew. He leads by example. People *want* to follow him. And yet, is he "too good"? Too good for his own good? Must he meet a tragic fate? And is Billy well suited to leadership? His innocence prevents him from fully engaging in a world where most others are not like him. His naïveté invites others to take advantage of him. Had Billy a few rough edges, had he a bit more understanding of just how cruel the world *can* be, he might have hardened himself for the task ahead. His destruction seems inevitable, unavoidable. Leaders must sometimes fight fire with fire. Billy does not know this and is unable to confront Claggart on a more even playing field.

Claggart is a brute, crude, at times vicious; he will go to any lengths to get what he wants. He is the polar opposite of Billy. Billy leads by example; Claggart is never a leader—he is a villain. He goes to extremes, is cruel simply to be cruel. He tries to rule by fear, yet his command fails to earn respect and legitimacy.

Vere is the most conflicted character in the film. He recognizes Billy's qualities of decency and seamanship but is responsible for enforcing the law. He knows Billy's act was neither premeditated nor intentional, yet he cannot allow a murder to go unpunished. Vere is a man torn between his admiration for Billy as a person and his apparently more compelling duty to his ship, his country, and the rule of law. Vere is genuinely torn. He is convinced that although Billy is an innocent person, he is not innocent of a crime. He sadly believes that "an angel must hang" yet immediately feels both helpless and misguided in this test of his decision making.

Lawrence of Arabia, 1962

Thomas Edward "T. E." Lawrence was a complex, paradoxical, extraordinary individual who attempted the impossible, tasted the fruits of victory, yet in the end was forced to accept defeat.[6] One of his biographers notes that the 1962 film has many inaccuracies and is obviously an incomplete portrait; yet, he adds, it is a masterpiece and "one of the longest, most beautiful, most ambitious and most honored films ever made." *Lawrence of Arabia* won seven Academy Awards and made a fortune for Columbia Pictures.[7]

During World War I, Lawrence, an officer in the British military, is assigned to the Arabian Peninsula as a representative to King Feisal. The British want to enlist Feisal and others in the war effort against the Turks, and Lawrence's job is to gain the support of the many disparate tribes in the battle.

Lawrence goes further. He becomes a leader of the Arab guerrilla war against the Turks and an advocate for Arab unity.

The various Bedouin tribes of the region have to join forces against the superior arms of the Turks, and it is the unlikely figure of T. E. Lawrence who helps bring them together and leads them to victory.

How odd a figure is this Oxford University–educated, slight, five-foot-five British officer in the Arabian desert? And how unlikely a leader of these fractious Bedouin tribes is he? (In the movie Lawrence is portrayed by six-foot-two Peter O'Toole.) What is it that allows the unlikely Lawrence to overcome the obvious liabilities and rise to leadership in a culture and setting so alien to all he knows? Not only is Lawrence an unlikely leader, the context seems ill suited to the achievement of his task. After all, Lawrence has to bring together in common purpose a slew of disparate tribes to fight the Turks, when these tribes are more accustomed to fighting each other than an outside enemy.

The simplistic (though profound) answer can be summed up in one word: Aqaba. They have to capture the port city of Aqaba.

Lawrence has a compelling and challenging *vision,* a *goal* that is as audacious as it is risky. If only he can get the tribes to *believe.*

Lawrence was a master of counterinsurgency, or guerilla warfare. In asymmetrical warfare, maneuvers and deception are keys. His basic principles were laid out in his short essay "Evolution of a Revolt."[8] He hit the Turks where they were most vulnerable, the railroads. He attacked their supply lines. He employed a hit-and-run strategy. Surprise was a key element, direct confrontation a rarity. This strategy was designed less to defeat the Turks on the battlefield than to undermine their morale, keep them confused and frustrated, and put them on the defensive. The Turks were flummoxed. They wanted direct combat; the Arabs denied them this goal.

The set of skills T. E. Lawrence employed in his quest for leadership was impressive. He was a renaissance man, gifted with natural skills as well as finely developed talents. Lawrence was a gifted writer and a voracious reader. Naturally curious, his interests were wide ranging and encompassing. He immersed himself in another culture to the point where his cross-cultural competence allowed him to be accepted and respected by the Arabs.

Lawrence was charismatic, excellent at self-dramatization, brilliant, visionary, goal oriented, inspirational. He had a powerful discipline, drive, persistence, and courage. His finely developed strategic sense allowed him to take intelligent risks and do the unexpected with good results. Both the movie and his biographers argue that he was ambitious more for results than for personal glory.

Lawrence was an adventurer and entrepreneur. He was flexible and highly adaptable. He oozed self-confidence even as he was torn from within. Lawrence was also a creative genius, able to see beyond conventional wisdom. His resilience got him through many tough times. And his persuasive skills usually enabled him to win over even the most skeptical of critics.

He had his flaws. Lawrence was brilliant yet his intensity and uncommon personal discipline often bordered on masochism. The British high command saw him as reckless, immature, undisciplined, a dreamer, and a loner. He was self-centered and at times driven by a ruthless desire to achieve greatness. He was a restless scholar and a mighty warrior. At times he displayed a shameless exhibitionism yet more often he cherished privacy and shunned honors and attention. As Crispin Burke notes,

> We must be aware that the great intuitive and creative skills we admire in Lawrence are often interpreted as their shadowy opposites. People of Lawrence's temperament are, to steal a term from pop-psychology, "right-brained," and often tend to have difficulty conforming to the norms of a bureaucratic professional military organization. As a result, they may seem "careless," as Lawrence's disheveled uniform suggested; "weird," as Lawrence's obsession for reading books in their original Latin or Greek might have seemed to other British officers; or worse yet, "insubordinate," as Lawrence and his ideas of Arab Revolt must have seemed to Murray and his staff.[9]

Patton, 1970

General George S. Patton, controversial, flamboyant, brilliant, known as "Old Blood and Guts," was admired, even loved, by many. Yet others hated him and found him dangerous.

In real life, George Patton was a larger-than-life figure. He was not a mellow, easygoing man but was intense, a demanding disciplinarian, bombastic, arrogant, temperamental, egomaniacal, harsh, at times brutal, and thoughtless. One time, he slapped an enlisted man who had disappointed him. Patton could be a brute and a thug. He was also a brilliant strategist and a much decorated war hero.

Patton was anything but simple or one-dimensional. He was a complex, ever contradictory figure. Of Patton it was often said, "He is his own worst enemy."

The movie *Patton* opens with the general (played by George C. Scott) delivering a long monologue as he stands in full dress uniform in front of a massive American flag. He says, in part,

> Now I want you to remember that no bastard ever won a war by dying for his country. He won it by making the other poor dumb bastard die for his country. Men, all this stuff you've heard about America not wanting to fight—wanting to stay out of the war, is a lot of horse dung. Americans traditionally love to fight. All

real Americans love the sting of battle. When you were kids, you all admired the champion marble shooter, the fastest runner, big league ball players, the toughest boxers. Americans love a winner and will not tolerate a loser. Americans play to win all the time. I wouldn't give a hoot in hell for a man who lost and laughed. That's why Americans have never lost and will never lose a war, because the very thought of losing is *hateful* to Americans.

Now, an army is a team—it lives, eats, sleeps, fights as a team. This individuality stuff is a bunch of crap. . . . Now, we have the finest food and equipment, the best spirit, and the best men in the world. You know, by god, I actually pity those poor bastards we're goin' up against. By god, I do. We're not just gonna shoot the bastards, we're going to cut out their living guts and use them to grease the treads of our tanks. . . . We're going to kick the hell out of him all the time and we're gonna go through him like crap through a goose.

Now, there's one thing that you men will be able to say when you get back home, and you may thank God for it. Thirty years from now when you're sitting around your fireside with your grandson on your knee, and he asks you: "What did you do in the great World War II?" You won't have to say, "Well, I shoveled s—t in Louisiana."

All right now, you sons-of-bitches, you know how I feel and I will be proud to lead you wonderful guys into battle anytime, anywhere. That's all.

The film then jumps to North Africa in 1943. Patton has just arrived to assume command of the failing American forces. "You know why these men lost? They don't look like soldiers," he says, "and they're scared." Patton lights a cigar and announces, "In fifteen minutes we're going to change all that. They're going to lose their fear of the Germans, because I'm gonna give them something to be fearful about."

When he gets to the officers' mess he is disturbed by the lack of military precision. He then goes through the men's barracks and again registers his disappointment. When he gets to the field hospital, he unloads on the attending physician.

"Doctor, am I to understand that you have a case here of battle fatigue?" "Yes we do, General," says the physician. "Well," intones Patton, "get him out of here. He doesn't belong in the same room with these brave men." The doctor responds, "But, General, he cannot recover unless we treat him here." The doctor feels the wrath of the General: "I don't care if he dies, just get him out of here!" With that, Patton leaves, then returns to confront the doctor. "Where is your helmet, doctor?" The doctor replies, "I can't use my stethoscope if I wear a helmet, General." Patton smiles and barks, "Well, doctor, have two holes cut in your helmet so you can."

Tough, demanding, military through and through, Patton insists on everyone's doing it his way, by the book. He is no mere barker of orders; Patton really lives this life and thus can lead by example. He is absolutely clear about what he expects (demands) of others and communicates with clarity and precision.

Patton was well suited to wartime leadership. He was able to get the most out of his troops because they knew precisely what he wanted, and what would result if they failed in their task. And yet one is left with the haunting suspicion that Patton was "a man for one season." Skilled in war, Patton probably would have been a fish out of water in peacetime. His temperament and skill fit the demands of war. Like Winston Churchill who performed magnificently during World War II yet was less able to adapt and adjust his style to the demands and needs of peacetime, Patton mastered war yet floundered in peace. When there is congruence between skill and task—Churchill and Patton in war—the leader can be highly successful, even if, at times, his methods are distasteful. Yet if that leader is unable to adjust to changing circumstances, he will fail to perform the task of effective leadership.

However, General George S. Patton, a West Point graduate and Olympic Games (1912) pentathlon competitor, was by far America's most successful fighting general in World War II. He may have been racist and at times even anti-Semitic, but he was a genius at getting his men to fight in the toughest battles. His military mantra seems to have been "The only way you can win a war is to attack and keep attacking, and after you have done that, keep attacking more." As one of his biographers writes, Patton "cultivated a complexity of character that defies explanation and developed a personality whose force was terrifying.... Patton defined and constructed himself as a hero. He spent his life preparing for the opportunity to fulfill his destiny on the battlefield, and when opportunity came ... he seized it with both hands."[10]

He died from traffic injuries in late 1945.

Norma Rae, 1979

Whereas most Hollywood films as well as popular myths and expectations focus on the individual—great man—leading and causing change, *Norma Rae* (played by Sally Field) takes a slightly different approach. Yes, there is the heroic leader (in this case, a woman),[11] but this is not the story of a leader alone. It is the tale of a leader *and* followers. In part, Norma Rae's success is dependent on concerted group action, on followers.

A careful reading of history, as well as a careful viewing of the film, should lead one to the conclusion that although leadership is important, followership is essential as well. Would Patton have won his many battles had his men failed to follow and execute? *The Godfather*'s Don Corleone, standing alone, is merely a man, easily disposed of. What is Lawrence without his Bedouin followers? Leaders need followers, as *High Noon*'s hero Will Kane so painfully discovered. This is the Yin and Yang of leadership. It is a two-way street, a symbiotic relationship; one can't exist without the other.

Unusual for Hollywood movies, *Norma Rae* explicitly recognizes the importance of followers and the impact of collective action in politics. The film pays proper tribute to leadership, yet not in the Gary Cooper/John Wayne tradition. Norma is a flawed person. She is presented warts and all. And yet, she, along with her coworkers, accomplishes a significant victory against considerable odds.

Norma is like us. And supporting the view that almost anyone can become a leader, she acts, leads, and wins. Not because of her superhuman skills but because, in the real world, real people often lead.

The movie is based on the life of Crystal Lee Sutton,[12] a labor organizer in North Carolina. It is the story of how one woman organizes her coworkers to form a union at the textile factory in which they work.

Norma Rae works for minimum wage. She and her coworkers are poorly treated and at first Norma sees no option but to put up with it. After all, her parents did, and most of her friends do. However, after hearing a speech by a visiting union organizer, Reuben Warshowsky, she decides to try to help start a union. After a long and difficult struggle, Norma Rae and her coworkers succeed in forming a union.[13]

Norma Rae is determined, focused, goal oriented, resilient, willing to risk a lot, able to motivate coworkers, willing to take on the boss, and able to articulate and sell a vision of a better tomorrow. She has little education but loads of determination. With the help of New York organizer Warshowsky, her teacher and mentor, she learns as she leads.

In one especially telling scene, Norma Rae faces defeat, for herself, her cause, and her coworkers. On the factory floor she climbs on a table and holds a sign that simply reads UNION. She stands there, sign held above her head, while the workers continue to work and the machinery continues to whir. She stands there on the edge of defeat for a full three minutes (which seem like a lifetime), and not one of her coworkers has the courage to stand up with her. She puts herself fully on the line for the union and her coworkers. Yet she stands alone. UNION, a one-word promise, a vision for the future. Norma Rae stands there, alone and frightened; yet she refuses to retreat, refuses to step down.

Finally, the factory workers slowly—one by one—turn off their machines. The factory that was buzzing with the sound of machinery in motion draws quiet until a deafening silence overtakes the factory floor. Norma Rae leads, her coworkers join her, and while later working together, they win a vote to unionize.

Gandhi, 1982

Gandhi is a Hollywood biopic of the inspirational advocate of nonviolence Mohandas Gandhi. The movie picks up Gandhi's life in 1893 when he lives in South Africa, follows him to India and the resistance movement against British imperial rule, and ends with his death at the hands of an assassin in 1948.

Gandhi was an unusual man and an unusual leader. He embraced nonviolence in spite of living in a violent world where might makes right, where disputes were often settled with bullets rather than ballots.

Gandhi had a profound impact on his world and ours. We can see his influence on some of the great leaders who followed and were influenced by him: notably, Martin Luther King Jr. (who once said that "Christ gave us the goals, and Gandhi gave us the tactics"), and Nelson Mandela of South Africa.

A slight man, shy, humbly dressed, Gandhi looked anything but a leader. Throughout the film, we see examples of his nonviolence in action.

His political commitment begins, the film suggests, in 1893 when, as a young (Indian-born, London-educated) lawyer living in South Africa, he is thrown off a moving train because he refuses to leave a first-class cabin, in spite of the fact he has bought a first-class ticket. From this and other events, he becomes sensitive to injustice and violence. He determines to live by a "better way." As he is pulled further and further into political action, his better way—nonviolence—becomes his source of power and leadership. His political metamorphosis leads to the blossoming of a leader who *earns* a following.

The movie unfolds by revealing leadership scene after leadership scene. When Gandhi emerges as a national leader in India, his nonviolent approach is in full operation. The British continue to apply conventional force, but they are flummoxed when confronting the unusual methods employed by Gandhi and his followers.

Finally, when independence is achieved, Gandhi is regarded as the father of the nation; yet he is not given a leadership position. He is seen as "mahatma" (saint), who inspires a people—not from a position of power or hierarchy—but as an extraordinary man.

What was it about this unlikely man that made him such an influential leader? Gandhi was well educated and well traveled. He was focused and disciplined. He possessed enormous moral capital. He not only talked the talk, he walked the walk. He genuinely lived a humble life and embraced nonviolence. His values were put to the test time and again, and yet he seldom faltered. His commitment to nonviolence was absolute, was tested under fire, and gave him a moral authority that attracted a devoted following.[14]

Moreover, Gandhi had a vision for a free India. He was inspirational and persuasive, determined and goal oriented. His use of nonviolence as a means of political action was unorthodox and threw his opponents off balance. Gandhi lived a humble lifestyle and gave as well as received respect.

Could Gandhi's method of leadership be applied elsewhere and under different circumstances? *Gandhi*, the movie, suggests that it was the man's sincerity, his genuineness, that compelled others to take him and his message of nonviolence seriously. It took a special man to convince a mass following that not only was he the real deal, but his unorthodox method was worth pursuing.

Primary Colors, 1998

Based on the 1996 best-selling book by "Anonymous" (later revealed to be journalist Joe Klein), *Primary Colors* follows the ups and downs of the 1992 presidential primary race with a not-so-hidden parallel to the Bill Clinton campaign.

We follow Jack Stanton, southern governor and presidential candidate, as he attempts to win his party's nomination for president. But Mr. Stanton (played by John Travolta) has a problem: he has a weakness for women with big hair and short skirts.

The film opens with political consultant Henry Burton, whom the Stanton campaign is trying to recruit, witnessing the "Stanton method" in action. Burton sees Stanton working the crowd, shaking hands, making eye contact with the voters, schmoozing. Stanton is a master at working the crowd. He oozes charm. Plus, he stands for all the "right" issues. He is a master politician with a progressive agenda. Burton is sucked into the Stanton vortex.

Quickly, things turn sour. Stanton, the incessant womanizer, is publicly accused of having a long-term affair with his wife's hairdresser, Cashmere McLeod. As the New Hampshire primary approaches, Stanton seems dead in the water. And yet, he fights on. And somehow he thrives and marches toward the nomination.

Jack Stanton is a sweet-talking seducer of both women and voters, a person of contradictions who cares deeply yet can be opportunistic and ruthless, and a man who cares passionately for reform yet is self-destructive. He is utterly exasperating to friend and foe, yet he is able to disarm even his toughest critics. A man with insatiable appetites, he seems always to have doughnut crumbs on his suit jacket and a big-haired woman in his sights. His empathy is genuine, as is his idealism. A skilled politician, he fends off crisis after crisis—most self-induced. He is a magnificent rascal who deeply cares about people and issues yet cynically manipulates those who come into his luminous orbit. He is a master seducer, both sexually and politically.

His wife Susan (Hillary), played by Emma Thompson, must deal not just with a philandering husband but with a political campaign about to be derailed by Jack's extracurricular activities. And yet, she, like Jack, really *believes.* She sees the good they can do for people—if only they can get elected. She alternately chews him out and saves him. If Jack exasperates her, she is also loyal both to him and to his political (if not his personal) ideals. Both Jack and Susan are painfully ambitious, but it is personal ambition mixed with the sincere belief that they can do good things. Susan puts up with her flawed husband because she is convinced that imperfect people can still make good policy, can still "change history."

Up to this point, our discussion of Hollywood leaders has taken a distinctly male tone. Apart from *Norma Rae* and a brief role in *High Noon,* women have been virtually silent and invisible. *Primary Colors* puts the candidate's spouse front and center and makes her an active participant in the drama that unfolds. This is one of the few leadership films that give a woman center stage (shared with a man, however).

Primary Colors is unusual in that it presents the political process not in black-and-white terms but in shades of gray. We are all human, with strengths and weaknesses. We must make tough choices in a complex world. Jack Stanton is deeply human and deeply flawed. And yet, he has positive qualities and is a gifted politician. Politics is a rough, tough, unsentimental, and often bruising, if not brutal, business. It is simultaneously compelling and repelling. It takes a tough-minded person to navigate the choppy waters of a presidential campaign, and if Jack Stanton has his flaws, we all do.

Real-world politics is not about achieving sainthood, it about gaining and using power wisely and well. Can a flawed man be a good president? We'd better hope so, as we are all flawed. Our heroes have feet of clay. In the real world, the search for perfection leads to disappointment.

At its best, *Primary Colors* reveals the ambiguity of politics. It raises the tough ethical questions we would rather avoid. Do the ends justify the means? Is there a distinction between one's private and public morality? Could a truly moral person—a Billy Budd or a Gandhi, for example—survive and rise in our political system? Can a flawed person be a good public servant?

These issues come to a head late in the film when the race boils down to two men. The Stanton campaign digs up damaging information about its opponent, Governor Fred Picker. What to do? They have the nomination in their grasp, yet, it requires a descent into the gutter to guarantee it. Some argue against releasing the information; but Stanton argues that if they don't release it, their opponents in the general election will, assuring the opposing party the presidency. Better, he argues, to get it out now. They struggle with both the political and the moral dimensions of their problems.

Primary Colors asks us, as it asks the characters in the film, to confront tough moral and political choices. It does not sugarcoat this dilemma. Whom do we want as leaders? Who can go through this process and not cross moral borders? Does the process corrupt? How can flawed leaders govern? Can a flawed person produce good, moral policies?

In *Primary Colors* we get an inside look at politics, and it isn't always pretty. But then, we are not always pretty. We cut corners, engage in all sorts of self-justifying behavior, assume the worst in others as we assume the best in ourselves. *Primary Colors* presents to us a *leadership context reality* that is unsettling yet relevant. It is a story of hope and pain, flaws and ideals, illusions and delusions, human flaws and human aspirations, highs and lows, image and reality. It places the leader in context, stripped of the glitz and glitter of campaign rhetoric and staged events. Our leaders occupy a morally ambiguous world. Few of us can be a Gandhi and succeed.

Milk, 2008

From apolitical outsider to activist, to insider, to martyr, Harvey Milk, the man, mattered; *Milk* the movie does as well.

In 1977, Harvey Milk was elected to the San Francisco board of supervisors, becoming the first openly gay man elected to public office in the United States. His journey to political prominence and leadership is as unlikely as his shocking death is tragic.

In 1972, living in New York City, Milk decides at age forty to change his life. Along with partner Scott Smith, Milk moves across the country, settling in San Francisco's Castro District, where he and Smith open a small camera shop. Soon, this outsider develops an interest in his community and plunges into the heated world of San Francisco politics.

With an interest in community economic development and gay rights, Milk begins to reach out to local small businesses, the gay as well as straight communities, and trade unions, building broad-based coalitions. For example, when the Teamsters want to strike against the Coors Company for refusing to sign a union contract, Milk gets the gay bars in the area to stop selling Coors beer. In exchange, Milk convinces the Teamsters to agree to hire more gay drivers. He then coaxes local Arab and Chinese grocers not to sell Coors beer. The boycott is successful and serves as a model of Milk's future coalitions that cut across political lines. He is soon dubbed "The Mayor of Castro Street."

Milk enjoys the attention and public spotlight his political activities afford him. He soon becomes the go-to guy in the Castro District as well as the lightning rod for the gay community. He decides to run for public office. In spite of his notoriety—perhaps because of it—he loses in three successive electoral efforts.

In 1977, he decides to give it one more try. In previous attempts, Milk has run in at-large races. Now, a new district system affords him a better chance.

As a politician, Milk tries to build bridges, forge coalitions, bring the gay community together, and reach out to senior citizens, union members, and small-business owners, developing a broad-based political coalition. To the surprise of many, he wins a seat on the board.

As a supervisor, Milk sponsors a civil rights bill that outlaws discrimination based on one's sexual orientation. Yet, Milk becomes much more than a gay politician, as he reaches out and promotes the interests of the broader community. Part of his coalition-building effort involves bringing another newly elected supervisor, Dan White, into his coalition. This proves problematic as their political agendas pull them apart and their personalities clash, leading to tragedy.

Dan White is clearly troubled. After serving for ten months as a supervisor, White resigns his position. Within days, he seeks reappointment to the same position. After initially agreeing, Mayor George Moscone reneges on his word and refuses to appoint White.

On November 27, 1978, Moscone plans to announce White's replacement. Shortly before the scheduled press conference, White sneaks into the basement of city hall, goes to Moscone's office, and shoots the mayor in the shoulder and chest; then, after Moscone has fallen to the floor, White shoots him twice in the head. He reloads his gun, walks to his former office, sees Milk, and asks for a meeting. White shoots Milk five times, including two close-range shots to the head.

In his actual trial, White's attorney claimed "diminished capacity," as the combination of White's anguished mental state and a steady diet of sugar-laden junk food that led him to explode. This was dubbed "the Twinkie defense." It worked.

Dan White was acquitted of first-degree murder but found guilty of two counts of voluntary manslaughter, and was sentenced to seven and two-thirds years in prison. His sentence was reduced for time served and good behavior, and he was released after five years. He committed suicide a couple of years later.

Harvey Milk, an outsider from a group discriminated against, was able to broaden his political appeal and garner coalition partners because he reached out, built bridges, was more than a one-issue advocate, saw injustice and fought it, saw needs and tried to fill them, had a vision, had a passion that was contagious, empowered and animated the gay and at times the straight communities, worked tirelessly, and cultivated both a personal and a political following. His was a politics of inclusion. *Milk,* the movie, gives us a portrait not of the leader as superhero, but of a real-life leader—warts and all. Yet, Milk does not solve problems alone. He enlists others; mobilizes, organizes, and empowers them; and helps to build a community on behalf of the shared common cause.

The Director as Leader: John Ford and Frank Capra

Having sampled several of Hollywood's provocative leadership films, we turn to two of the industry's most prolific and influential directors, John Ford and Frank Capra. These two men did more to shape our thinking of ourselves (as Americans) and of leadership than any other filmmakers. They were Hollywood's great mythmakers. Their vision of America became our narrative, the one we believed, passed down to our children, went to war over, and identified with. Their conception of leadership was passed down to us.

John Ford

Most famous for his classic westerns, John Ford did as much as anyone since Lincoln to shape America's self-image. His career spanned over fifty years, and he directed 140 films. Ingmar Bergman and Orson Welles believed Ford to be the greatest director of all time. A pioneer of on-location shooting and the development of the "long shot," Ford was seen as a master director and a commercial as well as an artistic success.

Born in 1894 to a large Irish immigrant family, Ford had a directing career that began in the silent era, and he became prominent in the 1930s. Best known for his westerns (a number of which starred John Wayne), Ford did not make the conventional bang-bang, shoot-'em-up westerns but wove complex myths of a time to which Ford longed to return.

In glorifying the ideals of the old West, Ford, like Capra, presented a clear-cut conflict between good and evil. But where Capra occasionally exhibited an inner conflict, Ford did not. So clear was Ford in his message, in fact, that his views seemed harsh and extremist. Called reactionary in his time, Ford's films did not, until recently, receive serious attention.

Ford respected tradition and honor. Home, family, law, decency, and a man's word were his primary values. His films centered on the myth of the old West as a metaphor for larger principles. His political values were conservative in a Burkean sense. His leadership themes were akin to those of Thomas Carlyle and Ralph Waldo Emerson.

Ford saw a natural and immutable order in life. His films were about the rules of civilization and the glorification of the heroic leader. The West was a world of Thomas Hobbes, where social Darwinism and Manifest Destiny came to life. There is no equality in Ford's world; there were only heroes and the meek. In his worship of the hero, Ford showed how different the hero was from the rest of the world. He served the people but could never be part of "the people."

He was different, he was above, and he was thus alone, a Christ-like figure who must die for our sins.

Two of Ford's films deserve attention, *The Searchers* and *The Man Who Shot Liberty Valance.* In *The Searchers* (named the greatest western of all time by the American Film Institute in 2008 and twelfth on its 2007 list of all-time greatest films), Ford presents the embodiment of the lone hero, the individual who almost single-handedly takes on great odds to emerge triumphant. The film opens with a wide shot, where in the distance we see a lone cowboy riding slowly toward the camera. It is Ethan Edwards (John Wayne), and he is going to visit his relatives. Soon, Edwards is on a mission to rescue his niece (played by Natalie Wood) who is kidnapped by Comanches. Edwards—of course—succeeds at his task; yet, rather than stay and receive the gratitude of his family, he rides off (into the sunset), as alone as when he arrived.

The Searchers (1956) helps establish the lone hero, the rugged individualist, and the romantic view of heroism so many of us have come to believe. Heroes are individuals. Rather than the hero's raising a posse—which is what almost always happened in reality—we romanticize individualism and convey the message that all that is necessary is individual action, the courage of one man. How much of our own conception of heroism stems from works such as *The Searchers*?

In *The Man Who Shot Liberty Valance* (1962), Ford presents an almost nostalgic tribute to the death of the old West and its rugged individualism. Starring John Wayne as Tom Doniphon and Jimmy Stewart as Ransom Stoddard, it is the story of a young attorney (Stoddard) who tries to bring the rule of law to Shinbone, a Wild West town. Outlaws, led by Liberty Valance (Lee Marvin), nearly kill Stoddard, but he is nursed back to life. Valance and his men continue to cause trouble for the good people of Shinbone, and the sheriff is unable to maintain law and order.

Doniphon, who embraces the values of the old West, believes that a man "needs a gun in these parts." Only he can stand up to Valance and his men. Doniphon sees Stoddard as well intentioned yet weak. Stoddard sees Doniphon as a dying breed. The future, Stoddard believes, will be to rely on the rule of law, not the rule of the gun.

In the end, Valance challenges Stoddard to a gunfight. Woefully ill suited to the task, Stoddard nonetheless feels he must agree to the fight. Shockingly, Stoddard "kills" Valance. Stoddard becomes a legend—the man who shot Liberty Valance.

As Stoddard's political star rises, he is torn with guilt because it was an act of violence that made Stoddard a hero. Then Doniphon tells Stoddard what really happened, that he, not Stoddard, was the one who, lurking in the darkness, shot Valance. Stoddard's political career takes off. He becomes a congressman, senator, ambassador to Great Britain, and an often-mentioned possibility for vice president.

Doniphon all but disappears from sight after revealing the truth to Stoddard. He dies alone. Stoddard returns to Shinbone for the funeral where he tells the editor of the local paper the real story of what happened the night Liberty Valance was shot. But the editor refuses to publish the story, telling Stoddard, "When the legend becomes fact, print the legend."

Ford seems to identify with the John Wayne character. He laments the death of the old West and the rise of "civilization." What is lost may not be worth what is gained, especially due to the fact that it is built on a lie. Gone are the days of rugged individualism and self-reliance. Ford recognizes this, even as he despairs over the change. The days of the individual are ending; the days of the collective are rising. It is no wonder that, in this period, Ford moves to the right politically.

Ford believes there are larger issues than "self." His heroes defend values and higher principles; and these values take precedence over all else, requiring us, on occasion, to sacrifice for these values.

Frank Capra

Frank Capra may well have invented America, at least the America many of us grew up believing in. It is the America of the dignity of the average man, of truth and justice, honesty and decency. It is the America of neighborhoods, friends, family, and of good triumphing over evil. Capra's works embody both the American dream and the American myth. In his work, we see the America that we wish existed. Frank Capra is in this sense the most "American" of all directors.

He was born in Palermo, Sicily, in 1897. The Capra family moved to Los Angeles when Frank was a boy. His family was poor, and young Frank was forced to work in order to keep the family afloat. In 1918 he graduated from the California Institute of Technology with a degree in chemical engineering. Unable to find steady work, he left home to become a wanderer.

Capra started working in the movies in the mid-1920s, and it wasn't long before he moved into the forefront. Yet in spite of his quick rise to fame, Capra never forgot his humble beginnings. His films were, in effect, glorifications of the average man and a celebration of middle-class values: optimism and the "never give up" attitude.

A recurring theme in his movies involves a confrontation between good and evil. The bad guys are rich and sophisticated: lawyers, tycoons, political bosses, bankers, and businessmen. They are preoccupied with power and money. The good guys are idealistic, simple, plain, everyday Americans.

To Capra the American system is essentially good. And when the unscrupulous employ their corrupt practices to gain control, in steps our hero. With goodness and truth on his side, he enters the fray and, because the system is essentially good, our hero triumphs. Goodness wins over evil.

Capra's hero is the American Everyman. Not "exceptional" or highly accomplished in conventional terms, the hero embodies small-town America and a composite of Jefferson, Lincoln, and Thoreau. Capra once said, "The common man idea, I didn't think he was common. I thought he was a hell of a guy. I thought he was the hope of the world."[15] Earlier he said that "the people are right. People's instincts are good, never bad."[16] Capra's average men could save the world from the corrupt political bosses and crooked Wall Street tycoons if only they would join forces. "We're the people and we're tough," says one of Capra's characters. "A free people can beat the world at anything ... if we all pulled the oars in the same direction."

Mr. Smith Goes to Washington (1939), starring Jimmy Stewart as Jefferson Smith, portrays a man of small-town virtue who is appointed to fill an unexpired term in the U.S. Senate. The corrupt Taylor political machine that controls Smith's state believes Smith will "follow orders," and for a time, Jefferson innocently complies.

But our hero gets an idea to build a youth camp, which he wants to build on land that the political bosses have other plans for. The bosses try to frame Smith, and it looks as if they will win. But Smith refuses to give in; after all, he has goodness on his side. He begins a filibuster and when Smith is near the point of exhaustion, one of Taylor's cronies bursts into the Senate chamber after a failed suicide attempt and clears Jefferson Smith.

For Capra it is a familiar theme and a familiar conclusion. The naïve innocent is bullied by corrupt men, evil begins to win, but in the end goodness triumphs. The system, we are told, is essentially good. There are just "a few rotten apples" spoiling the institution. If only we could elect "the right people" everything would be fine.

In *Meet John Doe* (1941), Capra shifts his emphasis. Faced with the rise of fascism in Europe, Capra seemed to have difficulty deciding just how to respond. Although Capra's previous films were dominated by a wide-eyed faith in the American system, *Meet John Doe* is a murkier vision of the dark side of America.

Meet John Doe is about a newspaper scheme in which a fake "John Doe" suicide note to the paper attracts mass attention. Ann Mitchell (Barbara Stanwyck), who wrote the letter, sets out to find the right man to play the part. She settles on Long John Willoughby (Gary Cooper), a would-be baseball pitcher in need of an arm operation.

The John Doe scheme captivates the public, and millionaire D. B. Norton (a fascist-like character) tries to use John Doe in his rise to power. Doe, relying mostly on a combination of common Christian parables and Hallmark card pieties, begins to speak to the problems of the common man. John Doe clubs spring up across America, and a John Doe convention is planned. D. B. Norton decides it is time to take control. Having financed the John Doe movement, Norton demands that Long John anoint Norton as the John Doe candidate for president.

But Long John refuses and plans to tell the convention of Norton's scheme. Before Willoughby (Doe) can do so, Norton rushes to the stage and reveals that Willoughby is a fake. The crowd turns against Willoughby, becoming a violent mob, and our hero barely escapes. Depressed, Long John decides that he will, as the original John Doe letter stated, commit suicide on Christmas Eve. As Long John walks toward the ledge of a tall office building, a group of John Does convinces Long John not to jump. The film ends (five different endings were shot) with no clear resolution. The film is a brutal, depressing portrait of America, presenting a pessimistic and disturbing picture of democracy and the people's inability to see through the corrupt power brokers.

To some critics, *Meet John Doe* Americanizes fascism. It portrays a public easily manipulated by the power brokers. The public can be turned into a mob, and if a political leader comes up with the right gimmick, the public may follow. In trying to oppose fascism, Capra paints a picture of how a fascist or other totalitarian could possibly assume power in America. Capra gives us two different types of American fascists: John Doe, the populist demagogue, and D. B. Norton, the authoritarian manipulator. Whereas Capra intended this film as a part of his formula of good versus evil, in the end, a darker conflict emerges.

Film critic Richard Glazer writes, "What began as Capra's denouncement of Nazi tactics finds the seeds of Fascism lying dormant in American Democracy. *Meet John Doe* presents America not with the good self-image that Deeds and Smith provided, but with the underside of that image with all of Capra's doubts about democracy and the American people."[17]

Still, in the end, the common man as hero rises above these feelings and goes on, against all odds, to beat those forces that have all the weapons, all the money, everything except goodness. To Capra, an average citizen, armed only with truth and goodness, can defeat the elites who control society. Capra may offer a misleading if not false promise. It gives the "little man" hope where sometimes little hope exists. It tells the common man to be good and not to envy the wealthy because poverty equals goodness and wealth equals corruption.

If Capra's common heroes win, real life gives the lone individual (no matter how "swell") little chance against the forces that help shape public policy today. But the Capra film remains a part of our national self-image. Capra may not have created America, yet he has captured its essence and embellished its aspirations. Frank Capra, like no other moviemaker, put America on the screen.

Conclusion

What does Hollywood teach us about leadership? The most pronounced message Hollywood sends is the glorification of the individual. Film after film presents the lone individual as the change agent, cause of all that happens, solution to our problems. A cult of heroic leadership is bolstered by Hollywood's representations of larger-than-life heroes as saviors.

Whether it is *High Noon* or *Mr. Smith Goes to Washington* or later films such as *Air Force One,* Hollywood's message to us too often is to sit back and wait for a knight in shining armor to save us. We give ourselves more willingly to the cult of leadership, and diminish our own power and responsibility when we succumb to this message.

Leadership, according to Hollywood, is a solitary act done by a lone, courageous person, without a team of followers. This message is both ahistorical and apolitical as well as antidemocratic, and is usually wrong.

Submitting to the cult of leadership saps power from the people who, in a democracy, are supposed to participate and govern. Relying on heroes to save us belittles popular sovereignty and leaves us waiting for someone else to solve our problems. It leaves us in awe of superstars and celebrities and encourages us to be sheep following the Pied Piper. It discourages citizen participation in politics and promotes apathy and passivity.

This celebration of romantic individualism makes citizens into observers rather than participants. Hollywood tells us (*Norma Rae* notwithstanding) that a hero solves our problems. We don't—perhaps can't—solve them ourselves. Wait on the sidelines, we are told, until our hero arrives. Organizing, working together, and building a popular mass movement are not the ways to solve problems. Only the lone hero can save us. Democracy, in this view, is merely a spectator sport.

Hollywood also tells us that good triumphs over evil. If we are only good, we can win against all odds. And of course, it is individual goodness that matters. The lone individual, armed with truth and goodness, can take on corrupt party bosses, evil tyrants, and greedy corporate moguls. "The system works," but only when goodness confronts evil.

Finally, followers, constituents, and subordinates rarely get the attention and praise they deserve. Part of the problem stems from the nature of Hollywood filmmaking. Focusing on a few key figures makes for better movies and so we get heroes and saviors, not mass movements or the complicated real politics of coalition building and negotiating, which are the hard work of both public and private sector leadership.

Unlike a novel where the author can take time developing plots and characters, filmmakers work under tight time constraints. They must condense reality, not having the luxury to introduce subplots, minor characters, and complex situations. They do not have the time to develop roles into nuanced, multidimensional characters.

Chapter Eleven
The Darker Side of Leadership

> There are aspects of power which are not attractive but repulsive.... Wanton brutality, hypocrisy and deceit, corruption and favoritism, inflexibility, indecision at important moments, falling behind cultural advancement; these are the underside of government [and leadership].
>
> —***Charles E. Merriam***[1]

We've all been there: the coach or supervisor who publicly humiliates us after we make an error, the parent who abuses a child, the teacher who brooks no questioning of his lectures, a president who compiles "enemies lists," the boss who barks orders and demands obedience. Negative leaders. Reverse or even perverse mentors, they infect virtually every aspect of life. And they can make work, or school, or sports, or home unbearable.

Such leaders (John W. Gardner calls them the "transgressors") come in all shapes and sizes. Some are the psychologically cruel, such as Idi Amin of Uganda; others may treat their followers well yet base their leadership on the encouragement of attaining evil ends, such as leaders of the Ku Klux Klan. Still others may not directly call for followers to engage in evil acts yet use hatred, fear, or prejudice to motivate followers. Other transgressors dominate and demean followers, making them dependent on the leader.[2] Dysfunctional leaders pose a grave danger to their organizations. As Algernon Sydney warns, "The rage of a private man may be pernicious to one or few of his neighbors; but the fury of an unlimited prince would drive whole nations into ruin." He adds, "And those very men, who have lived modestly when they had little power, have often proved the most savage of monsters when they thought nothing able to resist their rage."[3]

Toxic leaders engage in behaviors destructive or damaging to followers; "they leave their followers decidedly worse off than they found them."[4]

Political scientist Alan Wolfe defines political evil as the "willful, malevolent, and gratuitous death, destruction, and suffering inflicted upon innocent people by leaders of movements and states in their strategic efforts to achieve realizable objectives."[5]

Wolfe finds a world in which practitioners of everyday evil are with us in abundance. He agrees with James Madison that there are always some people, here and elsewhere, in politics as well as other walks of life, who can become so impressed with their importance that they no longer consider themselves subject to the rules of either God or man. "Power is, among other things, a temptation," he writes. "Some individuals will fall so totally under its appeal that laws, conscience, religious duties, or moral teachings will never stand in the way of their getting what they want."[6]

Humans are capable of great acts of kindness yet are also capable of horrendous acts of cruelty and destruction. Here is how James Madison characterized the paradoxical nature of this dilemma:

> If men were angels, no government would be necessary. If angels were to govern men, neither external nor internal controls on government would be necessary. In framing a government which is to be administered by men over men, the great difficulty lies in this: you must first enable the government to control the governed; and in the next place oblige it to control itself. A dependence on the people is, no doubt, the primary control on the government; but experience has taught mankind the necessity of auxiliary precautions.[7]

Leader or Tyrant?

Was Hitler a leader or merely a tyrant? Of course, if by "leader" we mean someone who attracted a following, had a vision for the future, and mobilized people and institutions to achieve his goals, then yes, Hitler indeed was a leader.[8]

Yet, some are loath to include Hitler and his ilk in the pantheon of leaders because of their morally toxic behavior. In his classic *Leadership,* James MacGregor Burns contends Hitler was a despot, not a leader: "his grotesque *führership* is solemnly examined as a doctrine of leadership. But Hitler, once he gained power and crushed the opposition, was no leader—he was a tyrant. A leader and a tyrant are polar opposites."[9] Thus, to exclude Hitler from the list of leaders, we must embrace in our definition of leadership some sort of moral standard.

Fair enough. Yet would not such a standard eliminate from the list of leaders many whom we today applaud and honor? Lincoln suspended habeas corpus and approved Sherman's devastating and brutal march across the South. Franklin D. Roosevelt had Japanese American citizens interned in detention centers during World War II and was an often deceptive and manipulative operative. The list could go on and on.

Although we may cringe at the thought of a bully "succeeding," it is nonetheless true that thugs sometimes get their way. Sadly, fear and intimidation often get results. Of course, this is not leadership, strictly speaking.

Toxic leaders have a strong need for power. In a narrow sense, this may make them more effective leaders as they "need" to get their way, to win, to get results. Yet this "positive" effort only works when the leader has his or her internal drives under control. McClelland and Burnham see the following motivations for leaders: a need for achievement, a need for affiliation, and a need for power. Toxic leaders are in the power category.[10]

Is there a means-ends test to clear this up? Lincoln and FDR, whose actions may have been questionable on some occasions, nonetheless had generally admirable social goals, while Hitler's means were as loathsome as his ends were objectionable. Is that too easy and self-justifying a definition?

Put another way, is there a morally neutral way of looking at leadership, or is a moral stance implicit in talking about leadership? And do moral positions differ from culture to culture? In the United States, our moral stance is influenced by our democratic values, plus our belief in individualism and free enterprise. Only recently have we learned to incorporate diversity into that schema. Our expectations of what makes a leader moral are based on these values. Yet not everyone shares our penchant for individualism or even individual freedom. Certain cultures value community cohesion over individual rights. Many Native American tribes or nations, for example, stress the group over the individual.

How would an Iranian Shiite, an Afghan opium farmer, a Saudi prince, a Mexican fisherman, a Russian miner, an Indian engineer, a Congolese teacher, and a young idealistic member of Earth First! define leadership and its connection to morals? Although most major religions agree on key principles such as thou shalt not kill innocents, or stealing is wrong, different cultures stress different values in living and in leadership. Certain cultures value religion over all else. Would they find it moral to follow a secular leader, even if the leader were elected? A society that honors religious laws above all others might want the state to be grounded in a rigid adherence to a strict religious code that subjugates women. In the West, we would call leadership that subjugates women barbaric, and yet in some deeply religious societies, to do otherwise is to violate the will of God. Which society, which culture, which leadership is "moral"?

Is it arrogant to impose the Western definition of moral leadership on all cultures, religions, societies? We need not be moral relativists to see the difficulty here. Our culture and our belief system tell us it is immoral to deny others equality; another culture says it is immoral to allow women to drive a car. Are we to deny others the right to believe and practice their chosen religion because it is anathema to ours?

Burns says we cannot separate leadership from morality, yet in connecting the two, at least definitionally, we run the risk of imposing our culture's version of morality on many who disagree with us for deeply, genuinely held, religious, historical, or cultural reasons. Is the only way out to divorce morality from leadership? Can a definition of leadership be morally neutral or even morally silent? Most leadership scholars today conclude that leadership is not a value-free concept.

To what extent must a leader be guided by high moral purpose? One response comes from Niccolò Machiavelli who, in *The Prince,* writes that "the man who wants to act virtuously in every way necessarily comes to grief among so many who are not virtuous. Therefore if a prince wants to maintain his rule he must learn how not to be virtuous."[11] Does being virtuous thus necessarily lead to defeat? If so, how can we ask or expect a leader to enter battle bound by moral principles when others are not so bound? At the other extreme, we find Immanuel Kant who argues that leaders must strictly follow the demands of high moral principle.[12] Are we thus stuck between a Machiavellian rock and a Kantian hard place?

Several leadership experts, among them Burns and Gardner, insist that there must be a link between leadership and morals.[13] And yet, must a leader choose one of the extremes, or is there a more reasonable and workable formula? Leaders can avoid the Machiavelli/Kant dilemma by looking to Aristotle for guidance.

Aristotle, as we discussed earlier, points the leader to *phronesis,* loosely translated as prudence and good political action in pursuit of a morally worthwhile goal. The purpose of employing *phronesis* is to "exercise judgment that unites moral and practical concerns in a world of conflict."[14]

Political prudence involves, among other things, disciplined reason, an openness to experience, a concern for the common good over the long term, a proper appreciation of means and ends, and a due diligence about the legitimacy and consequences of any decision.[15]

By practicing prudence or *phronesis,* leaders attach themselves to a morally sound goal while also operating in a politically complex world. Yes, leaders must be sensitive to the moral implications of their actions. A moral code is not a straightjacket that so binds leaders that they are unable to work effectively in a morally ambiguous world. Dysfunctional leaders eschew morals; effective leaders put morals in their proper place.

Loath as we may be to admit it, perhaps we are left with no other course but to concede that yes, Hitler *was* a leader. Yet, we need not let him off the hook quite so easily. Yes, he was a leader, but he was a dysfunctional or toxic leader.

Burns's linking of leadership to high moral purpose is appealing, and it should be the ideal toward which we strive. Yet, we cannot exclude Hitler, Mao, Pol

Pot, Idi Amin, Saddam Hussein, or Osama bin Laden from our list of leaders because we disapprove of the uses of their leadership skills.

Leaders have feet of clay. All are flawed, some tragically so. And yet, distinctions must be made, gradations noted. There *are* significant differences between Lincoln and Hitler.

Negative leaders can infect an organization like a virus, spreading uncivil behavior like a contagion. As Stanford University management science professor Robert I. Sutton warns, "*Assholes will breed like rabbits.*"[16] Sutton advises us to weed out dysfunctional leaders as well as workers and never let bullies have their way: "Bad things happen when 'the bullies win.'"[17]

Damaged or dysfunctional people are often drawn to leadership because it promises being on stage or in the limelight, in addition to glamour, celebrity status, power, and the possibility "to become someone special." Yet, as we know, power can corrupt. Often, people with power or celebrity status feel "entitled," feel they are owed special privileges, gifts, exceptions. They may begin to expect more, demand special treatment, insist on getting their own way. In the dysfunctional, power is certain to corrupt because it is tainted from the outset. Power can be poison; and in the dysfunctional, that poison spreads. All this reminds us of T. S. Eliot's line in *The Cocktail Party* that "half of the harm that is done in the world is due to people who want to feel important."

Leaders Who Mislead

"Man is born broken," wrote playwright Eugene O'Neill, a disturbing thought pregnant with menace. It is especially problematic when we focus on the role leaders play in the lives of citizens. When is "leadership" most likely to degenerate into dysfunctional leadership? There are several primary ways leadership becomes dysfunctional: (1) when ends completely justify the means; (2) when a single ideology becomes more important than anything else; and (3) when greed, love of power, excessive narcissism, or psychoses are unrestrained and dominate action.

Sadly, history offers us no shortage of such leaders.[18] Ironically, good leadership may involve small doses of all three of the factors mentioned in the previous paragraph. To lead, one must be focused on the end, the goal; and at times (Lincoln during the Civil War, for example), the means may be less than ideal. Also, an ideology or set of shared beliefs can motivate followers to get involved, help develop a consensus, animate behavior. Finally, all leaders—to be effective—must know how to harness and use power.

Although the lust for power is visible in every profession, it is more pronounced in societal governance than anywhere else. That is because it involves the exercise of power over so many others. This is what makes it dangerous.

Rather than understand these factors as discrete categories, it may be more useful to see each of these as a continuum. In the first, the means-ends continuum, we can see how easy it would be for the purist to argue that the ends do not justify unjust means (Gandhi said the means *are* the ends). And yet, Lincoln's ends were mostly noble—and successful—even if his means were at times distasteful. Life is so rarely lived at the extremes; so, too, does effective leadership require us to make tough choices.

In the second continuum, the ideological spectrum, we see a rigid ideology staked against a nonideological, purely pragmatic approach. Although it is easy to dismiss ideological leaders, one must note that they are passionate, committed (yes, some of them ought to be committed), focused, and goal oriented. This gives them a drive and will to win that are truly impressive. Yet, their narrow-mindedness, rigidity, and unwillingness to compromise make them all-or-nothing types of leaders. At the other end of the spectrum, purely pragmatic leaders have no backbone and no real principles. Again, life is best lived away from the extremes.

Finally, the category of love of power versus selflessness sees the dysfunctional leader as power hungry and, in many ways, blinded by a lust for power. At the other end of the spectrum, leaders can be too humble, too selfless, and insufficiently concerned with their power stakes. As always, life and leadership are usually lived between the extremes.

Power does not necessarily corrupt. And the absence of power is problematic as well. We are forever granting power to leaders to get things done, to solve problems. When kept within proper bounds, power can be used for good purposes. Yet, it will not always be the "healthiest" who wield power; and without checks, unbridled power may be used for the wrong ends.

It is no accident that free-market economist Friedrich A. Hayek chose as the title for Chapter 10 of his classic work *Road to Serfdom* "Why the Worst Get to the Top." Hayek is concerned not only with intrusive governmental power but also with the propensity of politics and power to attract the unsavory among us.[19]

Anthropologist F. G. Bailey also expresses suspicion of those attracted to power and politics, writing only slightly tongue in cheek that "leaders and gangsters have much in common." Bailey explains, "The leader must be partisan. He must use rhetoric. He must be ruthless, be ready to subvert values while appearing to support them, and be clever enough to move the discourse up to a level where opportunism can be successfully hidden by sermonizing about eternal virtues. Leadership is a form of cultivating ignorance, of stopping doubts, and stifling questions."[20]

One of the finest case studies in the uses of power can be found in Robert Caro's book *The Power Broker*.[21] Caro's work traces the career of Robert Moses (1888–1981), considered the "master builder" of the modern New York City regions. Although Moses never held elective office, for the twenty-year period between 1930 and 1950, he was the most powerful figure in New York. The New York City you see today owes much to the work of Moses, who once quipped, "If the ends don't justify the means, what does?" At the peak of his power, one-fourth of all federal construction dollars went to New York.

Moses was self-confident, focused, goal oriented, visionary, tenacious, and often ruthless. An able administrator, he had an iron will, fertile imagination, and an arrogance and sense of entitlement to rival anyone's. Over time, his idealism and desire to build and expand the metropolis gave way to a hunger for power and control and an increasingly expansive ego. His skill and power were used to bully others, and his arrogance closed Moses off to public input as well as advice from rivals and associates. Yet, in the end, Moses's power was his poison. As Caro writes, "Power is not an instrument that its possessor can use with impunity. It is a drug that creates in the user a need for larger and larger dosages."[22] Moses used power until power destroyed him. By the 1960s, urban planners began to condemn Moses's development schemes for New York, and he became more and more prickly, unnecessarily starting political fights he was doomed to lose. His downfall came from overreaching, with the demolition of Penn Station and the lukewarm reception for the 1964 New York World's Fair. By 1968, this led to a crescendo of public and political opposition that brought Moses down.

Paradoxically, some toxic leaders can and do have—at least to a degree—a positive impact. The semitoxic, bullying college basketball coach Bobby Knight won an impressive number of college basketball games. Former British prime minister Margaret Thatcher, somewhat of a bully within her own political party, managed to browbeat rivals and intimidate allies into compliance, ruling with an iron fist for more than a decade. Some of her accomplishments were the result of her aggressive style, and although in the end it was largely negative reactions to her approach that brought her demise, she was an influential political leader in the 1980s because of, not in spite of, her domineering presence. The case history of Apple's Steve Jobs is a complex one, yet it is clear he was rude to a great many people in- and outside his firm. He humiliated a number of his workers and rarely apologized for his tantrums. His excuse was that he was a perfectionist and had high (insanely high) expectations of others. Yet he was, everyone agrees, an enormously successful businessman. He also, or so it seems, won considerable loyalty from most of his employees.

We often assume that toxic leaders are mentally unbalanced—that there is something wrong with them. Sometimes this is the case. Psychiatrist Nassir Ghaemi contends that while in "normal" times we are probably well served by mentally sound leaders, in times of crisis we may be well served by somewhat less mentally balanced individuals. He argues that "most of us make a basic and reasonable assumption about sanity; we think it produces good results, and we believe insanity is a problem!" Yet Ghaemi argues that in "at least one vitally important circumstance *insanity* produces good results and *sanity* is a problem. In times of crisis, we are better off being led by mentally ill leaders than by mentally sound ones."[23]

Ghaemi is essentially contending there are different kinds of emotional or psychological makeups for different contexts. He also writes that the typical noncrisis leader may be too idealistic and overly optimistic to do what is needed in times of crisis. And accuracy of observation is likely better coming from a depressed leader.

Ghaemi's proposition, unconvincingly supported by some short biographical sketches, is that great crisis leaders are not, and need not be, like the rest of us. Indeed, he asserts that the best crisis leaders are either mentally abnormal or mentally ill while the worst crisis leaders are mentally healthy.

Ghaemi's is an unconventional and novel view. If he were even partially right, and we are not convinced, it would be an even harder challenge in constitutional democracies to design proper screening and discernment processes for those running for high office.

Leaders seldom lack self-confidence. After all, they put themselves out there, leap onto the stage, take risks, and accept responsibilities both personally and politically. Yet high levels of self-confidence can easily morph into narcissism—excessive self-love. (Narcissus was the mythical youth who fell in love with his own reflection in the water.) Studies show a clear link between narcissism and leader emergence.[24]

Narcissists often take excessive or unnecessary risks. The risky personal behavior of Gary Hart, Bill Clinton, Mark Sanford, Eliot Spitzer, James McGreevey, John Edwards, Larry Craig, John Ensign, Tiger Woods, Bernie Madoff—to name a few—suggests that narcissists see themselves as special, extraordinary, and entitled.

Somehow they interpret their hard work, leadership contributions, and special status as deserving of either special privileges and exceptions or immunity from normal standards of behavior. The Greeks called this *hubris*—which they considered an insulting or outsized pride, and even a haughty contempt toward the Greek gods.

It *is* about the power. And *yes*, perhaps power corrupts, at least some of us. But not in ways one might think. Researchers have found that when occupying positions of power, people act more impulsively and are so often focused on their own goals that they become "disinhibited" and less able to "see" and empathize with others. In effect, a selfish, risk-oriented approach often takes over and those in power find that their needs and desires become paramount. There may be, some research suggests, chemicals released by the brain that distort thinking and may make leaders less rational. This may lead them to see people as tools that can be used to achieve their goals. Such "leaders" probably become intoxicated with a swollen sense of entitlement.[25]

Because power can be disinhibiting, it reduces the ability to accurately read context, and releases one from the traditional normative and societal rules and norms designed to promote self-control and regulate behavior. People in power sometimes do feel that they are, and should be, special; that for some reason, the rules do not apply to them; that they are entitled to preferential treatment.

Freed of the confines of conventional restraints, some leaders and celebrities cannot see that their behavior might be risky or self-destructive. Power changes them, gives them illusions of grandeur, and distorts their reasoning capabilities. Many are able to channel this tendency in the service of others. Dysfunctional leaders allow the lure of power to dominate them. They end up going too far, expect too much, move beyond reason.

Leaders often must find the balance point between the extremes of pure self-interest and cynicism on the one hand, and selfless purity on the other. In accepting his Nobel Peace Prize in 2009, President Barack Obama spoke powerfully about the need to balance hope and peace with the baser demands of an occasionally dangerous world. Speaking of Martin Luther King Jr. and Gandhi, Obama noted, "As a head of state sworn to protect and defend my nation, I cannot be guided by their example alone. I face the world as it is, and cannot stand idle in the face of threats to the American people. For make no mistake: evil does exist in the world."

President Obama faced up to the challenge of "reconciling these two seemingly irreconcilable truths—that war is sometimes necessary, and war at some level is an expression of human folly." Wise leaders learn to live with, even creatively manage, these paradoxes. "We can," he said, "acknowledge that oppression will always be with us, and still strive for justice."

George Packer distilled the Obama worldview into the following: "What the President has is a sophisticated theology, an anti-utopian belief that human imperfection is inevitable but progress is possible if human beings remain self critical about what they can achieve."[26] Such introspection eludes the dysfunctional leader, who eschews balance and humility in favor of power and certitude. Simple truths trump complex reasoning in the world of the dysfunctional leader.

The dysfunctional leader may *know* what is wrong, yet be blind to his own transgressions, unable to turn the moral mirror on himself. One need only remember the horrific behavior of U.S. soldiers in Iraq's Abu Ghraib prison to understand this point. And political aide Andrew Young wrote of his former boss, John Edwards (the erstwhile former U.S. senator and presidential candidate): "Gifted, shamanistic, and mesmerizing, John Edwards knew what was right but was so blind to his own flaws—narcissism, greed, power, lust—and so determined to hide his shame even from himself that he couldn't correct them."[27] That's hubris.

Of course, self-confidence not only helps leaders, but it is essential.[28] The job is to find leaders who have their egos in check, who do not need adulation, who do not hunger for love, who are not self-destructively narcissistic. We want people with plenty of drive yet who are not driven.

Because we cannot always tell ahead of time which prospective candidates are and are not healthy, checks and balances are a necessary and positive antidote to narcissism. We always run the risk that the leader we love loves him- or herself more. Thus, unbridled power can corrupt and can become a poison.

Many politicians crave attention. Their big egos hunger for the applause of crowds. Yet in receiving this applause they can begin to see themselves as different, special, superior, entitled. They sometimes begin to believe the rules that apply to the rest of us do not especially apply to them.

They begin to take risks. A willingness to take risks is, of course, inherent in their profession. Who but risk takers would challenge an incumbent or put much of their lives and reputation on the line for the often-slim hope of getting elected?

Politicians are sometimes seduced by the rush and the thrill. And this need for excitement pushes them to go out on a limb, take chances, get up on the stage in hopes of being noticed and embraced. Wallflowers don't make it. Ambition, drive, and boldness sometimes bordering on recklessness are required. Yet, once in office and caught up in power transactions, these same extroverted, attention-seeking types can sometimes display elements of the darker, more toxic side of risk taking.

Italy's Silvio Berlusconi is one example. North Carolina's John Edwards, Illinois's Rod Blagojevich, and Providence, Rhode Island's Buddy Cianci are additional examples. The hunger for power and attention is a characteristic drive in elected officials and, it needs to be emphasized, is often harnessed on behalf of doing highly desirable acts of splendid public service. Often that hunger and appetite become a complicated part of the politician's larger character. And sometimes they gradually corrupt the soul and sensibility of the leader in question.

Leadership matters. It can enhance our lives or make them a living nightmare. Effective leaders can help improve the quality of our lives, and ineffective or corrupt leaders can greatly damage our lives. As all groups seek out leadership and direction, the ubiquitous nature of leadership means that we had better "get it right," as leadership—good or bad—is inevitable and unavoidable.

Hitler *was* a leader, but a *very* dysfunctional one. Why do dysfunctional leaders emerge, and why do we follow them?

The Scope of the Problem

We all know and have probably been at the mercy of a few dysfunctional leaders over the years. People with dysfunctional characters or psychological problems are attracted to power and its uses. Some are attracted to leadership for the "right" (or healthy) reasons: to do good, to solve tough problems, to help others, to make a better world or community. Others are attracted to leadership for the "wrong" reasons: to compensate for lack of self-esteem, to punish others for their own shortcomings, to feel powerful and loved, to dominate others. Here again it is more useful to envision leadership as a continuum, with functional and dysfunctional at the extremes, and a variety of gradations in between. Few are at either extreme. Most leaders have a mixture of pure and selfish motivations for getting into public service and leadership positions.

Why do we follow tyrants, bullies, and thugs? Usually, the *predicate* for the rise of a "popular" tyrant is social upheaval or crisis. This sets up the opportunity for a tyrant to gain attention, credibility, and a following. And yet, during the Depression and World War II, rather than follow a tyrant, England followed Churchill, and the United States followed FDR. So what else is required for a tyrant to take command?

Tyrants usually appeal to mass prejudices; they offer a beleaguered public a convenient scapegoat for their problems; they are often charismatic and experts at self-dramatization; they simplify complex realities and offer simple solutions to society's problems. In short, in an atmosphere of fear and uncertainty, they give us what we think we need, what psychologically seems satisfying; and they offer hope, albeit distorted hope, for the future. People sometimes follow a tyrant in the hope of being saved.

Such leaders offer reassurance and hope. They promise a better future, however distorted their means for attaining it. Their certainty gives us something to grab hold of amid confusion. They make us feel part of something. In exchange, we surrender our freedom and turn a blind eye to their barbarism.

We sometimes become eager to follow an investment banker like Bernie Madoff, or Enron's Jeff Skilling, or Wisconsin's former U.S. senator Joe McCarthy, or Louisiana's former governor and U.S. senator Huey Long, and even someone like Hitler. After all, they are persuasive performers, excellent at self-dramatization, skilled at the performance of a leadership role. They look and act like especially self-confident professionals. Many enjoy being taken for the ride. Freud wrote penetratingly of our deep need to idealize leaders and our wish to escape from responsibility and into the arms of the leader/father.

Dysfunctional leaders often rely upon and exploit what Harvard scholar Howard Gardner calls "chronic followers"—people who hunger for and willingly follow intriguing and often authoritarian leaders.[29] Such followers give their loyalty to leaders who appear charismatic, confident, and strong. They find that following such a "strong" leader gives them a sense of place, purpose, and meaning. They identify with, live through, and derive meaning by following.

Thus, the dark side of leadership cannot be divorced from the dark side of followership. Leaders may be evil, yet we may willingly, even eagerly, follow. And lest we think, "It can't happen here," we need only remember the mass hysteria and blind followership of the anti-Communist witch hunts of the post–World War II McCarthy era, the semiparanoid followers who went along with Huey Long or the KKK, or the hatred demonstrated by opponents of civil rights reforms.

If followers play a role in propping up or at times supporting dysfunctional leaders, they may also play a role in toppling them from power. Toxic leaders may rise up with promises of glory, yet disillusionment always follows. As followers can empower worthy leaders, so too can they withhold support, resist, and dissent when toxic leaders arise. Granted, speaking truth to power may exact a heavy penalty; yet history has demonstrated that such heroic followership does occur, and when followers join forces, they may find strength in numbers.

Negative leaders seduce us because many of us, on some level, want to be seduced by, want to give ourselves to, want to—perhaps need to—"fall in love" with the leader. We are seduced or led astray. One person—usually a man—presents himself, offers himself, seduces us to fall in love with him. And occasionally we do fall—literally. We give ourselves to the cult of leadership as we give ourselves or submit to a lover. And we are often—at least for a while—blinded by this love.

Once the process of seduction starts, we begin to see the leader as superhuman. Such wild conclusions are cultivated by the hero/leader who attempts to construct a narrative attributing legendary powers and accomplishments to himself. The leader is celebrated, made heroic, and morphs into myth.[30]

Being treated like a superhuman or even like a god has its impact on a leader as well as a follower. The leader may begin to believe the self-generated myth and see himself as deserving of worship, above criticism, and immune to the regular rules. "A range of narcissistic, ego-inflicted, sometimes neurotic and psychopathic behaviors can develop."[31]

Followers begin to fall prey to the cult of the heroic leader. It is as if they fall under the spell of these Pied Pipers, suspending disbelief and blindly following. Former White House aide John Dean recalled how during the Watergate crisis, he gave so much of himself to the cause of protecting President Nixon that he began to slide down a slippery slope of criminal activity that, with twenty-twenty hindsight, made absolutely no sense. How could this bright young attorney go so far astray? He was seduced by power and blinded by loyalty to the president and a burning ambition from within. In that context, a few crimes seemed a small price to pay to protect his leader.[32]

When our backs are to the wall, when things go from bad to worse, we sometimes revert to the ways of a child. We long for a father figure to step in and make things all right. We hunger for a leader who can relieve our stress, remove our problems, take care of us. The leader can thus become a god, a savior, a father who intervenes to lift us out of our despair and suffering. Our knight in shining armor is called to step in and perform heroic deeds. And yet, waiting for Godot or a savior means we too often passively sit back and wait. Rather than take responsibility, we give power and responsibility to another. We sell ourselves short as we somehow buy into the cult of leadership.

The cult of leadership that emerged out of the classic ancient tales of heroic deeds allows us to believe, to suspend disbelief, to surrender ourselves to the leader/tyrant. We *need* to feel better, and we *want* someone to solve our problems, slay our dragons, and make everything right again.

Although it is natural in times of great stress to want to escape into the arms of a savior, it is also dangerous. Tyrants end up doing great damage and perpetrate great misery on their subjects. Tyrants rarely emerge in stable, prosperous, calm times. They need the trigger of fear or dislocation to gain credibility and a platform.

Leaders can do great good or great harm. And some leaders—Caligula, Hitler, Pol Pot—cause horrific harm.

Of Demagogues and Democrats

The framers of the U.S. Constitution were deeply concerned about a powerful (monarchical) executive who might become a demagogue. Demagogues, leaders who inflame and manipulate the passions of the masses, use divisive rhetoric aimed at arousing the fears and insecurities of the people. And who shall rid us of these dangers? The leader, of course.

The framers sought a government that appeals to reason, that uses the brain to move the feet. Demagogues try to make an end run around the machinery of government, appealing directly to the people, stoking the flames of hatred and resentment, in hopes the mob will follow their lead.

James Madison spoke directly to this dilemma in *Federalist 49*: "The *passions,* therefore, not the *reason,* of the public would sit in judgment. But it is the reason, alone, of the public, that ought to control and regulate the government. The passions ought to be controlled and regulated by the government."

And how are these passions to be controlled? The framers developed an architectural means to regulate this problem: checks and balances and the separation of powers. As discussed earlier, if ambition could counter ambition, power counter power, an equilibrium or balance might be achieved that controls and regulates and tames the threats of the potential demagogue.

Mackerels in the Moonlight

Virginia congressman and aristocrat John Randolph once besmirched the reputation of his Kentucky colleague Henry Clay by characterizing him as brilliant yet corrupt, stigmatizing him famously as a man "like a rotten mackerel in the moonlight, [who] both shines and stinks."[33] As all our heroes have feet of clay, is it safe to say that there is a bit of the moonlight mackerel in all of us? All effective leaders are practitioners of high idealism *and* the sometimes low arts of politics. Leadership is not for the weak of spirit, and all leaders must, on occasion, make hard choices and painfully difficult decisions.

In war, leaders order soldiers into battle knowing that many will not return. In business, conditions may compel an executive to fire employees or eliminate departments. University leaders, on occasion, deny tenure to an aspiring academic or terminate a worthy yet expensive academic or athletic program.

Leadership is not about the easy cases—those are almost always handled somewhere down the food chain at lower levels of the organization. As noted earlier, those decisions that reach the top are usually the tough ones. Thus, leaders are required to manage deep-seated conflicts and choose from among a range of competing options.

Effective leaders make those tough choices based on evidence, information, and a thorough examination of options and possible consequences. And yes, on occasion they may end up as mackerels in the moonlight. How, given the human condition, could it be otherwise?

Dysfunctional leaders make tough choices by employing shortcuts, deciding based on prejudices or power considerations, with an eye toward self-interest and not the public interest. Driven by demons from within, the toxic leader will be self-serving, not one who serves others. Rather than being the occasional mackerels in the moonlight, these dysfunctional leaders may shine, yet they most often stink. It requires a bit of shine to achieve public recognition, but the stink corrupts from within. The shine is a necessary component of rising to the top; the stink is something inside that drives the dysfunctional leader to achieve power, recognition, domination, and control.

Dysfunctional leaders do not see the line beyond which they should not cross. Self-aware leaders know where the line is drawn and may from time to time feel compelled to cross that line; yet they are well aware that a certain "stink" may envelop them. It is a risk the prudent leader does not take lightly.

Dysfunctional Leadership

We are fascinated by powerful and successful leaders. In government and business, we celebrate charismatic leaders who transform the organization, win wars, and get their way. And yet, for every Steve Jobs, whom we generally applaud, there is a Kenneth Lay or Jeffrey Skilling who was once idolized but later condemned.[34]

There often seems a fine line between success and disaster, between the leaders who save us and those who damage us. What is heroic leadership today may be toxic tomorrow. In fact, many of the leadership traits we applaud are dangerously similar to those that feed the pathology of the dysfunctional leader. Today's strong leader may become tomorrow's toxic leader.

Negative leaders should not be confused with incompetent leaders. Toxic leaders are not merely mistake-prone, they are people who do great harm to themselves, to others, and to their organizations. They inflict serious damage due to their personality characteristics and leadership styles. They poison the atmosphere, demoralize, humiliate, and undermine their followers.

Although not ubiquitous, dysfunctional leadership is more common than we care to believe. And we are often the enablers who tolerate, even encourage, the rise of a toxic leader. Some negative leaders fulfill our basic material as well as psychological needs. Dysfunctional leaders may—for a time—provide material rewards to willing followers. They may also—for a time—satisfy psychological needs as we seek out strong leaders who reassure, represent strong authority or father figures, offer certainty in an uncertain world, promise security and protection.

And yet, this comes at a high cost. Like the evil Dementors from the *Harry Potter* book series, who "glory in decay and despair, and drain peace, hope, and happiness out of the air around them,"[35] toxic leaders suck the life out of people and organizations. They are, as political scientist Marcia Lynn Whicker describes, "maladjusted, malcontent, and often malevolent, even malicious. They succeed by tearing others down. They glory in turf protection, fighting and controlling rather than uplifting followers."[36]

Historian Stephen E. Ambrose in his book *Band of Brothers* sees the commander of Easy Company's 506th Parachute Infantry Regiment as a classic toxic leader. "Anyone who has ever been in the Army knows the type. [He] was the classic chickenshit. He generated maximum significance." He used poor judgment, yet that was not the larger problem. He "could not see the unrest and the contempt that was breeding in the troops. You led by fear or you led by example. We were being led by fear."[37] The soldiers talked about shooting him when the company went into battle.

Dysfunctional leaders employ many of the following characteristics: they are ambitious, hungry for power and attention (want it too much), selfish, callous, dishonest, cunning, arrogant, rigid and inflexible, self-serving, autocratic, impulsive, demanding, and blind to their own shortcomings. In addition to being bullies or tyrants, they violate the human dignity of and demoralize others, stifle creativity and criticism, demand obedience, need to be in control, have oversized egos, lack empathy, tend to be narcissistic, and demand obedience and admiration.[38]

We are here reminded of the adage "Happy people do not make history." Sadly, there is some truth in this. Happy, contented people rarely have the fire in their bellies to take on great odds, push through roadblocks and disappointments, keep driving when all seems lost. Unhappy or maladjusted people may well—for personal and psychological reasons—have the hunger and passion, even if derived from an unhealthy source, to tackle great odds. They may well *need* to.

Psychological research points to "the striking correlation between creative production and depressive disorders." Successful people, research suggests, "were eight times as likely as people in the general population to suffer from major depressive illness." So why did they succeed? One word: *persistence.* Depression "is intertwined with a 'cognitive style' that makes people more likely to produce successful art."[39] Perhaps the same could be said for leadership as well.

Things like anger, resentment, even depression can focus the brain, motivate the psyche, and animate behavior. They can give meaning—however distorted or negative—to action. Would a truly sane, balanced, psychologically healthy person be drawn to the trials and tribulations of the task of leadership? Yes, but not as passionately as the dysfunctional personality who truly needs, even hungers for, power. In the quest for leadership and power, the healthy and balanced individual is sometimes at a disadvantage.

The Isolation of a Negative Leader

The stories are legion of strong leaders who are predisposed toward disaster, where no one surrounding the leader has the nerve or strength to raise questions. A strong, determined leader needs constructive critics yet usually ends up surrounded by "yes people." Advisers want to remain close to the leader, and to do so, they feel the pressure to pander to the whims of the boss. This may ingratiate the staffer to the boss, yet disserves the needs and interests of the leader. If a person were about to drive off a cliff, they would want someone to warn them of the impending danger. And, although leaders "know" they need to encourage independent, even critical thinking among their advisers, they end up sending signals that warn staffers *not* to criticize the boss. If the coin of the realm is to have access to the leader, aides quickly get clued in as to how that is accomplished, and most often it is achieved by feeding the ego of the boss.

Healthy leaders neither want nor expect aides to treat them like gods. Dysfunctional leaders insist on it. Of course, this only increases the isolation in which dysfunctional leaders often find themselves. No one has the courage to tell the emperors they have no clothes.

John W. Gardner captures the paradoxical nature of our search for functional leadership: "Most of us want leaders who are not hungry for power, but some critics say we have created a system in which only the most power-hungry stay the course. We want leaders who serve the common good and at the same time serve our special interests, whatever these may be. We dislike paternalism, but we love father-figures. We bemoan the lack of leadership, but we do not treat our leaders very well."[40]

Strong leaders, and more so, dysfunctional leaders, expect, even demand to be treated with a deference and respect usually reserved for royalty if not divinity. Aides become servile, groveling sycophants, afraid to bring bad news to their boss. During the 2008 Democratic presidential primaries, John Edwards's aide Andrew Young went so far as to "take a bullet" for Edwards, only to be betrayed in the end.[41] Former White House staffer George Reedy noted how this tendency played out in the American presidency:

> There is built into the presidency a series of devices that tend to remove the occupant of the Oval Room from all of the forces which require most men to rub against the hard facts of life on a daily basis. The life of the White House is the life of a court. It is a structure designed for one purpose and one purpose only—to serve the material needs and the desires of a single man....
>
> He is treated with all the reverence due a monarch. No one interrupts presidential contemplation for anything less than a major catastrophe somewhere on the globe. No one speaks to him unless spoken to first. No one ever invites him to "go soak your head" when his demands become petulant and unreasonable.[42]

If these pressures exist in the United States where we have a free press, active opposition parties, and separation of powers, imagine how powerful the pressures must be in more autocratic systems. Albert Speer, who was minister of armaments and war production for the German Third Reich, noted this tendency, even by otherwise strong aides who buckled in the presence of the führer: "There is a special trap for every holder of power.... His favor is so desirable to his subordinates that they will sue for it by every means possible. Servility becomes endemic among his entourage, who compete among themselves in their show of devotion. This exercises a sway over the ruler who becomes corrupted in turn."[43]

In his memoirs, Khrushchev recalls how those around Stalin bent over backward to please their demanding boss. He recalls one particularly vexing day when a group of exhausted advisers met with the unreasonable demands of the boss:

> We would meet either in his study at the Kremlin or, more often, in the Kremlin movie theater. Stalin used to select the movies himself.... When a movie ended, Stalin would suggest, "Well, let's go get something to eat, why don't we?" By now it was usually one or two o'clock in the morning. It was time to go to bed.... But everyone would say, yes, he was hungry, too. This lie was like a reflex. We would all get into our cars and drive to the dacha.[44]

Two forces are at work here. First, aides are often intimidated by the aura of a strong leader and the trappings of the office. Second, in their desire to remain close to the leader and the levers of power, they are reluctant to contradict the leader. Thus, otherwise strong and intelligent assistants cower before the leader. The result? Ineffective or unhealthy leaders often end up making decisions based on misinformation or missing information.

Several studies of dysfunctional leadership are instructive and enrich our understanding of who these negative leaders are and why we occasionally follow them.

In *Bad Leadership,* political scientist Barbara Kellerman examines "the dark side" of the human condition and of leadership, and asks, "What does 'bad leadership' mean?"[45] Is it *immoral* behavior, *unethical, incompetent, ineffective* leadership?

Kellerman is concerned with what she refers to as "Hitler's Ghost," the haunting concern that in looking for good leadership, we ignore—to our own great cost—the bad side of leadership. "We cannot," she writes, "distance ourselves from even the most extreme example—Hitler—by bestowing on him another name, such as 'power wielder'"; after all, "he was brilliantly skilled at inspiring, mobilizing, and directing followers. His use of coercion notwithstanding, if this is not leadership, what is?"[46]

If the leader is so clearly dysfunctional, why do followers follow? Should we not see the impending problems? Ought we not to be aware of the flawed leaders before us? Kellerman sees a combination of *individual* and *group* needs conspiring against a healthy response to bad leadership.

What powerful *individual* needs might a toxic leader satisfy? The most basic of human needs: "safety, simplicity, and certainty." And what *group* needs might a bad leader satisfy? Primarily order, cohesion, identity, and the ability to foster collective work.

Additionally, the potential cost of not following can be great. "Not following is not in their interest. Not following can entail risk—to family, to position, and even to life. In particular, actively to protest against the powers that be takes time, energy, and, more often than not, courage."[47]

Organizational behavior expert Jean Lipman-Blumen explores the allure of toxic leaders who "first charm but then manipulate, mistreat, undermine, and ultimately leave their followers worse off than they found them."[48] She defines toxic leaders as those who "engage in numerous *destructive behaviors* and who exhibit certain *dysfunctional personal characteristics.*" She continues, "To count as toxic, these behaviors and qualities of character must inflict some reasonably serious and enduring harm on their followers and their organizations. The intent to harm others or to enhance the self at the expense of others distinguishes seriously toxic leaders from the careless or unintentional toxic leaders, who also cause negative effects."[49]

Toxic leaders "earn their toxic stripes through their cynicism, greed, corruptibility, moral blind spots, and stupidity. Narcissism, paranoia, grandiosity, and megalomania drive still other toxic leaders. Then there are leaders whom we recognize as toxic leaders because their actions spring from malevolence, even evil intent. Still other leaders may be toxic through sheer cowardice."[50]

Good/Bad, Effective/Ineffective

Clearly Hitler was an ethically bad leader, but was he an "effective" leader? And do bad means ever justify "good" ends or must leaders—to be truly *good*—be both ethically and substantially effective?

As Kellerman points out, bad leadership may be either *ineffective* or *unethical* (or both). Ineffective leaders fail to live up to the needs and/or expectations of the times. They are decision-making and skill deficient and are often strategically flawed. Their skill and performance simply fall short. These are not "bad" people, merely ineffective ones.

Unethical leaders, on the other hand, are morally flawed. They violate accepted codes of decency and morality. Their means violate codes of ethics and their ends tend to be selfish and narrow. Typically, they induce their followers to become dependent, childlike, and submissive. Ethical leaders, in contrast, empower their followers, educate, liberate, and help free them to become partners or even leaders in their own right.

Ethical leaders, in short, put the needs of their followers ahead of their own needs. They model decency and ethical behavior. They pursue shared good over their own good. They ennoble and help empower others.[51]

Conclusion

Although leadership is necessary, it is also always potentially dangerous. Just as leaders can help us reach much-desired breakthroughs and political heights, they may also bring us to the depths. As many would-be leaders seek power for the wrong reasons or become corrupted and intoxicated by power, we must be vigilant not only about the means of leadership but about the ends as well. Because leaders require followers, toxic or bad leaders are often as much our fault as that of the demonic leaders we now revile. Hitler *did* have a significant following, as did Stalin, Mao, Klan leaders, Huey Long, Joseph McCarthy, and other misguided, dysfunctional leaders. We cannot sit back and condemn them if we do not take some responsibility ourselves. After all, we colluded in some ways to allow, even encourage, the rise of some dysfunctional leaders.

"You cannot have power for good without having power for evil too," writes George Bernard Shaw. "Even mother's milk nourishes murderers as well as heroes."[52] So how do we find the leader elevated and inspired, not deluded and intoxicated, by power? That's the continuing challenge. We want leaders who seek and indeed need power in order to transcend it, redeem it, and use it to achieve mindful and purposeful ends.

It is easy to spot a Darth Vader as a dysfunctional leader, yet often difficult—at least in the early stages—to spot emerging unhealthy leaders. Are they strong and decisive or are they wrongheaded, driven bullies? Self-assured or arrogant? Confident or closed-minded? Demanding or belligerent? Determined or rigid? Having strong or swollen egos? Forceful or domineering? There are characteristics that, when kept within the proper bounds, can lead to success, but can lead to disaster when taken a step too far.

Leaders—even healthy ones—have a difficult time finding people who can and will speak truth to power, tell them when they are wrong, and challenge the accepted wisdom. Leaders who are unhealthy intimidate others into obedience and compliance. They brook little or no criticism. Those who most need constructive criticism are often the least likely to allow or accept it.[53]

How can we protect ourselves from tyrannical and undesirable leaders? Although no panacea exists, there are things we can do to decrease the likelihood that tyrants will get a free hand in exercising power over us.

The framers of the U.S. Constitution insisted on *separation of powers* within a system of *checks and balances.* They knew all too well and had firsthand experience with unacceptable kings and royal governors. A system of separation of powers along with regular elections, impeachment provisions, judicial review, and similar safeguards reduces the chances of a leader's becoming a despot. *Limited terms* of office also ensure that leaders do not overstay their welcome. An *aware and observant citizenry* also can limit the ability of a tyrant to seduce the public. A *free and unfettered press and Internet* may also help, as may *a culture that prizes learning.* Boards of directors must have at least a few truly independent members, and preferably an independent chair. A healthy dose of *skepticism* is likewise highly desirable.

In sum we need people like the legendary Golda Meir, who once said, "I'm not cynical—I've just lost my illusions, that's all." And we need people with the courage to tell our emperors, princes, and executives when they have lost their clothes or their positive values, or both.

Chapter Twelve
The Creative Side of Leadership

> It is not the strongest of the species that survives, nor the most intelligent, but the one most responsive to change.
>
> —***Attributed to Charles Darwin (1809–1882)***

Organizations constantly adapt to new challenges and reinvent or renew themselves to remain competitive. New ideas, new products, breakthroughs, and nimble coping with disruptive new technologies are essential. "The only sustainable competitive advantage comes," one management consultant put it, "from out-innovating the competition."[1]

Google's recruiting Web site proclaims, "Innovation is our bloodline." It sees, Google says, endless opportunity to create even more relevant, more useful, and faster products for its users. Its mantra, borrowed from *Star Trek*: "Boldly go where no one has gone before." Google says to its recruits, "Your creative ideas matter here and are worth exploring. You'll have the opportunity to develop innovative new products that millions of people will find useful."[2]

Leaders need not be particularly creative themselves, but they have to understand that success is in large part about making their colleagues smarter, bolder, more creative. The technology genius Steve Jobs wasn't an engineer or scientist in the traditional sense. He thought of himself as an artist. His genius came from his masterful orchestration of ideas, art, and new technologies and from his perfectionist drive to motivate his colleagues to come up with better and more beautiful products. He became an impressive marketer and promoter. He also hired thousands of very creative people.

What is creativity? What is innovation? Why are they essential? What are the tensions between leadership and creativity? How does intuition relate to creativity and innovation? What are the paradoxes of creative leadership? What responsibilities do leaders have to recruit and protect creative people and promote a culture of creativity and innovation in their organizations?

We explore the creative process and speculate about the possible role that "twice-born" or boundary-spanning people play in bringing about innovation. We also consider ways effective leaders unlock creative and innovative energies in complex organizations.

Creativity is an action that brings into existence something new and useful. Combining novelty and usefulness, it is the ability to reframe one's understanding of something in a not so obvious way.[3] The word comes from the Latin *creare,* meaning "to bring about, bring into existence, to originate."

Humans can't make something out of nothing, so creativity invariably involves the reframing or restructuring of existing materials or existing good ideas. Creativity is connecting things in some new and useful way. Something useful emerges from combining earlier concepts or physical materials.[4]

The cumulative character of scientific creation is widely acknowledged. Creative individuals build on the breakthroughs of predecessors. "Every inventor, however original he may appear to have been, is laying bricks upon a building which has long been in the course of construction from innumerable and many unknown hands."[5] What Pasteur or Edison or Watson and Crick "discovered" built on extensive previous research as well as their own labors. If they hadn't existed, their insights would doubtless have come about over the next few years. Artistic breakthroughs are more complicated, yet they too build upon earlier creative works. Picasso was clearly influenced by Cézanne, among others, and Shakespeare borrowed from Plutarch, Sophocles, Euripides, and others.[6] "Good artists borrow, great artists steal," quipped Picasso.

The psychologist Mihaly Csikszentmihalyi says we are all programmed from birth with two contradictory predispositions: a conservative tendency "made up of instincts for self-preservation, self aggrandizement, and saving energy" and a second disposition encouraging us to explore, enjoy novelty, and take risks. This second tendency gives us the curiosity that promotes creativity. It is human nature to have both inclinations, yet the second needs more encouragement.[7]

Creative people usually retain a childlike curiosity about the world, a spirit of playfulness. Picasso joked, it takes a long time "to become young." They strive to think outside the traditional rules of "this is how we have always done it." They draw outside the lines. Creativity involves asking a lot of why, what-if, and what-for questions. People become more creative when they are at play, when they allow their curiosity to flourish, when they discard preconceptions, and when they think in associational or recombining modes. Creative people perceive connections among diverse ideas and see possible connections among seemingly unrelated theories.

Creative people are usually smart, yet what sets them apart from countless other intelligent individuals is their willingness to disregard and challenge or defy rules and assumptions. Thomas Edison is alleged to have said, "Hell, there are no rules here, we're trying to accomplish something." Creative people look at things differently, explore beyond traditional boundaries, see things in a larger or different context. They learn from the past yet are not prisoners of the past.

Creative people balance contending incentives. "On the one side the Conformist attempts to restrain us in order to assure security, profit and safety. On the other side the Adventurer dares to embark on a journey of discovery—a gamble" that may be dangerous yet could lead to something novel and valuable.[8]

Creativity involves the capacity to engage in what psychologists call lateral or divergent thinking. Conventional or convergent thinking strives for a single rational or logical solution. "But creative people can free themselves from conventional thought patterns and follow new paths to unusual or distantly associated answers," writes Ulrich Kraft. "This ability is known as divergent thinking, which generates many possible solutions" and proceeds from various starting points to improvise new procedures or methodologies.[9]

Creative people such as poets, artists, and inventors often have a lover's quarrel with the world and sometimes just a plain old quarrel. In pursuing their conceptions of "what ought to be," they are more inclined than most of us to sail against the currents. Inventors and outliers relish breaking the norms. It is the fuel that drives their internal search engines.

"The creator stands out in terms of temperament, personality and stance," writes psychologist Howard Gardner. "She is perennially dissatisfied with current work, current standards, current questions, current answers. She strikes out in unfamiliar directions and enjoys—or at least accepts—being different from the pack."[10]

Both divergent thinking and convergent thinking are necessary to foster discovery. Creativity and logic are hardly mutually exclusive; they are companions. But giving logic too much weight can at times restrain creative tendencies.

Creative people are often generalists or even polymaths, well versed in more than one discipline, and their capacity to borrow ideas from one specialization to the next is a distinct advantage. People who know a lot about a great number of subjects are more likely to put together new combinations of ideas than are people who are less educated, less informed, or less experienced. Take Leonardo da Vinci, who was, among other things, a painter, musician, engineer, and neuroscientist.[11] Thomas Jefferson, likewise, was a diplomat, writer, inventor, farmer, architect, political leader, and much more, a man of multiple interests and talents. Creativity prospers when people are not only knowledgeable about their own discipline but can transcend it and make links with other methodologies that enrich perception, imagination, and recontextualization.

Borrowing has always been a part of the creative process. "Make it a habit to keep on the lookout for novel and interesting ideas that others have used successfully," advised Thomas Edison. "Your idea only needs to be original in its adaptation to the problem you are working on."[12]

Few acts of creativity, as noted, are entirely original. Most are new ways of using existing information, modifications, or upgrades on what has been previously tried. People develop solutions to problems by starting with what they already know and then improvising or modifying it to answer questions. At each step, the creative process involves adjustments from what we know to a tentative exploration of the unknown. But most of the process is anchored in previous knowledge and past experience.[13]

Thus gifted composers borrow or "quote," adapt and improvise. So too with artists, architects, scientists, politicians, novelists, and high-tech entrepreneurs.

There exist many impediments to creativity. A fear of looking foolish tops the list. Most of us fear rejection. We fear making mistakes. We fear being punished or chastised for mistakes. Pioneering artists, writers, composers, and scientists are often unaccepted, or even ridiculed and rejected in their early years and sometimes throughout their lifetime as well. Van Gogh sold few paintings while he was alive. Joyce's *Dubliners* was rejected by twenty-two publishers. Stravinsky's *Rite of Spring* was initially scorned. Melville's fame came mainly after he died. Even the *Harry Potter* series was rejected by numerous publishers. Think too of Copernicus and Galileo.

Creative people risk unpopularity and are often rebellious. They view themselves not as champions of lost causes, but as champions of new approaches, new ideas, or new products yet to be acclaimed. They are willing to defy conventional wisdom in search of what might become accepted. Theirs is the world of "what ifs" and "what might bes."

Another impediment is that most people lock on to quick yes-or-no answers. Breakthrough inventions take time and require a willingness to collaborate with others over long periods of intense concentration and tenacity. Creative individuals have a knack for questioning, probing, observing, experimenting, and networking. They know that the best way to come up with a compelling new idea is to have loads of ideas. Creative people come up with a lot of ideas, most of which don't work. Yet they keep trying; they are less afraid of failing than most of us. They are comfortable being nonconformists, experimenting and exploring.

Psychologist David Campbell suggests creativity is at least a five-step process. First comes a *preparation* stage. It involves becoming familiar with the challenge or the problem and undertaking the project. This can be a long process that can take many years. Creative ideas are usually rooted in a long history of earlier efforts that are not always apparent. Second comes a *concentration* stage. Creative people often have an amazing focus and intense concentration on their problem. It can dominate their lives. Edison, for example, conducted hundreds of experiments that failed before inventing a usable lightbulb.

Third comes an *incubation* period. Inventors often have to live with frustration and revisit their efforts with a new and perhaps more relaxed perspective. Fourth, after what may be an extensive and exhausting incubation stage with varying trials and multiple false starts, a *breakthrough* or "aha" stage can come. Insights and solutions become apparent. But the epiphany needs verification and often actualization or production. A creative idea is not just dumb luck. It must be verifiable, understandable, and *made to work*. It needs to be tested. The bugs need to be worked out.[14]

Much writing on creative thinking suggests that unleashing one's creative potential is merely a matter of removing barriers—barriers of fear, judgment, or habit—and letting one's inherent creative nature take the forefront. Notice, for example, the creative impulses in children, who are presumably free to be creative because they have less fear of looking foolish. This leaves the impression that mental activity is naturally creative. But this is perhaps an unnecessarily passive approach to creative thinking, prescribing little more than barrier removal for the promotion of innovative thought.

Edward de Bono, author of *Lateral Thinking*, says the "just get rid of the impediments" approach to creativity is misleading. Although he admits there are barriers to creativity, de Bono contends that the cultivation of creative thought requires an intensely focused, active, deliberate approach. In a sense, one has to be very disciplined in order to become free. Thus de Bono prescribes a conscious and deliberate approach to seeking innovative ideas.

The human brain is made up of many complex neural circuits, which funnel information and store impressions, ideas, and memories into set patterns. These "patterns of perception" are what make the brain efficient, by categorizing and channeling ideas along specific, well-worn neural channels. This is the way the brain is designed to function. It allows for neural efficiency, quickness of ideas, and perhaps is the primary underlying component of higher intelligence.[15]

Well-worn patterns of perception, although necessary for efficient thought patterning, can also work against creativity. Ideas are developed within specific delineated tracks, so it takes a considerable effort to break out of traditional thinking. Creativity is the ability to progress laterally, rather than sequentially, within neural channels. The key to innovative thought is this capacity to jump the tracks of mental reasoning and progress in fresh directions.

Creativity, scholars find, is not the same as intelligence. Creativity often takes a slower, more meandering path than intellectual thinking. "The brain appears to be an efficient superhighway that gets you from Point A to Point B," says Dr. Rex Jung. "But in the regions of the brain related to creativity, there appears to be lots of little side roads with interesting detours, and meandering little byways."[16]

Creating not only involves coming up with fresh, usable insights, it also involves "shutting down the brain's habitual response, or letting go of conventional solutions."[17] The key to breakthrough thinking is likely the confrontation of new modes of thought imposed by new stimuli while the subconscious is in a state of searching for the answers to long-standing questions.

A leader has many roles to fill, nearly all of which require in-depth knowledge of the way things currently work. To be creative, a leader must also seek to retain or regain the "freshness" that stems from a sense of innocence and naïveté.

The need to preserve freshness of thought means leaders must carefully evaluate the way in which they spend their time, energy, and thought on a given day. Individuals who spend their days consumed by management or logistical concerns are less likely to be able to see the workings and purpose of their organization from an innovative perspective. Likewise, people who are experts in their field, but who only study "relevant" information, are less likely to come up with innovative ideas. New information is quickly stored according to standard patterns of perception. Often, only "irrelevant" information can break old patterns of thinking.

Defining Intuition

Everyone lives in a world of uncertainty, including leaders. Leaders rely on reasoning and technology as much as possible. But at times leaders turn to "gut feelings" or intuition. Intuition plays an important role in creativity.

The term *intuition* is usually defined as a quick perception or insight with minimal conscious attention or reasoning. Others define intuition as a subconscious interpretation of the knowledge and cultural conditioning of one's lifetime. It differs from linear, rational, and logical thinking but isn't exactly contrary to reason. "Intuition is a highly complex and highly developed form of reason that is based on years of experience and learning and on facts, patterns, concepts, procedures and abstractions stored in one's head."[18]

Bruce Henderson of the Boston Consulting Group writes that "intuition is the subconscious integration of all the experiences, conditioning, and knowledge of a lifetime, including the cultural and emotional biases of that lifetime."[19]

Effective leaders accept the role intuition plays in their lives. They understand they cannot know everything and that having perfect information is an illusory goal. They understand, too, that not everything that can be counted counts, and not everything that counts is readily countable. Making decisions with incomplete information and solving wholly new problems become part of their job. Thus, they accept the role intuition, gut feelings, and "soft" data play in their lives. They accept that an organization's effectiveness lies in a blend of clearheaded reasoning, empirical analysis, imagination, and intuition.

Leaders also have to be aware of hidden or irrational biases that can shape both individual and organizational behavior. We are often unduly shaped by our expectations, marketing schemes, and other subtle framing and emotional influences. For example, "Our propensity to overvalue what we own is a basic human bias," writes psychologist Dan Ariely, "and it reflects a more general tendency to fall in love with, and be overly optimistic about, anything that has to do with ourselves."[20] Brafman and Brafman add, "We're all susceptible to the sway of irrational behaviors. But by better understanding the seductive pull of these forces, we'll be less likely to fall victim to them in the future."[21]

Inventive breakthroughs often defy conventional reasoning. Intuition supplements empirical testing. It helps us interpret and recontextualize facts. Creative people, along with intuitive leaders, say they can often rely on their greater peripheral vision and somehow see what others missed. They can sense the interrelationships and connections between relevant facts and past experiences. Intuition can be especially helpful when new trends are emerging, when new disruptive tipping points or technologies are on the horizon, when it is necessary to challenge critical assumptions, and when personnel decisions are being made.

Thoughtful, intuitive people don't guess wildly or overflow with insights. Rather they are people who combine a passion for rigorous analysis with a detachment from standard operations. They have a playfulness and appreciate that "whimsy and absurdity seem to favor intuition."[22] Commentators suggest that some of Steve Jobs's creative genius came from his experiences in the 1960s and 1970s California counterculture, his spiritual awakening when he lived for a while in India, his deeply held Zen perspectives, and perhaps even his Buddhism.

Jobs preached that one should neither live someone else's life nor be too guided by how other people think. "Don't be trapped by dogma, which is living with the results of other people's thinking," he told a Stanford University graduating class in 2005. "Don't let the noise of others' opinions drown out your own inner voice. And most important, have the courage to follow your heart and intuition. They somehow already know what you truly want to become."[23]

Just as with creativity, intuition is successful for individuals who are comfortable with themselves. They typically have a well-defined sense of self and seek out settings that allow for patience, reflection, and imagination.

The impediments to intuitive thinking parallel the constraints on creativity. People fear that relying on their intuition might make them look bad or invite organizational embarrassment. "Fear of failure," says David Kelley, "is rampant among students who have been drilled in standardized-test taking."[24] People who are afraid of change, fearful of risk, or overly self-critical are understandably less likely to listen to and nurture their intuition.

Most of us regularly use our intuitions and have an even greater capacity for enhancing and unlocking intuitive powers. Nowadays intuition is less likely to be dismissed as mere superstition. Instead, most executives at least guardedly acknowledge that intuition can at times be a positive asset in the decision-making process.

"Intuition is a gift that must be developed," write Stanford Business School professors Michael Ray and Rochelle Myers. "Because experiences with intuition so often seem to come out of the blue, you might assume that it is strictly a sometime thing, a matter of come-and-go lightning. It is equally easy to assume that intuition is the province of the gifted few, or, less charitably, of oddballs—that it is an innate talent that you either have or don't have."[25]

Not so. Intuition is a skill most executives can develop. No one suggests political or business decisions be made solely on intuition. But a combination of reason, experience, information, hard data, and simple cues in the environment, when added to intuition, can help shape informed decision making.

Beware: there are plenty of perils involved in the misguided use of intuition. Investors invariably lose money if they only follow their gut feelings. Gamblers have a lousy track record vis-à-vis gambling establishments. The so-called spiritual psychics, especially those who make predictions for tabloids like the *National Enquirer*, are almost always wrong. When making important decisions, "discerning people will welcome the powers of their gut wisdom, yet know when to restrain it with rational, reality-based, critical thinking," writes psychologist David G. Meyers. "By checking our intuitions—our hunches, our gut feelings, our voices within—against available evidence we can think smarter."[26]

Meyers acknowledges that we know more than we think we do. In addition to our rational, conscious mind we have a "backstage mind." People often respond emotionally to new situations and only later do our cognitive processes go to work.

A reliance on intuition can be taken to extremes, and thus professionals of all kinds, while being open to new ideas, must also be willing to apply hard-nosed scrutiny to every hunch. They should also consider conducting controlled experiments that can test their ideas and hunches. Rigorous experiments can often provide the hard evidence necessary for making major new investments in manufacturing or marketing.[27]

Moreover, intuition can be a dangerously unreliable method of decision making in complicated situations. It can be too tempting a shortcut and can at times be an unreliable guide. "The more options you have," writes Eric Bonabeau, "the more data you have to weigh, and the more unprecedented the challenge you face, the less you should rely on instinct and the more on reason and analysis."[28]

The difference between effective and ineffective intuitive leaders is twofold: effective leaders have a sense of when to trust their intuition or gut and when not to, and they also work hard to create an organizational culture that can help them and their colleagues discipline their intuitions in responsible ways.

On the Paradoxes of Creative Leadership

Creativity is full of paradox, and the very term "creative leadership" poses additional paradoxes. Creativity simultaneously "involves analysis and intuition, order and disorder, judgment and non-judgment ... fullness and emptiness, thinking and non-thinking."[29]

We can say that an organization is only as good as its capacity to generate new ideas, new products, and new services and creatively absorb and adapt to change. But consider these paradoxes.

> Leaders need to recruit, encourage, and protect highly creative people; yet creative inventors can take unnecessary, poorly thought-out, expensive risks that can not only result in failure but also be damaging to the larger organization.

Although everyone is creative to some degree, highly creative people often have trouble fitting into complex organizations. Creative types can be passionate, impatient, renegades, hotshots, and gadflies.[30] Creativity, as noted, is unpredictable, digressive, and capricious, and often can "disturb the peace" in negative as well as positive ways.

Mavericks in this sense can pose a serious challenge to their supervisors. They are generally inclined to break the rules, do things their way, and at times can become obnoxious and disruptive. The challenge for organizational leaders, as Warren Bennis has written, is, how do you get talented, incredibly bright, yet often self-absorbed and arrogant people to work effectively together?

Not surprisingly, many leaders and managerial types are threatened by creative people. Bursts of creativity can create confusion. Creative people sometimes get things wrong. Creativity involves risk. Excessive risk can be costly, destabilizing, and sometimes fatal. For example, Enron and AIG (the huge insurance conglomerate) became highly creative yet ethically and legally flawed.

Executives have to be concerned with budgets and returns on investment and broader public reception. They also have to involve themselves in the management of creativity and they have to have a moral compass. Yet a delicate balance must be reached. Leaders have to manage creativity, but creative individuals require autonomy.

If we accept the propositions that creativity is an inherently risky business and that many creative projects fail to produce useful results, then we come to another crucial role of the leader. Creative organizations tend to be those able to both embrace and absorb risks. To cultivate a vitally creative and enterprising organization, a leader must be willing to accept and fund failures. Yet a time always comes when a leader has to make crucial judgments about the future direction of new research projects.

Some potentially creative breakthrough projects, despite their prospect for brilliant payoff, may develop into sinkholes, and could wind up wasting scarce human and financial resources. Here again a sense of balance is needed. The effective leader provides the necessary resources for creativity to flourish, and has the wise judgment to let creative elements flourish unmolested, yet must stay prudentially involved in the creative process and know when and whether, in investment terms, to go long or short, to expand their commitment or cut losses. This is no job for the faint of heart.

A related paradox is:

> **Creativity and innovation are highly valued yet often become threatening and unpopular, especially when they first appear.**

John W. Gardner gets to the heart of this paradox:

> We must never forget that though the word may be popular the consequences of true creativity can never be assured of popularity. New ways threaten the old, and those who are wedded to the old may prove highly intolerant. Today Galileo is a popular historical figure, and we feel wise and emancipated as we reflect indignantly on his persecution for supporting Copernicus. But if he were to reappear today and assert something equally at odds with our own deepest beliefs, his popularity would plummet like one of those lead weights dropped from the Tower of Pisa. Our affection is generally reserved for innovators long dead.[31]

This is why creative people need protection. And it is similarly why a vigorous tradition of freedom and inquiry is absolutely vital for continuously self-renewing communities.

Gardner's point about the unpopularity of highly creative thinkers reminds us that vanguard political leaders are often more respected after they are gone than when they are in the saddle. Abraham Lincoln, Franklin D. Roosevelt, Harry Truman, and Martin Luther King Jr. were often mocked, scorned, and rebuked more than idolized during much of their time in the limelight.

Stanford Business School professor Harold Levitt says the same phenomenon can also occur when visionary entrepreneurs start pathfinding companies. "Very creative, very independent, very stubborn people are not usually easy to live with, especially in organizations."[32]

Creative people are barrier-breaking troublemakers, neither easy to love nor easy to manage. "Every company needs them and few tolerate them."[33]

The challenge is how to institutionalize creativity, how to guard against overly powerful leaders attracting overly loyal or subservient subordinates, and how to replace the highly creative founding visionary when an organization gets larger and more complex. IBM, Polaroid, Microsoft, and Apple all had to wrestle with this dilemma, with varying results.

Psychologists are not exactly sure how creative personalities are different from normal or less creative types. Yet one creativity scholar hazards that if he had to express in one word what makes creative personalities different from others, it would be *complexity*. "By this I mean that they show tendencies of thought and action that in most people are segregated." Thus they contain contradictory extremes: "Instead of being an 'individual', each of them is a 'multitude.'"[34] In his legendary "Song of Myself," the poet Walt Whitman aptly says, "Do I contradict myself? Very well then I contradict myself (I am large, I contain multitudes)."

Creative people have a higher comfort level for the contradictory or paradoxical. Although such qualities are present in most people, most develop only one pole of the dialectic. Creative people develop both. Novelist F. Scott Fitzgerald famously wrote in *The Crackup* that the "test of a first rate intelligence is the ability to hold two opposed ideas in mind at the same time and still retain the ability to function." This comfort with complexity lends itself to expressing a greater range of personal qualities and a greater ability to span boundaries when necessary. Here are a few examples Mihaly Csikszentmihalyi says are typical of creative people:

- They have great energy yet they can quietly concentrate with intensity.
- They can be both smart and naïve, "wise" and "childish," at the same time.
- They can be playful yet intensely disciplined, both irresponsible and responsible.
- They can be imaginative and intrigued by fantasy yet also deeply rooted in their evolving professional fields.
- They can be humble and selfless yet also ambitious, driven, narcissistic, and proud. They understand that humility can be admirable but that excessive humility paralyzes. Breakthroughs and inventions are usually made by people with more than a little irrational self-confidence.

Psychologist Csikszentmihalyi suggests, too, that creative people are often psychologically androgynous, having an ability to be both aggressive and nurturing, "sensitive and rigid, dominant and submissive, regardless of gender." They have the strengths of their own gender as well as those of the other. "A psychologically androgynous person in effect doubles his or her repertoire or responses and can interact with the world in terms of a much richer and varied spectrum of opportunities."[35]

The pioneering psychologist William James talked about the twice-born person having both tough-minded and tender-minded capabilities. Creative people can be driven, zealous, and dreamy. This can be both for good and for ill. Thus political historian Jay Winik writes:

> In history, nearly all leaders who have given birth to new nations or religious movements or empires or great discoveries were to one extent or another, fanatical. They had to be. From Caesar to Martin Luther, from Magellan to Napoleon, from Bolivar to Galileo, all these men shared common traits: stubborn, steel-willed, secretive, fastidious, zealous, short-tempered. Each, in his own way, was a profound dreamer.[36]

The Boundary-Spanning "Marginal Person" Theory of Creative Leadership

This is less a theory than a conceptual proposition. It is remarkable how often transforming leadership comes from individuals who have gone away or matured, both metaphorically and culturally, and have come back from their "wilderness years" to offer themselves as catalysts for major change.

Mohandas Gandhi is a prime example. As we discussed earlier, he left his neighborhood in colonial India in order to earn an education in London, the capital city of the empire. He took his training in law and after a while went to South Africa, where he was both an attorney and an activist organizer for several years.

He returned to his Indian community only in middle age, at which time his training, travels, and boundary-spanning marginality understandably enabled him to look at India's situation and opportunities with a wholly different perspective than would have been possible if he had never left his village. He knew things didn't have to be as they were. He lived among people who had not enjoyed freedom as he had experienced. He could now both dream of an independent India and conceive of strategies and tactics that could unleash the energies of his fellow countrymen.

Martin Luther King Jr. is another example. Born and bred in Atlanta, he migrated north, first to the Philadelphia area for seminary, and subsequently to Boston University for his doctoral studies. He lived, studied, and worked in decidedly different communities from those in his highly segregated Georgia.

Later he was hired to pastor a church in Montgomery, Alabama, at a time when civil rights protests were incubating throughout the South. King was reluctant about joining the movement, fearful of jeopardizing his new job and family responsibilities. But he could fully appreciate that the South and black southerners needed to be liberated and could and should be able to live with the freedom and respect he had seen others enjoy elsewhere in the country.

His understanding of the possibilities for desegregating and integrating was joined with his political and moral education about the rights of man, the promises of the American dream, and the examples of Gandhi, Henry David Thoreau, and others. Thus both his education and his travels encouraged an "otherness" or marginality that probably was not a factor that shaped his neighbors, who hadn't had such opportunities.

Winston Churchill was born of one English and one American parent and did not attend Oxford or Cambridge as most other members of his class did. He traveled extensively around the world, both in military service and as a journalist, prior to his remarkable roller coaster of a career in politics. Churchill, it is said, always felt something of an outsider to the establishment he would later govern, and this sense of being an outsider or marginalized individual may well have freed him from the inhibitions of England's establishment.

Perhaps Steve Jobs and his unusual Apple experience illustrate this "born-again" phenomenon in a corporate setting. Jobs, as is well known, co-founded Apple with a friend who had earlier gone to his high school. But as Apple grew larger and more complex, Jobs became an explosive and disruptive force within the firm. After some missteps and lagging sales, Jobs was surprisingly forced out of the firm he founded.

This was the second time Jobs had been abandoned by his "family." He was given away for adoption by his unwed birth mother in 1955; now Jobs was abandoned or given away (although this time at least with some valuable stock holdings) from the firm he had co-founded and nurtured from its birth. Jobs told many friends and biographers that he was hurt and shamed by these repudiations.

Most people would have been permanently set back by such an ouster at Apple. But Jobs was able to stage one of the greatest comebacks in corporate history.

His "wilderness years," if they can be called that, were spent inventing new companies and new products, the most successful of which was Pixar, a company that made digitally animated films.

Then, twelve years after he had been essentially fired, Jobs was called back to Apple, first as an adviser, and a few years later as the chief executive officer. In this "second coming of Steve Jobs," he emerged as one of the most inventive and stunningly successful corporate leaders America has ever had. He was still the stubbornly tenacious and often overbearing boss he had been in his first years at Apple, but he had doubtless learned a lot more about himself, about corporate America, and about ways to make his beloved Apple more competitive, more innovative, and more profitable. He was also happily married, very well-off, and a Silicon Valley celebrity. What is intriguing about Jobs is that he was neither a hardware engineer nor a software programmer. Nor did he consider himself an organizational manager. He reinvented himself as a "technology leader," choosing very bright people, setting incredibly high standards, encouraging and prodding people to make electronic devices that had uncommon and elegant style. Along the way he became an iconic promoter and a preeminent example of the modern-day entrepreneur.[37]

The Jobs story vivifies one of the old maxims about leaders and leadership: leaders can often redefine defeat, bad luck, setbacks, and personal crises as opportunities. He also plainly understood that lasting companies usually have to reinvent themselves, not just once but often.

Extensive travel, higher education, and the experience of multiple cultures are not sufficient causes for transformational or creative leadership. Yet people who have lived abroad, or served overseas in the military, or had Peace Corps types of experiences often return to their homes with a richer perspective than that of those without such experiences. Such people ask different questions, see different possibilities, and pay attention to things others take for granted. The solitary traveler often finds that exile elsewhere or "otherness" allows one to begin to understand who one is and what one's values are.

Yet the voyage of discovery or boundary-spanning depends less on visiting or living in distant places—although this often helps—than on developing the capacity to see problems with fresh eyes. Lincoln, for example, never traveled or lived abroad, yet he may have developed a fresher perspective on the central issue of his day by bringing a "Western perspective" to the growing North-South divide. He came from a southern heritage, was raised in border states, and learned his politics in what was then essentially the frontier. His lens for understanding the looming crisis among the states was honed by travels on the Mississippi, brief service in Congress, and extensive service in his state legislature and as a circuit-riding country attorney. He grew too from reading Shakespeare and the classics. He understood the imperfections of human nature, yet he developed a problem-solving instinct for the possibilities of progress. Both an optimist and a melancholy pessimist, he developed an ambition to go east and be a mediating and healing agent his country needed at that particular time.

Defining Innovation

Innovation is putting new ideas and technologies into practical use. It profits from inventions and creative discoveries, yet it is the enactment or implementation of these inventions and activity. It is inventiveness put to use. It is also the process of bringing about significant positive change.

Innovation is different from discovery or invention, yet innovations—both product innovations, such as the radio or Apple iPhones, iPods, and iPads, and process innovations, such as Amazon, Walmart, and McDonald's—can also be highly creative. It is in this sense that an innovation is the implementation of creative discoveries. Innovation can be more than launching successful products and services; it can also be about reframing organizational cultures.

Creativity is the cause, whereas innovation is the effect. Creativity is coming up with new ideas, whereas innovation is putting new ideas into action. Ideas or insights are usually not worth much until they are put into practice. Indeed, "invention without innovation is a pastime," writes Harold Evans. "Patents are important, very much so in some industries, like pharmaceuticals, and hardly at all in others, like machine building, but their role, like that of the inventor, has been overplayed. A patented invention is only a beginning. Less than 10 percent of patents turn out to have commercial importance."[38]

In today's borderless globalized markets, the innovative organization is constantly building new markets to meet untapped customer wants. It is also about picking which new ideas make the best sense, and executing the right strategies to quickly introduce them.[39]

Creativity and innovation are not easily compartmentalized. Innovation expert John Kao says the two are companions in the sense that "ideas are generated, developed, and transformed into value … [creativity] connotes both the art of giving birth to new ideas and the discipline of shaping and developing these ideas to the stage of realized value."[40]

Everyone wants to encourage innovation. But innovation is often messy, misunderstood, slow, and potentially disruptive to the stability of an organization. Innovation in the form of dazzling breakthroughs can be a powerful transforming force that shatters the status quo. But most innovations are undramatic and come to fruition only over an extended period. "Innovation is a daily struggle characterized by many false starts, mistakes and tiny advances, and only rarely by large leaps. It's not just invention and discovery," writes *Newsweek*'s Robert Samuelson. "It's the stretching of technologies and products to perform better and to meet new needs. In the 1980s, the spread of personal computers has seemed stunning. In fact, the invention that made them possible—the integrated circuit—occurred in the late 1950s. It took nearly two decades of improving electronic chips and fiddling with their possible uses to arrive at PC's."[41]

This was also the case with community colleges, online distance learning, and the implementation of electronic books and newspapers. First come the inventive insights and, later on, the often ingenious risk-taking experimentation, refinement, and large-scale implementation that create practical usage.

Thus innovation involves improvements and adjustments leading to advances in products, technologies, and services. "There's constant feedback between customers and suppliers, laboratories and factories, universities and companies. Innovation is a spirit; it subsists on trial and error."[42] No one has found a "once-and-for-all" formula for guaranteeing continuous innovation.

Innovation Realities

Leaders don't have any choice but to encourage constant innovation. Survival requires a constant flow of new ideas and a nimble responsiveness to change. As one CEO put it, "Whatever made you successful in the past won't in the future."[43] Effective companies, colleges, and nations almost always have more good ideas than they can support. The challenge is to know when to set aside older, less useful products and services and when to select and ramp up new innovations. A similar challenge for an innovating company is how to become independent of the founder's legacy or the organizational culture set in place by founders.[44]

Management guru Peter Drucker describes the relentless necessity for the ability to innovate continually and to have the managerial capacity to bring new products to market in record time: "Everybody in a pharmaceutical company or in a company making synthetic organic chemicals knows that the company's survival depends on its ability to replace three quarters of its products by entirely new ones every ten years."[45] The product life is now much shorter.

Studies find that smaller companies are responsible for an impressive number of innovations. Yet companies such as Google, Amazon, Apple, Procter & Gamble, 3M, GE, and Microsoft spend enormous funds trying to stay innovative.[46] They also spend lavishly acquiring small companies with promising innovative technologies. And the large cutting-edge firms do indeed come up with a large share of breakthrough inventions and patents.

A company's commitment to innovate may entail risks, yet far riskier is being unable to adapt to rapidly changing consumer tastes, fast-changing demographics, and market and technological disruptions.

Innovation is sometimes a function of luck and timing as much as of strategic thinking or having the best and brightest on your team. But there is widespread agreement that chief executive officers and top management are responsible for fostering and nurturing a culture of innovation. Without the right kind of senior leadership, a tolerance for risk taking, and major investment in research innovation, efforts take a backseat to short-term demands and routines.

Managers of large organizations are regularly tempted to direct their resources toward protecting established products by investing in incremental improvements rather than taking bolder, more radical risks in uncertain ventures.

Whether to postpone or to encourage innovation is a key strategic issue every leader faces. Most organizations have significant innovative potential, yet only a few embrace a continuous commitment to innovation.

Conventional wisdom often holds that innovation mainly comes about because of a genius working in a solitary lab somewhere who has an epiphany and singularly hits upon a brilliant new idea. The notion is that this type of person can't be managed or led in any predictable way. But this is largely a myth.

Most twentieth-century innovations of note came about gradually and without a grand epiphanic moment. "The World Wide Web, the web browser, the computer mouse, and the search engine—four pivotal developments in the history of business and technology—all involved long sequences of innovation, experimentation, and discovery." Scott Berkun writes that these innovations involved "contributions from dozens of different individuals and organizations, and took years (if not decades) to reach fruition."[47]

Innovation can be promoted and organizations that learn how to innovate have a competitive advantage over their rivals. McKinsey & Company director Richard N. Foster, in his *Innovation: The Attacker's Advantage*, writes about successful companies who "recognize that they must be close to ruthless in cannibalizing their current products and processes just when they are most lucrative, and begin the search, over and over. It is about the inexorable and yet stealthy challenge of new technology and the economics of substitution which force companies to behave like the mythical phoenix, a bird that periodically crashed to earth in order to rejuvenate itself."[48]

Foster's research contrasts aggressive companies that are constantly searching for ways to deal with technological or marketplace discontinuities with companies that defensively stick to their old products or old ways. Competitive companies understand both their customers and fast-developing technological change. They relentlessly study their direct and indirect competitors. They invest in enhanced productivity and try to estimate the economic consequences of new technological breakthroughs for both themselves and their competitors. They understand which of their products or services are most vulnerable to technical attack or disruptive technical shifts.

Producers and manufacturers are often slow to see the changes that are needed. Customers and product users are often the source of practical innovations. The user often needs something different or better or sees how a slightly improved product can have a different application. If, as research suggests, users are often responsible for suggesting useful ideas, innovative companies need to carefully listen to their smarter customers. Innovative manufacturers can and should stimulate user-fed innovation, not just by listening to customers but also by providing free or low-cost research and development help to users interested in applying a product to new applications. They can also form user groups to meet, exchange ideas, and even produce experimental product applications at customer request.[49]

Obstacles That Stifle Innovation

Organizations are naturally resistant to novel ideas, in part because most new ideas challenge the comfort of orthodoxy and often prove to be costly, ill-advised, or even foolish.

"Most novel ideas are quickly and beneficially extinguished," writes James G. March, "but for some reason, this does not seem to slow the flow of novelty."[50] Innovations and novelty are irrepressibly part of the human curiosity to improve things.

March cautions that "substantially novel ideas, routines, and properties are likely to deviate from established practices and knowledge. They will generally be identified as inferior to existing practice by conventional intelligence." In the overwhelming majority of cases, March adds, "rejection of new ideas by the application of intelligence proves sensible."[51]

Thus the organizational architecture or its DNA resists innovative tendencies. And, as March argues, this isn't all bad. Yet, as noted, innovation also supplies the new blood and the new yeast that fuel the sonic boom of globalization that is transforming today's world.[52]

Innovating, however, is seldom easy. Executives can't just exclaim, "We're going to be an innovative organization." Leaders understand there are plenty of barriers that discourage innovation.

Here are just a few:

Complacency. A sense of satisfaction or smugness can easily take hold in organizations that are enjoying success. For example, the company that produced and sold slide rules might well have believed business was fine, only to be done in by the unexpected success of the computer industry. Polaroid cameras were a smashing hit, yet the rise of digital camera technology plainly rained on their parade. Complacent organizations can mistakenly become inward rather than forward looking, can become defensive rather than pursuing the next generation of inventors that will help them evolve. GM and Sears were large, fat, and happy until Toyota and Walmart came along. Large is no longer an advantage, and fat and happy can be a liability.

Insularity and Compartmentalization. Most innovations don't come from a single genius working in some sequestered lab but rather through networking teams that collaborate across disciplines. Cross-pollination is essential. Innovations also come about from organizations listening to customers and engineers and marketers working together to adapt products to meet market and customer desires.

The way organizational communications are structured is key. "In any organization, there are many people who could almost certainly team up to produce new ideas—but often the structure of the company keeps them apart."[53] Sometimes it is a case of too much bureaucracy or different physical locations. Occasionally rival bosses who dislike each other can also inhibit collaboration.

Risk-Averse Cultures. Peter Drucker notes that all economic ventures are "high-risk" activities. Yet successful innovators, he says, are not necessarily risk takers. They are not "risk focused" so much as opportunity focused; "they try to define the risks they have to take and to minimize them as much as possible."[54]

The notion that entrepreneurs love risk is exaggerated, says Drucker. Excessive risk taking can obviously be costly, disruptive, and can lead to outright failure. On the other hand, organizations in highly competitive global markets have to be consistently on the lookout for new ideas, new products, new ways of doing things. To thrive is to innovate new technologies and new strategies, selecting fresh, usable ideas and then bringing them to the marketplace before rivals do so.

A company that is afraid of risk taking and afraid of investing in vigorous exploration of new ideas risks stagnation. The business models used by FedEx, Apple, Google, and Southwest Airlines, to take just a few examples, were based on trying something new, experimenting, and introducing new and profitable ways to provide services customers learned to appreciate. But each case involved risks; each case called for redefining what had been done previously. For-profit educational institutions such as the University of Phoenix and online colleges or educational service companies such as The Teaching Company are yet other examples of introducing services that appear to meet new markets and new demands.

Failure to Pay Attention to Customer Criticism, Advances Elsewhere, and Evolving New Technologies. Intel CEO Andy Grove titled one of his books *Only the Paranoid Survive.* His message was that a top executive has to be constantly listening and learning, especially learning about new innovations and new products and about how their rivals are inventing them and bringing new products to market.

Innovations rarely come from people in the front office. Innovative ideas are far more likely to come from younger people in research and development, engineering, or even marketing who are striving to make their mark. These potential innovators and their teams need to be encouraged, rewarded, and made aware that those in top leadership care a lot about creativity and innovation. Toxic bosses can kill the spirit of innovation by sneers, raised eyebrows, and the intimidation of those who have the passion to rethink, redefine, and restructure old ways of doing things.

Inadequate Resources. An obvious barrier to innovation is the failure to invest adequately in research and development. A culture of innovation not only needs articulation and celebration, it also needs money and brainpower. Companies who cut their investments in this area invite being bypassed by existing as well as start-up firms.

Organizations that care about innovation benefit from highly educated new blood and from proximity to and affiliations with leading intellectual centers. Cross-pollination counts. It's no surprise that Silicon Valley emerged in the shadow of great research institutions such as Stanford University and the University of California. Similar centers of innovation grew up in the Boston area, around Chicago, around Austin, around Seattle, at the North Carolina Research Triangle, and as offshoots of DuPont, Microsoft, and Hewlett-Packard. Intellectual energy is fueled by synergy and brainy collaboration.

The "Wet Blanket" and Killer Phrase Minefield. "It's essential to keep in mind that many great ideas were at first thought to be stupid ideas," write Jim Collins and William Lazier.[55] Indeed there is a long history of so-called leaders who failed to see the merits of breakthrough ideas.

One of the biggest barriers to innovation is a coolness to new ideas and a failure to appreciate innovative ideas from all kinds of predictable as well as unpredictable places.

Collins and Lazier cite a number of famous "wet blanket" innovation stiflers. Here are four such examples:

- "This 'telephone' has too many shortcomings to be seriously considered as a means of communication. The device is inherently of no value to us." Western Union internal memo in response to Bell's telephone, 1876.
- "The concept is interesting and well formed, but in order to earn better than a 'C' the idea must be feasible." [The alleged response of a Yale University professor] to Fred Smith's paper proposing reliable overnight delivery service. Smith went on to found FedEx.
- "Who the hell wants to hear actors talk?" H. M. Warner, Warner Brothers, 1927.
- "The television will never achieve popularity; it takes place in a semi-darkened rooms and demands continuous attention." Harvard professor Chester L. Dawes, 1940.[56]

Here are some additional "innovation killers" used by lazy and unimaginative managers: "We tried that already and it didn't work"; "Customers won't pay for something that expensive/technologically complex"; "That would be too big a departure for our company"; "It wouldn't make money"; and "We don't have the right people to build that."[57]

An old adage holds that "the only dumb question is the question you don't ask." The same can be said about the spirit of innovation. Innovative people ask a lot of dumb questions and develop a robust receptivity to questions, searching, edgy or crunchy ideas, and leaps of the imagination.

Encouraging Innovation

An innovative spirit can be one of an organization's greatest assets. Yet there is no magical formula for generating new ideas. Imaginative leaders first have to signal they not only welcome innovative ideas, but they are passionate about new ideas, change, and innovation of all kinds.

One of the more successful Wall Street bankers in recent years, Jamie Dimon of JPMorgan Chase, focused on where his company could improve. One of Dimon's favorite mantras is "More, better, faster, quicker, cheaper."[58] Leaders like Dimon understand that in today's entrepreneurial climate an organization may only be as good as its latest innovative idea. The rest, as an old saying has it, "is mere housekeeping."

Effective executives understand that innovation has its disruptive as well as constructive aspects. Both economists and artists agree that acts of innovation are in many ways acts of destruction.

Innovations and creative concepts in general "can shatter set patterns of thinking, threaten the status quo, or at least stir up people's anxieties. Often when people set out to sell or implement a creative idea, they are taking a big risk of failure, losing money, or simply making fools of themselves."[59] That's why senior executives have to nurture a culture that celebrates prudent risk taking and even failure and recognizes that an addiction to conventional wisdom leads to paradigm paralysis. Paradigms serve as a filter that screens most of the information we receive. If something nicely fits our preconceived notions, it's embraced. If it doesn't, we are taken aback. Thus most of us can't entertain ideas that don't fit our paradigms. And as one scholar warns, "If you see in any given situation only what everybody else can see, you can be said to be so much a representative of your culture that you are a victim of it."[60]

At W. L. Gore and Associates they celebrate, not stigmatize, failure. "When a project doesn't work out and the team kills it, they celebrate with beer or champagne just as they would if it had been a success." Why? "Celebrating a failure encourages risk-taking."[61]

If the people who work at Amazon "don't make some significant mistakes," says founder Jeff Bezos, "then we won't be doing a good job for our shareholders because we won't be swinging for the fences." Bezos adds, "We like to go down unexplored alleys and see what's at the end. Sometimes they're dead ends. Sometimes they open up into broad avenues and we find something really exciting."[62] Innovators almost by definition have a bias against the status quo, a yearning to experiment, and a passion for improving things.

Steve Jobs, after he had come back and taken over again at Apple, designed a brand campaign to celebrate both Apple and creativity. It was aimed at both his customers and Apple's employees, trying to emphasize what made them different. Jobs collaborated with his ad agency, and the ad read in part, "Here's to the crazy ones. The misfits. The rebels. The troublemakers. The round pegs in the square holes. The ones who see things differently. They're not fond of rules. And they have no respect for the status quo.... And while some people may see them as the crazy ones, we see genius. Because the people who are crazy enough to think they can change the world are the ones who do."[63]

Here are a few of the ways organizations institutionalize the spirit of enterprise:

1. They recognize innovation is a team sport.

Healthy organizations remind people that even Thomas Edison had at least a dozen associates who worked with him as he invented the lightbulb.

Creative people network and work with both similar-minded and alternative folks within their organizations. The "geeks" need to talk with the "suits," programmers need to talk with engineers, marketers need to mingle with manufacturers, and everyone needs to put themselves in the position of being a customer. Leaders have to break down the walls between different areas of a company. Insularity encourages inertia, not innovation. Leaders are responsible for "meshing things up" and for synchronization.

Talk and mingling are essential. Two MIT professors describe the top executive's role as that of a party host. The early stages of innovation, they suggest, have a lot in common with a cocktail party. "Diverse people gather and chat, casually but seriously, about a variety of topics. In a safe and stimulating environment, they explore ideas they wouldn't normally venture, eliciting frank reactions from listeners who might not otherwise take time to respond. Engaged, occasionally contentious conversations stimulate new ideas."[64]

The cocktail party metaphor may seem a bit whimsical. Yet most leaders learn that if necessity is often the mother of invention, playfulness is often the father. Innovative people need the freedom to look at things differently, to be playful in using their imaginations, and to have fun in what they are doing.

2. Innovative organizations celebrate brainstorming, questioning, discovery, and asking counterfactual "what if" and "why not" questions.

Asking the right questions is often as important as finding the right answers. Innovators question the unquestionable and think about how they can change the world. Innovators love brainstorming, love mixing it up with other bright people who are excited about ideas, love learning how things work.

Michael Dell, founder of Dell Computing, says his venture started when he wondered why it was that most computers at the time cost five times as much as the sum of their parts. "In chewing over the question, he hit on his revolutionary business model."[65]

Google founders Larry Page and Sergey Brin flourished in the intellectual brainstorming hothouse of Stanford University's legendary computer science department in the 1990s. They profited from brilliant professors and brilliant fellow graduate students and from the fact that several of these professors and classmates had founded a score of pathbreaking innovative technology companies in the area. It was in this greenhouse of brainstorming that the Google search engine was incubated and turned into a gold mine.[66]

Innovative people, writes John Kao, run best on the high-octane fuels of play and freedom. Leaders, he adds, need to appreciate that like jazz musicians, innovators need to improvise. Perpetually innovative organizations benefit not only from formal brainstorming or "skunk work" teams but also from bringing in outsiders to help mix things up. "Recruiting outsiders to 'sit in' and jam—perhaps on a just-in-time basis—on specific projects has become common in business. Like jazzmen, outside musicians who sit in and shake up a tired tune, these migrant virtuosos are never more essential than when in-house creativity flags."[67]

In sum, organizational leaders need both to invest in brainstorming and to create safe havens for it. They also need to encourage everyone from vice presidents to the landscape and custodial crews to think about new ways the organization can improve, discover, and prosper. In innovative organizations, innovation becomes everyone's business.

3. Innovations often are smaller adjustments or reconfigurations than startling mega departures.

The glorification of "Mount Rushmore" visionaries or genius inventors tends to overshadow the greater reality of those who adapt and upgrade existing products or technologies.

"Innovators carefully, intentionally, and consistently look out for small behavioral details—in the activities of customers, suppliers, and other companies—in order to gain insights about new ways of doing things."[68] That's how hybrid cars came about. That's how iPods, iPads, BlackBerries, YouTube, Facebook, and e-commerce emerged in the marketplace.

It is a mistake to unduly celebrate the most spectacular innovators in history. They deserve praise, yet many of the major changes in history have also come about through small successive innovations, most of them anonymous. "Our dramatic sense leads us to seek out the person 'who started it all' and to heap on his or her shoulders the whole credit for a prolonged, diffuse and infinitely complex process," writes John W. Gardner. This is a misplaced preoccupation, for many of today's most challenging problems defy resolution by any single dramatic mega-solution. Think of energy independence, for example. "This will yield, if at all, only to a whole series of innovations," Gardner writes. "An example may be found in the renewal of our metropolitan areas. To bring these sprawling giants back under the rational control of the people who live in them will require a prolonged burst of political, economic and social innovation."[69]

4. Hierarchy and bureaucracy are often the enemy of innovation.

There is a power in small teams and fluid structures. Google and W. L. Gore pride themselves on keeping teams small. They prefer it if everyone can get to know one another and the rules are few.

Former DuPont engineer Bill Gore, who founded W. L. Gore and Associates, discarded the conventional rules of how companies operate. "He created a place with hardly any hierarchy and few ranks and titles. He insisted on direct, one-on-one communication; anyone in the company could speak to anyone else. In essence, he organized the company as though it were a bunch of small task forces." Alan Deutschman, writing for *Fast Company*, describes it this way: "To promote this idea, he limited the size of teams—keeping even the manufacturing facilities to 150 to 200 people at most. That's small enough so that people can get to know one another and what everyone is working on, and who has the skills and knowledge they might tap to get something accomplished—whether it's creating an innovative product or handling the everyday challenges of running a business."[70]

Innovative organizations flatten the pyramid, empower as many associates as possible, and preach the doctrine of "using your good judgment" rather than writing lengthy rule books full of restrictions. They minimize rules and fight hierarchy, fancy titles, and compartmentalization.

The goal is to create community, celebrate the spirit of enterprise, and have fun. "Innovation is a serious business but being serious does not help you get started. Humor involves challenging conventions, poking fun at taboos and coming up with the unexpected."[71] Thus humor, playfulness, and laughter are natural allies of innovation and creativity.

Other characteristics of innovative leaders and innovative organizations are:

- They take the long view. They understand it often takes years before truly innovative products or services can be brought to market.

- They hire smart, creative people who have a passion for inventing things and contributing to society, and they work hard to provide the training, space, and incentives to keep them.
- They encourage networking, relevant travel, attending "idea conferences," retooling sabbaticals, and similar self-renewal initiatives.
- Innovative organizations make sufficient room for unorthodox and unusual people and for mavericks, "geeks," "nerds," and explorers, yet are understandably less tolerant of cynics, whiners, and toxic managers.
- Innovative organizations understand that change is inevitable and that crises and disruptive technologies provide as many opportunities as they do challenges.
- Innovative organizations design their self-renewing organizations as questioning, learning, and idea-generating enterprises.
- Innovative leaders understand that innovation and peak performance are most often the result of years and years of arduous practice, discipline, and incredible tenacity.[72]
- Finally, the innovative leader understands that just like civilization, innovation is a movement not a condition, a voyage not a harbor.[73]

On Encouraging an Innovative Nation

Dozens of nations have adopted innovation as a top priority. China, South Korea, Singapore, Brazil, Israel, and Finland are just a few nations that are investing heavily in some aspect of technology or design to enhance their ability to compete in the age of globalization.[74]

The United States has been one of the most innovative nations in the world. It has the greatest number of patents and has witnessed more inventions turned into practical products than any other country. This has been especially true in Internet and computer technology, pharmaceutical drugs, DNA sequencing, GPS, chemistry, physics, social network inventions, robotics, and related fields. The United States has also built the most impressive research universities and leading professional schools.

In many ways the United States' Manhattan Project, the secret government-sponsored, government-funded invention and development of atomic weapons that took place during the 1940s, is Exhibit A of a focused and brute-force national initiative to promote innovative breakthroughs.

The Chinese government is investing enormous resources in educating scientists working on alternative energy development, automobile design and manufacturing, and a host of related engineering ventures.

Singapore is investing heavily in life sciences and biomedical research. Its Biopolis, a huge research center, is aggressively recruiting top scientists from all over the world to work on stem cell research and related possible breakthroughs.

South Korea, a well-known leader in electronics and automobiles, is also becoming a leader in bringing new automotive battery technologies to market, and it has won big contracts from General Motors and others. It has also won big contracts for designing and installing nuclear energy facilities in the Middle East.

Nations are trying to position themselves to compete in the borderless economy. To do this they try to predict how they can capitalize on their strengths in order to win a competitive edge. "Singapore offers tax relief, employee training, and R & D grants to life sciences firms that locate there. India provides talent management for some of the world's most sophisticated technological development work. Finland is becoming a global center for innovative design."[75]

Until World War II much of the inventive and innovative progress took place in Europe. Isaac Newton, Charles Darwin, Albert Einstein, and Guglielmo Marconi are examples. "It's no secret why the West now dominates invention and innovation," writes Robert J. Samuelson. "One requirement for success is a belief that science and technology matter for national power, human well-being and economic growth."[76] This idea was a product of the Renaissance and became a Western idea.

In the 1990s the United States invested more in basic research than the next four or five countries combined. But Asian nations now fully understand the drive to invent, discover, and bring new innovations to the marketplace. And nations like Israel and Finland have become hotbeds for start-up entrepreneurial ventures.[77]

The United States strategically invested in military, space, and health sectors. It subsidized agriculture research and technology. And more recently it began investing in alternative energy research and development.

But has innovation in the United States started slowing down in recent years? This is a big debate as of this writing. Much debated also, especially in America, is how directly the government should be involved in picking potential winners, that is, steering government resources toward targeted areas rather than letting the use of resources be decided by the private sector and the marketplace.

America has long prided itself on being a pro-business, pro–private enterprise nation and has opposed, at least in principle, a centralized planning process with a focused and defined national industrial policy. The American dream has always been of an enduring economic experiment that encourages bottom-up innovation, with the federal government playing only a minor role as encourager, facilitator, and gentle regulator. The reality, of course, is more complicated.

Everyone agrees, however, that every nation can indirectly encourage its citizens and its economics to be innovation friendly.

A nation's innovation agenda should include the following:

1. Make sure imaginative patent laws and intellectual property right protections are in place that adequately protect the rights of inventors yet are not used to discourage innovative practices.
2. Overhaul the financial system so that innovation gets adequate investment. "Opportunities in clean technologies and nanotechnology require large-scale, long-term investments.... Business innovation ought to be declared a public policy objective—one at least as important as boosting home ownership and agriculture."[78]
3. Invest heavily in pathbreaking basic research as the United States has done in semiconductors, lasers, DNA sequencing, and the development of alternative energies and a new energy grid.
4. Invest strategically in education at all levels but especially push for greater quality in math, engineering, and advanced science learning. This requires both infrastructure investments and financial help for advanced studies in these and related science ventures.[79]
5. Encourage flexible visa policies that will attract talented and highly skilled immigrants. The importance of this is that nearly a quarter of international patent applications filed from the United States are the work of immigrants here. Nearly a quarter of America's engineering and technology firms in recent years were founded by immigrants or children of immigrants. Andrew Grove, who helped found Intel Corporation, immigrated as a youth from Hungary, as did Wall Street legend George Soros. Sergey Brin, co-founder of Google, immigrated to the United States from Russia; Jeff Bezos, founder of Amazon, is the son of a Cuban immigrant; and Steve Jobs of Apple was the son of a Syrian graduate student at the University of Wisconsin.
6. Consider what Manhattan (1940s) or "Man to the Moon" projects are worth mounting on a massive scale. Fighting cancer? Energy security? Rebuilding failed American cities? Revitalizing railroads or the American automotive industry? And decide how much should be a public as opposed to private sector commitment.
7. Recognize and celebrate too that many if not most innovative ideas emerge out of dreams, serendipity, and the relatively amateur individual who explores, invents, and collaborates more for the love of it than for immediate capital rewards. "The roots of great innovation are never just in technology itself," writes David Brooks. "They are always in the wider historical context. They require new ways of seeing."[80]

Such an agenda "would steer and spark innovation without controlling it, which is what government has done since the days of Alexander Hamilton."[81]

Conclusion

Creativity, invention, intuition, and innovation matter in how leaders go about designing and running organizations. Most individuals and organizations have the capacity to innovate. It is the job of a leader to unlock and encourage creativity and invention. Many leaders are not necessarily the most creative, smartest, or best-educated people in the room but they learn how to creatively manage, encourage, and liberate talented people of all kinds. They recruit the creatively talented, they set high standards (sometimes insanely high standards), they inspire and motivate talented colleagues, and they ensure their organizations are tackling the toughest challenges while still being highly innovative and fun places for learning, self-renewal, and personal satisfaction. Managers, an old saying has it, make "to-do" lists; leaders make "to-invent, to-create, and to-imagine" lists.

Companies as well as countries must regularly court the kinds of creativity and innovative ideas that will enrich them. The creative side of leadership is the process of bringing the results of change and renewal into line with an organization's purposes and aspirations.

Chapter Thirteen
Leadership as a Performing Art

> We should be clear from the start that leadership is not a science but an art; it is a performance not a recipe; it is an invention not a discovery. If it was a science, we could reduce the essence down to a parsimonious set of rules and apply the result with confidence. Unfortunately this is not the case.
>
> —*Keith Grint*[1]

Civilizations die. Empires collapse. Nation-states can become failed states. Cities and states can go bankrupt. Companies and colleges can go out of business.[2]

People and societies that don't master the arts of renewal decay, and people and societies that don't provide for the development of leaders invite a downward spiral. Healthy ventures depend on leaders, talent, energy, and a sense of purpose that can help guide them in achieving mutual aspirations.

Leaders matter just as composers, conductors, coaches, teachers, inventors, physicians, architects, and military commanders matter. A guiding question in this concluding chapter comes from people who regularly ask: "How can I better prepare myself for playing an effective leadership role in my community, my profession, my country?"

Leadership, like empathy and love, is a central aspect of being human, of connecting us to one another, and an essential part of living a life of purpose. As noted, we believe leaders are mostly made, not born, and that leadership can be learned and most people can prepare for at least some form of leadership service. Not everyone can become a Mount Rushmore leader, but everyone can become a better leader.

"All the effective ones have had to learn to be effective," writes Peter Drucker. "And all of them had to practice effectiveness until it became habit. But all the ones who worked on making themselves effective executives succeeded in doing so. Effectiveness can be learned."[3]

Exploration of the full range of one's possibilities is not something self-renewing people leave to the chances of life. It is something they pursue systematically and strategically.

Making it to the top always requires discipline, practice, hard work, and tenacity, as well as a bit of luck and good timing.[4]

John W. Gardner once mentioned to one of us that large numbers of individuals level off far earlier in their careers than need be the case. He wondered aloud about the barriers that prevent people from becoming more fully realized citizen leaders. Poverty, ignorance, illiteracy, alcoholism, and physical and sensory handicaps all drag people down. But, he believed, mental and emotional factors are also key. Anything that nibbles away at a person's self-esteem and self-confidence, Gardner thought, inhibits their development toward emotional fullness and detracts from what they could otherwise contribute.

Such people, especially those with low self-esteem and low self-efficacy, are at least partially fatalistic. They are people who feel they don't have much control over their lives. There is some scattered research on locus of control, where at one extreme people sense they have little or no control over what goes on in their lives. At the other extreme are people who feel they are totally in charge. Each extreme may be pathological, yet the further one comes to the low-control end of this spectrum, the less one has the courage, confidence, self-identity, or self-awareness to take on leadership responsibilities.

Leaders, with some notable exceptions, are people who have self-confidence, are self-renewing, emotionally healthy, and develop plans and convictions that steer their lives. They have a good sense of who they are and who they could become.

Would-be leaders regularly make "appointments" with themselves in order to evaluate their strengths and deficiencies. They are self-reflective. They lead an examined life. It's what we learn (about self and life) after we think we know it all that really matters. Would-be leaders, John Gardner suggested, learn that self-pity and resentment are like toxic substances. Leaders understand the old truth that most people are neither for you nor against you but rather preoccupied with themselves. Would-be leaders break out of their comfortable imprisonments, cast aside dull routines, and make commitments to larger causes beyond the self.[5]

Such people set high expectations for themselves. They plan. They dream. They develop multiple skills. They become more self-aware and more balanced and they learn, in Warren Bennis's words, that becoming a "leader is synonymous with becoming yourself."[6]

Decoding the Mystery of Leadership

We understand most of what is involved in leadership—vision, strategy, collaboration, trust, goal setting, recruiting, integrative thinking, synthesizing, contextual and emotional intelligence, integrity, innovation, judgment, adaptive decision making, renewal, and the ability to ignite others to rise to high levels of cooperation, courage, imagination, and productivity.

Yet precise definition, as discussed, remains elusive. Something remains mysterious or even magical about leadership, something hard to reduce to an equation or a handful of principles.

Leadership defies formulaic prescriptions. It is more art than science. Indeed, it is an always evolving ensemble of art, invention, and improvisation. As leadership is connective and relational, it involves human interactions, yet the precise chemistry between leaders and followers is extremely hard to measure.

Leaders seldom follow a set recipe; they create their own path, improvise a lot, take advantage of opportunities and challenges, persuade and cajole, and do countless little things. As management consultant Tom Peters argues, the little things, like civilities, listening, initiative, complimenting, networking, and presentation skills, well executed, often make or break a leader's performance.[7]

Heifetz and Linsky contend that leadership is typically more improvisational than scripted: "Leadership is an improvisational art. You may have an overarching vision, clear, orienting values, and even a strategic plan, but who you actually are from moment to moment cannot be scripted. To be effective, you must respond to what is happening ... you take action, step back and assess the results of the action, reassess the plan, then ... make the next move."[8]

Effective leadership remains in many ways the most baffling of the performing arts. There is an element of mystery about it. Intuition, flare, risk taking, improvisation, and even theatrical ability come into play. Leadership needs vary from organization to organization, culture to culture. There is no set formula. Individuals with ample leadership qualities and skills do not necessarily become effective leaders, often because of cultural or timing factors. The genius of leadership sometimes comes too early or too late, and an effective person in one setting can be a failure in another.

We know, as discussed, that leadership needs in complex organizations and societies have to be viewed as an engagement between partners and collaborators. At times all of us are followers and, in a sense, all of us can lead. Followers, as we have emphasized, often have considerable influence on their leaders. Leaders model follower behaviors as well as leader behaviors and create cultures that value both roles.[9] Even the often autocratic Steve Jobs said that he liked to hire people not to tell them what to do but to have them tell him and Apple what they should be doing. James MacGregor Burns warns us, too, that we're never quite sure when it is that a follower becomes a leader. The line is typically blurry, as we saw in the 2011 revolutions in Egypt, Tunisia, and Libya.

There is yet another paradoxical aspect of leaders. We yearn for leaders to serve us, yet somewhere built into our DNA is a suspicion about leaders. Perhaps it is our wariness about the darker side of power and leadership. Shakespeare, as discussed, most assuredly was similarly wary of the state and its leaders.

Thus in looking for leadership, in almost any organizational affiliation, people are seeking competence, affirmation, significance, meaning, direction, results, and fairness. In joining an organization, individuals give up some aspect of their own uniqueness, perhaps sometimes even part of their soul. There is a price for affiliating, following, joining with a group. Leaders often serve as a magnet and an attraction in the organization, yet psychologically there can be a latent repulsion to the leader—in part because of a dependence on the leader, and perhaps in part because of the loss of individuality we pay to join.

We don't fully understand it, but it is a reality, sometimes a painful reality, that both leaders and followers pay a price for their respective roles in most organizations.

The Leader and Ideas

Leaders come in all sizes, shapes, and colors, with varying dispositions and multiple styles. But virtually every leader has ideas and contributes to the substantive thinking necessary to move an organization beyond problems and toward achieving mutual goals.

The best leaders think strategically, help define reality, clarify options, and work to remove the obstacles that prevent an organization and its members from succeeding.

Leaders infuse vision and meaning into an enterprise. They are preoccupied with purpose and the longer-range aspirations of their organizations. They manage the dream, but first they have to help their colleagues to invent the dream.

This requires a leader to be a planner and an uncommonly able integrative thinker. It requires as well a sense of history: Where has the organization come from? What are the competing possibilities going forward? What are the critical personnel and resource issues that will shape the organization's immediate future?

A leader is constantly wrestling with critical ends and means considerations. What are the best paths, the best strategies, the best teams to get an organization to achieve its purpose? What are our nonnegotiable values? What are our ethical principles? What are the key decisions that have to be made, in what sequence, and what are the critical tipping points along the way? In this sense leaders function as organizational architects.

Leaders celebrate what an organization is going to become without unduly criticizing what it has been. Leaders insist on flexible organizational architecture and understand when an organization's structure and practices are outdated. They develop effective programs for recruiting talent, training and inspiring them, and learning from customers and competitors. Leaders develop processes that help them to transcend or bypass the sclerotic vested interests that are too wedded to the status quo.

All this requires a leadership of ideas, of breadth, of reading people and context, and considering alternative futures. As discussed earlier, leaders define, defend, and promote values. And they help redefine values and understand when the dogmas or structures of the past have become antiquated. They understand that new circumstances call for new ideas, new goals, new vision.

To paraphrase an observation from historian Max Lerner, effective leaders must have a sense of the past without getting overwhelmed by it, a sense of the present without becoming one-dimensional, and a sense of the future without shrinking from it or becoming an obsessed zealot.

Unlocking the imagination is also essential. Leaders, like poets, artists, and composers, look at things differently; they question conventional assumptions, offer fresh perspectives, and help us not only understand the paradoxes of the human condition but also see, in William Faulkner's words, that the problem of the human heart is that it is often in conflict with itself.

The Leader as Motivator

Effective leaders learn how to serve as morale builders and renewers of purpose, able to motivate people to rededicate themselves and give their best to achieve mutual goals. *Motivation* is central to the leadership enterprise.

Leadership involves the power to motivate and persuade. People are motivated by words and inspiring stories, by narratives and examples. Leaders communicate in the language of their followers and provide the meaning that inspires loyalty, productivity, and a sense of pride and purpose.

Leadership and politics are, in many ways, applied rhetoric, the art of using words to help people to achieve goals. Leaders frame and reframe issues, use metaphors, parables, stories, and humor to create the reality they want others to understand.

Common values motivate. Common commitments motivate. Fear can be a motivator. So can the hunger for liberty and dignity. Leaders learn that constituents prize progress and achievement and they learn how to unlock human energies in pursuit of these very real human aspirations.

Leaders, at their best, conceive and articulate "goals that lift people out of their petty preoccupations, carry them above the conflicts that tear a society apart, and unite them in pursuit of objectives worthy of their best efforts."[10]

The Leader as Listener

Listening sounds easy. Yet listening turns out to be more complicated—and is probably one of the most difficult but least appreciated skills a leader must develop. Active, reflective, and disciplined listening drains energy and time. Few people are superb listeners—people who listen so carefully that they really hear you and in doing so both respect and empower you.

Nobody can fake listening. Listening involves perception, attention, and comprehension. The listening needed to lead requires one to comprehend not only the content of what is said but also context.

Effective listeners are able to put aside their own ideas and prejudices and listen openly—with their eyes and heart as much as with their ears. To inspire others, you must understand them—their wants, needs, fears, and dreams. Effective listening involves getting inside another person's mind and trying to see things from his or her point of view.

Professional listeners, with their trained "third ear," are able to pick up on what others are feeling and thinking as well as what they are not saying. The leader as listener learns that empathetic listening is a form of therapy. A lot of people need listeners not for any answer or specific solution to their problem so much as to work out, vent, or verbalize what they feel. The mere act of attentive listening—to complaints and hurts and explanations—is often enough of an answer.

Bill Clinton won the U.S. presidency in part because he mastered the art of listening and conversation at "town-hall meetings" at his various 1992 campaign stops. Clinton transformed himself and his image into that of a talk-show host, putting a premium on letting his audience "pass the microphone" and speak their minds.

Candidate Clinton made a conscious effort to listen, understand, and empathize with these representatives of the electorate. Showing he was "in tune" with voters became a personal strength for him in that campaign—and helped revive his candidacy against the more aloof George H. W. Bush and the quirky billionaire Ross Perot.

Listening is an art, and like most arts it can, with extensive practice, be nurtured, developed, and eventually mastered. Trainers in this skill have a whole array of strategies for listening enhancement. Much of what they teach may strike one as obvious, yet most people fully understand less than half of what is said to them and then forget even this in a matter of hours.

Leadership involves listening and understanding, and being able to convince and mobilize people. Underestimating the importance of listening is one of the mistakes failed leaders routinely make. Such was the case with Sophocles' King Creon, or Melville's Captain Vere, or America's Richard Nixon.

The Leader as Speaker and Debater

Effective leaders develop the ability to reason and define, defend, and convincingly argue their views. Those who can speak and debate well enjoy a disproportionate voice in policy-making deliberations; those who cannot often become spectators.

Politics, governance, and leadership are, in many ways, one long conversation about how best to provide for the common good, the common security, and the common future. The ability to communicate an idea is sometimes as important as the idea itself. Just as it is said that the world belongs to those with energy and passion, so also the audience belongs to speakers who have important things to say—and have the ability to persuade, convince, and inspire.

Nobody is born a great speaker. It is a performance skill that people can learn. A good speaker has to invent his or her own rules for speaking. This is because the key strength of a speaker lies in effectively putting their inner self, in some way, into their talking. No rule can prescribe the best way to do this.

One of the best ways to begin to learn about speakers is to study classic addresses. Abraham Lincoln's Gettysburg Address and his acclaimed Second Inaugural Address deserve a careful reading. Pericles' famed Funeral Oration found in Thucydides' *History of the Peloponnesian War* warrants scrutiny. Martin Luther King Jr.'s "I Have a Dream" speech, delivered at the March on Washington in 1963, and his "Letter from a Birmingham Jail" are prime illustrations of reasoned argumentation. Several anthologies exist of great speakers from Cicero to Churchill and beyond.[11]

The first law of public speaking is to know one's audience. The best speakers use simple language and talk *with* rather than lecture *to* their audience. Most ineffective talks suffer from being too long and making too many points.

Effective speakers are guides as well as performers. Thus an effective presentation needs a compelling introduction and thesis, clear transitions from one point to the next, and a forceful conclusion.

An effective speech often uses various techniques to keep listeners on edge and, like Shakespeare's and Beethoven's, introduce minor tensions and resolutions as they build toward a climax. Designing an elegant persuasive speech is ultimately an art form.

Effective leaders also develop the ability to debate. Our judicial, legislative, and election processes are all structured around formal debates. The philosophy behind formal policy debates is that, with informed and constructive adversarial deliberation, understanding and truths ideally will emerge.

Being prepared in a debate requires knowing as much as possible about both sides of a question. Skillful debaters know they can concede some of the other side's points and actually be in a stronger position to attack the strategically weak points in the opposition's argument.

Debating tests one's capacity to listen and speak as nothing else does. Most people avoid debates just as they avoid giving speeches to large audiences. Yet those who aspire to be leaders learn that the ability to debate is an invaluable leadership skill.

The Leader as Writer

Writing well is yet another form of leadership. Good writing helps us think clearly, express ideas, heighten consciousness, inspire, and promote community and shared values.

Plato, Niccolò Machiavelli, Karl Marx, Harriet Beecher Stowe, Henry David Thoreau, Rachel Carson, Martin Luther King Jr., and Aleksandr Solzhenitsyn all have in common that through their writings, they changed how people thought, dreamed, and behaved.

A writer with a sense of justice can remind us of when we have failed and who we are capable of becoming. Writers can help vanquish lies. They can encourage moral outrage and suggest strategies for breakthroughs. The writer as leader can remind us of the blessings of liberty and the hope that life can get better.

Thomas Jefferson and his colleagues rallied a new nation as it fought for independence and staked out the aspirational ideals of a people searching for a better way of governing themselves. The "first politicians" who drafted the U.S. Constitution in the summer of 1787 in Philadelphia wrote as both political philosophers and political architects as they merged experience and theory in the formation of practical political institutions.

Active, clear writing informs, persuades, entertains, empowers, and liberates.

Students of leadership adopt favorite writers such as Jefferson, Lincoln, Ralph Waldo Emerson, Winston Churchill, Arthur M. Schlesinger Jr., Peter Drucker, and others. We suggest reading their best works and discovering why they are so good by trying a little of what is called "reverse engineering." How do they provide a clear, logical outline? How do they frame their argument? How do they marshal evidence? What do they do to simplify, clarify, and persuade?

Writing matters. Great writing is often an act of courage. Just as leaders help define, defend, and promote important values, so also writers help define and clarify critical choices. Writing can be a superb opportunity for introducing and explaining fresh ideas. A writer writes to understand, teach, persuade, celebrate, criticize, caution, inspire, lead, and share important values and realities.

Great writers help shape their times. The power of the pen (or electronic communication device) may be considerably different from the power of the sword or the power of the purse, yet the compelling argument persuasively expressed may prove more powerful as well as more enduring. Just ask King George III about the Declaration of Independence. Or the white southern clergy so eloquently addressed in King's remarkable "Letter from a Birmingham Jail."

The Leader as Community Builder

It is nearly impossible for leadership to be exercised without community. The absence of shared values and social cohesion makes leadership success improbable. The art of leadership is in many ways the art of creating and sustaining communities of shared purpose. Divided, fractured societies repel leadership efforts.

Factions, as James Madison, Marx, and Yale law professor Amy Chua point out, arise in every society.[12] The unequal distribution of property and wealth guarantees conflict and the rise of factions. Race, religion, and ethnic or national identity also divide, as we have painfully seen in Iraq, Palestine, Northern Ireland, Rwanda, and so many other places.

Community building may also sound easy, yet it is one of the hardest jobs a leader can tackle. Community building necessarily involves creative listening and open communications across functional and territorial boundary lines, and across horizontal as well as vertical separations.

Healthy organizations encourage candid discussions and even encourage some level of disagreement to surface. Although these are risky, leaders instill "a philosophy of pluralism, an open climate for dissent, and an opportunity for subcommunities to retain their identity and share in the setting of larger goals."[13]

Leaders are invariably networkers. They help promote shared values and common ground. They are seldom able to win agreement on everything. The goal is to unite people to decide what is important and what their common goals and priorities are.

We laugh a lot at politicians, yet the best of them are skilled networkers, skilled mediators among disparate and sometimes warring factions. They are often indispensable in helping us to transcend polarizing self-interests. Politics, at its best, is the art of listening to, and accommodating, a diversity and variety of public views. It is also the indispensable art of making possible tomorrow what appears impossible today.

Politicians, as agreement makers and community builders, accentuate shared values and work out acceptable compromises in an effort to prevent us from shooting at one another. Moreover, they can also provide a much-desired alternative to living under a dictator.

The Leader as Negotiator and Bargainer

Life is full of diversity and conflict, and leaders are expected to bring about a creative balance. The point of negotiating is to achieve an accord that is mutually advantageous to two or more parties. And although "compromise" often has a negative connotation in our society, pragmatic compromise, as discussed, is the glue that helps get things done and keeps our pluralistic society together.

On one level negotiating is relatively simple: know your position, know your opponent's position, understand all the incentives involved, and find some agreeable middle ground. But in practice—in politics, international diplomacy, and business deals—negotiating is exacting.

A negotiator has to have multiple skills: listening, the ability to collaborate, the ability to read an adversary, and the ability to bargain and persuade. A skilled negotiator is able to peer across a table and deconstruct the demands, needs, and wants of opponents. Knowing what motivates your opponents is fundamental. Negotiation as collaboration is the process in which contending parties see different aspects of a problem and creatively explore differences and solutions.

Equally important, of course, is understanding your side's interests, what is nonnegotiable, what are the best possible settlements you can hope to achieve, and what would be the worst possible deal your side would be willing to accept.

Negotiators who enter a negotiation with higher aspiration levels than their rivals', research finds, do better in achieving favorable settlements. It is axiomatic in negotiations that both sides approach a negotiation with contending positions. Positions in and of themselves are not bad; it is how these positions are abandoned and new positions are arrived at that become important.

Roger Fisher and William Ury of the Harvard Negotiation Project developed what they called "Principled Negotiation." Their process sought results in which both sides could win.[14] Their model of principled negotiation rests on four basic principles: separate the people from the issues, focus on *interests not positions,* generate a variety of possibilities before deciding what to do, and insist on some objective standard by which to judge the mutual decision.

Looking behind the announced positions of the contending parties at their real interests allows the negotiation to focus on the goals of the process, not merely a set of compromises. Interests, not positions, define the problem. They can also depersonalize the process, thereby moving egos to the background. Generating multiple options encourages many different possibilities and may result in the discovery of a solution that neither party believed existed before.

Negotiators, like politicians, are trying to mediate or resolve conflict and transcend narrow, selfish position taking. It requires patience, discipline, homework, and uncommon focus. It also requires using emotions as a positive tool in the process.

Roger Fisher and Daniel Shapiro, in *Beyond Reason,* note that we cannot stop having emotions any more than we can stop having thoughts.[15] The challenge, they write, is learning to stimulate *helpful emotions* in those with whom we negotiate as well as in ourselves.

The Leader as Teacher

Great teachers give us a sense not only of who they are, but more importantly, of who we are and who we might become. They unlock our energies, imaginations, courage, and minds. Effective teachers, like the best leaders, pose compelling questions, explain options, teach us to reason, suggest possible new directions, and urge us on. Good teachers and good leaders have an uncanny ability to step outside themselves and become liberating forces in the lives of others.

Inspirational teachers are typically psychologically centered. They know who they are and are self-confident. They are vital and full of passion. For them, teaching is fun.

Great teachers know they are always on stage and that when they are, how they act and what they believe are sometimes as important as what they teach. Just as a good example is often the best sermon, a teacher's contribution often is less the subject taught than the role model caught.

The first law of effective teaching is to "know your stuff," to be exceptionally well versed in your subject area. Effective teachers have a passion for their field. Memorable teachers are enthusiastic about their subject and teach with a joy and intensity that are often contagious. A teacher can fool a colleague, yet rarely can he or she fool students. Students rightly expect teachers to serve as interpreters of what is known, important, and fundamental. Great teachers not only know their subject well, they radiate it. Our most memorable teachers are men and women who have enormous enthusiasm about their subjects, who teach with joy, intensity, and a love of their subjects. Great teachers are curious; they are explorers; they are puzzle solvers; they persevere, persist, and find the threads that connect, unite, and integrate. They convey the importance and relevance of their subjects and the amazement of discovery. As an old proverb puts it, the mediocre teacher tells, the good teacher explains, the superior teacher demonstrates, and the great teacher inspires.

We ask the same of political and business leaders. We want not just competence but mastery.

We expect the same passion, dedication, and flair from effective executives in every field. The effective leader, in common with the effective teacher, clearly defines new or unfamiliar terms, answers questions thoroughly, and explains complex problems in language largely free of jargon.

The best of teachers help liberate and free us from prejudice, dogmatism, and parochialism; from complacency, sentimentality, and hypocrisy; from sloppy reasoning and careless writing. The best teachers, like the best leaders, encourage people to discover themselves and their obligations to others. The message is the same one Pericles encouraged in Athens—that a flourishing community is everyone's business, and that an ethic of collaboration and empathy for others is critical for resolving society's problems.

Effective teaching makes us understand that although truths may make us free, they often at first will be disturbing, even order shattering; and that the uncommitted as well as the unexamined life is not worth living. Aldous Huxley joked, "Ye shall know the truth and the truth shall make you mad." Great teachers ask us: What is worth knowing? What are justice, beauty, courage, and virtue? They insist we ask both "what if" and "what for" questions.

Great teachers understand that all serious thinking starts with wonder. To be educated, they insist, is to develop a sense of wonder, to imagine, to think differently, to reexamine one's principles, and to qualify what one says with the word *perhaps*. They help us to realize it is a mistake to be afraid of making mistakes; new challenges and risk taking have a genius, power, and magic in them for those who are unafraid of a life of continuous learning.

Effective leaders share these same qualities: unlocking our imaginations, defining our central challenges, urging us to look at our longer-term horizons, and clarifying our choices for both the short and longer terms.

The Leader and Social, Emotional Intelligence

"Strong people," writes management guru Peter Drucker, "always have strong weaknesses."[16] Leaders know as much as possible about their strengths, weaknesses, prejudices, and motivations.

Most leaders have a natural optimism about their own abilities and the possibilities for progress. Sometimes they are too optimistic about their abilities. Since every leader deals with conflict and occasional setbacks, a leader needs to learn how to bounce back and to turn failure, rejection, and liabilities into opportunities and advantages.

Leaders are self-evaluating, accepting their failures yet constantly working to improve themselves. In his book *Emotional Intelligence,* Daniel Goleman says emotional intelligence is knowing what you are feeling, managing those feelings, and developing the ability to read the emotions of others as well as to empathize with others and control one's impulses.[17] Emotional and social intelligence, or personal self-efficacy, is not fixed at birth—everyone has to learn, and can learn, to balance these key emotions.

America's three greatest presidents, Washington, Lincoln, and Franklin D. Roosevelt, all had their personal challenges, which included vanity, melancholy, and physical disability among other things; yet they also had an uncommon sense of who they were, and were sure of themselves in social settings, including when they were in the presence of strangers. Each also had an ability to reassure people, call for sacrifice, and encourage as well as radiate hope.

Leaders have guts, judgment, and the ability to take risks. They make themselves vulnerable by regularly putting themselves and their reputations on the line, in full view of large numbers of people. Such leaders must be strong enough to have other strong people around them. Doris Kearns Goodwin's best-selling *Team of Rivals* vividly documents how Lincoln recruited into his administration his three adversaries for the Republican nomination for president in the 1860 campaign—and successfully put them to work as key advisers and top cabinet members.[18] In doing so, he converted rivals into colleagues and it served him and the country well in a time of crisis.

Other writers warn us to beware of would-be leaders who lack emotional intelligence or positive emotional character.[19] Those who are involved in politics and leadership at the highest levels must like both people and politics and must be able to control their flaws, acknowledge their fallibility, and yet still believe in themselves and in the possibilities for breakthroughs.

Effective leaders are reasonably comfortable with who they are—their strengths, their deficiencies, and their humanity. They have to like themselves and recognize the truism that vitality and morale seldom flourish in an organization based primarily upon fears. They learn how to forgive and move on.

The Leader and Stagecraft

Political and societal leadership involves stagecraft skills. Leaders are very much on stage and need to project confidence, strength, and courage, as well as empathy and a reassuring optimism that problems can be solved. Certain leaders such as Theodore Roosevelt, Winston Churchill, Fidel Castro, Ronald Reagan, Richard Branson, and Steve Jobs had a special gift for theater.

Noted playwright Arthur Miller suggests that "the closer one approaches any kind of power, the more acting is required." The question is, Miller says, "how much? Masks and makeup go back to primitive times.... Men transform how they look and talk in order to draw down power upon themselves which their ordinary behavior cannot possess."[20]

Ronald Reagan said politics was a lot like show business, by which he meant one's presence matters, and relaxed sincerity and storytelling skills are important. Another actor who tried his hand at political leadership, former California governor Arnold Schwarzenegger, says that in acting as well as in government, "what is important is that it's organic." In acting, you have to connect to the people so they can look at a scene and buy in. It's the same in government, says Schwarzenegger. "You have to connect with the people, and the more organic you are ... that's what then makes people buy in."[21]

Effective leaders artfully combine a sense of theater, a debater's skill in simplifying and making an argument, and a storyteller's narrative ability.

Being a skilled actor or performer, of course, can only be a *means* for effective leadership, not an end in itself. No amount of acting skills can be substituted for the purpose, policies, goals, and artful judgment and compromises leaders must offer. We may want relaxed sincerity and charisma, yet we detest fakery and inauthenticity. We rightly expect purposeful leadership that links appropriate means and ends.

Leaders also need to understand important cultural traditions. We have discussed at length that people expect many things from their leaders, including good judgment, competence, integrity, priority setting, crisis leadership, and much more. But we also want a certain amount of tribal, cultural, or spiritual leadership that we might associate with primitive or religious communities. We want leaders who, for example, remind us of our obligations to one another, our shared beliefs, and the ties, traditions, and trust that can bind us together.

Leadership, like great acting, is often a matter of timing and improvising. The difference between integrity and duplicity and between success and failure often resides in the perspective of time. Leadership often involves the necessity of having to make a decision in a timely manner yet almost always with incomplete information, or doing something that may be unpopular today but might be respected later on.

Both leaders and actors learn to improvise. Lincoln and Reagan sometimes won support as much for their extemporaneous storytelling and weaving of parables as for their policy positions.[22]

What Leaders Understand

- Leaders understand that good judgment—the ability to synthesize hard data, questionable data, and intuition to arrive at reflective decisions—is key.
- Leaders understand that things need to be done and find a way to mobilize people to do them. Leaders don't blame circumstances or other people; they roll up their sleeves and accept responsibility.

- Would-be leaders travel, read widely (especially the classics), understand other languages and cultures, welcome diversity as an opportunity, and continually embrace challenge, change, and opportunities for self-renewal. And they call upon both their masculine and feminine strengths in a creative ambidextrous or androgynous way.
- Leaders collaborate with co-leaders, build teams, delegate wisely, and celebrate the contributions of everyone, yet leaders are relentlessly competitive on behalf of both their own and their organizations' aspirations.
- Leaders understand that values and purposes matter, but that power, influence, and persuasion also matter.
- Leaders understand their strengths and weaknesses, learn from mistakes, and develop both their intuition and their emotional, social, cultural, and political intelligence. They also understand the Thoreau paradox: being objective about your shortcomings is about as hard as it is for people to look behind them without turning around.
- Leaders are optimistic, yet theirs is a tough-minded optimism rather than a naïve optimism. Leaders understand how things may be, yet keep searching for the possibilities.
- Leaders understand that ambition and leadership are uneasy yet indispensable companions. Leaders need to have a strong dose of ambition, pride, and egotism—strong egos, not swollen ones or what is called a narcissistic personality disorder. They understand too that ambition can be both a good servant and a dangerous master. The ideal leader understands that "appropriate ambition is directed toward achieving the goals of an institution and realizing the [valid] needs of followers."[23]
- Leaders understand that leadership effectiveness is highly correlated with the strength of a community. Strong communities empower their leaders and often point the way. Weak communities struggle to understand who they are and what their needs are, and thus make it hard for leadership to develop.
- Leaders learn that their primary challenge is less to produce followers than to produce community, meaning, and more leaders.

Effective leaders understand all of the above, and understand, too, that paradoxes, dilemmas, and quandaries are everywhere. Leaders embrace paradoxes and learn to reconcile them when they can, yet coexist with them when they cannot. The best of leaders learn to exploit paradoxes, transcend either/or choices, and, where possible, unlock the power and advantages of paradox.

As emphasized, leaders find it useful to view paradoxes in a dialectical manner, in which a thesis often gets matched in creative ways by an antithesis, and these seeming opposites call on the leader for a reframing synthesis. Ideal leaders are integrative and synthesizing thinkers; they can think fast, slow, and smartly as they resiliently adapt to opportunities, paradoxes, and the luck that confront every venture.

Acknowledgments

At least a score of generous scholars have inspired and encouraged us over the years leading up to this book. We especially thank John W. Gardner, James MacGregor Burns, Arthur M. Schlesinger Jr., and Warren Bennis.

Several friends read substantial portions of the manuscript and provided encouragement and suggestions for improvement: Warren Bennis, David P. Campbell, Joanne B. Ciulla, David D. Crislip, Nicole Cundiff, James O'Toole, Norman W. Provizer, Ronald E. Riggio, William E. Rosenbach, and W. Thomas Wren.

We have profited from the steadily growing interdisciplinary scholarship on leadership and acknowledge our debts to its many contributors in footnotes and in the bibliography. We were supported financially by the Henry Luce Foundation, the McHugh Family Endowments at Colorado College, and the Loyola Chair of Leadership Endowments at Loyola Marymount University.

Tom Cronin wants to thank David Lowland, Holly Ornstein Carter, Jeff Brune, Mark Hummels, Charles P. Barkley, Tom Ori, Alex Traux, Bill Hochman, Tim Fuller, Jenn Sides, and Hank Luce. He also thanks Kim-Marie Coons for her expert help in preparing the manuscript.

Michael Genovese thanks Brian Whitaker, Matt Candau, Kelsey Flott, Brianna Bruns, and Rebecca Hartley.

We thank the always helpful librarians at Colorado College, Loyola Marymount University, and Whitman College.

Paradigm Publishers' Vice President and Executive Editor Jennifer Knerr has wonderfully advised us and helped make this a much better book. We thank Production Editor Ashley Moore for her splendid help, President and Publisher Dean Birkenkamp for his leadership, Sales and Marketing Manager Pete Hammond for his guidance, College Marketing Associate Maggie Faber for her help, copyeditor Sharon Schwoch for her rigorous reading, proofreader Lori Kranz for her sharp eyes, and indexer Christine Arden. They and their colleagues provided the indispensable leadership needed to convert our inchoate manuscript into this book. Thank you.

Tom Cronin
Colorado Springs

Michael Genovese
Los Angeles

Notes

Notes for Chapter One

1. Jack Walsh, *Winning* (New York: Harper Business, 2005), p. 64.
2. William Manchester, *American Caesar: Douglas MacArthur* (New York: Dell, 1978), p. 15.
3. Vaclav Havel, "Reflections on a Paradoxical Life," in *The New York Times Review of Literature,* June 14, 1990, 38; drawn from Havel's larger work, *Disturbing the Peace.*
4. Roderick M. Kramer, "The Great Intimidators," *Harvard Business Review,* February 2006, 96.
5. See especially Jim Collins, *Good to Great: Why Some Companies Make the Leap and Others Don't* (New York: Harper Business, 2001).
6. Schumpter, "The Cult of the Faceless Boss," *Economist,* November 14, 2009, 80.
7. Ibid.
8. See, for example, "Looking for a Democratic Tough Guy or Girl," by Maureen Dowd, *New York Times,* January 18, 2006, A23.
9. Charles de Gaulle, *The Edge of the Sword,* trans. by Gerald Hopkins (London: Faber and Faber, 1960, originally published in 1932), p. 96.
10. Richard Nixon, *Leaders* (New York: Warner Books, 1983), p. 341.
11. Clinton Rossiter, *The American Presidency,* 2nd ed. (New York: Harcourt, Brace and World, 1960), p. 180.
12. Marshall E. Dimock, *The Executive in Action* (New York: Harper & Brothers, 1945), p. 91.
13. Ibid., pp. 92–93.
14. Saul Alinsky, *Rules for Radicals: A Pragmatic Primer for Realistic Radicals* (New York: Vintage, 1972), p. 51.
15. Machiavelli, *The Prince,* Quentin Skinner, ed. (Cambridge: Cambridge University Press, 1988), p. 62.
16. Terry L. Price, *Understanding Ethical Failures in Leadership* (New York: Cambridge University Press, 2006), pp. 25–27.
17. For an excellent overview of leadership and morals, see Joanne B. Ciulla, Terry L. Price, and Susan E. Murphy, *The Quest for Moral Leaders* (Cheltenham, UK: Edward Elgar, 2005).
18. Michael Walzer, "Political Action: The Problem of Dirty Hands," *Philosophy and Public Affairs* 2 (1973). See also the useful discussion of this quandary in Joseph S. Nye Jr., *The Powers to Lead* (New York: Oxford University Press, 2008), Chapter 5.

19. John W. Gardner, *Morale* (New York: W. W. Norton, 1987), p. 152.
20. Quoted in the *New York Times,* October 17, 1981, 30.
21. Ibid. Ironically, or perhaps paradoxically, Dayan, during the 1973 Yom Kippur War, was so rattled and defeatist that Prime Minister Golda Meir prevented him from appearing on television. We are indebted to Norman Provizer for this information.
22. John Keegan, *The Mask of Command* (New York: Viking, 1987), p. 11. See also Michael Korda, *Hero: The Life and Legend of Lawrence of Arabia* (New York: HarperCollins, 2010).
23. Peter Drucker, *The Effective Executive* (New York: Harper & Row, 1966), p. 87.
24. See Daniel Goleman, Richard Boyatzis, and Arnie McKee, *Primal Leadership: Learning to Lead with Emotional Intelligence* (Boston: Harvard Business School Press, 2002).
25. This contrast is suggested in Charles J. Palus and John B. McGuire, "From Lone Hero to a Culture of Leadership," *Harvard Business Review,* November 2010, 144–146.
26. Sophocles, *Antigone,* from *The Theban Plays,* E. F. Watling, trans. (Middlesex, UK: Penguin Books, 1947), p. 145.
27. Morgan W. McCall Jr., Michael M. Lombardo, and Ann N. Morrison, *The Lessons of Experience: How Successful Executives Develop on the Job* (Lexington, MA: Lexington Books, 1988), p. 144.
28. Daniel Kahneman, *Thinking, Fast and Slow* (New York: Farrar, Straus and Giroux, 2011), pp. 417–418.
29. Harold J. Laski, *The American Presidency: An Interpretation* (New York: Harper & Brothers, 1940), p. 38.
30. Woodrow Wilson, "Leaders of Men," speech delivered on more than one occasion in 1890 and 1899, in *The Papers of Woodrow Wilson,* vol. 6, Arthur S. Link, ed. (Princeton: Princeton University Press, 1970), p. 666.
31. Walter Lippmann, *A Preface to Morals* (New York: Macmillan, 1929), p. 282.
32. Hans J. Morgenthau, *The Purpose of American Politics* (New York: Vintage, 1960), p. 317.
33. James MacGregor Burns, *Leadership* (New York: Harper & Row, 1978), p. 461.
34. Rosabeth M. Kanter, *When Giants Learn to Dance* (New York: Simon & Schuster, 1989), p. 20.
35. Quoted in William Davison Johnston, *TR, Champion of the Strenuous Life* (New York: Theodore Roosevelt Association, 1958), p. 95.
36. J. William Fulbright, *The Price of Empire* (New York: Pantheon, 1989), p. 89. See also Tip O'Neill with Gary Hymel, *All Politics Is Local* (New York: Times Books, 1994).
37. Woodrow Wilson, "Leaders of Men," in Arthur Link, *The Papers of Woodrow Wilson,* vol. 6 (Princeton: Princeton University Press, 1970), pp. 663, 664.
38. Quoted in Rexford G. Tugwell, *The Brains Trust* (New York: Viking, 1968), p. 410.
39. Warren Bennis, *On Becoming a Leader* (Reading, MA: Addison-Wesley, 1990), pp. 42, 47.
40. Ibid., p. 50.
41. Charles de Gaulle, *The Edge of the Sword,* p. 117.
42. Ibid., p. 96. See also Arthur Miller, *On Politics and the Art of Acting* (New York: Viking, 2001).
43. Portia Isaacson, quoted in Thomas R. Horton, *"What Works for Me"* (New York: AMACON, 1986), p. 322.
44. Meg Greenfield, "Mandela's Discipline," *Newsweek,* July 9, 1990, 68.
45. Aaron Wildavsky, *The Nursing Father: Moses as a Political Leader* (Tuscaloosa, AL: University of Alabama Press, 1984), p. 192.
46. Michael Korda, "How to Be a Leader," *Newsweek,* January 5, 1981. Reprinted in William Rosenbach and Robert Taylor, eds., *Contemporary Issues in Leadership* (Boulder, CO: Westview Press, 1984), p. 63.
47. See Gary C. Jacobson, *A Divider, Not a Uniter* (New York: Pearson, 2007).
48. Niccolò Machiavelli, *The Prince and the Discourses* (New York: Modern Library, 1940), p. 21.

49. Saul Alinsky, *Rules for Radicals* (New York: Vintage, 1972).

50. Richard T. Pascale, *Managing on the Edge: How the Smartest Companies Use Conflict to Stay on the Edge* (New York: Simon & Schuster, 1990), p. 110. See also Tom Peters, *The Little Big Things: 163 Ways to Pursue Excellence* (New York: Harper Studio, 2010).

51. Mortimer B. Zuckerman, "The Indispensable Man," *U.S. News and World Report,* January 16, 2006, 72.

52. From a speech by Bob Galvin on leadership in "Bob Galvin and Motorola, Inc.," *Harvard Business School Case* (9-487-062, 1987), 13–14.

53. Chester I. Barnard, *The Functions of the Executive* (Cambridge: Harvard University Press, 1938), p. 163.

54. Burns, *Leadership,* p. 461.

55. Robert E. Kelley, "In Praise of Followers," *Harvard Business Review,* November–December 1989, 144.

56. Warren Bennis, "Followers Make Good Leaders Good," *New York Times,* December 1989.

57. Robert K. Greenleaf, *The Servant as Leader* (Petersborough, NH: Windy Row Press, 1970), p. 4.

58. Arnold "Red" Auerbach, "Misleading Followers," letters to the editor, *Harvard Business Review,* January–February 1989, 152.

59. John Lewis, *Walking with the Wind: A Memoir of the Movement* (New York: Harcourt, Brace & Co., 1998), p. 499.

60. William Rosenbach, personal communication to the authors, December 3, 2011.

61. Communication to the authors from David Crislip, December 15, 2011. See David D. Crislip and Carl E. Larson, *Collaborative Leadership: How Citizen and Civic Leaders Make a Difference* (San Francisco: Jossey-Bass, 1994). See also Frank LaFasto and Carl E. Larson, *The Humanitarian Leader in Each of Us* (Los Angeles: Sage, 2012).

62. Thomas Carlyle, *On Heroes, Hero-Worship and the Heroic in History,* originally published in 1840 (Garden City, NY: Dolphin Books, 1963). See also Fred Kaplan, *Thomas Carlyle* (Ithaca, NY: Cornell, 1983).

63. William James, "The Social Values of the College-Bred," in *Memories and Studies* (New York: Best Books, 1911), p. 318.

64. See, for example, the writings of Robert Caro on Robert Moses and Lyndon Johnson or the writings of Carl Sandburg and Doris Kearns Goodwin on Lincoln; Dumas Malone on Thomas Jefferson; or David McCullough on George Washington, John Adams, and Harry Truman. See also James M. McPherson's prizewinning *Tried by War: Abraham Lincoln as Commander-in-Chief* (New York: Penguin Books, 2008).

65. McPherson, public talk at Colorado College, April 1, 2009.

66. Harry S. Truman, quoted in Robert A. Fitton, ed., *Leadership: Quotations from the Military Tradition* (Boulder, CO: Westview Press, 1990), p. 151.

67. Lee Iacocca, *Where Have All the Leaders Gone?* (New York: Scribner, 2008).

68. Herbert Kaufman, *The Administrative Behavior of Federal Bureau Chiefs* (Washington, DC: The Brookings Institution, 1981), p. 135.

69. James G. March, "How We Talk and How We Act: Administrative Theory and Administrative Life," in Michael D. Cohen and James G. March, *Leadership and Ambiguity,* 2nd ed. (Boston: Harvard Business School Press, 1986), pp. 277 and 288–289. See also March, *The Ambiguities of Experience* (Ithaca, NY: Cornell University Press, 2010).

70. James R. Meindle, Stanford B. Ehrlich, and Janet M. Dukerich, "The Romance of Leadership," *Administrative Science Quarterly,* March 1985, 99, 10. See also Jeffrey Pfeffer, "The Ambiguity of Leadership," *Academy of Management Review,* January 1977, 104–112.

71. Kahneman, *Thinking, Fast and Slow,* p. 205.

72. Wildavsky, p. 188.

73. See also Jared Diamond's provocative *Guns, Germs, and Steel* (New York: W. W. Norton, 1997).

74. One helpful interpretation of Tolstoy is found in James G. March and Thierry Weil, *On Leadership* (Oxford: Blackwell, 2005). Not everyone agrees with Tolstoy's interpretation of Russian history. See, for example, Dominic Lieven, *Russia Against Napoleon* (New York: Viking, 2010). See also Norman Provizer's analysis that Tolstoy had a certain attraction to certain leaders despite his rhetoric: "On Hedgehogs, Foxes and Leadership: Uncovering the Other Tolstoy," *Leadership Quarterly,* August 2008, 453–458.

75. For two instructive biographies of Washington and Lincoln as leaders, see Ron Chernow, *Washington: A Life* (New York: Penguin, 2010); and Eric Foner, *The Fiery Trial: Abraham Lincoln and American Slavery* (New York: W. W. Norton, 2010).

76. Charles Handy, *The Age of Paradox* (Boston: Harvard Business School Press, 1994), p. 47.

77. See Roger Cohen, "The Unquiet American," *New York Times,* December 17, 2010, A31.

78. Roger Martin, *The Opposable Mind: How Successful Leaders Win Through Integrative Thinking* (Boston: Harvard Business School Press, 2007), p. 144.

79. John Heider, *The Tao of Leadership* (Toronto: Bantam, 1986), p. 71.

80. Howard Gardner, *Five Minds for the Future* (Boston: Harvard Business Press, 2008), p. xiii.

Notes for Chapter Two

1. Quoted in Lorne Adrian, *The Most Important Thing I Know* (Kansas City, MO: Andrews McMeel Publishing, 1997).

2. Historians continue to reassess this battle and exactly what went on. The French, some say, suffered from a devastating plague, terrible weather, a civil war, and a possibly insane king. See James Glanz, "Historians Reassess Battle of Agincourt," *New York Times,* October 25, 2009. Also see Anne Curry, *Agincourt: A New History* (Stroud, Gloucestershire, UK: Tempus Publishing Group, 2005); Ian Mortimer, *1415: Henry V's Year of Glory* (London: Bodley Head, 2009); and Matthew Strickland and Robert Hardy, *The Great Warbow* (Stroud, Gloucestershire, UK: Sutton, 2005).

3. See, among other works, Max Hastings, *Winston's War: Churchill, 1940–1945* (New York: Knopf, 2010).

4. George W. Breslauer, *Gorbachev and Yeltsin as Leaders* (Cambridge: Cambridge University Press, 2002).

5. Akan Malici, *When Leaders Learn, and When They Don't* (Albany: SUNY Press, 2008).

6. Tom Lodge, *Mandela: A Critical Life* (Oxford: Oxford University Press, 2006).

7. Robert Michaels, *Political Parties: A Sociological Study of the Oligarchical Tendencies of Modern Democracy* (New York: Free Press, 1915).

8. Ronald A. Heifetz, *Leadership Without Easy Answers* (Cambridge, MA: Belknap Press, 1994), p. 28.

9. Ibid., p. 69. See also Ronald A. Heifetz and Marty Linsky, *Leadership on the Line: Staying Alive Through the Dangers of Leading* (Boston: Harvard Business Press, 2002).

10. See Joseph S. Nye Jr., *The Powers to Lead* (New York: Oxford University Press, 2008); and John J. Mearsheimer, *Why Leaders Lie* (New York: Oxford University Press, 2011).

11. For a few overviews of the ideas and theories of leadership that do exist, see Bernard Bass, *Bass and Stogdill's Handbook of Leadership,* 3rd ed. (New York: Free Press, 1990); James MacGregor Burns, *Leadership* (New York: Harper & Row, 1978); Kenneth E. and Miriam C. Clark, eds., *Measures of Leadership* (West Orange, NJ: Leadership Library of America, 1990); and Nitin Nohria and Rakesh Khurana, eds., *Handbook of Leadership Theory and Practice* (Boston: Harvard Business Press, 2010). See also George R. Goethals

and Georgia Sorenson, eds., *The Quest for a General Theory of Leadership* (Cheltenham, UK: Edward Elgar, 2007).

12. James MacGregor Burns, *Leadership* (New York: Harper & Row, 1978), p. 1.

13. John W. Gardner, *On Leadership* (New York: Free Press, 1990).

14. Bernard M. Bass, *Bass and Stogdill's Handbook of Leadership*, 3rd ed. (New York: Free Press, 1990), p. 20.

15. Mary Parker Follett, *The New State* (New York: Longman's, 1923), p. 230.

16. Gary A. Yukl, *Leadership in Organizations* (Englewood Cliffs, NJ: Prentice Hall, 1981), p. 10.

17. Keith Grint, *The Arts of Leadership* (Oxford: Oxford University Press, 2000), p. 419.

18. Crispin Burke, "T. E. Lawrence: A Leadership Vignette for the Successful Counter-Insurgent," *Small Wars Journal*, posted by SLOJ Editors, February 19, 2009, www.smallwarsjournal.com.

19. David J. Garrow, *Bearing the Cross: Martin Luther King and the Southern Leadership Conference* (New York: Vintage Books, 1986), p. 625. See also the helpful essay by Clayborne Carson, "Martin Luther King, Jr.: Charismatic Leadership in a Mass Struggle," *Journal of History* 74 (September 1987): 448–454.

20. Fred E. Fiedler and Joseph E. Garcia, *New Approaches to Effective Leadership* (New York: Wiley, 1987), p. 2.

21. Quoted in Noel Tichy and Ram Charan, "Speed, Simplicity, Self-Confidence: An Interview with Jack Welch," *Harvard Business Review*, September–October 1989, 113. See also Jack Welch with Suzy Welch, *Winning* (New York: Harper Business, 2005).

22. Jim Collins, *Good to Great: Why Some Companies Make the Leap and Others Don't* (New York: Harper Business, 2001), Chapter 3.

23. Ed Peters, ed., *Mountaineering: The Freedom of the Hills*, 4th ed. (Seattle: The Mountaineers, 1982), p. 414. But see the vivid case study of a failed Everest expedition in Jon Krakauer, *Into Thin Air* (New York: Anchor Books, 1997).

24. Proctor and Gamble CEO A. G. Lafley reflects on these responsibilities in "What Only the CEO Can Do," *Harvard Business Review*, May 2009, 54–62.

25. Walter Isaacson, *Steve Jobs* (New York: Simon & Schuster, 2011).

26. See, in general, Kay Redfield Jamison, *Exuberance: The Passion for Life* (New York: Knopf, 2004).

27. On Lawrence, see Michael Korda, *Hero: The Life and Legend of Lawrence of Arabia* (New York: HarperCollins, 2010).

28. Harold D. Lasswell, *Power and Personality* (New York: Viking Press, 1962; originally published in 1948), p. 38.

29. Alexander L. and Juliette L. George, *Woodrow Wilson and Colonel House: A Personality Study* (New York: Dover, 1956). But see the differing views of Arthur M. Schlesinger Jr., "Can Psychiatry Save the Republic?" *Saturday Review/World*, September 7, 1974, 10–16.

30. Manfred F. R. Kets de Vries, "The Dark Side of Entrepreneurship," *Harvard Business Review*, November–December 1985, 69.

Notes for Chapter Three

1. Joseph S. Nye Jr., *The Powers to Lead* (New York: Oxford University Press, 2008), p. 19.

2. Some of our thoughts here have been influenced over the years by discussions with Jim Burns, Harlan Cleveland, John Gardner, Joseph S. Nye Jr., Barbara Kellerman, Ron Riggio, and Ronald Heifetz. See especially Ronald A. Heifetz, *Leadership Without Easy Answers* (Cambridge, MA: Belknap/Harvard University Press, 1994).

3. Heifetz, p. 28.

4. Ibid., p. 35.

5. Bruce Mazlish, "History, Psychology and Leadership," in *Leadership: Multidisciplinary Perspectives,* Barbara Kellerman, ed. (Englewood Cliffs, NJ: Prentice Hall, 1984), p. 13.
6. Robert C. Tucker, *Politics as Leadership* (Columbia: University of Missouri Press, 1981), pp. 71–76.
7. For different explorations of leadership and justice, see Michael J. Sandal, *Justice: What's the Right Thing to Do?* (New York: Farrar, Straus and Giroux, 2009); and Waller R. Newell, *The Soul of a Leader* (New York: HarperCollins, 2009).
8. Niccolò Machiavelli, *The Prince* (New York: Bantam Books, 1966) pp. 53, 54.
9. Address by General Douglas MacArthur at West Point, May 12, 1962.
10. Theodore M. Hesburgh quoted in "What Works for Me," *16 CEOs Talk About Their Careers and Commitments,* Thomas R. Horton, ed. (New York: AMACON, 1986), p. 157.
11. GE chairman Jack Welch, quoted in Noel Tichy and Ram Charan, "Speed, Simplicity, Self-Confidence: An Interview with Jack Welch," *Harvard Business Review,* September–October, 1989, 113.
12. See Peter B. Vaill, *Managing as a Performing Art: New Ideas for a World of Chaotic Change* (San Francisco: Jossey-Bass, 1989), p. 2.
13. Herbert A. Simon, "Making Management Decisions: The Role of Intuition and Emotion," *Academy of Management Executive* 1, no. 1 (February 1987): 63.
14. James M. Kouzes and Barry Z. Posner, *The Leadership Challenge* (San Francisco: Jossey-Bass, 1987), p. 93.
15. Harlan Cleveland, "Training Intuitive Leaders," *Minneapolis Star Tribune,* July 9, 1989, 23A. For the Kissinger view, see Hugh Sidey, "Is Bush Bold Enough?" *Time,* October 6, 1989, 28.
16. Henry Mintzberg, *Mintzberg on Management* (New York: Free Press, 1989), p. 54. See also Philip Goldberg, *The Intuitive Edge* (Los Angeles: Jeremy Tarcher, 1983); Roy Rowan, *The Intuitive Manager* (Boston: Little, Brown, 1986); Frances E. Vaughan, *Awakening Intuition* (New York: Anchor Books, 1979); and Weston H. Angor, *Intuition in Organizations* (Newbury Park, CA: Sage Publications, 1989). But also see, on the limits of intuition, Daniel Kahneman, *Thinking, Fast and Slow* (New York: Farrar, Straus and Giroux, 2011).
17. See Steven Johnson, *Where Good Ideas Come From: The Natural History of Innovation* (New York: Riverhead Books, 2010). See also Malcolm Gladwell, *Blink: The Power of Thinking Without Thinking* (New York: Back Bay Books, 2007).
18. Kahneman, *Thinking, Fast and Slow.*
19. Benjamin R. Barber, and Debs quote, "Neither Leaders nor Followers . . . ," in *Essays in Honor of James MacGregor Burns,* Michael Beschloss and Thomas E. Cronin, eds. (Englewood Cliffs, NJ: Prentice-Hall, 1989), p. 123.
20. F. G. Bailey, *Humbuggery and Manipulation: The Art of Leadership* (Ithaca, NY: Cornell University Press, 1988), p. 2.
21. See, for example, the writings of David Shapiro, *Neurotic Styles* (New York: Basic Books, 1965); Otto F. Kernberg, *Borderline Conditions and Pathological Narcissism* (New York: Jason Aronson, 1975). See also Jerrold M. Post, *Leaders and Their Followers in a Dangerous World* (Ithaca, NY: Cornell University Press, 2004); and Manfred Kets de Vries, *The Leader on the Couch* (San Francisco: Jossey-Bass, 2006).
22. See the preliminary work of Robert Hogan, Robert Raskin, and Dan Fazzini, "The Dark Side of Charisma," paper delivered at the Conference on the Measurement of Leadership, San Antonio, October 1988, reprinted in *Measures of Leadership,* Kenneth C. Clark and Miriam B. Clark, eds. (West Orange, NJ: Leadership Library of America, 1990), pp. 343–354. See also Manfred F. R. Kets de Vries, *Prisoners of Leadership* (New York: Wiley, 1989), Chapters 5–9; and Jay Conger, *The Charismatic Leader* (San Francisco: Jossey-Bass, 1989), Chapter 8.
23. James MacGregor Burns, *Leadership* (New York: Harper & Row, 1978), pp. 37–44.
24. See, for example, Marcia Cohen, *The Sisterhood: The Inside Story of the Women's Move-*

ment and the Leaders Who Made It Happen (New York: Fawcett Columbine, 1988). See also Saul Alinsky, *Rules for Radicals* (New York: Vintage, 1971).

25. Harvey C. Mansfield Jr., in *Taming the Prince: The Ambivalence of Modern Executive Power* (New York: Free Press, 1989), traces the evolution of notions of executive power and the necessity for a single leader to serve at the helm of large complex organizations such as the nation-state.

26. Malcolm Gladwell, "The Act of Failure," *The New Yorker,* August 21 and 28, 2000.

27. Jonathan Alter, "Leadership," *Newsweek,* December 31, 1990, 25.

28. Warren Bennis and Burt Nanus, *Leaders* (New York: Harper & Row, 1985). See also the writings of Peter Drucker; see also John P. Kotter, *Leading Change* (Boston: Harvard Business Press, 1996); and Kotter, *A Sense of Urgency* (Boston: Harvard Business Press, 2008).

29. John P. Kotter, "What Leaders Really Do," originally in *Harvard Business Review*; republished in *The Leader's Companion: Insights on Leadership Through the Ages,* J. Thomas Wren, ed. (New York: Free Press, 1995), p. 115.

30. Max De Pree, *Leadership Is an Art* (New York: Doubleday, 1989), p. 16. See also John Kotter, *A Force for Change: How Leadership Differs from Management* (New York: Free Press, 1990).

31. Abraham Zaleznik, *The Managerial Mystique* (New York: Harper & Row, 1989), p. 23. See also Tom Peters, *Thriving on Chaos: Handbook for a Management Revolution* (New York: Knopf, 1987).

32. John W. Gardner, "Effective Leadership," address to Independent Sector Meeting, Washington, DC, May 12, 1988.

33. See, for example, the stories in Rod Blagojevich, *The Governor* (Beverly Hills, CA: Phoenix Books, 2009).

34. Noel M. Tichy and Warren Bennis, *Judgment: How Winning Leaders Make Great Calls* (New York: Penguin Books, 2007), pp. 4–5.

35. De Pree, *Leadership Is an Art,* p. 51. For another view of what motivates people, see Daniel H. Pink, *Drive* (New York: Riverhead Books, 2009).

36. Swanee Hunt, "Let Women Rule," *Foreign Affairs* 86 (2007), 109–120; Sally Helgesen, *The Female Advantage* (New York: Doubleday, 1990); Michael A. Genovese, ed., *Women as National Leaders,* 2nd ed. (New York: Psychology Press, 2012); and Dee Dee Myers, *Why Women Should Rule the World* (New York: Harper, 2008).

37. Joseph S. Nye Jr., *The Powers to Lead* (New York: Oxford, 2008), p. 50. See the useful review by Robin J. Ely and Deborah L. Rhode, "Women and Leadership: Defining the Challenges," in Nitin Nohria and Rakesh Khurana, eds., *Handbook of Leadership Theory and Practice* (Boston: Harvard Business Press, 2010), pp. 377–410.

38. Nannerl O. Keohane, *Thinking About Leadership* (Princeton: Princeton University Press, 2010), pp. 152–153.

39. Ibid., p. 154.

40. Mihaly Csikszentmihalyi, *Creativity: Flow and the Psychology of Discovery and Invention* (New York: Harper, 1996), p. 71.

41. Nye, *The Powers to Lead*; and Nye, *The Future of Power* (New York: Public Affairs, 2011).

42. George Bernard Shaw, *Saint Joan* (New York: Penguin Books, 1957), first published in 1924. See also Kathryn Harrison, "Joan of Arc: Enduring Power," New York Times, January 6, 2012, p. A23.

43. Theodore Hesburgh, "The College Presidency: Life Between a Rock and a Hard Place," *Change,* May–June 1979, 44.

44. Fred E. Fiedler and Joseph E. Garcia, *New Approaches to Effective Leadership* (New York: John Wiley, 1987), p. 51.

45. Aaron Wildavsky, "A Cultural Theory of Leadership," in *Leadership and Politics,* Bryan D. Jones, ed. (Lawrence: University Press of Kansas, 1989), p. 108. See also Wildavsky, *The Nursing Father: Moses as a Political Leader* (Tuscaloosa, AL: University of Alabama Press, 1984).

46. Wildavsky, "A Cultural Theory of Leadership," p. 108.
47. See, for example, the writings of anthropologist Clifford Geertz.

Notes for Chapter Four

1. Cornelius Tacitus, *The Annals of Imperial Rome,* Alfred John Church and William Jackson Brodribb, trans. (originally published 1864–1877; reprinted Lawrence, KS: Digireads .com, 2005), p. 220.
2. Maureen Gallery Kovacs, trans., *The Epic of Gilgamesh* (Stanford: Stanford University Press, 1990).
3. Seamus Heaney, trans., *Beowulf: A New Verse Translation* (New York: W. W. Norton, 2001).
4. Daniel J. Boorstin, *The Creators* (New York: Random House, 1992), pp. 9–17.
5. See Annping Chin, *The Authentic Confucius: A Life of Thought and Politics* (New York: Scribner, 2007); Jonathan Clemens, *Confucius: A Biography* (Stroud: Sutton, 2004); B. W. Van Norden, ed., *Confucius and the Analects: New Essays* (New York: Oxford University Press, 2001).
6. All quotes from Confucius, *The Analects* (Minneapolis: Filiquarian Publishing, 2006).
7. Arthur Waley, *The Way and Its Power: Lao Tzu's Tao Te Ching and Its Place in Chinese Thought* (New York: Grove Press, 1958); Hans-George Moeller, *The Philosophy of the Daodejing* (New York: Columbia University Press, 2006).
8. See Craig Johnson, "Taoist Leadership Ethics," *The Journal of Leadership Studies* 7, no. 1 (2000).
9. On Herodotus and this debate, see David Asheri et al., *A Commentary on Herodotus* (New York: Oxford University Press, 2007), pp. 471–478.
10. Thucydides, *The History of the Peloponnesian War* (New York: Penguin, 1954).
11. Guy Cromwell Field, *Philosophy of Plato* (New York: Oxford University Press, 1969).
12. Plato, *The Republic,* translated by Desmond Lee, introduction by Melissa Lane (New York: Penguin Classics, 2007).
13. Robert D. Kaplan, "A Historian for Our Time," *The Atlantic,* January–February 2007, 82.
14. Kaplan, p. 83.
15. Cicero, *On Government,* Michael Grant, trans. (London: Penguin Books, 1993), p. 45.
16. Ibid., p. 193.
17. Anthony Everitt, *Cicero: The Life and Times of Rome's Greatest Politician* (New York: Random House, 2001).
18. See Scott Gordon, *Controlling the State: Constitutionalism from Ancient Athens to Today* (Cambridge: Harvard University Press, 1999).
19. Quoted in *The Week,* June 19, 2009, 21.
20. Plutarch, *The Rise and Fall of Athens: Nine Greek Lives* (London: Penguin, 1960), p. 17.
21. Ibid., p. 281.
22. Robin Lane Fox, *Alexander the Great* (New York: Penguin, 2004).
23. Plutarch, *Makers of Rome* (London: Penguin Books, 1965), p. 31.
24. Plato, *The Republic,* G. M. A. Grube and C. D. C. Reeve, trans. (Indianapolis: Hackett, 1992), Book VI.
25. Thad Williamson, "The Good Society and the Good Soul: Plato's Republic on Leadership," *The Leadership Quarterly* 19, no. 4 (August 2008): 397–408.
26. On Philosopher-Kings, the ruler Dionysus of Syracuse once asked the philosopher Aristippus why philosophy paid court to princes, and not vice versa. Aristippus replied, "Philosophers know what they need, and princes do not."
27. Quoted in James O'Toole, *Creating the Good Life* (Emmaus, PA: Rodale, 2005), p. 9.

28. O'Toole, p. 11.
29. Aristotle; *Nicomachean Ethics* and *Politics* are his two masterpieces.
30. O'Toole, *Creating the Good Life*; Tom Morris, *If Aristotle Ran General Motors* (New York: Holt Paperbacks, 1998).
31. Hermann Hesse sees a similar path-oriented or journey-driven search for truth as the true meaning of life. See *Siddhartha* (Scotts Valley, CA: Createspace, 2008).
32. Alan M. Dershowitz, *The Genesis of Justice* (New York: Warner Books, 2002).
33. See Hershey H. Friedman and Mitchell Langbert, "Abraham as a Transformational Leader," *The Journal of Leadership Studies* 7, no. 2 (2002).
34. Robert Alter, *The David Story* (New York: W. W. Norton, 2000).
35. Martin Buber, "Biblical Leadership," in *Biblical Humanism,* Nahum Glatzer, ed. (London: MacDonald, 1968).
36. See Michael Keren, "Moses as a Visionary Realist," *International Political Service Review,* 1998, 71–84.
37. See Aaron Wildavsky, *The Nursing Father: Moses as a Political Leader* (Tuscaloosa, AL: University of Alabama Press, 1984); and Michael Walzer, *Exodus and Revolution* (New York: Basic Books, 1985).
38. Keren, "Moses as a Visionary Realist," p. 79.
39. Matthew 7:12.
40. Matthew 5:43–45.
41. Matthew 5:38–39.
42. Matthew 5:9.
43. Warren Bennis, *On Becoming a Leader* (New York: Basic Books, 2003), p. 39.
44. John Beverly Butcher, *The Tao of Jesus* (San Francisco: Harper San Francisco, 1994).

Notes for Chapter Five

1. Niccolò Machiavelli, *The Prince* (New York: Random House, 1940), p. 21.
2. For a fuller explanation and further quotes, see Maurizio Viroli, *Niccolò's Smile: A Biography of Machiavelli* (New York: Farrar, Straus and Giroux, 2000). Also of interest is Noccolo Capponi, *An Unlikely Prince: The Life and Times of Machiavelli* (Cambridge, MA: Da Capo, 2010).
3. See Reinhold Niebuhr, *Moral Man, Immoral Society* (New York: C. Scribner's Sons, 1952).
4. James MacGregor Burns, *Leadership* (New York: HarperCollins, 1978), p. 180.
5. Quoted in Robin Headlam Wells, *Shakespeare's Politics* (London: Continuum, 2009), p. 90.
6. Harold Bloom, *Shakespeare: The Invention of the Human* (New York: Riverhead, 1998), p. 321.
7. See Allan Bloom and Henry V. Jaffa, *Shakespeare's Politics* (New York: Basic Books, 1964); and Michael Platt, *Rome and Romans According to Shakespeare* (Lanham, MD: University Press of America, 1982).
8. Hugh Grady, *Shakespeare, Machiavelli, and Montaigne: Power and Subjectivity from Richard II to Hamlet* (Oxford: Oxford University Press, 2002); and John Roe, *Shakespeare and Machiavelli* (Cambridge: D. S. Brewer, 2002).
9. William Shakespeare, *Henry IV,* Part I, Act 5, Scene 4.
10. William Shakespeare, *Hamlet,* Act 3, Scene 3.
11. William Shakespeare, *The Tragedy of Coriolanus.*
12. Plutarch, *The Lives of Noble Grecians and Romans* (Oxford: Benediction Classics, 2010).
13. See Malcolm Gladwell, "Cocksure," *The New Yorker,* July 27, 2009, 24–28.

14. William Shakespeare, *The Tragedy of Othello, the Moor of Venice.*

15. John Mearsheimer, *Why Leaders Lie* (New York: Oxford University Press, 2010). See also Hugh Shelton, *Without Hesitation* (New York: St. Martin's Press, 2010), p. 419.

16. See Michael A. Genovese, *The Nixon Presidency: Power and Politics in Turbulent Times* (Westport, CT: Greenwood Press, 1990); and Stanley Kutler, *The Wars of Watergate* (New York: W. W. Norton, 1992).

17. See Joseph Conrad, *Heart of Darkness,* the novella on which Francis Ford Coppolla's *Apocalypse Now* is based. *Heart of Darkness* was first published as a book in 1902. It originally appeared as a three-part series in *Blackwood's Magazine* in 1899.

18. *Julius Caesar,* introduction by William and Barbara Rosen (New York: Signet, 1998), p. lxvi. See also the lucid essay by David Bromwich, "What Shakespeare's Heroes Learn," *Raritan* XXIX, no. 4 (Spring 2010): 132–148.

19. See the useful portraits of them in Bruce Miroff's splendid *Icons of Democracy* (New York: Basic Books, 1993).

20. Ibid., p. 354. See also Joseph S. Nye Jr., *The Powers to Lead* (New York: Oxford, 2008); and Nannerl O. Keohane, *Thinking About Leadership* (Princeton: Princeton University Press, 2010).

Notes for Chapter Six

1. Thomas Jefferson, *The Kentucky Resolutions of 1798.* Available: www.constitution.org/cons/kent1798.htm.

2. Christopher Hibbert, *Charles I* (New York: Palgrave Macmillan, 2007).

3. Geoffrey Robertson, *The Tyrannicide Brief* (London: Vintage Books, 2005).

4. Edmund S. Morgan, *Inventing the People: The Rise of Popular Sovereignty in England and America* (New York: W. W. Norton, 1988).

5. In the Old Testament, Leviathan was a giant sea monster that devoured all in its path.

6. Michael A. Genovese, *Presidential Prerogative* (Palo Alto, CA: Stanford University Press, 2011).

7. Scott Gordon, *Controlling the State: Constitutionalism from Ancient Athens to Today* (Cambridge, MA: Harvard University Press, 1999).

8. Bert A. Rockman, *The Leadership Question: The Presidency and the American System* (New York: Praeger, 1984), pp. 39–43.

9. See Bruce Miroff, *Pragmatic Illusions: The Presidential Politics of John F. Kennedy* (New York: Longman, 1979).

10. Quoted in Thomas E. Cronin, "Presidential Power Revisited and Reappraised," *Western Political Quarterly,* December 1979, 338.

11. James Bryce, *The American Commonwealth,* vol. 2 (New York: Macmillan & Co., 1888), p. 460.

12. Arthur M. Schlesinger Jr., *The Cycles of American History* (Boston: Houghton Mifflin, 1986), p. 430. See also Bruce Miroff, *Icons of Democracy* (New York: Basic Books, 1993), p. 1.

13. Abraham Lincoln, *The Gettysburg Address.* See Mario Cuomo and Harold Holzer, eds., *Lincoln on Democracy* (New York: HarperCollins, 1990).

14. William Sterne Randall, *Thomas Jefferson: A Life* (New York: Henry Holt, 1993). See also Merrill D. Peterson, ed., *The Portable Thomas Jefferson* (New York: Viking Press, 1975).

15. Miroff, *Icons of Democracy,* p. 354.

16. We are indebted to James O'Toole for bringing the Ensor painting to our attention; see James O'Toole, *Leading Change* (San Francisco: Jossey-Bass, 1995), pp. 1–5.

Notes for Chapter Seven

1. Tom Peters, *Thriving on Chaos* (New York: Knopf, 1987), p. 391.

2. Morgan W. McCall Jr. and Michael M. Lombardo, "What Makes a Top Executive?" *Psychology Today,* February 1983, 31.

3. David Gergen, Foreword, *True North: Discover Your Authentic Leadership,* ed. Bill George and Peter Sims (New York: Wiley, 2007), p. xviii.

4. Ibid., p. xiii.

5. Fred J. Greenstein, *The Presidential Difference* (New York: Free Press, 2000), pp. 199–200.

6. Walter Isaacson, *Steve Jobs* (New York: Simon & Schuster, 2011). Still, Jobs was seen by some as unnecessarily flawed in the way he occasionally treated other people, especially those over whom he exercised power.

7. Michael Ignatieff, Address at Whitman College, May 2004.

8. See Michael Maccoby, "Narcissistic Leaders," *Harvard Business Review,* January–February 2000, reprinted in *Harvard Business Review, Leadership Insights* and article collection, not dated, pp. 53–61. See also Maccoby, *The Productive Narcissist: The Promise and Perils of Visionary Leadership* (New York: Broadway Books, 2003).

9. Maccoby, *The Productive Narcissist,* p. 244.

10. Manfred F. R. Kets de Vries, *Prisoners of Leadership* (New York: Wiley, 1989), p. 10. See also Amanda Sinclair, *Leadership for the Disillusioned: Moving Beyond Myths and Heroes to Leading That Liberates* (Crows Nest, NSW: Allen & Unwin, 2007), Chapters 1 and 2.

11. Kets de Vries, *Prisoners of Leadership,* p. 98.

12. Peter Drucker, *The Effective Executive* (New York: Harper & Row, 1966), p. 45.

13. Andrew S. Grove, *High Output Management* (New York: Vintage, 1985), Chapter 4.

14. See, for example, Warren Bennis, *On Becoming a Leader* (Reading, MA: Addison-Wesley, 1990); and Warren Bennis and Burt Nanus, *Leaders: Strategies for Taking Charge* (New York: Harper & Row, 1985).

15. This parable can be found, among other places, in Jan Carlzon, *Moments of Truth: New Strategies for Today's Customer Driven Economy* (New York: Harper & Row, 1989), p. 135.

16. John W. Gardner, *Self-Renewal* (New York: Harper & Row, 1963). See also his valuable book *On Leadership* (New York: Free Press, 1990).

17. Tom Peters, *Thriving on Chaos: Handbook for a Management Revolution* (New York: Knopf, 1987), p. 396.

18. Warren Bennis and Patricia Ward Biederman, *Organizing Genius—The Secrets of Creative Collaboration* (Reading, MA: Addison-Wesley, 1997), p. 199.

19. Robert Maynard Hutchins, 1934 speech at Oberlin College.

20. James C. Collins and Jerry I. Porras, *Built to Last: Successful Habits of Visionary Companies* (New York: Harper Business, 1997), pp. 44, 45.

21. See Jim Collins, *Good to Great: Why Some Companies Make the Leap and Others Don't* (New York: Harper Business, 2001).

22. Louis V. Gerstner Jr., *Who Says Elephants Can't Dance? Inside IBM's Historic Turnaround* (New York: Harper Business, 2002), p. 235.

23. Ibid., p. 238.

24. See Bill George, *True North*; Max De Pree, *Leadership Is an Art* (New York: Doubleday, 1989); and Don Frick and Larry Spears, eds., *On Becoming a Servant Leader: The Private Writings of Robert K. Greenleaf* (San Francisco: Jossey-Bass, 1996).

25. See, for example, James M. McPherson, *Tried by War: Abraham Lincoln and Commander-in-Chief* (New York: Penguin Books, 2008).

26. George Tenet with Bill Harlow, *At the Center of the Storm: My Years at the CIA* (New York: HarperCollins, 2007), p. 494. See also Hugh Shelton, *Without Hesitation* (New York: St. Martin's Press, 2010).

27. Michael O'Brien, *Vince: A Personal Biography of Vince Lombardi* (New York: Morrow, 1987), p. 189.
28. Louis B. Lundborg, *The Art of Being an Executive* (New York: Free Press, 1981), p. 85.
29. Perry M. Smith, *Rules and Tools for Leaders* (New York: Perigee, 2002), p. 17.
30. Jeffrey Sonnenfeld and Andrew Ward, *Firing Back: How Great Leaders Rebound After Career Disaster* (Cambridge, MA: Harvard Business Press, 2007).
31. Barbara Tuchman, *The March of Folly* (New York: Ballantine Books, 1984), p. 4.
32. Ibid., p. 7.
33. *Growing a Business* (New York: Simon & Schuster, 1987), p. 204.
34. Lisa Endlich, *Goldman Sachs: The Culture of Success* (New York: Touchstone, 1999), p. 119.
35. Michael Dell, *Direct from Dell* (New York: Harper Business, 1999), p. 130.
36. Michael D'Antonio, "The Advantage of Falling Short," *Los Angeles Times Magazine,* July 14, 2002.
37. Peter F. Drucker, *The Essential Drucker* (New York: Collins Business, 2001), p. 28.
38. Stanley Marcus, *Minding the Store* (Boston: Little, Brown, 1974), p. 3.
39. Carl Sewell and Paul B. Brown, *Customers for Life: How to Turn That One-Time Buyer into a Lifetime Customer* (New York: Doubleday, 1990), p. 3.
40. Ibid., p. 13.
41. Jan Carlzon, *Moment of*Truth, p. 74.
42. Gerstner, *Who Says Elephants Can't Dance?,* p. 50.
43. Anthony Ulwick, *What Customers Want* (New York: McGraw Hill, 2005), p. xxv.
44. Adam Richardson, *Innovation X* (San Francisco: Jossey-Bass, 2010), Chapter 3.
45. Chris Denove and James D. Power IV, *Satisfaction: How Every Great Company Listens to the Voice of the Customer* (New York: Portfolio, 2006), p. 180.
46. Welch quoted in Robert Slater, *Jack Welch and the GE Way* (New York: McGraw Hill, 1999), p. 104. See also Justin Fox, Interview with Whole Foods CEO John Mackey, "What Is It That Only I Can Do?" *Harvard Business Review,* January–February 2011, 119–123.
47. Dell, *Direct from Dell,* pp. 166–167.
48. Andrew S. Grove, *Only the Paranoid Survive* (New York: Doubleday, 1996), p. 31.
49. Ibid., pp. 117–118.
50. Paul Hawken, *Growing a Business* (New York: Simon & Schuster, 1987), p. 213.
51. Dell, *Direct from Dell,* p. 110.
52. Collins, *Good to Great,* p. 62.
53. Lundborg, *The Art of Being an Executive,* pp. 33–34.
54. Discussed in James M. Kilts, *Doing What Matters* (New York: Crown, 2007), pp. 136–137.
55. Drucker, *The Effective Executive,* p. 99.
56. Jack Welch, *Jack: Straight from the Gut* (New York: Warner Books, 2001), p. 128.
57. Ibid.
58. Robert I. Sutton, *The No Asshole Rule: Building a Civilized Workplace and Surviving One That Isn't* (New York: Warner Business Books, 2007).
59. Drucker, *The Effective Executive,* p. 89.
60. Perry Smith, *Rules and Tools for Leaders* (New York: Perigee, 2002), p. 215.
61. Rosabeth Moss Kanter, *SuperCorp: How Vanguard Companies Create Innovation, Projects, Growth, and Social Good* (New York: Crown Business, 2009), p. 254. See also the fascinating case study of *Interface* by Ray C. Anderson, *Confessions of a Radical Industrialist: Prophets, People, Purpose—Doing Business by Respecting the Earth* (New York: St. Martin's Press, 2009).
62. Gerstner, *Who Says Elephants Can't Dance?,* p. 187.
63. Ibid., p. 213.

64. Quoted in David A. Vise, *The Google Story* (New York: Bantam Dell, 2005), p. 197.

65. Virginia Scott, *Google* (Westport, CT: Greenwood, 2008), pp. 58–59.

66. To cite just a few, see David Packard, *The HP Way* (New York: Harper Business, 1995); Jeffrey K. Liker, *The Toyota Way* (New York: McGraw-Hill, 2004); Robert Slater, *Jack Welch and the GE Way* (New York: McGraw-Hill, 1999); Sam Walton with John Huey, *Sam Walton: Made in America* (New York: Doubleday, 1992); Vise, *The Google Story*; Collins, *Good to Great*; and Kanter, *SuperCorp*. See also Michael L. Tushman and Charles A. O'Reilly III, *Winning Through Innovation: A Practical Guide to Leading Organizational Change and Renewal* (Boston: Harvard Business School Press, 1997).

67. Collins and Porras, *Built to Last*, p. 123.

68. Grove, *Only the Paranoid Survive*, p. 118.

69. Three works from the past emphasize these values: Gardner, *Self-Renewal*, 1963; Tom Peters, *Thriving on Chaos*, 1987; and John F. Kotter, *A Sense of Urgency* (Boston: Harvard Business Press, 2008).

70. Kotter, p. 185.

71. Michael E. Porter, Jay W. Lorsch, and Nitin Nohria, "Seven Surprises for New CEO's," *Harvard Business Review*, October 2004, 65.

72. Alfred P. Sloan Jr., *My Years with General Motors* (Garden City, NY: Doubleday, 1964), p. 139.

73. This is an idea suggested in Marshall Edward Dimock, *The Executive in Action* (New York: Harper & Brothers, 1945), p. 176.

74. Sloan, p. 129.

75. Drucker, *The Essential Drucker*, p. 73.

76. Ibid., p. 74.

77. Carlzon, *Moments of Truth*, p. 68.

78. Ibid., p. 74.

79. Ken Blanchard, "Turning the Organizational Pyramid Upside Down," in *The Leader of the Future*, Frances Hesselbein et al., eds. (San Francisco: Jossey-Bass, 1996), p. 84.

80. Ibid., p. 85.

Notes for Chapter Eight

1. Frederick Scott Oliver, *Politics and Politicians* (London: Macmillan, 1934), p. 39.

2. H. L. Mencken, "Why Nobody Loves a Politician," originally published on October 27, 1934, reprinted in the *New York Times*, September 13, 1980, 21.

3. Harold D. Lasswell, *World Politics and Personal Insecurity* (first published in 1934); reprinted in Lasswell et al., *The Study of Power* (Glencoe, IL: Free Press, 1956), p. 3.

4. Joseph S. Nye Jr., *The Powers to Lead* (New York: Oxford, 2008), p. 27.

5. For a useful study of the power of nuclear weapons, see Garry Wills, *Bomb Power: The Modern Presidency and the National Security State* (New York: Penguin Press, 2010). But for stories of how persuasion, collaboration, and coalition building are powerful in making things happen, see Bill Bradley, *Time Present, Time Past* (New York: Knopf, 1996); Leverett Saltonstall, *Salty: Recollections of a Yankee in Politics* (Boston: Boston Globe, 1976); Warren Rudman, *Combat* (New York: Random House, 1996); and William K. Muir Jr., *Legislature* (Chicago: University of Chicago Press, 1982).

6. Daniel Kemmis, *The Good City and the Good Life* (Boston: Houghton Mifflin, 1995), p. 159.

7. John F. Kennedy, *Profiles in Courage* (New York: Harper & Row, 1955).

8. Tip O'Neill with Gary Hymel, *All Politics Is Local* (New York: Times Books, 1994), p. xvi.

9. Chris Matthews, *Hardball*, rev. ed. (New York: Free Press, 2004), p. 48.

10. See Mike Stanton, *The Prince of Providence* (New York: Random House, 2004). He tells his own story in Vincent Cianci Jr. with David Fisher, *Politics and Pasta* (New York: St. Martin's Press, 2011).

11. For his story, see Willie Brown, *Basic Brown: My Life and Our Times* (New York: Simon & Schuster, 2008).

12. Alan Ehrenhalt, *The United States of Ambition* (New York: Times Books, 1991), p. 17.

13. Louis Sandy Maisel, *From Obscurity to Oblivion: Running in the Congressional Primary* (Knoxville: University of Tennessee Press, 1982), p. 15.

14. William M. Bulger, *While the Music Lasts: My Life in Politics* (Boston: Houghton Mifflin, 1996), p. 326.

15. John Margolis, *The Quotable Bob Dole* (New York: Avon Books, 1986), p. 71.

16. See David Mayhew, *Congress: The Electoral Connection* (New Haven, CT: Yale University Press, 1974).

17. Stanton, *The Prince of Providence,* p. 29.

18. Quoted in Myra MacPherson, *The Power Lovers: An Intimate Look at Politicians and Their Marriages* (New York: Putnam, 1975), p. 19. On this and other dangers and pitfalls of the profession of politics, see Arnold Ludwig, *King of the Mountain: The Nature of Political Leadership* (Lexington: University Press of Kentucky, 2002), Chapter 4.

19. Maisel, *From Obscurity to Oblivion,* p. 128.

20. For Blagojevich's own story, see Rod Blagojevich, *The Governor* (Beverly Hills, CA: Phoenix Books, 2009). On John Edwards, see the critical analysis by badly bruised aide Andrew Young, *The Politician* (New York: St. Martin's Press, 2010); and on Cianci, see Stanton, *The Prince of Providence.*

21. Brown, *Basic Brown,* pp. 29, 30, and 32.

22. Stephen Marks, *Confessions of a Political Hitman: My Secret Life of Scandal, Corruption, Hypocrisy and Dirty Attacks That Decide Who Gets Elected (and Who Doesn't)* (Naperville, IL: Sourcebooks, 2008), p. 8.

23. Quoted in Muir, *Legislature,* p. 31.

24. Bradley, *Time Present, Time Past,* p. 74.

25. Garry Wills, "Hurrah for Politicians," *Harper's,* September 1975, 48.

26. Newt Gingrich, *Lessons Learned the Hard Way* (New York: HarperCollins, 1998), p. 36.

27. Quoted in Chris Matthews, *Life's a Campaign* (New York: Random House, 2007), p. 159.

28. Marks, *Confessions of a Political Hitman,* p. 8.

29. Chris Matthews, *Hardball: How Politics Is Played by One Who Knows the Game* (New York: Free Press, 1988), p. 136.

30. Barry M. Goldwater with Jack Casserly, *Goldwater* (New York: Doubleday, 1988), p. 108.

31. On the necessity and political pragmatism of legislative compromise, see the classic by James L. Sundquist, *Politics and Policies* (Washington, DC: Brookings Institution, 1968); and Richard J. Fenno, *The Making of a Senator—Dan Quayle* (Washington, DC: Congressional Quarterly Press, 1989).

32. O'Neill, *All Politics Is Local,* p. 93.

33. Charles Handy, *The Age of Paradox* (Boston: Harvard Business School Press, 1994), pp. 90, 94.

34. Matthews, *Hardball,* p. 183.

35. Jesse Ventura, *I Ain't Got Time to Bleed* (New York: Penguin Books, 1999), p. 297.

36. Alan K. Simpson, *Right in the Old Gazoo: A Lifetime of Scrapping with the Press* (New York: Morrow, 1997), p. 260.

37. See, for example, Bobby Baker, *Wheeling and Dealing* (New York: W. W. Norton, 1978); Robert A. Caro, *Means of Ascent* (New York: Knopf, 1989); and Caro, *Master of the Senate* (New York: Knopf, 2002).

38. Hubert Humphrey quoted in *New York Times,* October 19, 1974, E18.

39. See, for example, Tim Wirth, "Diary of a Dropout," *The New York Times Magazine,* August 9, 1992, 16–18, 26, 34–36.

40. William Shakespeare, *The Tragedy of King Lear* (New York: Pocket Books, 1957), p. 99; and Shakespeare, *The Tragedy of Hamlet, Prince of Denmark* (New York: New American Library, 1963), pp. 151–152.

41. See Henry Adams, *The Education of Henry Adams* (Boston: Houghton-Mifflin Co., 1918); and Adams, *Democracy: An American Novel* (New York: Henry Holt and Co., 1883).

42. Quoted in Charles A. Madison, *Critics and Crusaders* (New York: Henry Holt, 1947), p. 184.

43. The Shelley quote and related themes come from William M. Gibson, *Theodore Roosevelt Among the Humorists: W. D. Howells, Mark Twain and Mr. Dooley* (Knoxville: University of Tennessee Press, 1980).

44. E. L. Doctorow, "The Case for the Writer as Politician," *Washington Post National Weekly,* May 28–June 3, 1990, 25.

45. Nelson Polsby, *Political Innovation in America: The Politics of Policy Institution* (New Haven, CT: Yale University Press, 1984), p. 5.

46. They are often going on in major interest groups and are reflected in Congress and in the opposition party. See, for example, James L. Sundquist, *Politics and Policy: The Eisenhower, Kennedy and Johnson Years* (Washington, DC: Brookings Institution, 1968).

47. Frederick Douglass, "Oration in Memory of Abraham Lincoln," April 14, 1876, reprinted in *The World's Great Speeches,* 3rd ed., Lewis Copeland and Lawrence W. Lamm, eds. (New York: Dover Publications, 1973), pp. 808, 809. See also Richard Hofstadter, *The American Political Tradition* (New York: Vintage, 1948), Chapter 5; and David H. Donald, *Lincoln* (New York: Simon & Schuster, 1995); Ronald C. White, *A. Lincoln: A Biography* (New York: Random House, 2009); and Eric Foner, *The Fiery Trial: Abraham Lincoln and American Slavery* (New York: W. W. Norton, 2010).

48. Douglass, "Oration," p. 812.

49. We borrow and adapt here from Thomas E. Cronin, *On the Presidency* (Boulder, CO: Paradigm Publishers, 2009), Chapter 3.

50. Albert O. Hirschman, "Underdevelopment, Obstacles to the Perception of Change, and Leadership," *Daedalus,* Summer 1968, 933.

51. See the general treatment of this in Thomas Kuhn, *The Structure of Scientific Revolutions* (Chicago: University of Chicago Press, 1962); Roger Fisher and Daniel Shapiro, *Beyond Reason* (New York: Penguin Books, 2005); and James L. Adams, *The Care and Feeding of Ideas* (Stanford, CA: Stanford Alumni Association, 1986).

52. Charles A. Madison, *Critics and Crusaders: A Century of American Protest* (New York: Henry Holt, 1947), p. 14.

53. Wallace Stegner letter in Richard Manning, "Abbey's Clan Gathers to Rededicate Itself," *High Country News,* June 5, 1989, 3.

54. See, for example, Alma Lutz, *Susan B. Anthony: Rebel, Crusader, Humanitarian* (Boston: Beacon Press, 1969).

55. Howard Jarvis, *I'm Mad as Hell* (New York: Times Books, 1979).

56. See Christopher Ketcham, "The New Populists?" *Los Angeles Times,* October 6, 2011, A19.

57. March quoted in Diane Couth, "Ideas as Art," *Harvard Business Review,* October 2006, 85. See also James G. March and Thierry Weil, *On Leadership* (Cambridge, UK: Blackwell, 2005).

58. See the classic by David Mayhew, *Congress: The Electoral Connection* (New Haven, CT: Yale University Press, 1974); and Kevin Phillips, *American Theocracy: The Peril and Politics of Radical Religion, Oil, and Borrowed Money in the 21st Century* (New York: Viking, 2006).

59. See, for example, the examination of a large number of crucial leaders in David J. Garrow, *Bearing the Cross: Martin Luther King, Jr., and the Southern Christian Leadership*

Conference; Juan Williams, *Eyes on the Prize: America's Civil Rights Years, 1954–1965* (New York: Viking, 1987); and Taylor Branch, *Parting of the Waters* (New York: Simon & Schuster, 1988).

60. See the splendid treatment of Long and Coughlin and their followers in Alan Brinkley, *Voices of Protest: Huey Long, Father Coughlin, and the Great Depression* (New York: Vintage, 1983).

61. Torri Minto, "She Rages No More," *San Francisco Chronicle,* October 3, 1999, B3.

62. See, for example, Alan Light, "Bono: The Rolling Stone Interview," *Rolling Stone,* March 4, 1993, 43–46 and 77; and Ron Suskind, *The Price of Loyalty* (New York: Simon & Schuster, 2004), Chapter 7.

63. Illustrative examples of this type of analysis are James MacGregor Burns, *Running Alone* (New York: Basic Books, 2006); and Bruce Miroff, *Pragmatic Illusions: The Presidential Politics of John F. Kennedy* (New York: David McKay, 1976).

64. Personal interview with Tom Cronin.

65. Garry Wills, *Certain Trumpets: The Call of Leaders* (New York: Simon & Schuster, 1994), p. 16.

66. Personal interview with Tom Cronin.

67. On Steve Jobs, see Virginia Brackett, *Steve Jobs: Computer Genius and Apple* (Springfield, NJ: Enslow, 2003). See also Walter Isaacson, *Steve Jobs* (New York: Simon & Schuster, 2011).

68. Garry Wills, "Dishonest Abe," *Time,* October 5, 1992, 42.

69. Ibid., p. 42.

70. Attributed to Frederick Douglass.

Notes for Chapter Nine

1. Multiple translations, quoted in *The Art of War,* Andrew Roberts, ed. (London: Quercus, 2008); see also R. L. Wing's translation entitled *The Art of Strategy* (New York: Doubleday, 1988). *The Art of War* can also be found in whole on the Internet under Sun Tzu.

2. Adapted from Will and Ariel Durant, *The Lessons of History* (New York: Simon & Schuster, 1968), p. 81.

3. Stephen E. Ambrose, *Duty, Honor, Country: A History of West Point* (Baltimore: Johns Hopkins University Press, 1999); and Larry E. Donnithorne, *The West Point Way of Leadership* (New York: Doubleday, 1993). See also Tom Kolditz, "Why the Military Produces Great Leaders," *Harvard Business Review,* February 2009; for some contrarian ideas, see Martin van Creveld, *The Training of Officers: From Military Professionalism to Irrelevance* (New York: Free Press, 1990).

4. Jonathan Fenby, "Sun Tzu," in *The Art of War,* ed. Andrew Roberts (London: Quercus, 2008), p. 65.

5. Ibid., p. 63.

6. From a translation by R. L. Wing, *The Art of Strategy* (New York: Doubleday, 1988), p. 97.

7. "Sun Tzu and the Art of Soft Power," *The Economist,* December 17, 2011, pp. 71–74.

8. Edith Hamilton, *The Greek Way* (New York: New American Library, 1948), p. 134.

9. See John Finley, *Thucydides* (Cambridge, MA: Harvard University Press, 1947); and Donald Kagan, *The Peloponnesian War* (New York: Viking, 2003).

10. Neal Wood, Introduction, *Machiavelli: The Art of War* (Indianapolis: Bobbs-Merrill, 1965), p. xxv.

11. Most of these prescriptions come from Wood's invaluable Introduction, ibid., adapted from various pages, pp. xii–xxvii.

12. Machiavelli, *The Art of War,* revised edition of the Ellis Farnsworth translation (Indianapolis: Bobbs-Merrill, 1965), p. 202.

13. Ibid., p. 175.

14. Ibid., pp. 203–204.

15. Miles J. Unger, *Machiavelli: A Biography* (New York: Simon & Schuster, 2011), p. 303.

16. Carl von Clausewitz, in *Principles of War,* Hans Gatzke, trans. and ed. (Harrisburg, PA: Military Service Publishing Company, 1942), p. 47.

17. Ibid., p. 67.

18. Carl von Clausewitz, in *On War,* Michael Howard and Peter Paret, trans. and eds. (Princeton: Princeton University Press, 1976), p. 105.

19. Quoted from *The Oxford Companion to Military History,* Richard Holmes, ed. (Oxford: Oxford University Press, 2001), p. 209.

20. Ibid., p. 209.

21. On Clausewitz, see also *Clausewitz and Modern Strategy,* Michael E. Handel, ed. (London: Frank Cass, 1986); and Michael Howard, *Clausewitz* (Oxford: Oxford University Press, 1983).

22. John Keegan, *The Mask of Command* (New York: Penguin Books, 1987), p. 90.

23. Robin Lane Fox, in *The Art of War,* Andrew Roberts, ed. (London: Quercus, 2008), p. 131.

24. Julius Caesar, *The Conquest of Gaul,* S. A. Handford, trans. (New York: Penguin Books, 1982), Book II, Section 2.

25. For helpful analysis of Grant and his relationship with Lincoln, see Eliot A. Cohen, *Supreme Command* (New York: Anchor, 2003); John Keegan, *The Mask of Command* (New York: Penguin Books, 1987); and James M. McPherson, *Tried by War: Abraham Lincoln as Commander in Chief* (New York: Penguin Books, 2008).

26. See Ronald Lewin, *Rommel as Military Commander* (Princeton: D. Van Nostrand, 1968). See also Dennis Showalter, *Patton and Rommel* (New York: Berkley, 2005).

27. Christopher R. Paparone and James A. Crupi, "The Principles of War as Paradox," *Proceedings,* October 2005, 40, www.navalinstitute.org.

28. Christopher R. Paparone, "Deconstructing Army Leadership," *Military Review,* January–February 2004, 5.

29. Ibid., p. 3.

30. Ibid., pp. 9–10.

31. Perry M. Smith, *Rules and Tools for Leaders* (New York: Perigee, 2002), pp. 90–91.

32. Eliot A. Cohen, *Supreme Commanders* (New York: Anchor, 2002), pp. 50 and 51.

33. Colin Powell quoted in Karen DeYoung, *Soldier: The Life of Colin Powell* (New York: Knopf, 2006), p. 209.

34. Hugh Shelton, *Without Hesitation: The Odyssey of an American Warrior* (New York: St. Martin's Press, 2010), p. 485.

35. Andrew J. Bacevich, *Washington Rules: America's Party to Permanent War* (New York: Metropolitan Books, 2011). See also the criticism from a Navy Seal operative toward the Clinton White House in Howard E. Wasdin and Stephen Templin, *Seal Team Six: Memoirs of an Elite Navy Seal Sniper* (New York: St. Martin's Press, 2011); and the criticism of the Bush administration in Bing West, *No True Glory: A Front-Line Account of the Battle of Fallujah* (New York: Bantam, 2006). See also H. R. McMaster, *Dereliction of Duty: Lyndon Johnson, Robert McNamara, the Joint Chiefs of Staff and the Lies That Led to Vietnam* (New York: Harper Perennial, 1997).

36. See the useful writings of Gary Hart, *The Shield and the Cloak: The Security of the Commons* (New York: Oxford University Press, 2006); and Garry Wills, *Bomb Power: The Modern Presidency and the National Security State* (New York: Penguin, 2010).

37. DeYoung, *Soldier,* p. 91.

38. See, for example, Colonel Denise F. Williams, *Toxic Leadership in the U.S. Army,* USAWC Strategy Research Project, U.S. Army War College, March 18, 2005.

39. Matthew B. Ridgway, "Leadership," in *Military Leadership: In Pursuit of Excellence,* Robert L. Taylor and William E. Rosenbach, eds. (Boulder, CO: Westview Press, 1984), p. 27.
40. General Bruce C. Clarke, *Thoughts on Leadership* (Ft. Belvoir, VA: U.S. Army Engineer School, n.d.).
41. See, for example, Donnithorne, *The West Point Way of Leadership.*
42. Department of the Army, *Leadership and Command at Senior Levels,* 1987, p. 26.
43. Ibid., p. 8.
44. David H. Hackworth, "A Soldier's Plan for Better Leaders," *Christian Science Monitor,* July 3, 1989, 18. For a different yet similarly scathing indictment, see H. R. McMaster, *Dereliction of Duty.*
45. Mathew B. Ridgway, "Leadership," *Military Review,* October 1966, p. 40.
46. Mark H. Gerner, "Leadership at the Operational Level," *Military Review,* June 1987, p. 29.
47. George S. Patton Jr. quoted in Robert A. Fitton, ed., *Leadership* (Boulder, CO: Westview Press, 1990), p. 83.
48. Norman Schwarzkopf, Introduction, *West Point: Two Centuries of Honor and Tradition,* Robert Cowley and Thomas Guinsburg, eds. (New York: Warner Books, 2002), p. 15.
49. David McCullough, *1776* (New York: Simon & Schuster, 2005), p. 293. See also Ron Chernow, *Washington: A Life* (New York: Penguin Books, 2010).
50. Martin van Creveld, *Command in War* (Cambridge: Harvard University Press, 1985), p. 268.
51. Frederick the Great, *Instructions for His Generals,* 1747; this quote was drawn from Fitton, ed., *Leadership,* p. 141.
52. See the long list of sought-after qualities in Department of the Army, "Army Leadership," Army Regulation 600-100 (Washington, DC, March 8, 2007).
53. Larry H. Ingraham, "An Uninvited Talk to Army Leaders," *Military Review,* December 1987, p. 46.
54. Quoted in Fitton, ed., *Leadership,* p. 287. For a firsthand account by a marine platoon leader in Iraq of the costs involved when inadequate training and preparation have taken place, see Donovan Campbell, *Joker One: A Marine Platoon's Story of Courage* (New York: Random House, 2009).
55. Showalter, *Patton and Rommel,* p. 421.
56. Jeff Weiss, Aram Donigan, and Jonathan Hughes, "Extreme Negotiations," *Harvard Business Review,* November 2010, p. 68.
57. See Thomas A. Kolditz, *In Extremis Leadership: Leading as If Your Life Depended on It* (San Francisco: Jossey-Bass, 2007). See also Bing West, *No True Glory*; and West, *The Wrong War: Grit, Strategy and the Way Out of Afghanistan* (New York: Random House, 2011).
58. See the fascinating biographies: Michael Korda, *Hero: The Life and Legend of Lawrence of Arabia* (New York: Harper, 2010); and William Manchester, *American Caesar: Douglas MacArthur, 1880–1964* (Boston: Little, Brown, 1978).

Notes for Chapter Ten

1. Terry Christensen and Peter J. Haas, *Projecting Politics* (Armonk, NY: M. E. Sharpe, 2005), p. 13.
2. In focusing on Hollywood films, we exclude several foreign-made films that rank among the best political films ever made, such as *The Battle of Algiers* (Italy, 1966), *Ran* (Japan, 1985), *Kagemasha* (Japan, 1980), and the British classics *A Very British Coup* (1988) and *House of Cards* (1993).
3. Peter C. Rollins and John E. O'Connor, eds., *Hollywood's White House: The American*

Presidency in Film and History (Lexington: University Press of Kentucky, 2005). See also John K. Clemens and Melora Wolff, *Movies to Manage By* (Chicago: Contemporary Books, 1999); Ralph R. DiSibio, *Reel Lessons in Leadership* (Aiken, SC: Paladin Group, 2006); and Michael A. Genovese, *The Political Film* (Needham Heights, MA: Simon & Schuster, 1998).

4. John Wayne called *High Noon* "the most un-American thing I've ever seen in my whole life." The *Playboy* interview, *Playboy Magazine*, May 1971, Vol. 18, Number 5. Yet both Dwight D. Eisenhower and Bill Clinton referred to *High Noon* as their favorite film.

5. See also the excellent 2003 Academy Award–winning documentary *The Fog of War*, 2003, directed by Errol Morris, in which former Kennedy and Johnson defense secretary Robert McNamara discusses, often painfully and with convoluted remorse, his role in the war in Vietnam and other conflicts.

6. As an interesting side note, the film *Lawrence of Arabia* does not contain a single female-speaking role.

7. Michael Korda, *Hero: The Life and Legend of Lawrence of Arabia* (New York: HarperCollins, 2010), p. 690.

8. T. E. Lawrence, "Evolution of a Revolt," which became a part of his magisterial work *Seven Pillars of Wisdom* (New York: First Anchor Books, 1991), first published in 1926.

9. Crispin Burke, "T. E. Lawrence: A Leadership Vignette for the Successful Counter-Insurgent," *Small Wars Journal*, posted by *SWJ*, editors, February 19, 2009, http://www.smallwarsjournal.com. These and similar Lawrence paradoxes are splendidly discussed in Michael Korda, *Hero: The Life and Legend of Lawrence of Arabia* (New York: Harper Perennial, 2011).

10. Dennis Showalter, *Patton and Rommel* (New York: Berkley Caliber, 2005), pp. 421, 424.

11. For "heroic" women in political films, see also *Silkwood* (1983), in which Meryl Streep plays a worker in a nuclear power plant who, after an accident at the plant, is contaminated by radiation. It is based on a true-life story: Karen Silkwood investigates the tragedy and discovers a cover-up by the plant owners. See also *Erin Brockovich* (2000), with Julia Roberts playing the title role as a legal clerk who takes on the Pacific Gas and Electric Company of California, which was polluting the city's water supply.

12. See Henry P. Liefermann, *Crystal Lee: A Woman of Inheritance* (New York: Macmillan, 1975).

13. Robert Nathan and Jo-Ann Mort, "Remembering 'Norma Rae,'" *The Nation*, February 26, 2007.

14. For a probing look at Gandhi's complicated personal and political life, see Joseph L. Lelyveld, *Great Soul: Mahatma Gandhi and His Struggle with India* (New York: Knopf, 2011).

15. Geoffrey Hellman, "Thinking in Hollywood," *The New Yorker*, February 24, 1940, 23–24.

16. Frank Capra interview with Steve Mamber, "One Man—One Film," *American Film Institute*, Discussion No. 3 (Washington, DC: AFI, 1971).

17. Richard Glazer, "Meet John Doe: An End to Social Mythmaking," in John Raeburn, ed., *Frank Capra: The Man and His Films* (Ann Arbor: University of Michigan Press, 1975), p. 146.

Notes for Chapter Eleven

1. Charles E. Merriam, *Political Power* (Glencoe, IL: Free Press, 1950), p. 153.

2. John W. Gardner, *On Leadership* (New York: Free Press, 1990), pp. 67–68.

3. Quoted in James MacGregor Burns, *Leadership* (New York: HarperCollins, 1978), pp. 148–149.

4. See Jean Lipman-Blumen, "Toxic Leadership," in *Political and Civic Leadership: A Reference Handbook,* Richard A. Cuoto, ed. (Los Angeles: Sage, 2010), p. 652.

5. Alan Wolfe, *Political Evil: What It Is and How to Combat It* (New York: Knopf, 2011), p. 4.

6. Ibid., p. 292.

7. Alexander Hamilton, James Madison, and John Jay, *The Federalist Papers,* No. 51.

8. Ron Rosenbaum, "Explaining Hitler," *The New Yorker,* May 1, 1995, 50–70.

9. Burns, *Leadership,* p. 3.

10. See David C. McClelland and David H. Burnham, "Power Is the Great Motivation," *Harvard Business Review* 54, no. 2 (2000): 100–110.

11. Niccolò Machiavelli, *The Prince,* George Bull, trans. (New York: Penguin Books, 1973), p. 15.

12. Immanuel Kant, *Perpetual Peace,* I. W. Beck, trans. (New York: Bobbs Merrill, 1957).

13. Burns, *Leadership*; and Gardner, *On Leadership.*

14. J. Patrick Dobel, "Political Prudence and the Ethics of Leadership," *Public Administration Review* 58, no. 1 (January–February 1998): 75.

15. Ibid. See also Michael J. Sandel, *Justice: What Is the Right Thing to Do?* (New York: Farrar, Straus and Giroux, 2009).

16. Robert I. Sutton, *The No Asshole Rule: Building a Civilized Workplace and Surviving One That Isn't* (New York: Warner Business Books, 2007), p. 66.

17. Ibid., p. 80.

18. See H. E. Barnes, *The Story of Punishment: A Record of Man's Inhumanity to Man,* 2nd rev. ed. (Glen Ridge, NJ: Patterson Smith, 1996); Benjamin Valentino, *Final Solutions: Mass Killings and Genocide in the Twentieth Century* (Ithaca, NY: Cornell University Press, 2004); Eric Alterman, *When Presidents Lie: A History of Official Deception and Its Consequences* (New York: Viking, 2004).

19. Friedrich A. Hayek, *Road to Serfdom* (Chicago: University of Chicago Press, 1944).

20. F. G. Bailey, *Humbuggery and Manipulation: The Art of Leadership* (Ithaca, NY: Cornell University Press, 1988), pp. xii and 2.

21. Robert A. Caro, *The Power Broker: Robert Moses and the Fall of New York* (New York: Vintage Books, 1974).

22. Ibid., p. 19.

23. Nassir Ghaemi, *A First-Rate Madness: Uncovering the Links Between Leadership and Mental Illness* (New York: Penguin Books, 2011), pp. 2–3.

24. Amy B. Brunell, William A. Gentry, W. Keith Campbell, Brian J. Hoffman, Karl W. Kuhnert, and Kenneth G. De Marree, "Leader Emergence: The Case of the Narcissistic Leader," *Personality and Social Psychology Bulletin* 34, no. 12 (2008): 1663–1676.

25. Deborah Gruenfeld, "Power, Approach, and Inhibition," *Psychological Review,* Keith Rayner, ed. (Washington, DC: American Psychological Association, 2003); and Gruenfeld, "From Power to Action," *Journal of Personality and Social Psychology,* Charles M. Judd, Jeffry A. Simpson, and Laura A. King, eds. (Washington, DC: American Psychological Association, 2003).

26. George Packer, "Comment: Peace and Wars," *The New Yorker,* December 21 and 28, 2009, 46.

27. Andrew Young, *The Politician* (New York: St. Martin's Press, 2010), p. 300.

28. Ronald J. Deluga, "Relationship Among American Presidential Charismatic Leadership, Narcissism, and Rated Performance," *The Leadership Quarterly* 8, no. 1 (1997): 49–65. See also Michael Maccoby, *The Productive Narcissist* (New York: Broadway Books, 2003).

29. Howard Gardner, *Leading Minds: An Anatomy of Leadership* (New York: Basic Books, 1996), p. 35.

30. Amanda Sinclair, *Leadership for the Disillusioned* (Sydney: Allen & Unwin Academics, 2008).

31. Ibid., p. 7.

32. John Dean, *Blind Ambition* (Palm Springs, CA: Polimedia, 2009).

33. Alan Ehrenhalt, "The Paradox of Corrupt Yet Effective Leadership," *New York Times,* September 30, 2002, op-ed page.

34. Bethany McLean and Peter Elkind, *The Smartest Guys in the Room: The Amazing Rise and Scandalous Fall of Enron* (Honolulu, HI: Portfolio Trade, 2004). For an informative discussion of a whole range of business types, see Joe Nocera, *Good Guys and Bad Guys* (New York: Penguin Books, 2011). See also a case study of erratic and dysfunctional leadership that afflicted the giant pharmaceutical company Pfizer, by Peter Elkind and Jennifer Reingold, "Inside Pfizer's Palace Coup," *Fortune,* August 15, 2011, 76–91.

35. J. K. Rowling, *Harry Potter and the Prisoner of Azkaban* (London: Bloomsbury, 1999), p. 140.

36. Marcia Lynn Whicker, *Toxic Leaders: When Organizations Go Bad* (New York: Doubleday, 1996), p. 11.

37. Stephen E. Ambrose, *Band of Brothers* (New York: Simon & Schuster, 1992), pp. 15, 17.

38. See Gary L. McIntosh and Simon D. Rima, *Overcoming the Dark Side of Leadership* (New York: Baker Books, 1998); Manfred Kets de Vries, *Prisoners of Leadership* (New York: Wiley and Sons, 1989); and Maccoby, *The Productive Narcissist.*

39. Jonah Lehrer, "Depression's Upside," *The New York Times Magazine,* February 28, 2010, 43.

40. John W. Gardner, *On Leadership,* p. 71.

41. Andrew Young, *The Politician: An Insider's Account of John Edwards's Pursuit of the Presidency and the Scandal That Brought Him Down* (New York: Thomas Dunne Books, 2010).

42. George E. Reedy, *The Twilight of the Presidency* (New York: Mentor, 1970), pp. 17–18.

43. Albert Speer, *Inside the Third Reich* (New York: Macmillan, 1970).

44. Nikita Khrushchev, *Khrushchev Remembers* (Boston: Little, Brown, 1970).

45. Barbara Kellerman, *Bad Leadership: What It Is, How It Happens, Why It Matters* (Boston: Harvard Business School Press, 2004), p. xv.

46. Ibid., p. 11.

47. Ibid., p. 25.

48. Jean Lipman-Blumen, *The Allure of Toxic Leaders* (New York: Oxford University Press, 2005), p. 17.

49. Ibid., p. 18.

50. Ibid., p. 21.

51. See Joanne Ciulla, ed., *Ethics: The Heart of Leadership* (Portland: Praeger, 2004).

52. George Bernard Shaw, *Major Barbara* (New York: Penguin Books, 1968). See also the helpful distinction about different types of evil and what our responses should be in Alan Wolfe, *Political Evil* (New York: Knopf, 2011).

53. John J. Mearsheimer, *Why Leaders Lie* (New York: Oxford University Press, 2011).

Notes for Chapter Twelve

1. James Morse quoted in Tom Peters, *The Circle of Innovation* (New York: Vintage, 1999), p. 29.

2. Cited in Ann Scott, *Google* (Westport, CT: Greenwood, 2008), pp. 58, 59.

3. See related definitions in Patricia Cohen, "Charting Creativity: Signposts of a Hazy Territory," *New York Times,* May 8, 2010, C1, C7.

4. See Frank Barron, *Creative Person and Creative Process* (New York: Holt, Rinehart and Winston, 1969). See also Howard Gardner, *Creating Minds* (New York: Basic Books, 1993); and Paul Johnson, *Creators* (New York: HarperCollins, 2006).

5. John Jewkes, David Sawers, and Richard Stillerman, *The Sources of Invention,* 2nd ed.

(New York: W. W. Norton, 1969), p. 27. See also John Diebold, *The Innovators* (New York: E. P. Dutton, 1990); Harold Evans, *They Made America* (New York: Back Bay Books, 2004); and Steven Johnson, *Where Good Ideas Come From: The Natural History of Innovation* (New York: Riverhead Books, 2010).

6. See Gunther S. Stent, "Prematurity and Uniqueness in Scientific Discovery," *Scientific American* 227, no. 6 (December 1972).

7. Mihaly Csikszentmihalyi, *Creativity* (New York: HarperCollins, 1996), p. 11.

8. Linda S. Leonard, *The Call to Create* (New York: Harmony Books, 2000), p. 140.

9. Ulrich Kraft, "Unleashing Creativity," *Scientific American Mind* 16, no. 1 (2005): 19.

10. Howard Gardner, *Five Minds for the Future* (Boston: Harvard Business School Press, 2008), pp. 83, 99.

11. See Charles Nicholl, *Leonardo da Vinci: The Heights of the Mind* (New York: Penguin, 2005).

12. Quoted in Alex Osborn, *Applied Imagination*, 3rd ed. (New York: Charles Scribner's Sons, 1963), p. 242.

13. See Robert W. Weisburg, *Creativity: Genius and Other Myths* (New York: W. H. Freeman, 1986), p. 50.

14. Digested from interviews with David Campbell and from his tapes and writings sponsored by the Center for Creative Leadership. For similar notions, see also Frank Barron, *Creative Person and Creative Process.*

15. Edward de Bono, *Lateral Thinking* (New York: Harper & Row, 1970). See also Kenneth M. Heilman, *Creativity and the Brain* (New York: Psychology Press, 2005).

16. Jung quoted in Cohen, "Charting Creativity," C7.

17. Ibid. Cohen cites the work of neurologist Heilman, *Creativity and the Brain*, p. C7.

18. Kurt Matzler, Johannes Kepler, Franz Bailom, and Todd A. Mooradiam quoted in "Some Hunches About Intuition," *New York Times*, November 17, 2007, 135.

19. Henderson quoted in Eric Bonabeau, "Don't Trust Your Gut," *Harvard Business Review*, May 2003, 118.

20. Dan Ariely, *Predictably Irrational: The Hidden Forces That Shape Our Decisions*, rev. ed. (New York: Harper Perennial, 2009), p. 182.

21. Ori Brafman and Ron Brafman, *Sway: The Irresistible Pull of Irrational Behavior* (New York: Broadway Books, 2008), p. 7. See also Sheena Iyengar, *The Art of Choosing* (New York: Twelve Books, 2010).

22. Philip Goldberg, *The Intuitive Edge* (Los Angeles: Jeremy P. Tarcher, 1983), p. 157.

23. Steve Jobs, Commencement Address, Stanford University, Palo Alto, CA, June 12, 2005.

24. Quoted in Carolyn Geer, "Innovation 101," *Wall Street Journal*, October 17, 2011, R5.

25. Michael Ray and Rochelle Meyers, *Creativity in Business* (New York: Doubleday, 1986), pp. 163–164.

26. David G. Myers, *Intuition: Its Powers and Perils* (New Haven, CT: Yale University Press, 2002), p. 129. See also the many cautions about relying on past experiences in James G. March, *The Ambiguities of Experience* (Ithaca, NY: Cornell University Press, 2010). And, on the limits and complexity of intuition, see Daniel Kahneman, *Thinking, Fast and Slow* (New York: Farrar, Straus and Giroux, 2011).

27. See Dan Ariely, *Predictably Irrational* (New York: HarperCollins, 2009); and Ariely, "Why Businesses Don't Experiment," *Harvard Business Review*, April 2010, 34.

28. Bonabeau, "Don't Trust Your Gut," p. 117.

29. Ray and Meyers, *Creativity in Business*, p. 137.

30. See the discussion in Donald W. Blohowiak, *Mavericks!* (Homewood, IL: Business One Irwin, 1992).

31. John W. Gardner, *Self-Renewal: The Individual and the Innovative Society*, rev. ed. (New York: W. W. Norton, 1981), p. 32.

32. Harold Levitt, *Corporate Pathfinders* (New York: Penguin Books, 1987), p. 189.
33. Evans, *They Made America*, p. 627.
34. Csikszentmihalyi, *Creativity*, p. 71.
35. Ibid.
36. Jay Winik, *April 1865* (New York: Harper Perennial, 2002), p. 333.
37. See John Markoff, "A Visionary Who Transformed the Digital Age," *New York Times*, October 6, 2001, 1, A24. See also Walter Isaacson, *Steve Jobs* (New York: Simon & Schuster, 2011).
38. Evans, *They Made America*, p. 7.
39. For a fascinating discussion of how new Internet technologies are creating new markets and marketing innovations, see Chris Anderson, *The Long Tail: Why the Future of Business Is Selling Less of More*, 2nd ed. (New York: Hyperion, 2008). See also Adam Richardson, *Innovation X* (San Francisco: Jossey-Bass, 2010).
40. John Kao, *Jamming: The Art and Discipline of Business Creativity* (New York: Harper Business, 1996), p. xvii. See also Kao, *Innovative Nation* (New York: Free Press, 2007).
41. Robert J. Samuelson, "Innovation Is Messy," *Newsweek*, June 13, 1988, p. 55.
42. Robert J. Samuelson, "Secrets of Success," *Newsweek Special Issue* on "The Power of Invention" (Winter 1997–1998), 79.
43. Lee Platt of Hewlett-Packard quoted in Peters, *The Circle of Innovation*, p. vii.
44. On this point, see James C. Collins and William C. Lazier, *Beyond Entrepreneurship* (Englewood Cliffs, NJ: Prentice Hall, 1992), p. 136; and Louis C. Gerstner, *Who Says Elephants Can't Dance?* (New York: Harper Business, 2002).
45. Peter F. Drucker, *The Practice of Management* (New York: HarperCollins, 1954), p. 70.
46. See Jena McGregor, "The World's Most Innovative Companies," *Business Week*, April 24, 2006, 63–74.
47. Scott Berkun, *The Myths of Innovation* (Sebastopol, CA: O'Reilly, 2010), p. 14.
48. Richard N. Foster, *Innovation: The Attacker's Advantage* (New York: Summit Books, 1986), p. 21.
49. Some of these ideas are discussed at length in Eric Von Hippel, *The Sources of Innovation* (New York: Oxford University Press, 1988). But see also Richardson, *Innovation X*.
50. James G. March, *The Ambiguities of Experience* (Ithaca, NY: Cornell University Press, 2010), p. 80.
51. Ibid., p. 91.
52. See, for example, Gregg Easterbrook, *Sonic Boom: Globalization at Mach Speed* (New York: Random House, 2009).
53. Rob Cross et al., "Together We Innovate," *Wall Street Journal*, September 15–16, 2007, R6.
54. Peter F. Drucker, *Innovation and Entrepreneurship* (New York: Harper & Row, 1985), p. 199.
55. Collins and Lazier, *Beyond Entrepreneurship*, p. 137.
56. Ibid., pp. 138–139.
57. Some of these and others are discussed in Berkun, *The Myths of Innovation*, Chapter 6.
58. Dimon quoted in Duff McDonald, *Last Man Standing: The Ascent of Jamie Dimon and J. P. Morgan Chase* (New York: Simon & Schuster, 2009), p. 222.
59. Kenichi Ohmae, *The Mind of the Strategist* (New York: McGraw Hill, 1982), p. 276.
60. S. I. Hayakawa quoted in Ray and Myers, *Creativity in Business*, p. 113.
61. Alan Deutschman, "The Fabric of Creativity," *Fast Company*, December 2004, 59.
62. Quoted in Daniel Lyons, "Jeff Bezos," *Newsweek*, December 28, 2009–January 4, 2010, 85.
63. Quoted in Isaacson, *Steve Jobs*, p. 329.
64. Richard Lester and Michael Piore, *Innovation: The Missing Dimension* (Cambridge,

MA: Harvard University Press, 2004), as quoted in *Harvard Business Review*, November 2004, 31.

65. Jeffrey H. Dyer, Hal B. Gregersen, and Clayton M. Christensen, "The Innovator's DNA," *Harvard Business Review*, December 2009, 63.

66. The story is told in John Battelle, *The Search: How Google and Its Rivals Rewrote the Rules of Business and Transformed Our Culture* (New York: Penguin Books, 2005). See especially Chapter 4.

67. Kao, *Jamming*, p. 117.

68. Dyer, Gregersen, and Christensen, "The Innovator's DNA," p. 64.

69. John W. Gardner, *Self-Renewal*, rev. ed., p. 31.

70. Deutschman, "The Fabric of Creativity," p. 58.

71. Paul Sloane, *The Innovative Leader* (London: Kogan Page, 2007), p. 144. See also Roger Von Oech, *A Whack on the Side of the Head: How You Can Be More Creative*, 25th anniversary edition (New York: Business Plus, 2008); and Tom Kelley with Jonathan Littman, *The Art of Innovation: Lessons from IDEO, America's Leading Design Firm* (New York: Doubleday, 2001).

72. See Matthew Syed, *Bounce: Mozart, Federer, Picasso, Beckham, and the Science of Success* (New York: HarperCollins, 2010).

73. See this spirit discussed in Richard Branson, *Business Stripped Bare: Adventures of a Global Entrepreneur* (New York: Penguin Books, 2011).

74. See the useful essay "The New Incubators," *World Policy Journal*, Fall 2011, 23–34.

75. John Kao, "Tapping the World's Innovative Hot Spots," *Harvard Business Review*, March 2009, 114.

76. Samuelson, "Secrets of Success," p. 79.

77. See Dan Senor and Saul Singer, *Start-Up Nation: The Story of Israel's Economic Miracle* (New York: Twelve, 2009).

78. Edmund S. Phelps and Leo M. Tilman, "Wanted: A First National Bank of Innovation," *Harvard Business Review*, January–February 2010, 103.

79. See also Adam Segal, *Advantage: How American Innovation Can Overcome the Asian Challenge* (New York: W. W. Norton, 2011).

80. David Brooks, "Where Are the Jobs?" *New York Times*, October 7, 2011, A23.

81. David Brooks, "An Innovation Agenda," *New York Times*, December 8, 2009, A31. See also Kao, *Innovation Nation*, 458.

Notes for Chapter Thirteen

1. Keith Grint, *The Arts of Leadership* (Oxford: Oxford University Press, 2000), p. 147.

2. See, for example, Jared Diamond, *Guns, Germs, and Steel: The Fates of Human Societies* (New York: W. W. Norton, 1997).

3. Peter F. Drucker, Preface, *The Effective Executive* (New York: Harper Colophon Books, 1985), p. vii.

4. On the realities and virtues of practice see Matthew Syed, *Bounce: Mozart, Federer, Picasso, Beckham and the Science of Success* (New York: HarperCollins, 2010). On taking advantage of luck, see Jim Collins and Morten Hansen, "What's Luck Got to Do with It?" *New York Times*, October 20, 2011, pp. 1, 10, business section.

5. John W. Gardner. These themes pervade his speeches and books, but see especially his *On Leadership* (New York: Free Press, 1990) and his earlier classic *Self Renewal: The Individual and the Innovative Society* (New York: Harper & Row, 1963).

6. Warren Bennis, *On Becoming a Leader* (Reading, MA: Addison-Wesley, 1989), p. 9.

7. Tom Peters, *The Little Big Things: 163 Ways to Pursue Excellence* (New York: Harper Studio, 2010).

8. Ronald A. Heifetz and Marty Linsky, *Leadership on the Line* (Boston: Harvard Business School Press, 2002), p. 73.

9. We are grateful to Bill Rosenbach for this formulation.

10. John W. Gardner, *No Easy Victories* (New York: Harper & Row, 1968), p. 134. See also S. Alexander Haslam, Stephen Reicher, and Michael Platow, *The New Psychology of Leadership: Identity, Influence and Power* (New York: Psychology Press, 2011).

11. See, for useful examples, Garry Wills, *Lincoln at Gettysburg: The Words That Remade America* (New York: Simon & Schuster, 1992); and Keith Grint's splendid analysis of Martin Luther King's 1963 "I Have a Dream" speech in Keith Grint, *The Arts of Leadership* (Oxford: Oxford University Press, 2000), pp. 359–408. See also Garry Wills, *Rome and Rhetoric: Shakespeare's Julius Caesar* (New Haven: Yale University Press, 2011).

12. See, for example, Amy Chua, *World on Fire* (New York: Anchor Books, 2004).

13. John W. Gardner, *Living, Leading and the American Dream* (San Francisco: Jossey-Bass, 2003), p. 182.

14. Roger Fisher and William Ury, *Getting to Yes* (Boston: Houghton Mifflin, 1981). See also the valuable insights on negotiating in Dennis Ross, *Statecraft* (New York: Farrar, Straus and Giroux, 2007), Chapters 8 and 9.

15. Roger Fisher and Daniel Shapiro, *Beyond Reason* (London: Penguin Books, 2005).

16. Peter Drucker, *The Effective Executive* (New York: Harper & Row, 1966), p. 72.

17. Daniel Goleman, *Emotional Intelligence* (New York: Free Press, 2000). See also Goleman, Richard Boyatis, and Annie McKee, *Primal Leadership: Learning to Live with Emotional Intelligence* (Boston: Harvard Business School Press, 2002).

18. Doris Kearns Goodwin, *Team of Rivals: The Political Genius of Abraham Lincoln* (New York: Simon & Schuster, 2005).

19. Fred I. Greenstein, *The Presidential Difference* (New York: Free Press, 2000); and James David Barber, *The Presidential Character* (Englewood Cliffs, NJ: Prentice Hall, 1972).

20. Arthur Miller, *On Politics and the Art of Acting* (New York: Viking, 2001), p. 26.

21. Schwarzenegger, quoted in Connie Brack, "Supermoderate," *The New Yorker,* June 28, 2004, 27.

22. On the importance of storytelling, see Howard Gardner, *Leading Minds* (New York: Basic Books, 1995).

23. James O'Toole, *Leadership A to Z* (San Francisco: Jossey-Bass, 1999), p. 91.

Selected Bibliography

Anderson, Chris. *The Long Tail: Why the Future of Business Is Selling Less of More.* 2nd ed. New York: Hyperion, 2008.

Anderson, Ray C. *Confessions of a Radical Industrialist: Prophets, People, Purpose—Doing Business by Respecting the Earth.* New York: St. Martin's Press, 2009.

Ariely, Dan. *Predictably Irrational: The Hidden Forces That Shape Our Decisions.* Rev. ed. New York: Harper Perennial, 2009.

———. *The Upside of Irrationality: The Unexpected Benefits of Defying Logic at Work and at Home.* New York: HarperCollins, 2010.

Bailey, F. G. *Humbuggery and Manipulation: The Art of Leadership.* Ithaca, NY: Cornell University Press, 1988.

Barnard, Chester I. *The Functions of the Executive.* Cambridge: Harvard University Press, 1938.

Barron, Frank. *Creative Person and Creative Process.* New York: Holt, Rinehart and Winston, 1969.

Bass, Bernard. *Bass and Stogdill's Handbook of Leadership.* 3rd ed. New York: Free Press, 1990.

Bennis, Warren. *On Becoming a Leader.* Reading, MA: Addison-Wesley, 1990.

Bennis, Warren, and Burt Nanus. *Leaders: Strategies for Taking Charge.* New York: Harper & Row, 1985.

Bennis, Warren, and Patricia Ward Biederman. *Organizing Genius—The Secrets of Creative Collaboration.* Reading, MA: Addison-Wesley, 1997.

Brafman, Ori, and Ron Brafman. *Sway: The Irresistible Pull of Irrational Behavior.* New York: Broadway Books, 2008.

Bulger, William M. *While the Music Lasts: My Life in Politics.* Boston: Houghton Mifflin, 1996.

Bullitt, Stimson. *To Be a Politician.* Garden City, NY: Doubleday-Anchor, 1961.

Burns, James MacGregor. *Leadership.* New York: HarperCollins, 1978.

———. *Transforming Leadership.* New York: Atlantic Monthly Press, 2003.

Campbell, David. *Take the Road to Creativity.* Allen, TX: Argus, 1977.

Carlyle, Thomas. *On Heroes, Hero-Worship and the Heroic in History.* Garden City, NY: Dolphin Books, 1963. Originally published in 1840.

Carlzon, Jan. *Moment of Truth: New Strategies for Today's Customer-Driven Economy.* New York: Harper & Row, 1989.

Caro, Robert A. *The Power Broker: Robert Moses and the Fall of New York.* New York: Vintage Books, 1974.
Chrislip, David D., and Carl E. Larson. *Collaborative Leadership: How Citizens and Civic Leaders Can Make a Difference.* San Francisco: Jossey-Bass, 1994.
Christensen, Clayton M. *The Innovator's Dilemma: The Revolutionary Book That Will Change the Way You Do Business.* New York: Harper Business, 2000.
Ciulla, Joanne, ed. *Ethics: The Heart of Leadership.* 2nd ed. Westport, CT: Praeger, 2004.
Ciulla, Joanne B., Terry L. Price, and Susan E. Murphy. *The Quest for Moral Leaders.* Cheltenham, UK: Edward Elgar, 2005.
Cohen, Marcia. *The Sisterhood: The Inside Story of the Women's Movement and the Leaders Who Made It Happen.* New York: Fawcett Columbine, 1988.
Collins, James C., and William C. Lazier. *Beyond Entrepreneurship.* Englewood Cliffs, NJ: Prentice Hall, 1992.
Collins, James C., and Jerry I. Porras. *Built to Last: Successful Habits of Visionary Companies.* New York: Harper Business, 1997.
Collins, Jim. *Good to Great: Why Some Companies Make the Leap and Others Don't.* New York: Harper Business, 2001.
Conger, Jay. *The Charismatic Leader.* San Francisco: Jossey-Bass, 1989.
Conger, Jay A., and Ronald E. Riggio, eds. *The Practice of Leadership: Developing the Next Generation of Leaders.* San Francisco: Jossey-Bass, 2007.
Crick, Bernard. *In Defense of Politics.* Rev. ed. New York: Penguin Books, 1983.
Cronin, Thomas E. *Direct Democracy: The Politics of the Initiative, Referendum and Recall.* Cambridge: Harvard University Press, 1989.
———. *On the Presidency.* Boulder, CO: Paradigm, 2009.
Cronin, Thomas E., and Michael A. Genovese. *The Paradoxes of the American Presidency.* 4th ed. New York: Oxford University Press, 2013.
Csikszentmihalyi, Mihaly. *Creativity: Flow and the Psychology of Discovery and Invention.* New York: HarperCollins, 1996.
de Bono, Edward. *Lateral Thinking.* New York: Harper & Row, 1970.
De Pree, Max. *Leadership Is an Art.* New York: Doubleday, 1989.
de Gaulle, Charles. *The Edge of the Sword.* Trans. Gerald Hopkins. London: Faber and Faber, 1960. Originally published in 1932.
Diebold, John. *The Innovators.* New York: E. P. Dutton, 1990.
Dimock, Marshall Edward. *The Executive in Action.* New York: Harper & Brothers, 1945.
Donald, David H. *Lincoln.* New York: Simon & Schuster, 1995.
Drucker, Peter F. *The Effective Executive.* New York: Harper & Row, 1966.
———. *The Essential Drucker.* New York: Collins Business, 2001.
———. *The Practice of Management.* New York: HarperCollins, 1954.
Ernst, Chris, and Donna Chrobot-Mason. *Boundary Spanning Leadership.* New York: McGraw Hill, 2004.
Evans, Harold. *They Made America.* New York: Back Bay Books, 2004.
Fiedler, Fred E., and Joseph E. Garcia. *New Approaches to Effective Leadership.* New York: John Wiley, 1987.
Fisher, Roger, and Daniel Shapiro. *Beyond Reason.* New York: Penguin Books, 2005.
Fisher, Roger, and William Ury. *Getting to Yes.* Boston: Houghton Mifflin, 1981.
Foster, Richard N. *Innovation: The Attacker's Advantage.* New York: Summit Books, 1986.
Freiberg, Kevin, and Jackie Freiburg. *Nuts! Southwest Airlines' Crazy Recipe for Business and Personal Success.* Austin, TX: Bard, 1996.

Fuller, Timothy, ed. *Leading and Leadership*. Notre Dame, IN: University of Notre Dame Press, 2000.

Gardner, Howard. *Creating Minds*. New York: Basic Books, 1993.

———. *Five Minds for the Future*. Boston: Harvard Business School Press, 2008.

Gardner, John W. *Living, Leading and the American Dream*. San Francisco: Jossey-Bass, 2003.

———. *On Leadership*. New York: Free Press, 1990.

———. *Self-Renewal: The Individual and the Innovative Society*. New York: Harper & Row, 1963.

Genovese, Michael A. *Memo to a New President*. New York: Oxford University Press, 2008.

———. *The Political Film*. Needham Heights, MA: Simon & Schuster, 1998.

George, Alexander L. and Juliette L. *Woodrow Wilson and Colonel House: A Personality Study*. New York: Dover, 1956.

George, Bill. *True North: Discover Your Authentic Leadership*. New York: Wiley, 2007.

Gerstner, Louis V. Jr. *Who Says Elephants Can't Dance?: Inside IBM's Historic Turnaround*. New York: Harper Business, 2002.

Ghaemi, Nassir. *A First-Rate Madness: Uncovering the Links Between Leadership and Mental Illness*. New York: Penguin Books, 2011.

Goleman, Daniel. *Emotional Intelligence*. New York: Free Press, 2000.

Goleman, Daniel, Richard Boyatzis, and Arnie McKee. *Primal Leadership: Learning to Lead with Emotional Intelligence*. Boston: Harvard Business School Press, 2002.

Gordon, Scott. *Controlling the State: Constitutionalism from Ancient Athens to Today*. Cambridge: Harvard University Press, 1999.

Grady, Hugh. *Shakespeare, Machiavelli, and Montaigne: Power and Subjectivity from Richard II to Hamlet*. Oxford: Oxford University Press, 2002.

Greenleaf, Robert K. *The Servant as Leader*. Petersborough, NH: Windy Row Press, 1970.

Grint, Keith. *The Arts of Leadership*. Oxford: Oxford University Press, 2000.

Grove, Andrew S. *High Output Management*. New York: Vintage, 1985.

Handy, Charles. *The Age of Paradox*. Boston: Harvard Business School Press, 1994.

Heifetz, Ronald A. *Leadership Without Easy Answers*. Cambridge, MA: Belknap/Harvard University Press, 1994.

Heifetz, Ronald A., and Marty Linsky. *Leadership on the Line: Staying Alive Through the Dangers of Leading*. Boston: Harvard Business Press, 2002.

Heilman, Kenneth M. *Creativity and the Brain*. New York: Psychology Press, 2005.

Iyengar, Sheena. *The Art of Choosing*. New York: Twelve Books, 2010.

Jewkes, John, David Sawers, and Richard Stillerman. *The Sources of Invention*. 2nd ed. New York: W. W. Norton, 1969.

Johnson, Paul. *Creators*. New York: HarperCollins, 2006.

Johnson, Steven. *Where Good Ideas Come From: The Natural History of Innovation*. New York: Riverhead Books, 2010.

Kahneman, Daniel. *Thinking, Fast and Slow*. New York: Farrar, Straus and Giroux, 2011.

Kanter, Rosabeth M. *When Giants Learn to Dance*. New York: Simon & Schuster, 1989.

Kao, John. *Innovative Nation*. New York: Free Press, 2007.

———. *Jamming: The Art and Discipline of Business Creativity*. New York: Harper Business, 1996.

Katzenbach, Jon R., and Douglas K. Smith. *The Wisdom of Teams: Creating the High-Performance Organization*. Boston: Harvard Business School Press, 1993.

Kearns Goodwin, Doris. *Team of Rivals: The Political Genius of Abraham Lincoln*. New York: Simon & Schuster, 2005.

Keegan, John. *The Face of Battle: A Study of Agincourt, Waterloo, and the Somme.* New York: Penguin, 1978.
———. *The Mask of Command.* New York: Viking, 1987.
Kellerman, Barbara. *Bad Leadership: What It Is, How It Happens, Why It Matters.* Boston: Harvard Business School Press, 2004.
———, ed. *Leadership: Essential Selections on Power, Authority and Influence.* New York: McGraw Hill, 2010.
Kelley, Tom, and Jonathan Littman. *The Art of Innovation: Lessons from IDEO, America's Leading Design Firm.* New York: Doubleday, 2001.
Keohane, Nannerl O. *Thinking About Leadership.* Princeton: Princeton University Press, 2010.
Kets de Vries, Manfred. *The Leader on the Couch: A Clinical Approach to Changing People and Organizations.* San Francisco: Jossey-Bass, 2006.
———. *Prisoners of Leadership.* New York: Wiley, 1989.
Koestler, Arthur. *The Act of Creation.* New York: Macmillan, 1964.
Korda, Michael. *Hero: The Life and Legend of Lawrence of Arabia.* New York: HarperCollins, 2010.
Kotter, John P. *A Force for Change: How Leadership Differs from Management.* New York: Free Press, 1990.
———. *A Sense of Urgency.* Boston: Harvard Business Press, 2008.
Kouzes, James M., and Barry Z. Posner. *The Leadership Challenge.* 4th ed. San Francisco: Jossey-Bass, 2007.
Lasswell, Harold D. *Power and Personality.* New York: Viking Press, 1962. Originally published in 1948.
Lester, Richard, and Michael Piore. *Innovation: The Missing Dimension.* Cambridge, MA: Harvard University Press, 2004.
Levitt, Harold. *Corporate Pathfinders.* New York: Penguin Books, 1987.
Lewis, John. *Walking with the Wind: A Memoir of the Movement.* New York: Harcourt, Brace & Co., 1998.
Lipman-Blumen, Jean. *The Allure of Toxic Leaders.* New York: Oxford University Press, 2005.
———. *Connective Leadership: Managing in a Changing World.* New York: Oxford University Press, 2000.
———. *Hot Groups: Seeding Them, Feeding Them and Using Them to Ignite Your Organization.* New York: Oxford University, 1995.
Lodge, Tom. *Mandela: A Critical Life.* Oxford: Oxford University Press, 2006.
Ludwig, Arnold M. *King of the Mountain: The Nature of Political Leadership.* Lexington: University of Kentucky Press, 2002.
Lundborg, Louis B. *The Art of Being an Executive.* New York: Free Press, 1981.
Maccoby, Michael. *The Productive Narcissist: The Promise and Perils of Visionary Leadership.* New York: Broadway Books, 2003.
Machiavelli, Niccolò. *The Prince and the Discourses.* New York: Modern Library, 1940.
Madison, Charles A. *Critics and Crusaders: A Century of American Protest.* New York: Henry Holt, 1947.
Malici, Akan. *When Leaders Learn, and When They Don't.* Albany: SUNY Press, 2008.
Manchester, William. *American Caesar: Douglas MacArthur.* New York: Dell, 1978.
Mansfield, Harvey C., Jr. *Taming the Prince: The Ambivalence of Modern Executive Power.* New York: Free Press, 1989.
March, James G. *The Ambiguities of Experience.* Ithaca: Cornell University Press, 2010.
March, James G., and Thierry Weil. *On Leadership.* Oxford: Blackwell, 2005.

Martin, Roger. *The Opposable Mind: How Successful Leaders Win Through Integrative Thinking*. Boston: Harvard Business School Press, 2007.
May, Rollo. *Power and Innocence*. New York: Mentor, 1972.
McCall, Morgan W., Jr., Michael M. Lombardo, and Ann N. Morrison. *The Lessons of Experience: How Successful Executives Develop on the Job*. Lexington, MA: Lexington Books, 1988.
McIntosh, Gary L., and Simon D. Rima. *Overcoming the Dark Side of Leadership*. New York: Baker Books, 1998.
McPherson, James M. *Tried by War: Abraham Lincoln as Commander-in-Chief.* New York: Penguin Books, 2008.
Mearsheimer, John J. *Why Leaders Lie*. New York: Oxford University Press, 2011.
Miller, Arthur. *On Politics and the Art of Acting*. New York: Viking, 2001.
Mintzberg, Henry. *Mintzberg on Management*. New York: Free Press, 1989.
Miroff, Bruce. *Icons of Democracy*. New York: Basic Books, 1993.
Moss Kanter, Rosabeth. *SuperCorp: How Vanguard Companies Create Innovation, Projects, Growth, and Social Good*. New York: Crown Business, 2009.
Myers, David G. *Intuition: Its Powers and Perils*. New Haven, CT: Yale University Press, 2002.
Newell, Waller R. *The Soul of a Leader*. New York: HarperCollins, 2009.
Niebuhr, Reinhold. *Moral Man, Immoral Society*. New York: C. Scribner's Sons, 1952.
Nohria, Nitin, and Rakesh Khurana, eds. *Handbook of Leadership Theory and Practice*. Boston: Harvard Business Press, 2010.
Nye, Joseph S. Jr. *The Future of Power*. New York: Public Affairs, 2011.
———. *The Powers to Lead*. New York: Oxford University Press, 2008.
O'Toole, James. *Creating the Good Life*. Emmaus, PA: Rodale, 2005.
———. *The Executive Compass: Business and the Good Society*. New York: Oxford University Press, 1993.
———. *Leading Change*. San Francisco: Jossey-Bass, 1995.
Ohmae, Kenichi. *The Mind of the Strategist*. New York: McGraw Hill, 1982.
Olson, Robert W. *The Art of Creative Thinking*. New York: Harper & Row, 1980.
Osborn, Alex. *Applied Imagination*. 3rd ed. New York: Charles Scribner's Sons, 1963.
Peters, Tom. *The Little Big Things: 163 Ways to Pursue Excellence*. New York: Harper Studio, 2010.
———. *Thriving on Chaos: Handbook for a Management Revolution*. New York: Knopf, 1987.
Pink, Daniel H. *Drive*. New York: Riverhead Books, 2009.
Plutarch. *The Rise and Fall of Athens: Nine Greek Lives*. London: Penguin, 1960.
Post, Jerrold M. *Leaders and Their Followers in a Dangerous World*. Ithaca, NY: Cornell University Press, 2004.
Ray, Michael, and Rochelle Meyers. *Creativity in Business*. New York: Doubleday, 1986.
Redfield Jamison, Kay. *Exuberance: The Passion for Life*. New York: Knopf, 2004.
Richardson, Adam. *Innovation X*. San Francisco: Jossey-Bass, 2010.
Riggio, Ronald E., et al., eds. *The Art of Followership: How Great Followers Create Great Leaders and Organizations*. San Francisco: Jossey-Bass, 2008.
Roe, John. *Shakespeare and Machiavelli*. Cambridge: D. S. Brewer, 2002.
Rowan, Roy. *The Intuitive Manager*. Boston: Little, Brown, 1986.
Schlesinger, Arthur M. Jr. *The Cycles of American History*. Boston: Houghton Mifflin, 1986.
Schultz, Howard. *Onward: How Starbucks Fought for Its Life Without Losing Its Soul*. New York: Rodale, 2011.

Senge, Peter M. *The Fifth Discipline: The Art and Practice of the Learning Organization.* New York: Doubleday, 1990.
Senor, Dan, and Saul Singer. *Start-Up Nation: The Story of Israel's Economic Miracle.* New York: Twelve, 2009.
Simonton, Dean Keith. *Genius, Creativity, and Leadership: Histriometric Inquiries.* Cambridge: Harvard University Press, 1984.
Sinclair, Amanda. *Leadership for the Disillusioned: Moving Beyond Myths and Heroes to Leading That Liberates.* Crows Nest, NSW: Allen and Unwin, 2007.
Slater, Robert. *Jack Welch and the GE Way.* New York: McGraw Hill, 1999.
Sloan, Alfred P. Jr. *My Years with General Motors.* Garden City, NY: Doubleday, 1964.
Smith, Perry M. *Rules and Tools for Leaders.* New York: Perigee, 2002.
Syed, Matthew. *Bounce: Mozart, Federer, Picasso, Beckham, and the Science of Success.* New York: HarperCollins, 2010.
Thucydides. *The History of the Peloponnesian War.* New York: Penguin, 1954.
Tichy, Noel M., and Warren Bennis. *Judgment: How Winning Leaders Make Great Calls.* New York: Penguin Books, 2007.
Tuchman, Barbara. *The March of Folly.* New York: Ballantine Books, 1984.
Tugwell, Rexford G. *The Art of Politics.* Garden City, NY: Doubleday & Co., 1958.
Tushman, Michael L., and Charles A. O'Reilly III. *Winning Through Innovation: A Practical Guide to Leading Organizational Change and Renewal.* Boston: Harvard Business School Press, 1997.
Unger, Miles J. *Machiavelli: A Biography.* New York: Simon & Schuster, 2011.
Vaill, Peter B. *Managing as a Performing Art: New Ideas for a World of Chaotic Change.* San Francisco: Jossey-Bass, 1989.
Vaughan, Frances E. *Awakening Intuition.* New York: Anchor Books, 1979.
von Clausewitz, Carl. *On War.* Princeton: Princeton University Press, 1976. Originally published in 1832.
Von Hippel, Eric. *The Sources of Innovation.* New York: Oxford University Press, 1988.
Weisburg, Robert W. *Creativity: Genius and Other Myths.* New York: W. H. Freeman, 1986.
Welch, Jack. *Jack: Straight from the Gut.* New York: Warner Books, 2001.
Welch, Jack, and Suzy Welch. *Winning.* New York: Harper Business, 2005.
Whicker, Marcia Lynn. *Toxic Leaders: When Organizations Go Bad.* New York: Doubleday, 1996.
White, Ronald C. *A. Lincoln: A Biography.* New York: Random House, 2009.
Wildavsky, Aaron. *The Nursing Father: Moses as a Political Leader.* Tuscaloosa, AL: University of Alabama Press, 1984.
Wills, Garry. *Certain Trumpets: The Call of Leaders.* New York: Simon & Schuster, 1994.
———. *A Necessary Evil: A History of American Distrust of Government.* New York: Simon & Schuster, 1999.
———. *Rome and Rhetoric: Shakespeare's Julius Caesar.* New Haven: Yale University Press, 2011.
Wolfe, Alan. *Political Evil.* New York: Knopf, 2011.
Wren, J. Thomas, ed. *The Leader's Companion: Insights on Leadership Through the Ages.* New York: Free Press, 1995.
Wren, J. Thomas, Ronald E. Riggio, and Michael A. Genovese, eds. *Leadership and the Liberal Arts.* New York: Palgrave, 2009.
Yukl, Gary A. *Leadership in Organizations.* Englewood Cliffs, NJ: Prentice Hall, 1981.
Zaleznik, Abraham. *The Managerial Mystique.* New York: Harper & Row, 1989.

Index

About the Authors

Thomas E. Cronin is the McHugh Professor of American Institutions and Leadership at Colorado College. He is president emeritus of Whitman College (1993–2005) and a former acting president of Colorado College (1991). He earned a PhD in political science from Stanford University, and is author, coauthor, or editor of a dozen books on politics and government. Cronin is a past president of both the Western Political Science Association and the Presidency Research Group and was honored by the American Political Science Association with the Charles E. Merriam Award recognizing outstanding contributions to the art of government.

Michael A. Genovese is Director of the Institute for Leadership Studies and holds the Loyola Chair of Leadership as Professor of Political Science at Loyola Marymount University in Los Angeles. He received his PhD in political science from the University of Southern California, has authored over 30 books, and edits a series on the presidency. Genovese has won numerous awards for outstanding teaching and scholarship.